NEGIMA! 12

Ken Akamatsu

TRANSLATED BY
Toshifumi Yoshida

ADAPTED BY
T. Ledoux

LETTERING AND RETOUCH BY
Steve Palmer

BALLANTINE BOOKS · NEW YORK

Negima! volume 12 is a work of fiction. Names, characters, places, and incidents are the products of the author's imagination or are used fictitiously. Any resemblance to actual events, locales, or persons, living or dead, is entirely coincidental.

A Del Rey Trade Paperback Original

Published in the United States by Del Rey, an imprint of The Random House Publishing Group, a division of Random House, Inc., New York.

DEL REY is a registered trademark and the Del Rey colophon is a trademark of Random House, Inc.

Publication rights arranged through Kodansha Ltd.

First published in Japan in 2005 by Kodansha Ltd., Tokyo

ISBN-10: 0-345-49463-6
ISBN-13: 978-0-345-49463-4

Printed in the United States of America

www.delreymanga.com

9 8 7 6 5 4 3 2 1

Translator—Toshifumi Yoshida
Adaptor—T. Ledoux
Lettering and retouch—Steve Palmer
Cover design—David Stevenson

Honorifics Explained

Throughout the Del Rey Manga books, you will find Japanese honorifics left intact in the translations. For those not familiar with how the Japanese use honorifics and, more important, how they differ from American honorifics, we present this brief overview.

Politeness has always been a critical facet of Japanese culture. Ever since the feudal era, when Japan was a highly stratified society, use of honorifics—which can be defined as polite speech that indicates relationship or status—has played an essential role in the Japanese language. When addressing someone in Japanese, an honorific usually takes the form of a suffix attached to one's name (example: "Asuna-san"), or as a title at the end of one's name, or in place of the name itself (example: "Negi-sensei," or simply "Sensei!").

Honorifics can be expressions of respect or endearment. In the context of manga and anime, honorifics give insight into the nature of the relationship between characters. Many translations into English leave out these important honorifics, and therefore distort the "feel" of the original Japanese. Because Japanese honorifics contain nuances that English honorifics lack, it is our policy at Del Rey not to translate them. Here, instead, is a guide to some of the honorifics you may encounter in Del Rey Manga.

-*san*: This is the most common honorific, and is equivalent to Mr., Miss, Ms., or Mrs. It is the all-purpose honorific and can be used in any situation where politeness is required.

-*sama*: This is one level higher than "-san." It is used to confer great respect.

-*dono*: This comes from the word "tono," which means "lord." It is even a higher level than "-sama," and confers utmost respect.

-kun: This suffix is used at the end of boys' names to express familiarity or endearment. It is also sometimes used by men among friends, or when addressing someone younger or of a lower station.

-chan: This is used to express endearment, mostly toward girls. It is also used for little boys, pets, and even among lovers. It gives a sense of childish cuteness.

Bozu: This is an informal way to refer to a boy, similar to the English term "kid" or "squirt."

Senpai/sempai: This title suggests that the addressee is one's senior in a group or organization. It is most often used in a school setting, where underclassmen refer to their upperclassmen as "senpai." It can also be used in the workplace, such as when a newer employee addresses an employee who has seniority in the company.

Kohai: This is the opposite of "sempai," and is used toward underclassmen in school or newcomers in the workplace. It connotes that the addressee is of lower station.

Sensei: Literally meaning "one who has come before," this title is used for teachers, doctors, or masters of any profession or art.

Anesan (or *nesan*): A generic term for a girl, usually older, that means sister.

Ojôsama: A way of referring to the daughter or sister of someone with high political or social status.

-[blank]: Usually forgotten in these lists, but perhaps the most significant difference between Japanese and English. The lack of honorific means that the speaker has permission to address the person in a very intimate way. Usually, only family, spouses, or very close friends have this kind of permission. Known as *yobisute*, it can be gratifying when someone who has earned the intimacy starts to call one by one's name without an honorific. But when that intimacy hasn't been earned, it can also be very insulting.

A Word from the Author

Thanks for your patience. It's now Day Two, and we're in the middle of the Mahora "Budōkai" Martial Arts Tournament. Most of this volume's pretty much taken up with fighting; those of you who're in for the *moe* ("cute"), my apologies. (^^;)

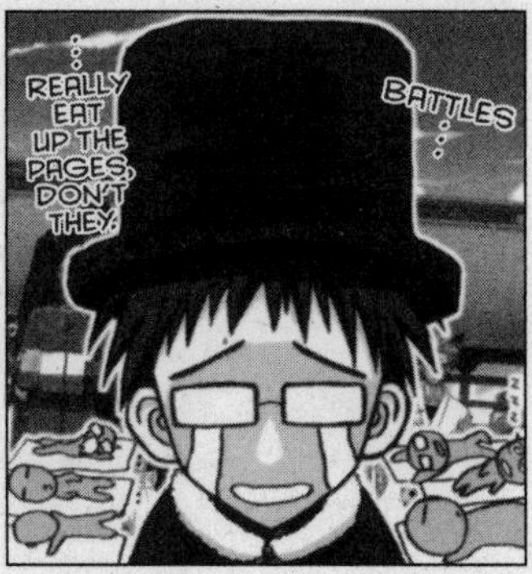
REALLY EAT UP THE PAGES, DON'T THEY.
BATTLES

My work "*Itsudatte* (Always) My Santa" has been made into an Original Animation Video (OAV). Please see my home page for more details!

Ken Akamatsu
www.ailove.net

魔法先生 ネギま!

MAGISTER NEGI MAGI

12

赤松 健

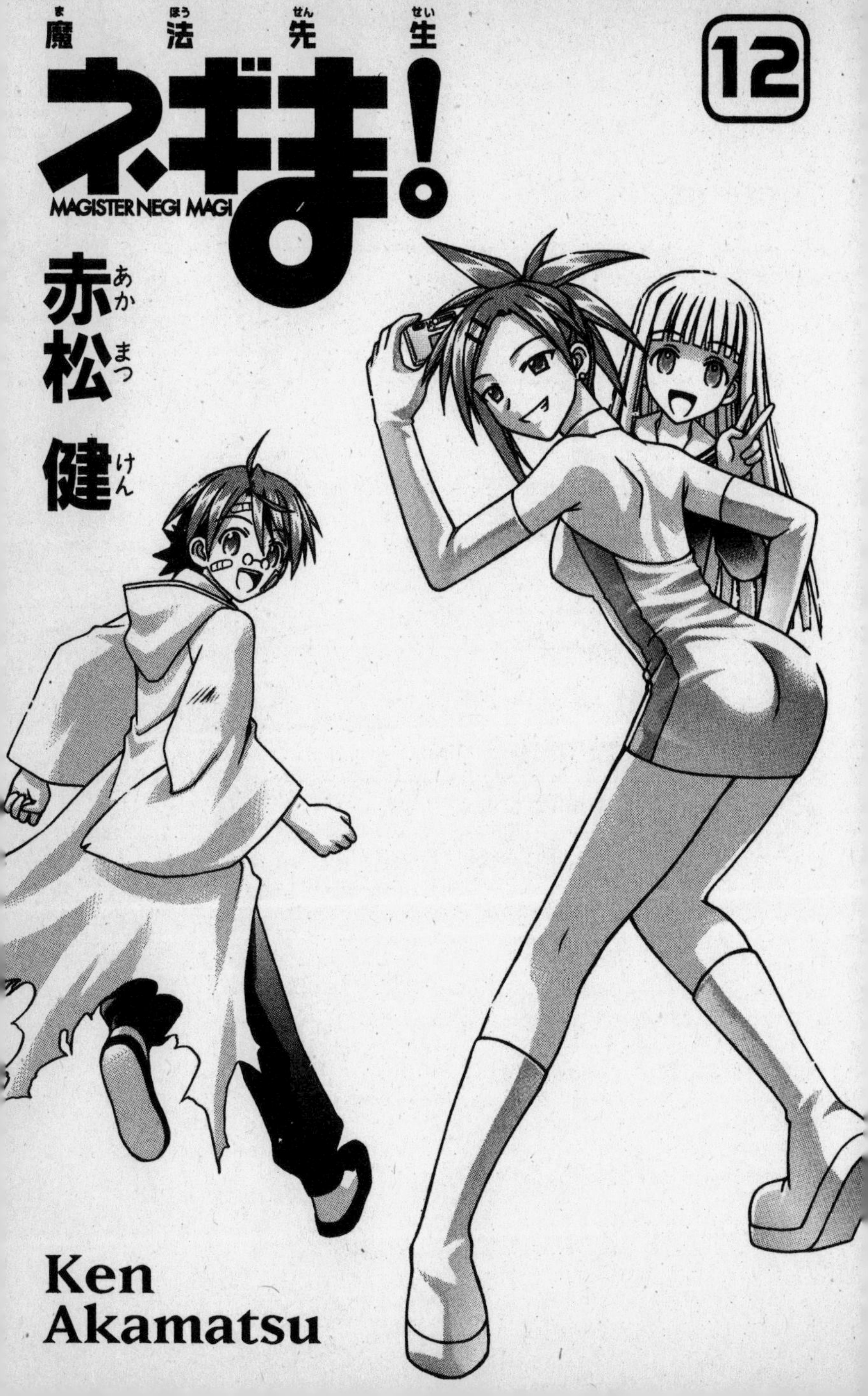

Ken Akamatsu

Contents

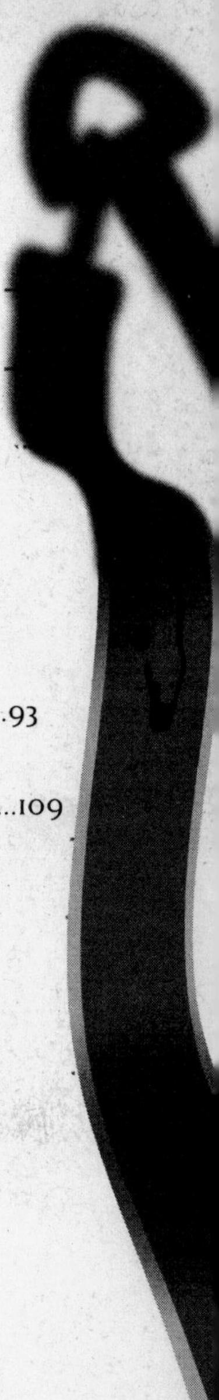

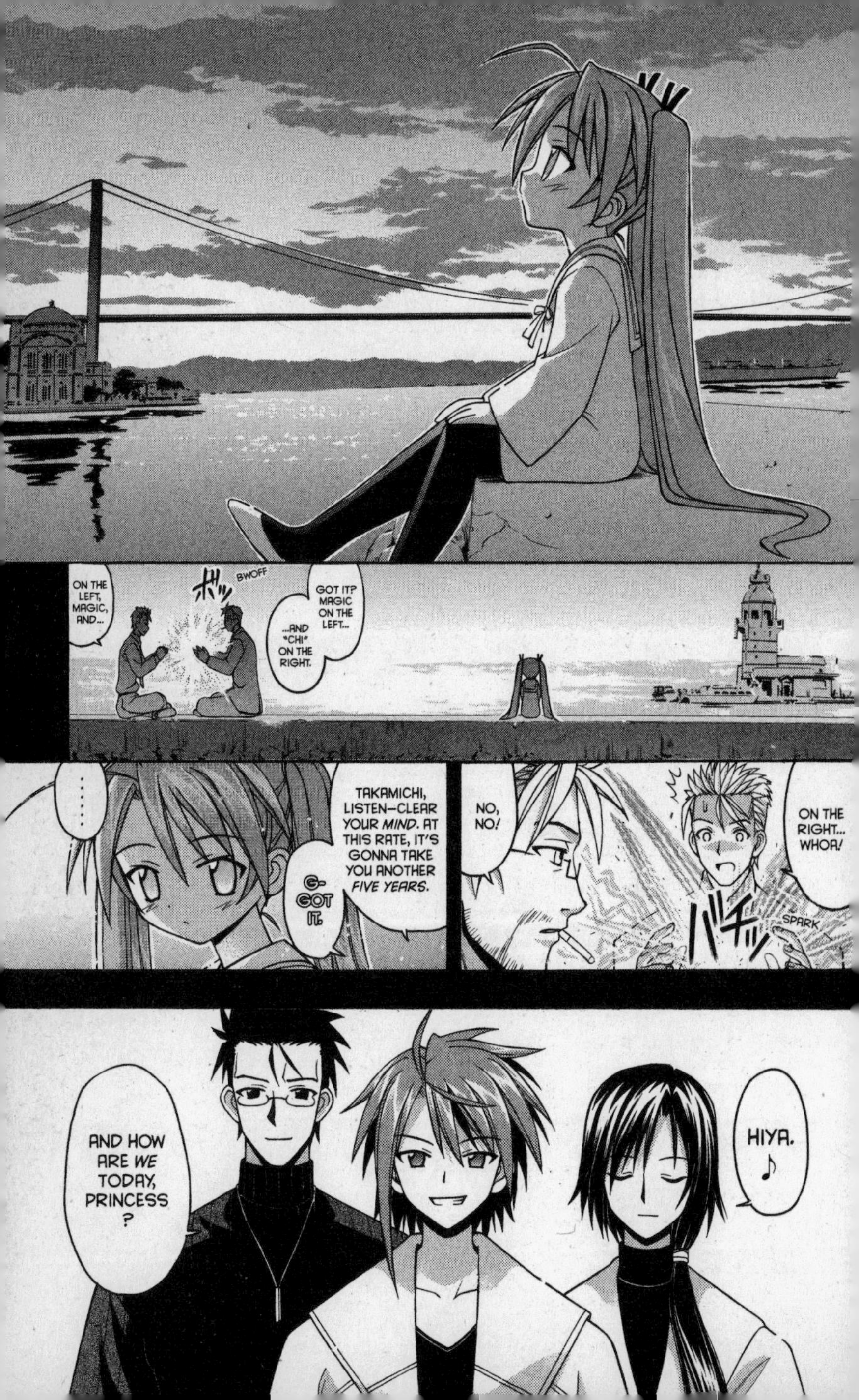
GOT IT? MAGIC ON THE LEFT...
...AND "CHI" ON THE RIGHT.
BWOFF
ON THE LEFT, MAGIC, AND...
ON THE RIGHT... WHOA!
SPARK
NO, NO!
TAKAMICHI, LISTEN—CLEAR YOUR *MIND*. AT THIS RATE, IT'S GONNA TAKE YOU ANOTHER *FIVE YEARS*.
G-GOT IT.
......
HIYA. ♪
AND HOW ARE *WE* TODAY, PRINCESS?

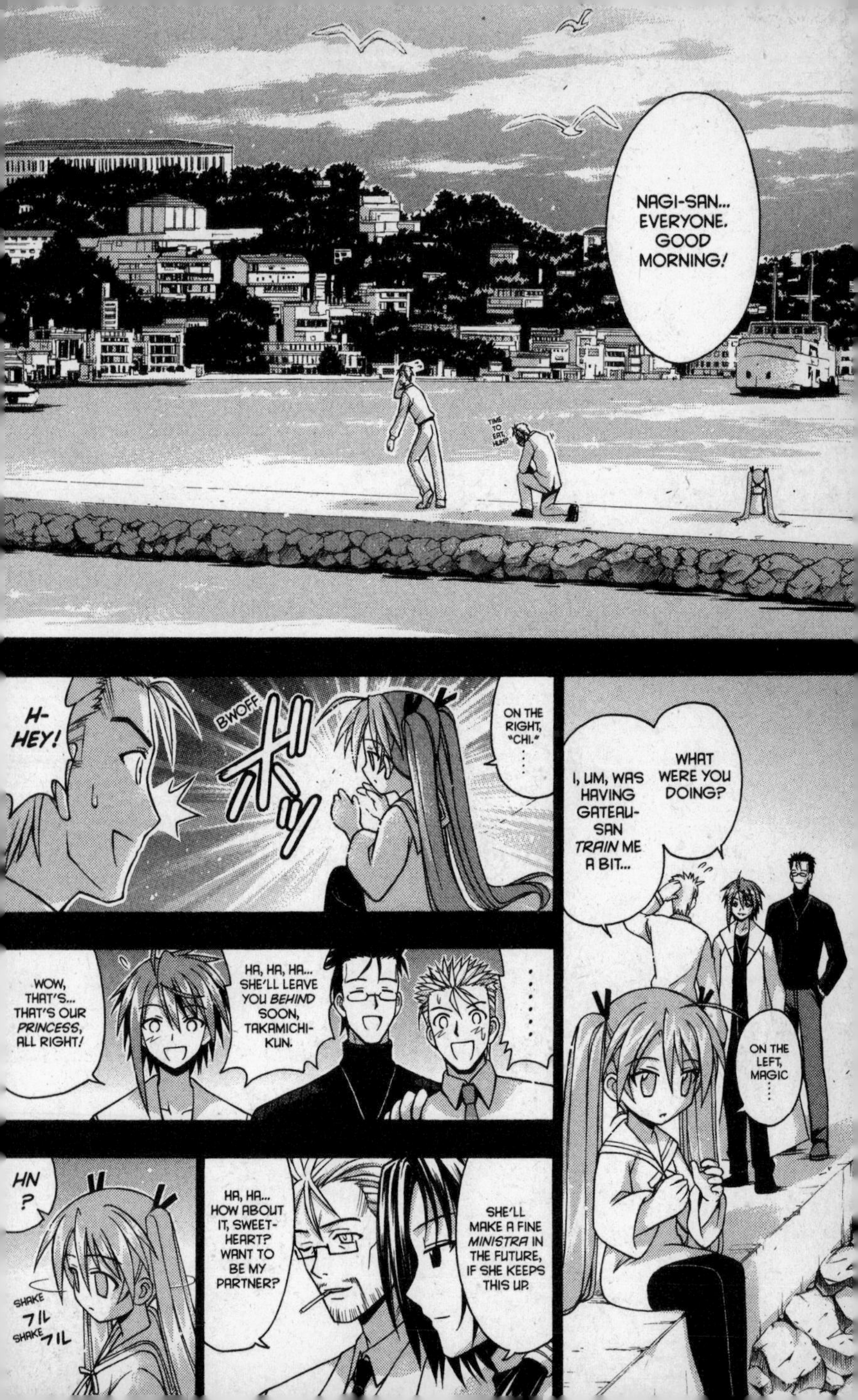
NAGI-SAN... EVERYONE. GOOD MORNING!
TIME TO EAT, HUH?
WHAT WERE YOU DOING?
I, UM, WAS HAVING GATEAU-SAN *TRAIN* ME A BIT...
ON THE LEFT, MAGIC ....
ON THE RIGHT, "CHI." ....
BWOFF
H-HEY!
......
HA, HA, HA... SHE'LL LEAVE YOU *BEHIND* SOON, TAKAMICHI-KUN.
WOW, THAT'S... THAT'S OUR *PRINCESS*, ALL RIGHT!
SHE'LL MAKE A FINE *MINISTRA* IN THE FUTURE, IF SHE KEEPS THIS UP.
HA, HA... HOW ABOUT IT, SWEET-HEART? WANT TO BE MY PARTNER?
HN ?
SHAKE フル
SHAKE フル

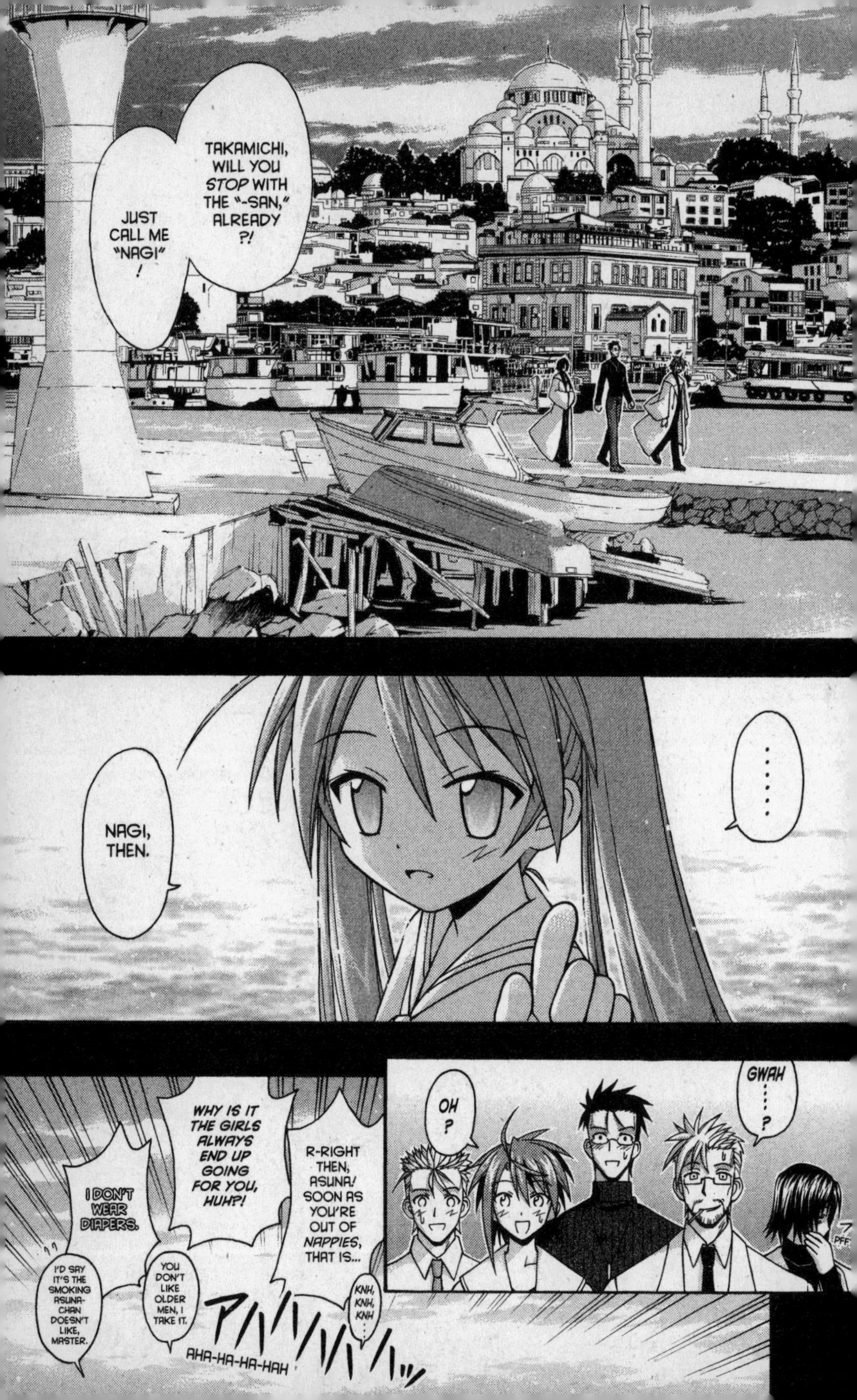
TAKAMICHI, WILL YOU *STOP* WITH THE "-SAN," ALREADY ?!
JUST CALL ME "NAGI" !
......
NAGI, THEN.
GWAH ....?
OH ?
PFF
R-RIGHT THEN, ASUNA! SOON AS YOU'RE OUT OF *NAPPIES*, THAT IS...
WHY IS IT THE GIRLS ALWAYS END UP GOING FOR YOU, HUH?!
I DON'T WEAR DIAPERS.
KNH, KNH, KNH...
YOU DON'T LIKE OLDER MEN, I TAKE IT.
I'D SAY IT'S THE SMOKING ASUNA-CHAN DOESN'T LIKE, MASTER.
AHA-HA-HA-HAH

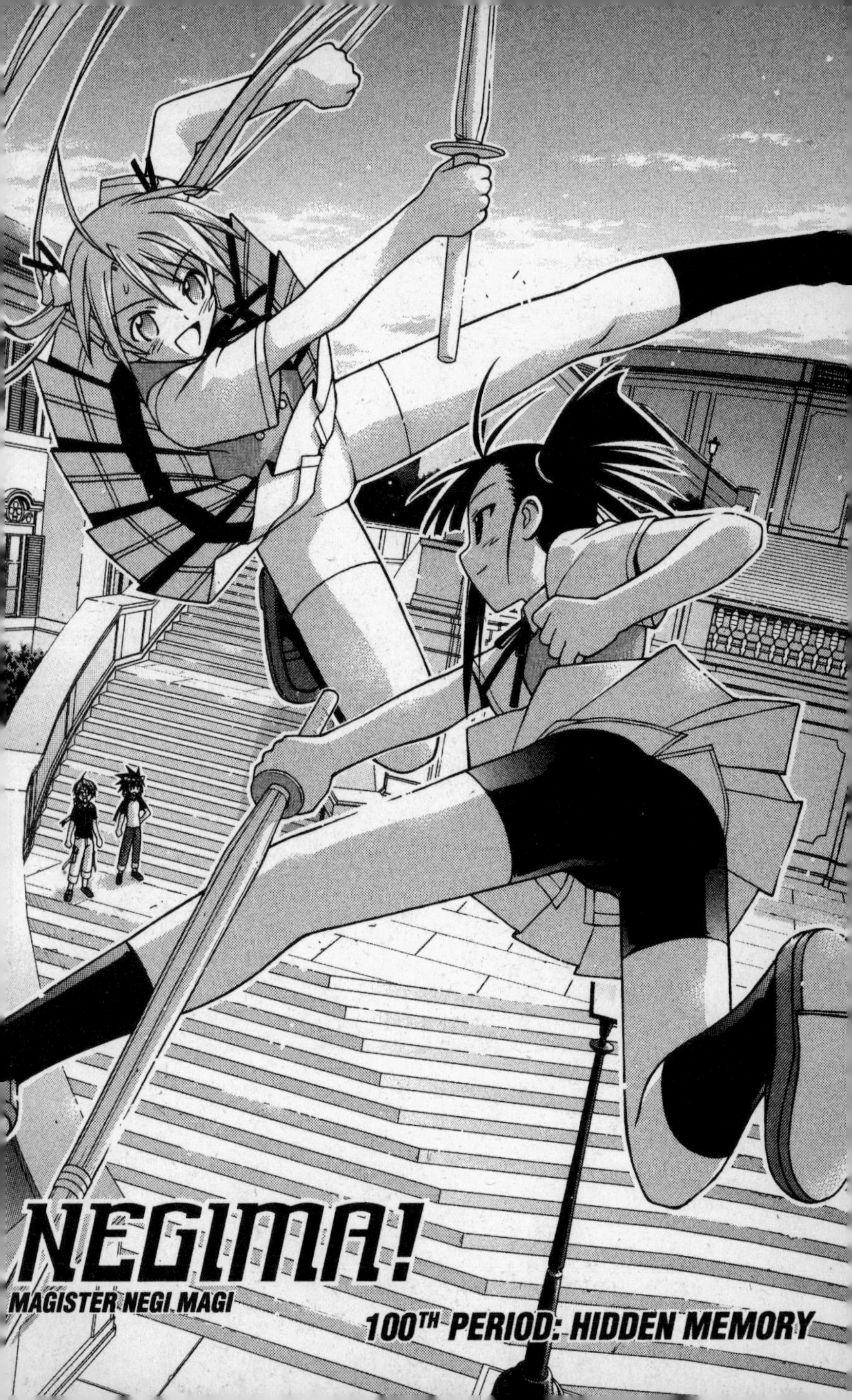
NEGIMA!
MAGISTER NEGI MAGI
100TH PERIOD: HIDDEN MEMORY

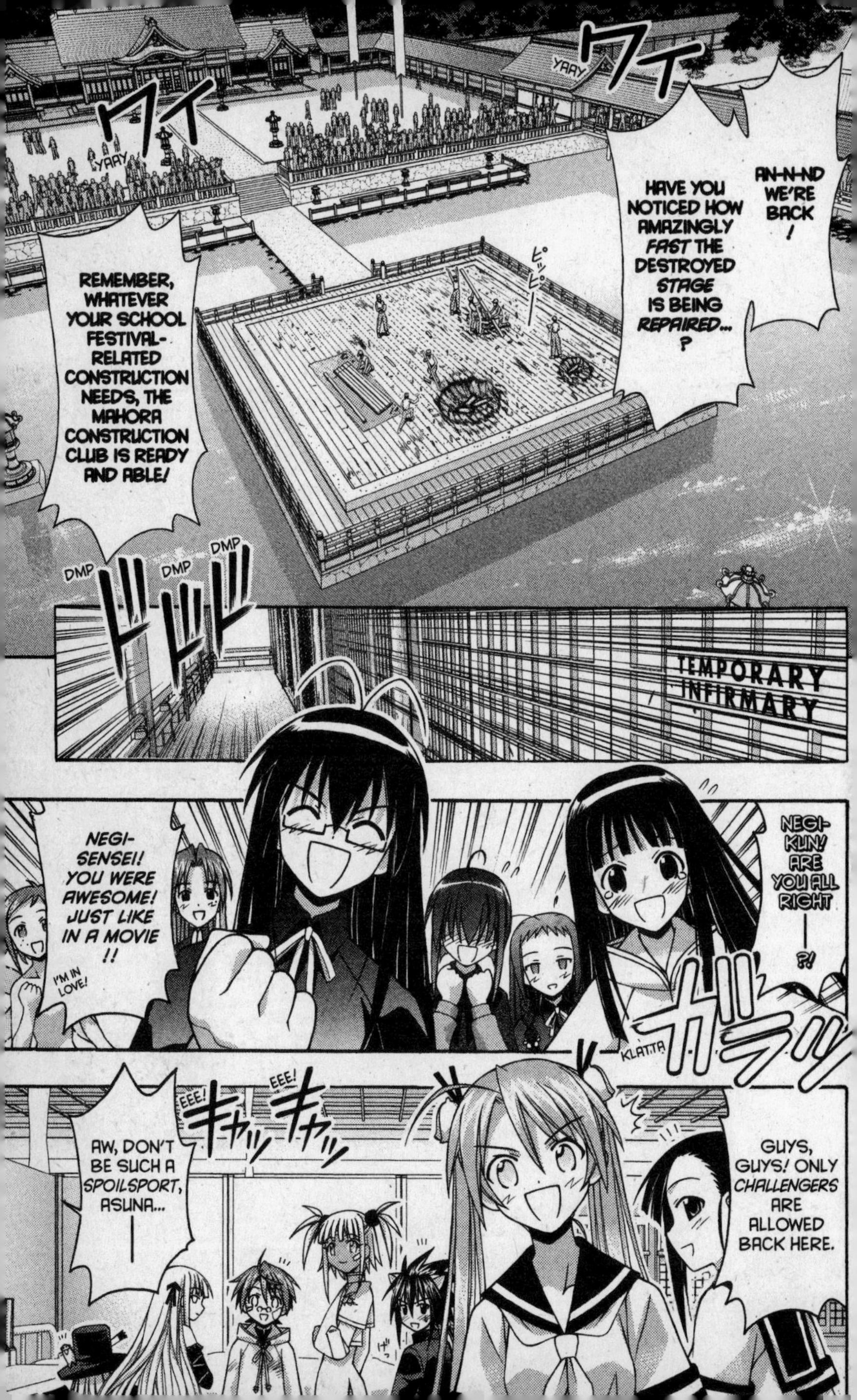
YAAY
YAAY
AN-N-ND WE'RE BACK!
HAVE YOU NOTICED HOW AMAZINGLY FAST THE DESTROYED STAGE IS BEING REPAIRED...?
REMEMBER, WHATEVER YOUR SCHOOL FESTIVAL-RELATED CONSTRUCTION NEEDS, THE MAHORA CONSTRUCTION CLUB IS READY AND ABLE!
DMP
DMP
DMP
TEMPORARY INFIRMARY
NEGI-KUN! ARE YOU ALL RIGHT—?!
KLATTA
NEGI-SENSEI! YOU WERE AWESOME! JUST LIKE IN A MOVIE!!
I'M IN LOVE!
GUYS, GUYS! ONLY CHALLENGERS ARE ALLOWED BACK HERE.
EEE!
EEE!
AW, DON'T BE SUCH A SPOILSPORT, ASUNA...—

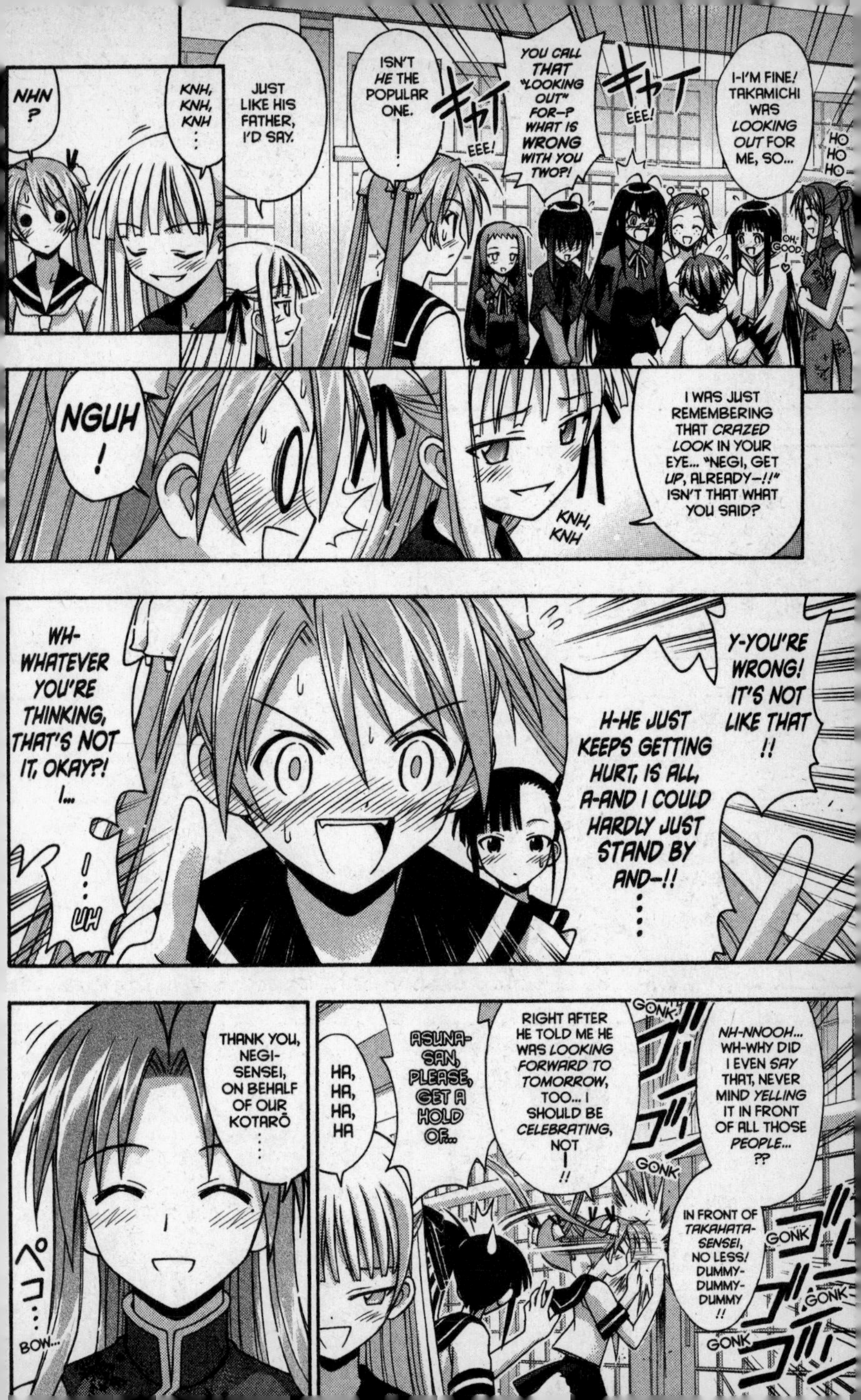
I-I'M FINE! TAKAMICHI WAS LOOKING OUT FOR ME, SO...
HO HO HO
OH, GOOD. ♡
EEE!
YOU CALL THAT "LOOKING OUT" FOR—? WHAT IS WRONG WITH YOU TWO?!
EEE!
ISN'T HE THE POPULAR ONE. ...
JUST LIKE HIS FATHER, I'D SAY.
KNH, KNH, KNH ...
NHN ?
I WAS JUST REMEMBERING THAT CRAZED LOOK IN YOUR EYE... "NEGI, GET UP, ALREADY—!!" ISN'T THAT WHAT YOU SAID?
KNH, KNH
NGUH !
Y-YOU'RE WRONG! IT'S NOT LIKE THAT !!
H-HE JUST KEEPS GETTING HURT, IS ALL, A-AND I COULD HARDLY JUST STAND BY AND—!! ....
WH-WHATEVER YOU'RE THINKING, THAT'S NOT IT, OKAY?! I...
!... UH
NH-NNOOH... WH-WHY DID I EVEN SAY THAT, NEVER MIND YELLING IT IN FRONT OF ALL THOSE PEOPLE... ??
GONK
RIGHT AFTER HE TOLD ME HE WAS LOOKING FORWARD TO TOMORROW, TOO... I SHOULD BE CELEBRATING, NOT I !!
GONK
IN FRONT OF TAKAHATA-SENSEI, NO LESS! DUMMY-DUMMY-DUMMY !!
GONK
GONK
GONK
ASUNA-SAN, PLEASE, GET A HOLD OF...
HA, HA, HA, HA
THANK YOU, NEGI-SENSEI, ON BEHALF OF OUR KOTARŌ ...
BOW...

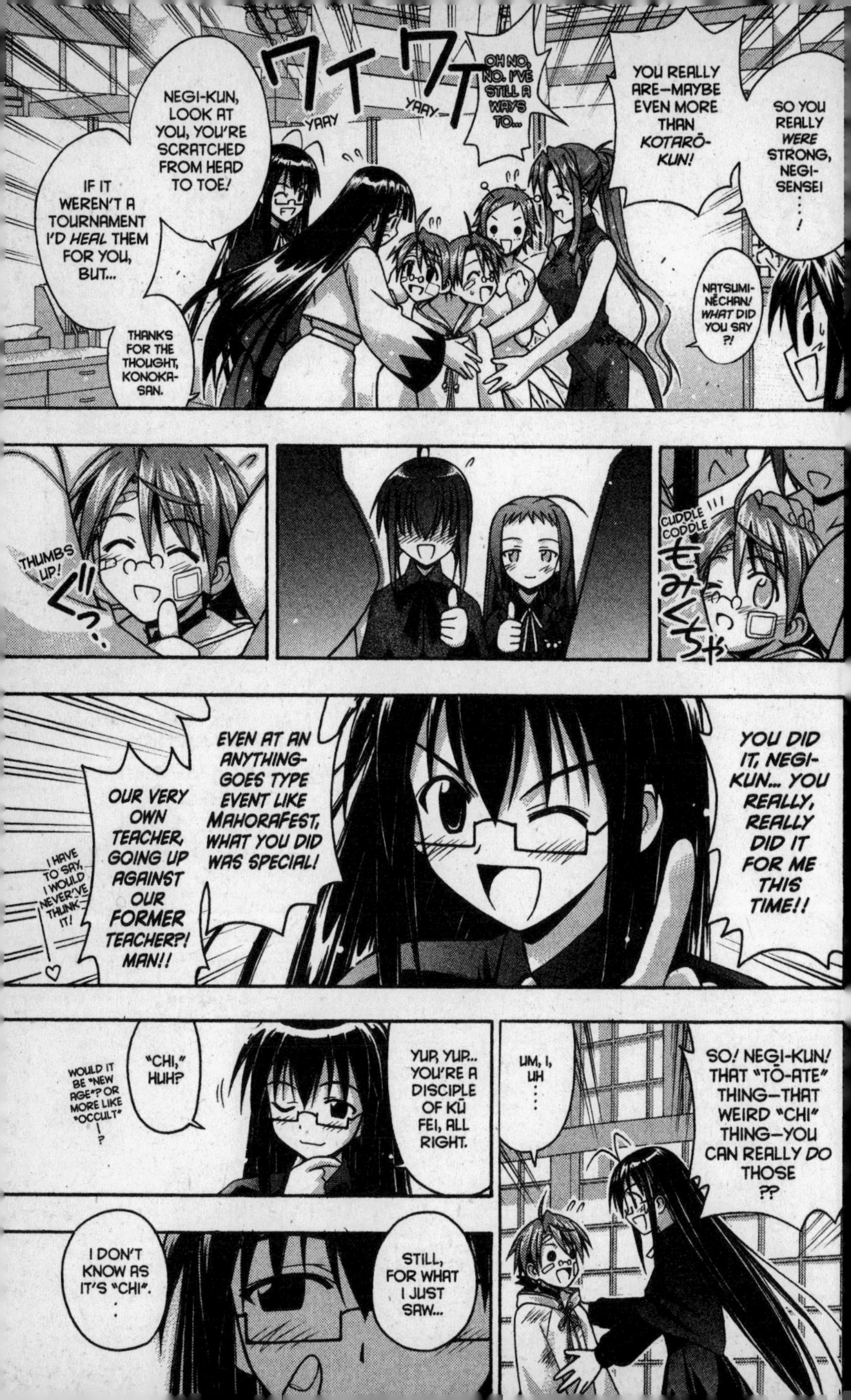
SO YOU REALLY WERE STRONG, NEGI-SENSEI...!
YOU REALLY ARE—MAYBE EVEN MORE THAN KOTARŌ-KUN!
NATSUMI-NĒCHAN! WHAT DID YOU SAY?!
OH NO, NO. I'VE STILL A WAYS TO...
ワイ ワイ
YAAY YAAY
NEGI-KUN, LOOK AT YOU, YOU'RE SCRATCHED FROM HEAD TO TOE!
IF IT WEREN'T A TOURNAMENT I'D HEAL THEM FOR YOU, BUT...
THANKS FOR THE THOUGHT, KONOKA-SAN.
CUDDLE CODDLE
もみくちゃ
THUMBS UP!
ぐっ
YOU DID IT, NEGI-KUN... YOU REALLY, REALLY DID IT FOR ME THIS TIME!!
EVEN AT AN ANYTHING-GOES TYPE EVENT LIKE MAHORAFEST, WHAT YOU DID WAS SPECIAL!
OUR VERY OWN TEACHER, GOING UP AGAINST OUR FORMER TEACHER?! MAN!!
I HAVE TO SAY, I WOULD NEVER'VE THUNK IT! ♡
SO! NEGI-KUN! THAT "TŌ-ATE" THING—THAT WEIRD "CHI" THING—YOU CAN REALLY DO THOSE??
UM, I, UH....
YUP, YUP... YOU'RE A DISCIPLE OF KŪ FEI, ALL RIGHT.
"CHI," HUH?
WOULD IT BE "NEW AGE"? OR MORE LIKE "OCCULT"...?
STILL, FOR WHAT I JUST SAW...
I DON'T KNOW AS IT'S "CHI"...

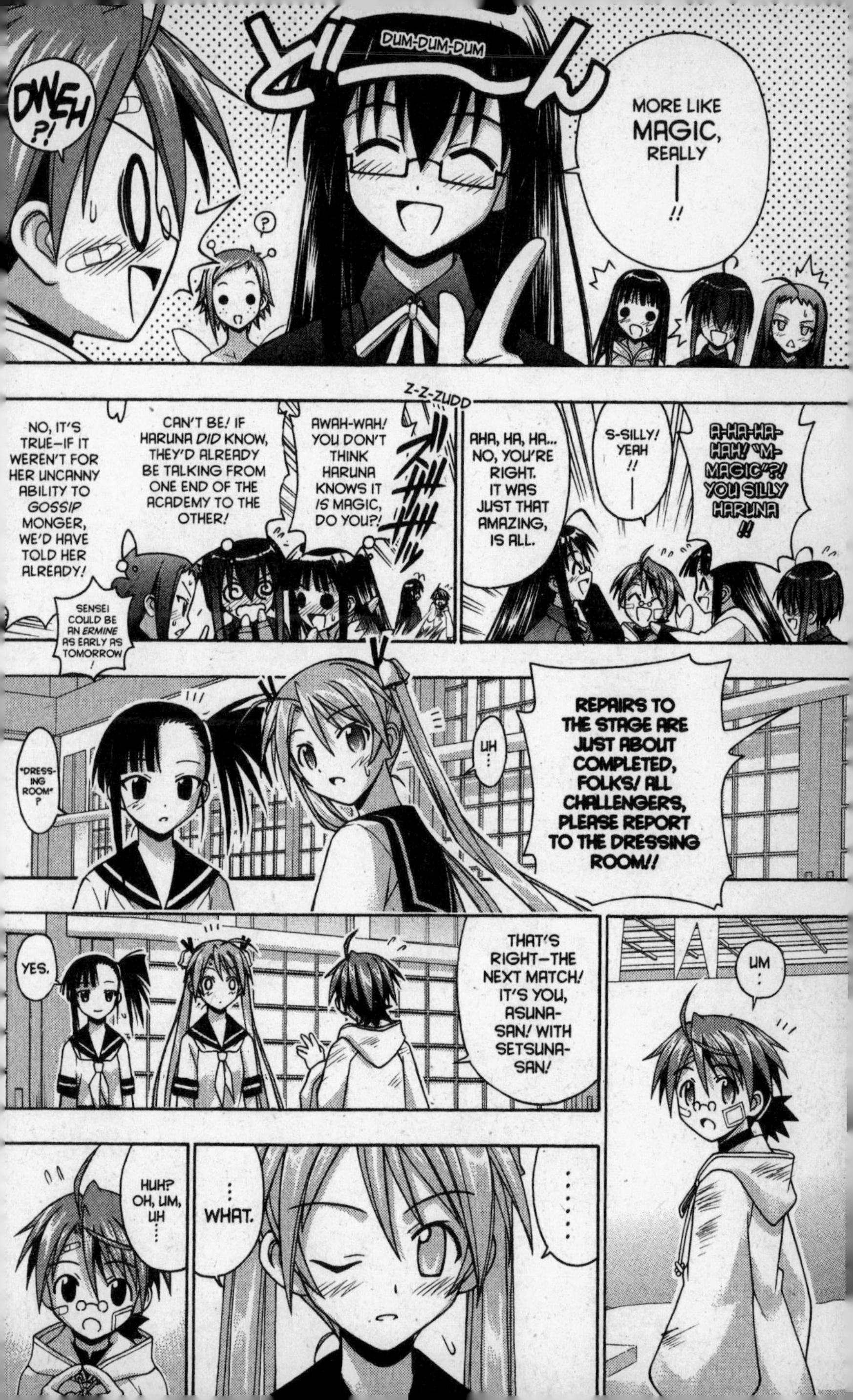
DUM-DUM-DUM
MORE LIKE MAGIC, REALLY —!!
DWEH ?!
?
A-HA-HA-HAH! "M-MAGIC"?! YOU SILLY HARUNA!!
S-SILLY! YEAH!! —
AHA, HA, HA... NO, YOU'RE RIGHT. IT WAS JUST THAT AMAZING, IS ALL.
Z-Z-ZUDD
AWAH-WAH! YOU DON'T THINK HARUNA KNOWS IT *IS* MAGIC, DO YOU?!
CAN'T BE! IF HARUNA *DID* KNOW, THEY'D ALREADY BE TALKING FROM ONE END OF THE ACADEMY TO THE OTHER!
NO, IT'S TRUE—IF IT WEREN'T FOR HER UNCANNY ABILITY TO *GOSSIP* MONGER, WE'D HAVE TOLD HER ALREADY!
SENSEI COULD BE AN *ERMINE* AS EARLY AS TOMORROW!
REPAIRS TO THE STAGE ARE JUST ABOUT COMPLETED, FOLKS! ALL CHALLENGERS, PLEASE REPORT TO THE DRESSING ROOM!!
UH...
"DRESSING ROOM"?
UM...
THAT'S RIGHT—THE NEXT MATCH! IT'S YOU, ASUNA-SAN! WITH SETSUNA-SAN!
YES.
......
... WHAT.
HUH? OH, UM, UH......

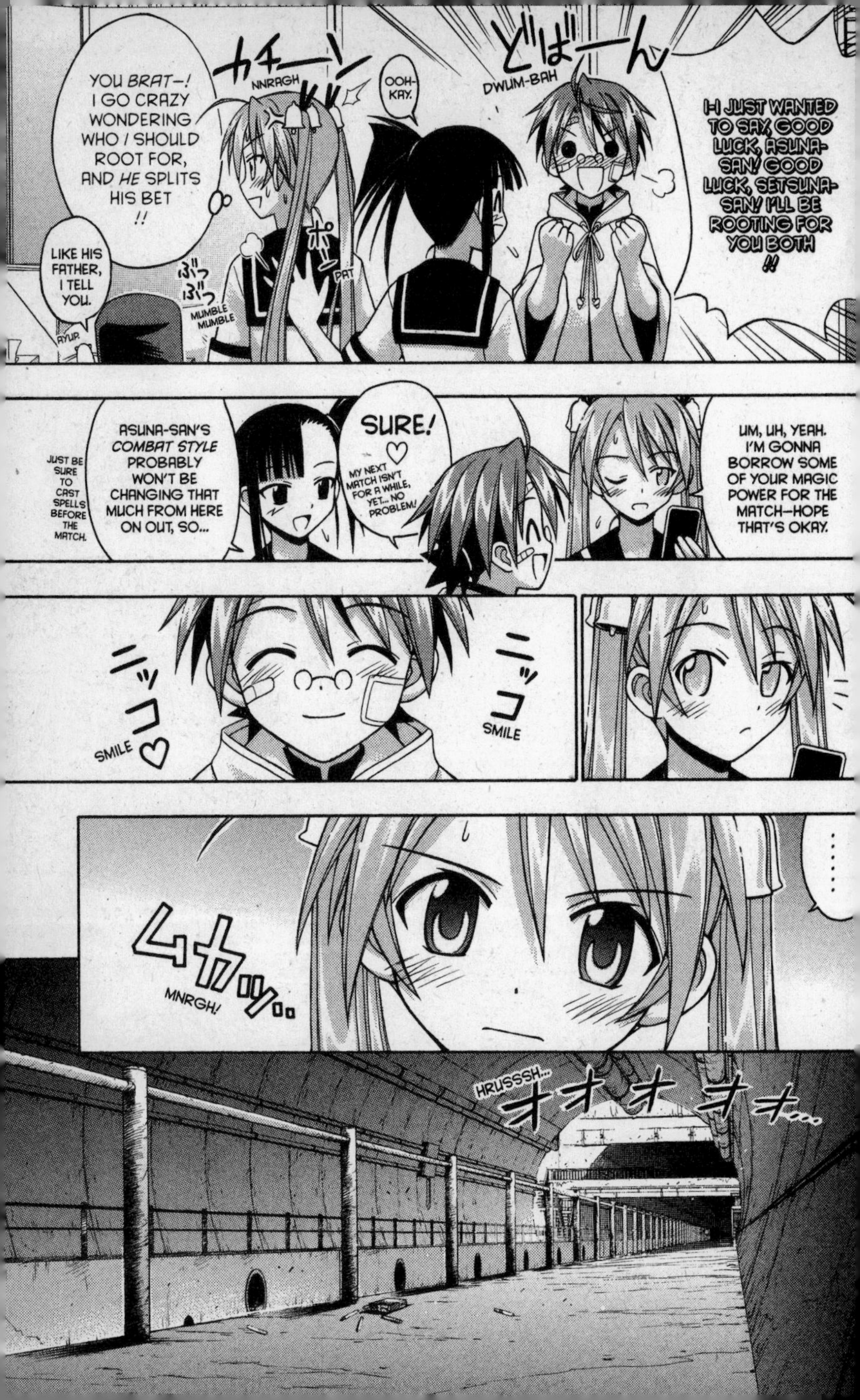
I-I JUST WANTED TO SAY, GOOD LUCK, ASUNA-SAN! GOOD LUCK, SETSUNA-SAN! I'LL BE ROOTING FOR YOU BOTH!!
どばーん
DWUM-BAH
OOH-KAY.
カチーン
NNRAGH
ポン
PAT
YOU BRAT-! I GO CRAZY WONDERING WHO I SHOULD ROOT FOR, AND HE SPLITS HIS BET!!
ぶつぶつ
MUMBLE MUMBLE
LIKE HIS FATHER, I TELL YOU.
AYUP.
UM, UH, YEAH. I'M GONNA BORROW SOME OF YOUR MAGIC POWER FOR THE MATCH—HOPE THAT'S OKAY.
SURE!
MY NEXT MATCH ISN'T FOR A WHILE, YET... NO PROBLEM!
ASUNA-SAN'S COMBAT STYLE PROBABLY WON'T BE CHANGING THAT MUCH FROM HERE ON OUT, SO...
JUST BE SURE TO CAST SPELLS BEFORE THE MATCH.
ニッコ
SMILE
ニッコ
SMILE
......
ムカッ
MNRGH!
HRUSSSH...
オオオオオ...

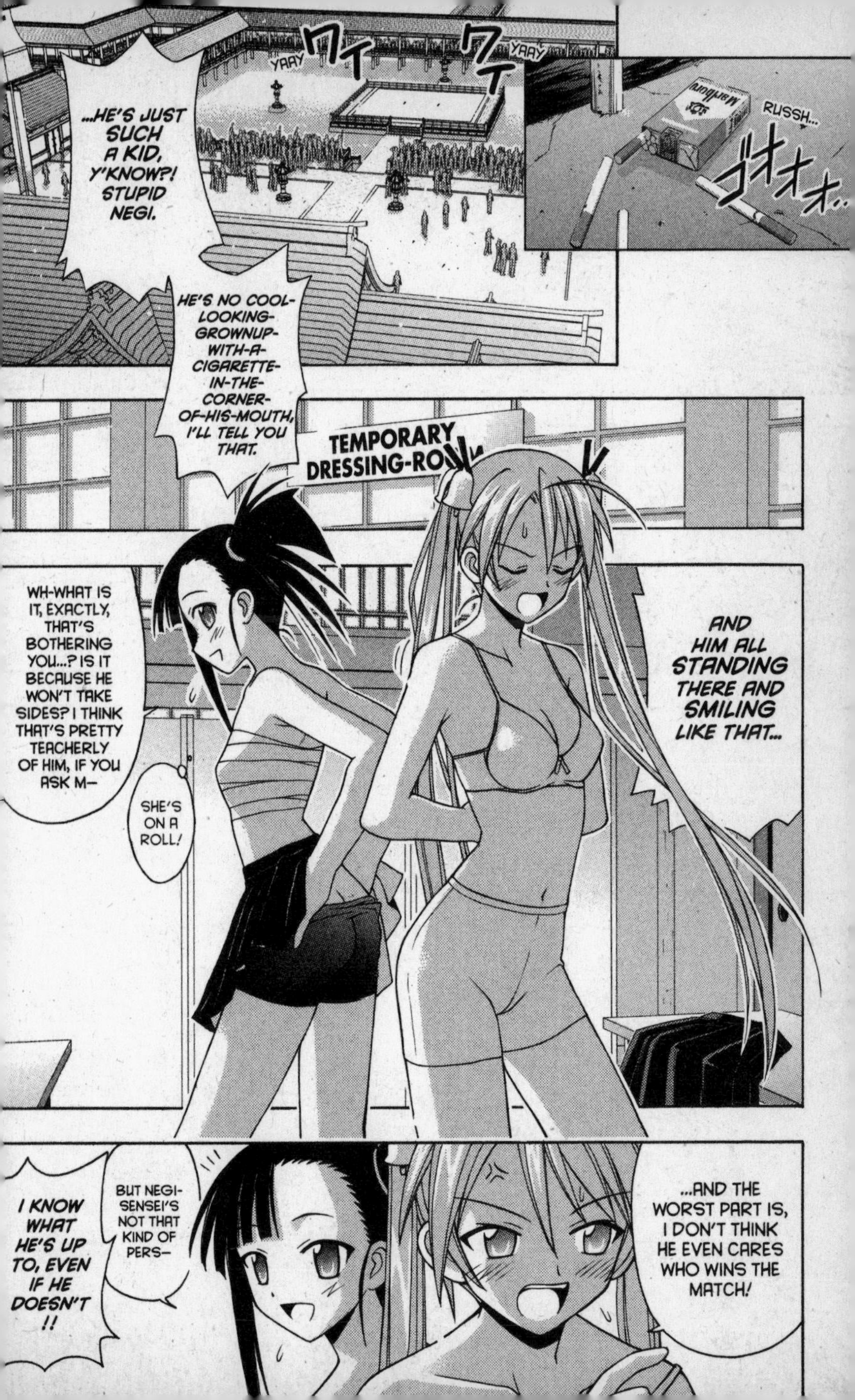

RUSSH...
ゴオオオ...
YAAY
ワイワイ
YAAY
...HE'S JUST SUCH A KID, Y'KNOW?! STUPID NEGI.
HE'S NO COOL-LOOKING-GROWNUP-WITH-A-CIGARETTE-IN-THE-CORNER-OF-HIS-MOUTH, I'LL TELL YOU THAT.
TEMPORARY DRESSING-RO
AND HIM ALL STANDING THERE AND SMILING LIKE THAT...
WH-WHAT IS IT, EXACTLY, THAT'S BOTHERING YOU...? IS IT BECAUSE HE WON'T TAKE SIDES? I THINK THAT'S PRETTY TEACHERLY OF HIM, IF YOU ASK M—
SHE'S ON A ROLL!
...AND THE WORST PART IS, I DON'T THINK HE EVEN CARES WHO WINS THE MATCH!
BUT NEGI-SENSEI'S NOT THAT KIND OF PERS—
I KNOW WHAT HE'S UP TO, EVEN IF HE DOESN'T!!

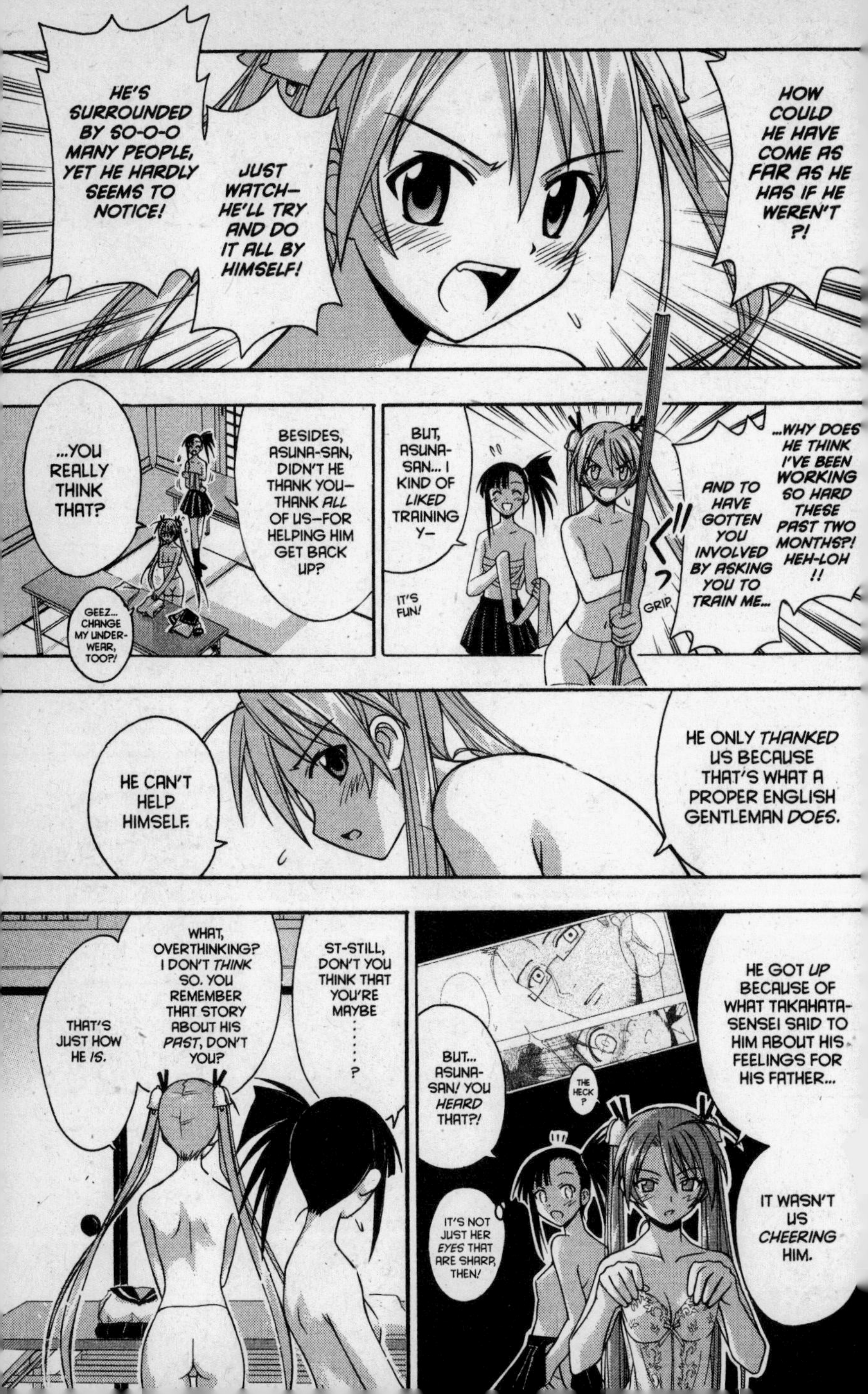
HOW COULD HE HAVE COME AS FAR AS HE HAS IF HE WEREN'T ?!
JUST WATCH— HE'LL TRY AND DO IT ALL BY HIMSELF!
HE'S SURROUNDED BY SO-O-O MANY PEOPLE, YET HE HARDLY SEEMS TO NOTICE!
...WHY DOES HE THINK I'VE BEEN WORKING SO HARD THESE PAST TWO MONTHS?! HEH-LOH !!
AND TO HAVE GOTTEN YOU INVOLVED BY ASKING YOU TO TRAIN ME...
GRIP
BUT, ASUNA-SAN... I KIND OF LIKED TRAINING Y—
IT'S FUN!
BESIDES, ASUNA-SAN, DIDN'T HE THANK YOU—THANK ALL OF US—FOR HELPING HIM GET BACK UP?
...YOU REALLY THINK THAT?
GEEZ... CHANGE MY UNDERWEAR, TOO?!
HE ONLY THANKED US BECAUSE THAT'S WHAT A PROPER ENGLISH GENTLEMAN DOES.
HE CAN'T HELP HIMSELF.
HE GOT UP BECAUSE OF WHAT TAKAHATA-SENSEI SAID TO HIM ABOUT HIS FEELINGS FOR HIS FATHER...
IT WASN'T US CHEERING HIM.
THE HECK?
BUT... ASUNA-SAN! YOU HEARD THAT?!
IT'S NOT JUST HER EYES THAT ARE SHARP, THEN!
ST-STILL, DON'T YOU THINK THAT YOU'RE MAYBE ......?
WHAT, OVERTHINKING? I DON'T THINK SO. YOU REMEMBER THAT STORY ABOUT HIS PAST, DON'T YOU?
THAT'S JUST HOW HE IS.

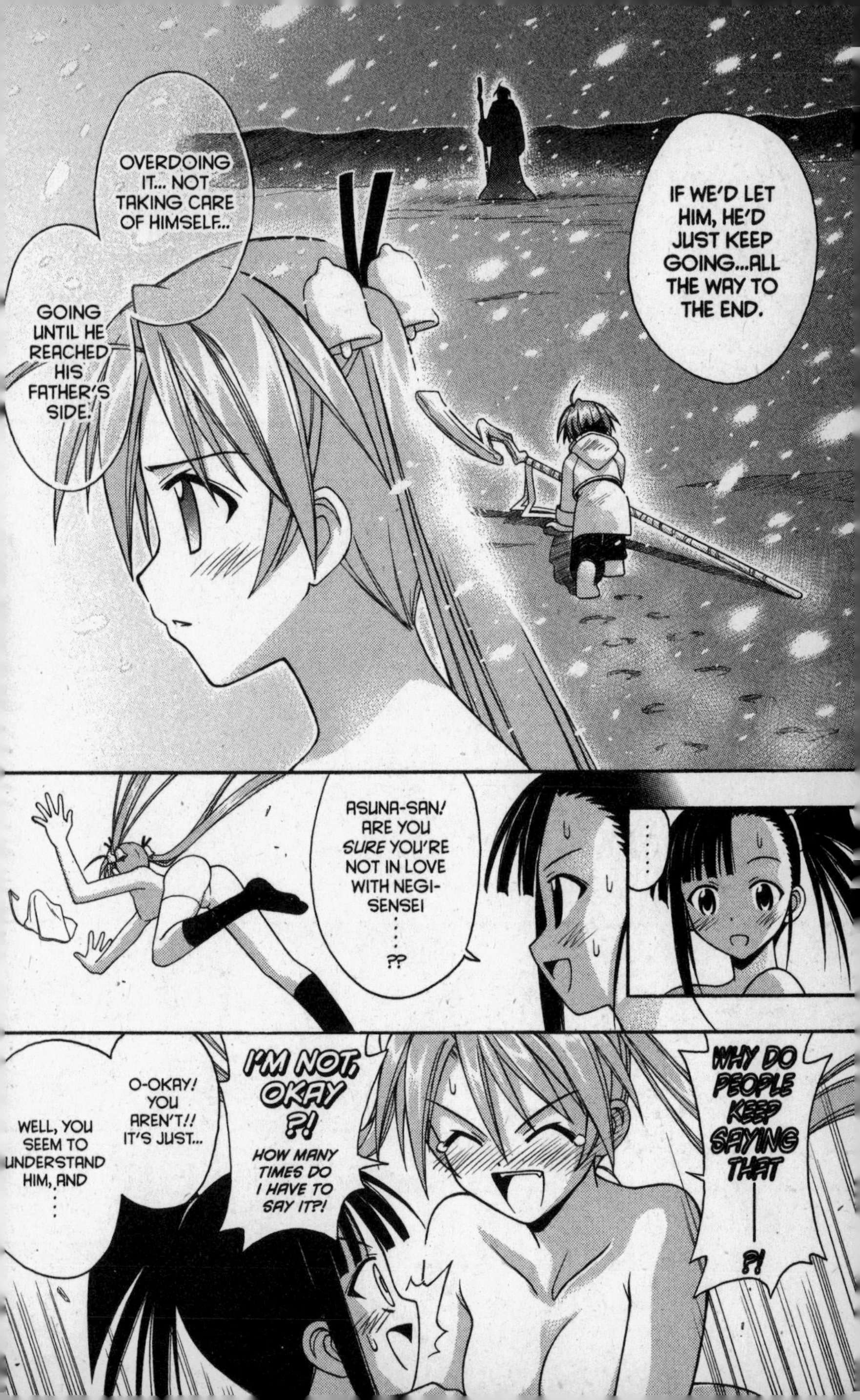
IF WE'D LET HIM, HE'D JUST KEEP GOING...ALL THE WAY TO THE END.
OVERDOING IT... NOT TAKING CARE OF HIMSELF...
GOING UNTIL HE REACHED HIS FATHER'S SIDE.
......
ASUNA-SAN! ARE YOU *SURE* YOU'RE NOT IN LOVE WITH NEGI-SENSEI ......??
WHY DO PEOPLE KEEP SAYING THAT——?!
I'M NOT, OKAY?!
HOW MANY TIMES DO I HAVE TO SAY IT?!
O-OKAY! YOU AREN'T!! IT'S JUST...
WELL, YOU SEEM TO UNDERSTAND HIM, AND ......

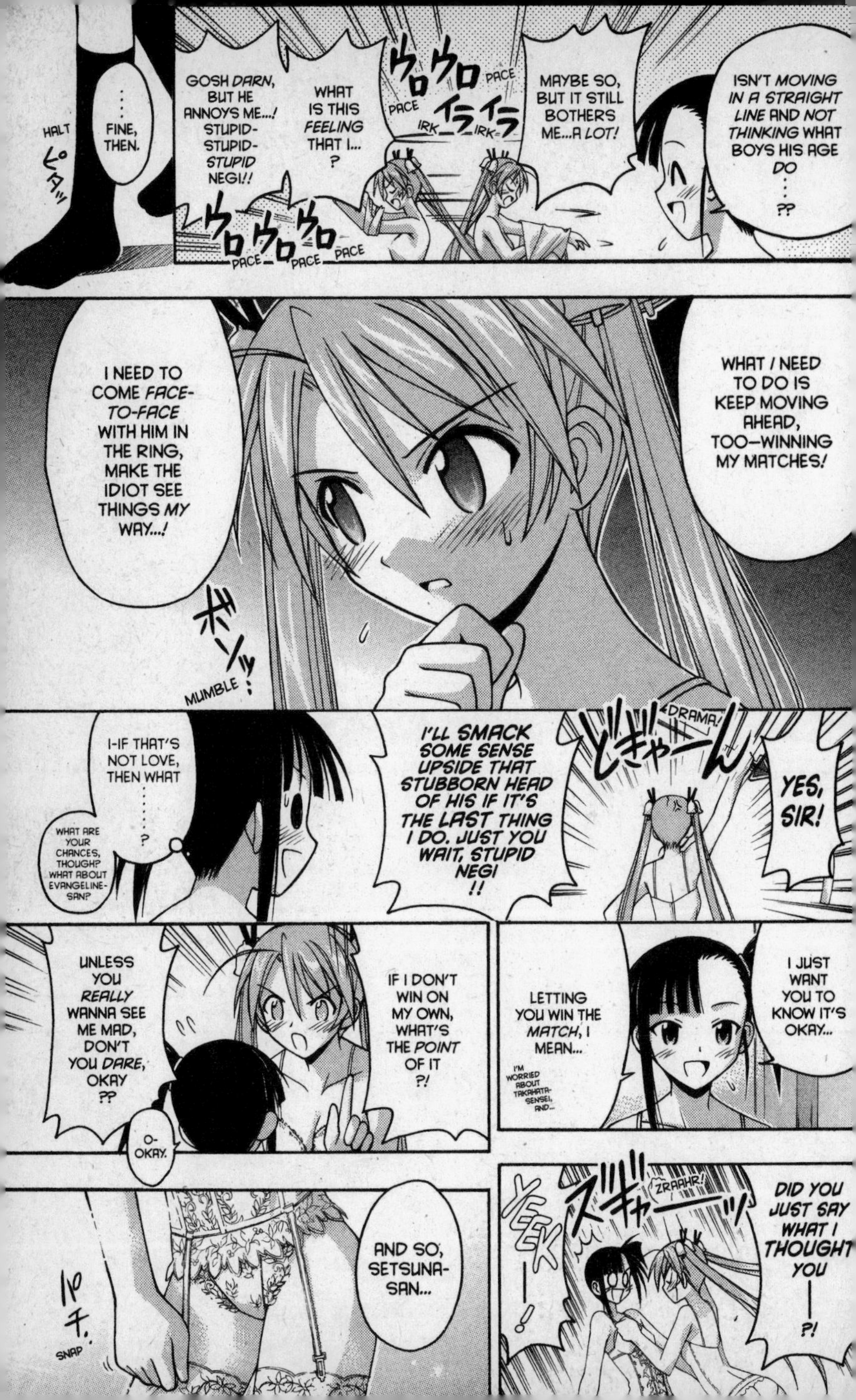
ISN'T MOVING IN A STRAIGHT LINE AND NOT THINKING WHAT BOYS HIS AGE DO ...??
MAYBE SO, BUT IT STILL BOTHERS ME...A LOT!
PACE
PACE
IRK
IRK
WHAT IS THIS FEELING THAT I... ?
GOSH DARN, BUT HE ANNOYS ME...! STUPID-STUPID-STUPID NEGI!!
PACE
PACE
PACE
... FINE, THEN.
HALT
WHAT I NEED TO DO IS KEEP MOVING AHEAD, TOO—WINNING MY MATCHES!
I NEED TO COME FACE-TO-FACE WITH HIM IN THE RING, MAKE THE IDIOT SEE THINGS MY WAY...!
MUMBLE
DRAMA!
YES, SIR!
I'LL SMACK SOME SENSE UPSIDE THAT STUBBORN HEAD OF HIS IF IT'S THE LAST THING I DO. JUST YOU WAIT, STUPID NEGI !!
I-IF THAT'S NOT LOVE, THEN WHAT ...... ?
WHAT ARE YOUR CHANCES, THOUGH? WHAT ABOUT EVANGELINE-SAN?
I JUST WANT YOU TO KNOW IT'S OKAY...
LETTING YOU WIN THE MATCH, I MEAN...
I'M WORRIED ABOUT TAKAHATA-SENSEI, AND...
IF I DON'T WIN ON MY OWN, WHAT'S THE POINT OF IT ?!
UNLESS YOU REALLY WANNA SEE ME MAD, DON'T YOU DARE, OKAY ??
O-OKAY.
DID YOU JUST SAY WHAT I THOUGHT YOU —?!
ZRAAHR!
YEEK—!
AND SO, SETSUNA-SAN...
SNAP

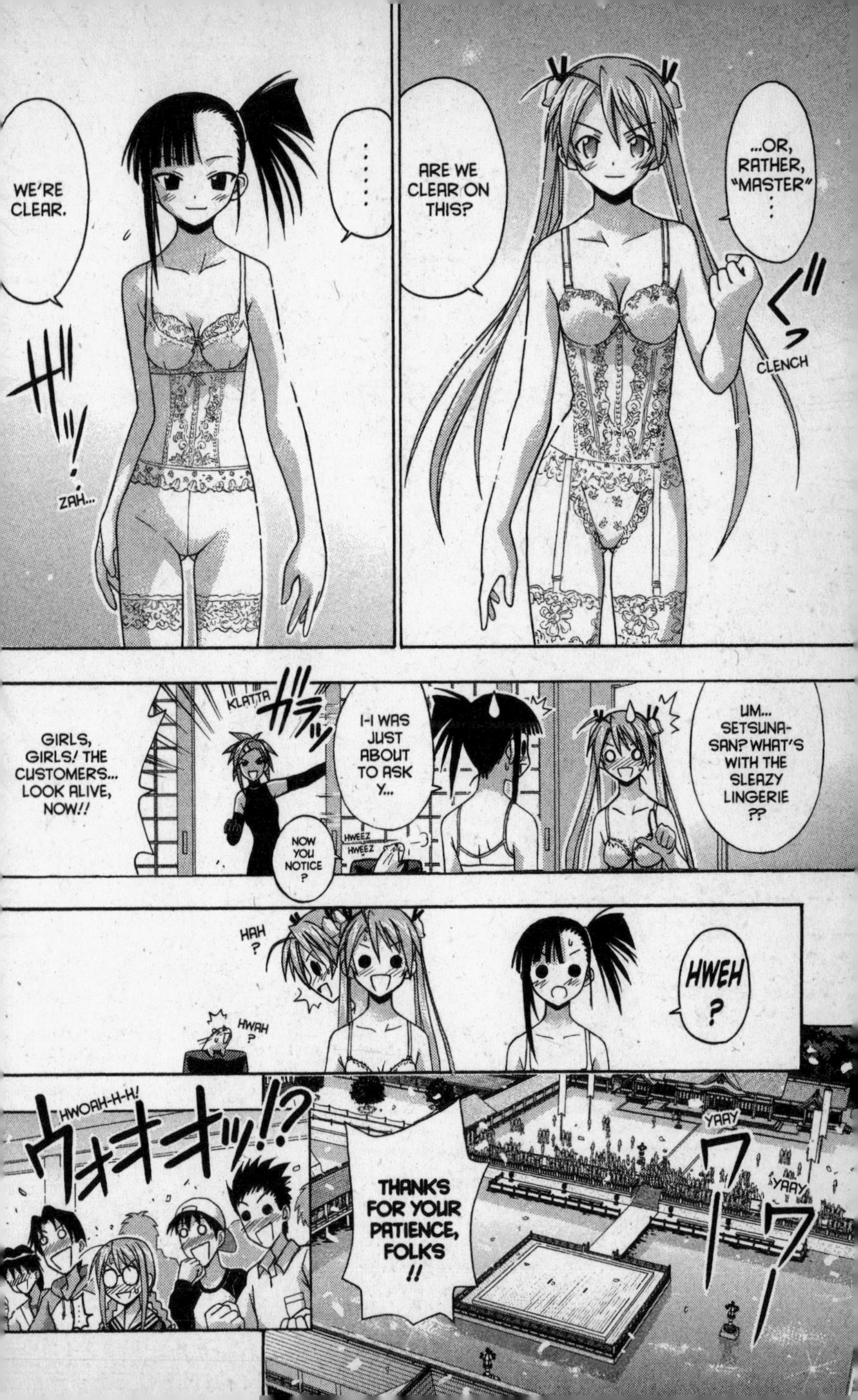

...OR, RATHER, "MASTER" ...
ARE WE CLEAR ON THIS?
CLENCH
......
WE'RE CLEAR.
ZAH...
UM... SETSUNA-SAN? WHAT'S WITH THE SLEAZY LINGERIE ??
I-I WAS JUST ABOUT TO ASK Y...
HWEEZ HWEEZ
NOW YOU NOTICE ?
KLATTA
GIRLS, GIRLS! THE CUSTOMERS... LOOK ALIVE, NOW!!
HWEH ?
HAH ?
HWAH ?
YAAY
YAAY
THANKS FOR YOUR PATIENCE, FOLKS !!
HWOAH-H-H!

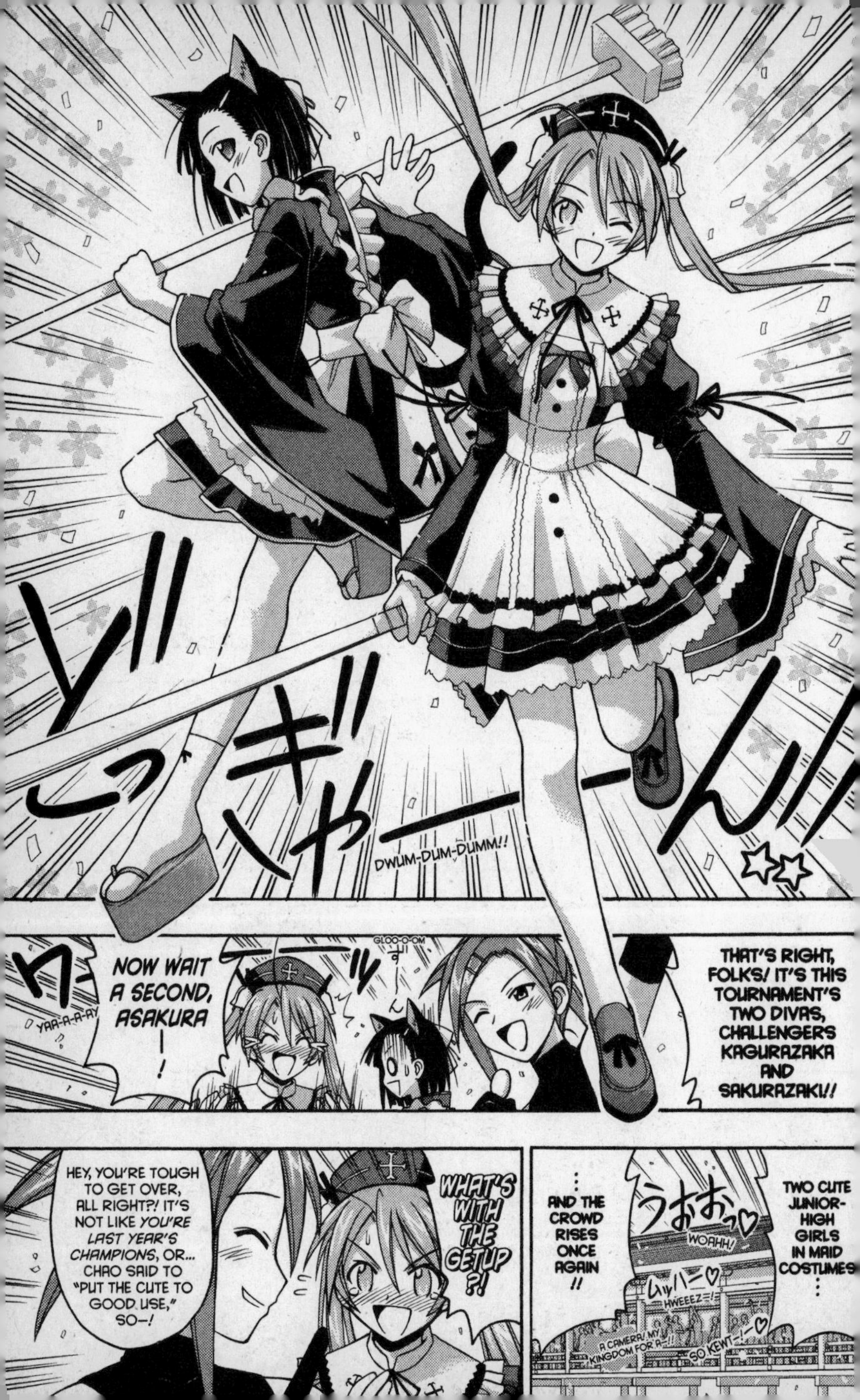
どっぎゃーーん!!
DWUM-DUM-DUMM!!
THAT'S RIGHT, FOLKS! IT'S THIS TOURNAMENT'S TWO DIVAS, CHALLENGERS KAGURAZAKA AND SAKURAZAKI!!
GLOO-O-OM
ず~ん
NOW WAIT A SECOND, ASAKURA—!
わー
YAA-A-A-AY
TWO CUTE JUNIOR-HIGH GIRLS IN MAID COSTUMES...
...AND THE CROWD RISES ONCE AGAIN!!
うおおっ♡
WOAHH!
ムッハー♡
HWEEEZ—!
A CAMERA! MY KINGDOM FOR A—!
SO KEWT—!—♡
WHAT'S WITH THE GETUP?!
HEY, YOU'RE TOUGH TO GET OVER, ALL RIGHT?! IT'S NOT LIKE *YOU'RE LAST YEAR'S CHAMPIONS*, OR... CHAO SAID TO "PUT THE CUTE TO GOOD USE," SO—!

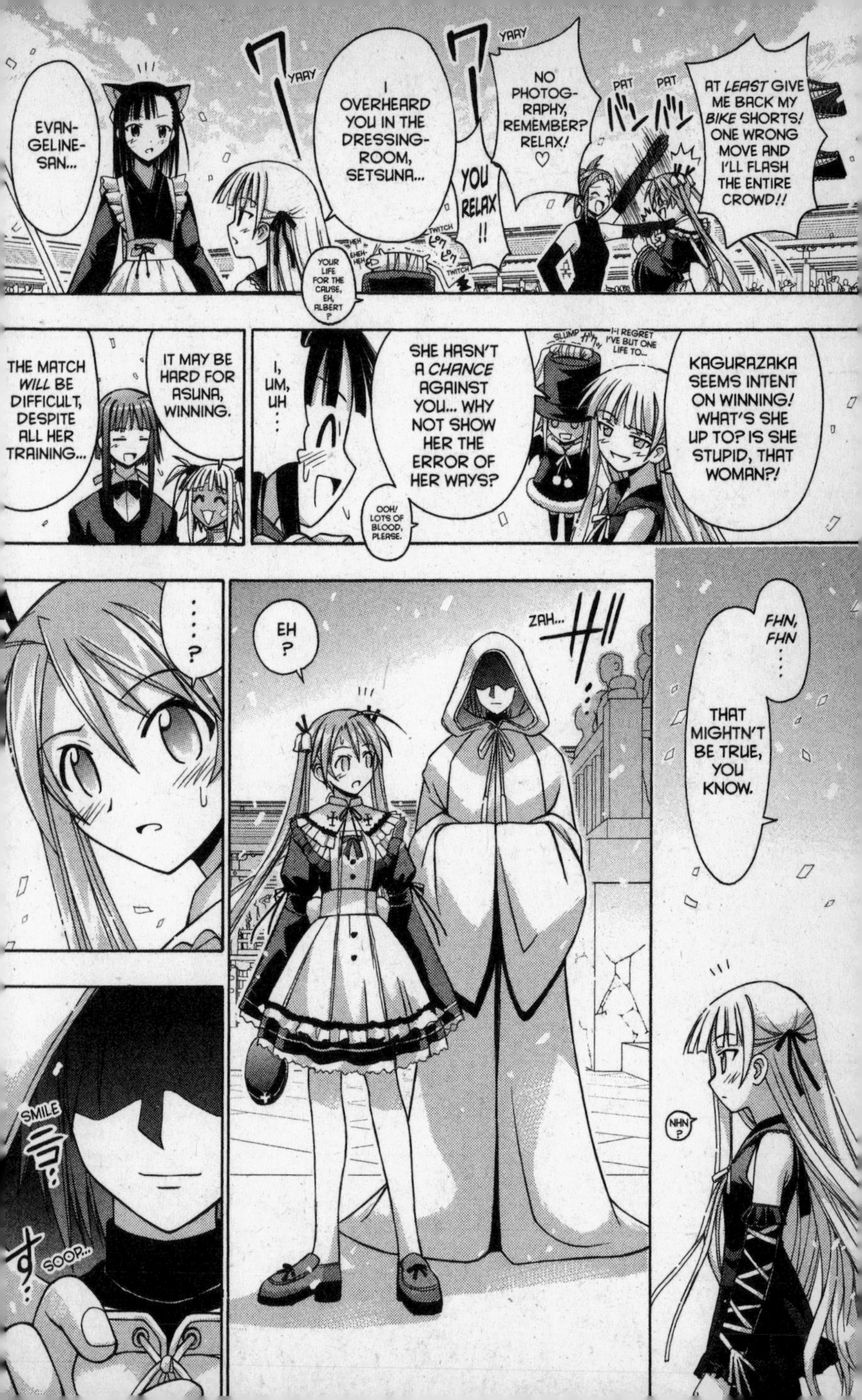
AT LEAST GIVE ME BACK MY BIKE SHORTS! ONE WRONG MOVE AND I'LL FLASH THE ENTIRE CROWD!!
PAT PAT
NO PHOTOG-RAPHY, REMEMBER? RELAX! ♡
YAAY
YOU RELAX!!
TWITCH TWITCH
I OVERHEARD YOU IN THE DRESSING-ROOM, SETSUNA...
YAAY
HEH EHEH-HEH
YOUR LIFE FOR THE CAUSE, EH, ALBERT?
EVAN-GELINE-SAN...
KAGURAZAKA SEEMS INTENT ON WINNING! WHAT'S SHE UP TO? IS SHE STUPID, THAT WOMAN?!
I-I REGRET I'VE BUT ONE LIFE TO...
SLUMP
SHE HASN'T A CHANCE AGAINST YOU... WHY NOT SHOW HER THE ERROR OF HER WAYS?
OOH! LOTS OF BLOOD, PLEASE.
I, UM, UH...
IT MAY BE HARD FOR ASUNA, WINNING.
THE MATCH WILL BE DIFFICULT, DESPITE ALL HER TRAINING...
FHN, FHN....
THAT MIGHTN'T BE TRUE, YOU KNOW.
NHN?
ZAH...
EH?
....?
SMILE
SOOP...

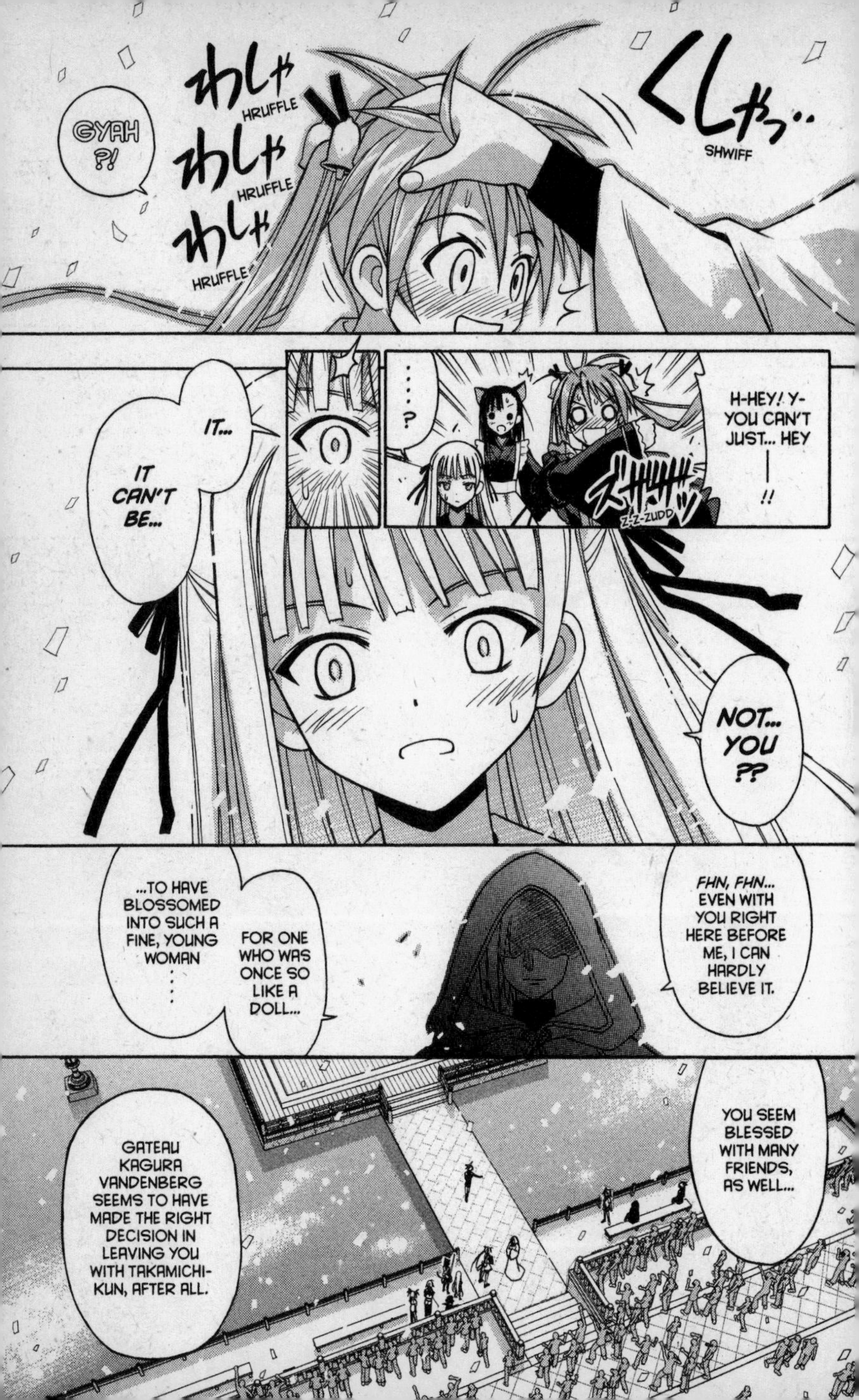
くしゃっ‥
SHWIFF
わしゃ
HRUFFLE
わしゃ
HRUFFLE
わしゃ
HRUFFLE
GYAH ?!
H-HEY! Y-YOU CAN'T JUST... HEY —!!
ズザザザッ
Z-Z-ZUDD
...?
IT...
IT CAN'T BE...
NOT... YOU??
FHN, FHN... EVEN WITH YOU RIGHT HERE BEFORE ME, I CAN HARDLY BELIEVE IT.
FOR ONE WHO WAS ONCE SO LIKE A DOLL...
...TO HAVE BLOSSOMED INTO SUCH A FINE, YOUNG WOMAN...
YOU SEEM BLESSED WITH MANY FRIENDS, AS WELL...
GATEAU KAGURA VANDENBERG SEEMS TO HAVE MADE THE RIGHT DECISION IN LEAVING YOU WITH TAKAMICHI-KUN, AFTER ALL.

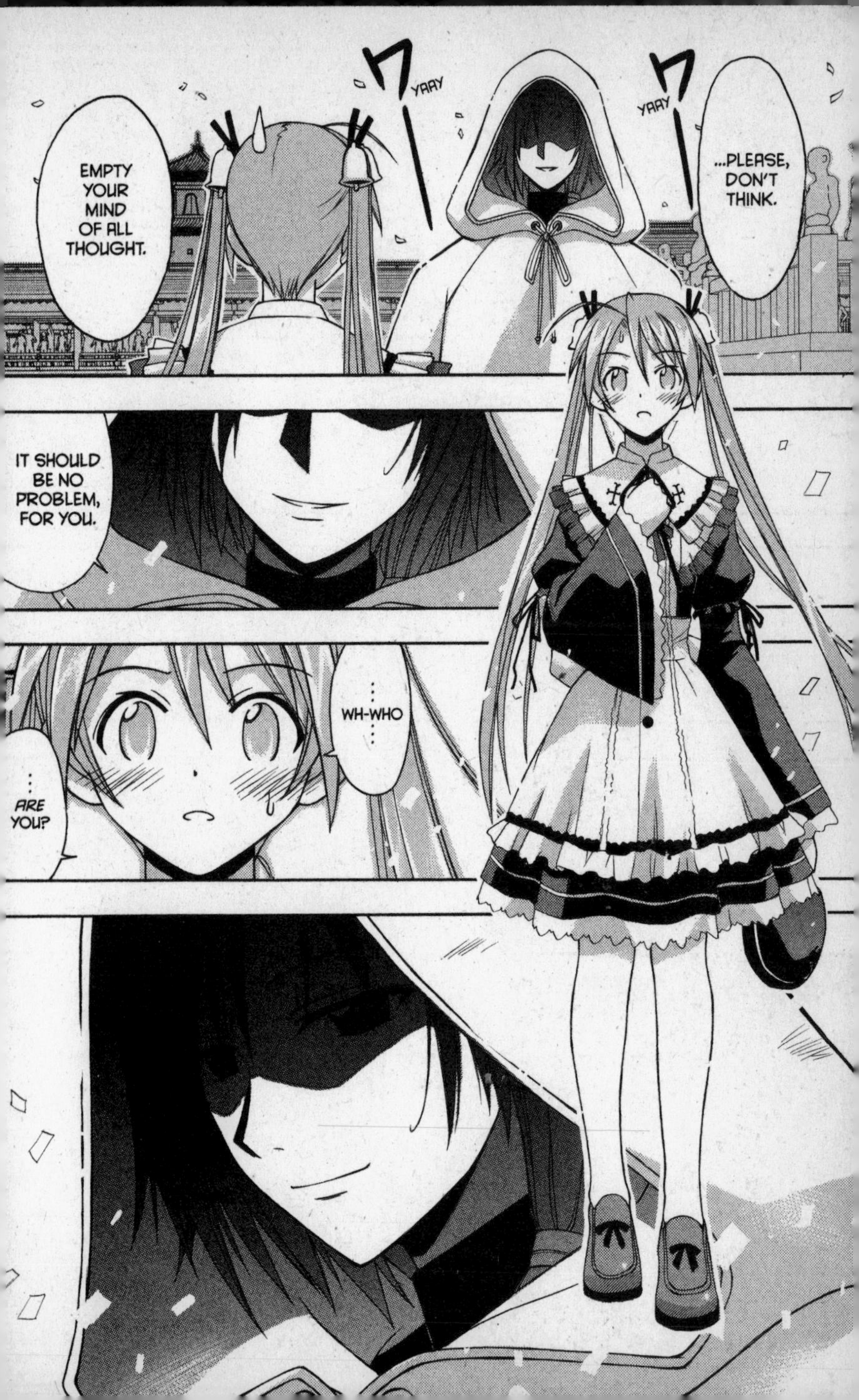
YAAY
...PLEASE, DON'T THINK.
YAAY
EMPTY YOUR MIND OF ALL THOUGHT.
IT SHOULD BE NO PROBLEM, FOR YOU.
...WH-WHO...
...ARE YOU?

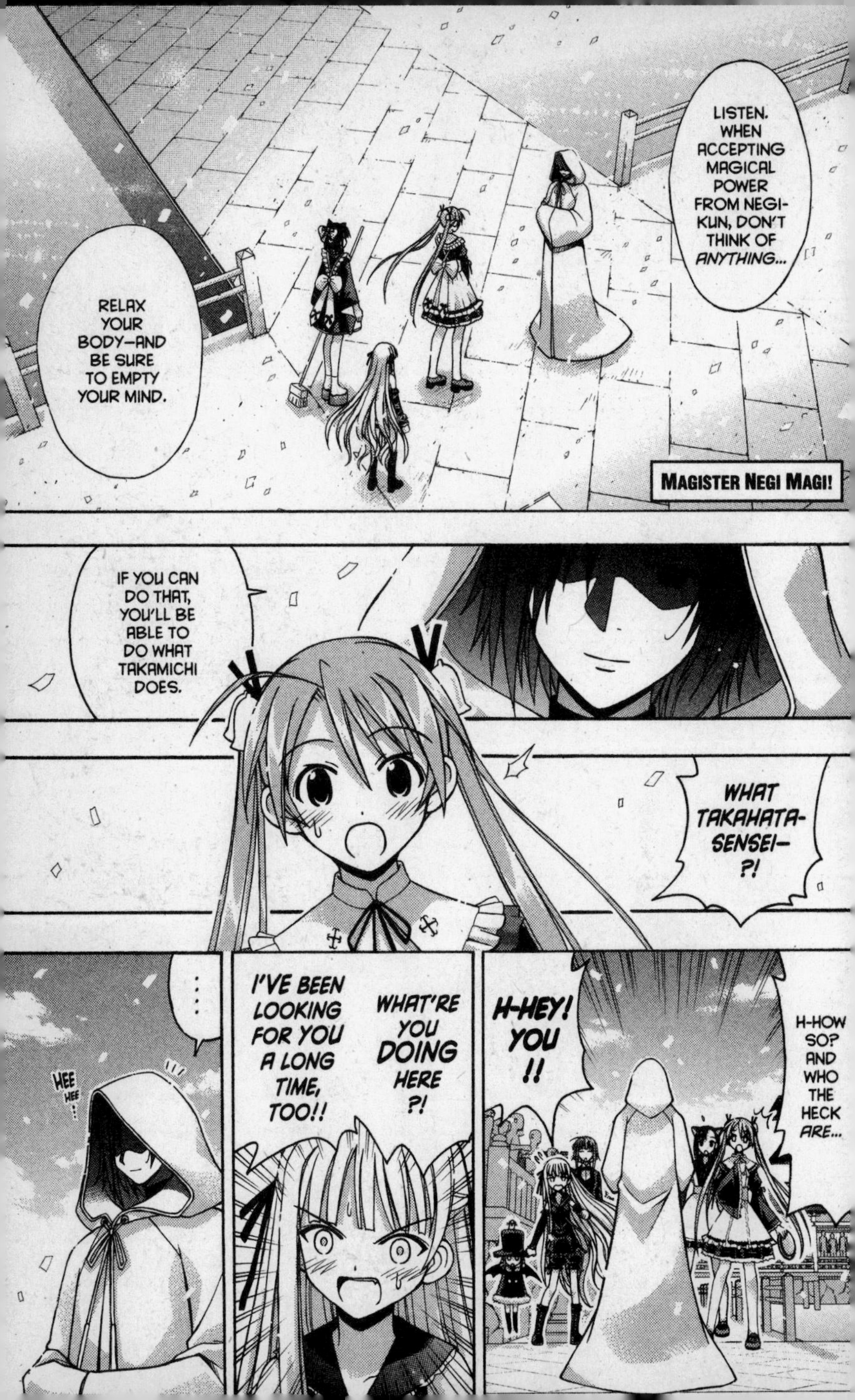
LISTEN. WHEN ACCEPTING MAGICAL POWER FROM NEGI-KUN, DON'T THINK OF *ANYTHING*...
RELAX YOUR BODY—AND BE SURE TO EMPTY YOUR MIND.
MAGISTER NEGI MAGI!
IF YOU CAN DO THAT, YOU'LL BE ABLE TO DO WHAT TAKAMICHI DOES.
WHAT TAKAHATA-SENSEI—?!
H-HOW SO? AND WHO THE HECK *ARE*...
H-HEY! YOU!!
WHAT'RE YOU DOING HERE?!
I'VE BEEN LOOKING FOR YOU A LONG TIME, TOO!!
....
HEE HEE

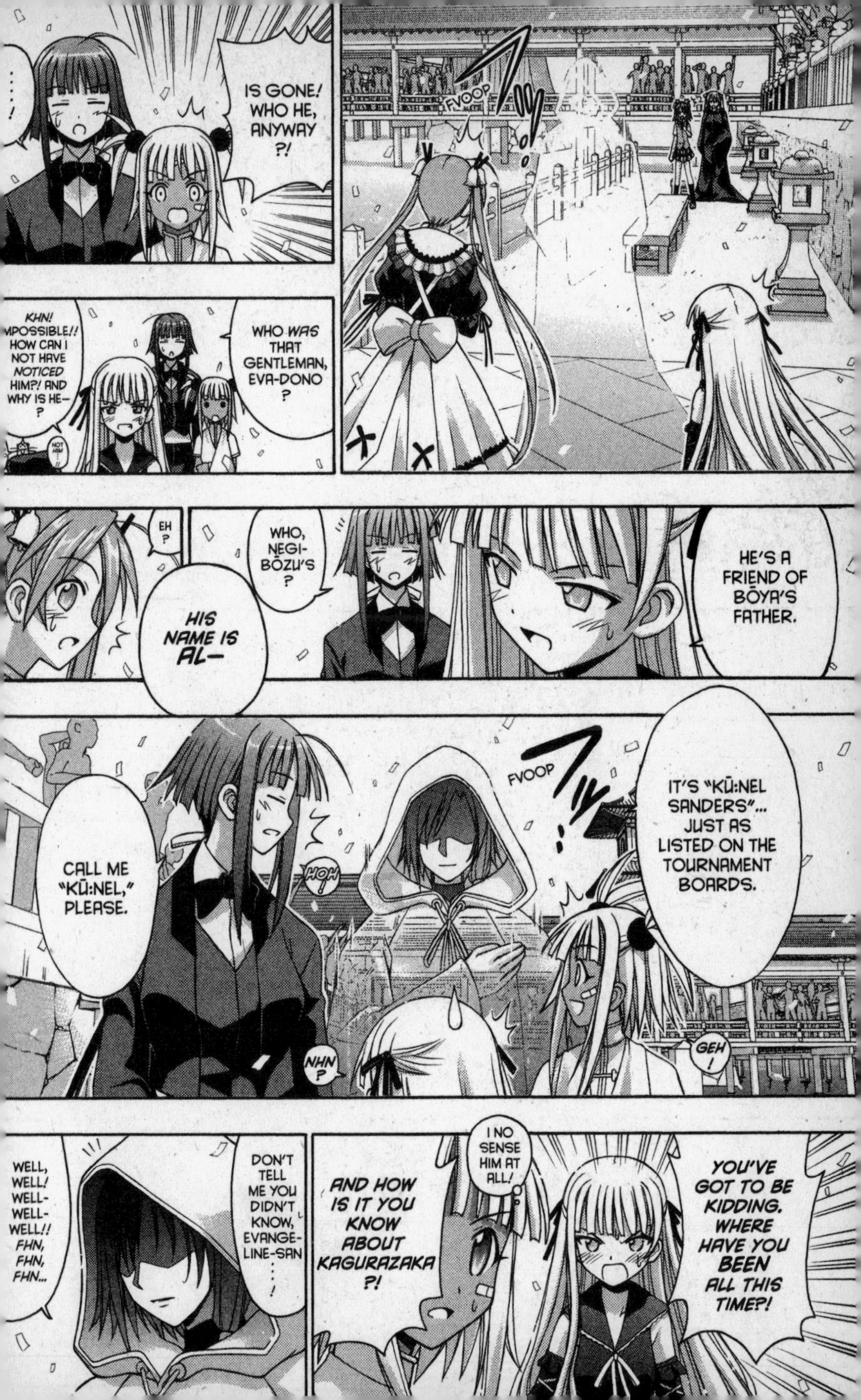
FVOOP
....!
IS GONE! WHO HE, ANYWAY?!
WHO WAS THAT GENTLEMAN, EVA-DONO?
KHN! IMPOSSIBLE!! HOW CAN I NOT HAVE NOTICED HIM?! AND WHY IS HE—?
NOT HIM...!!
HE'S A FRIEND OF BŌYA'S FATHER.
WHO, NEGI-BŌZU'S?
HIS NAME IS AL—
EH?
IT'S "KŪ:NEL SANDERS"... JUST AS LISTED ON THE TOURNAMENT BOARDS.
FVOOP
GEH!
HOH!
CALL ME "KŪ:NEL," PLEASE.
NHN?
YOU'VE GOT TO BE KIDDING. WHERE HAVE YOU BEEN ALL THIS TIME?!
I NO SENSE HIM AT ALL!
AND HOW IS IT YOU KNOW ABOUT KAGURAZAKA?!
DON'T TELL ME YOU DIDN'T KNOW, EVANGELINE-SAN...!
WELL, WELL! WELL-WELL-WELL!! FHN, FHN, FHN...

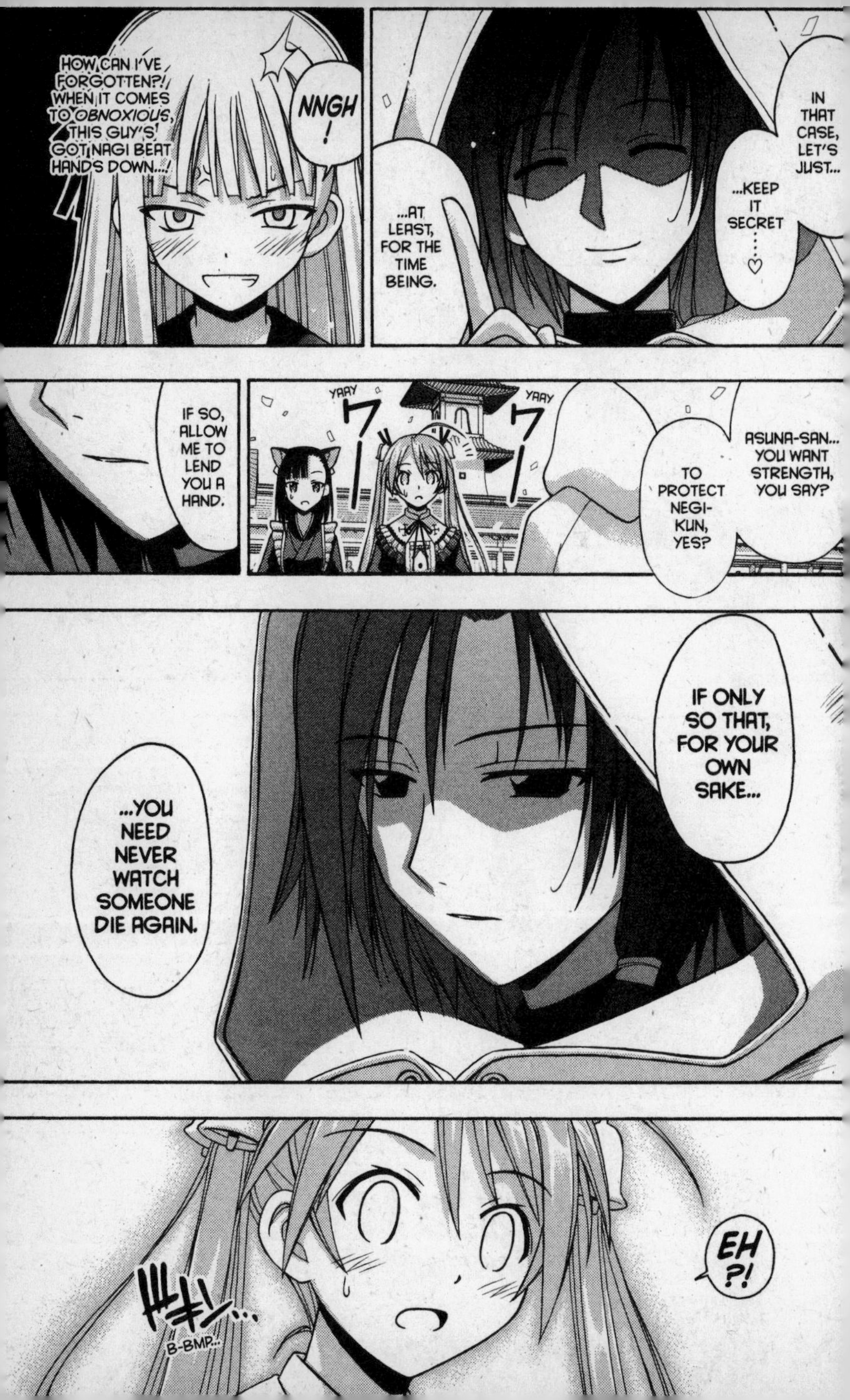
IN THAT CASE, LET'S JUST...
...KEEP IT SECRET ♡
...AT LEAST, FOR THE TIME BEING.
NNGH!
HOW CAN I'VE FORGOTTEN?! WHEN IT COMES TO *OBNOXIOUS*, THIS GUY'S GOT NAGI BEAT HANDS DOWN...!
ASUNA-SAN... YOU WANT STRENGTH, YOU SAY?
TO PROTECT NEGI-KUN, YES?
YAAY
YAAY
IF SO, ALLOW ME TO LEND YOU A HAND.
IF ONLY SO THAT, FOR YOUR OWN SAKE...
...YOU NEED NEVER WATCH SOMEONE DIE AGAIN.
EH?!
B-BMP...

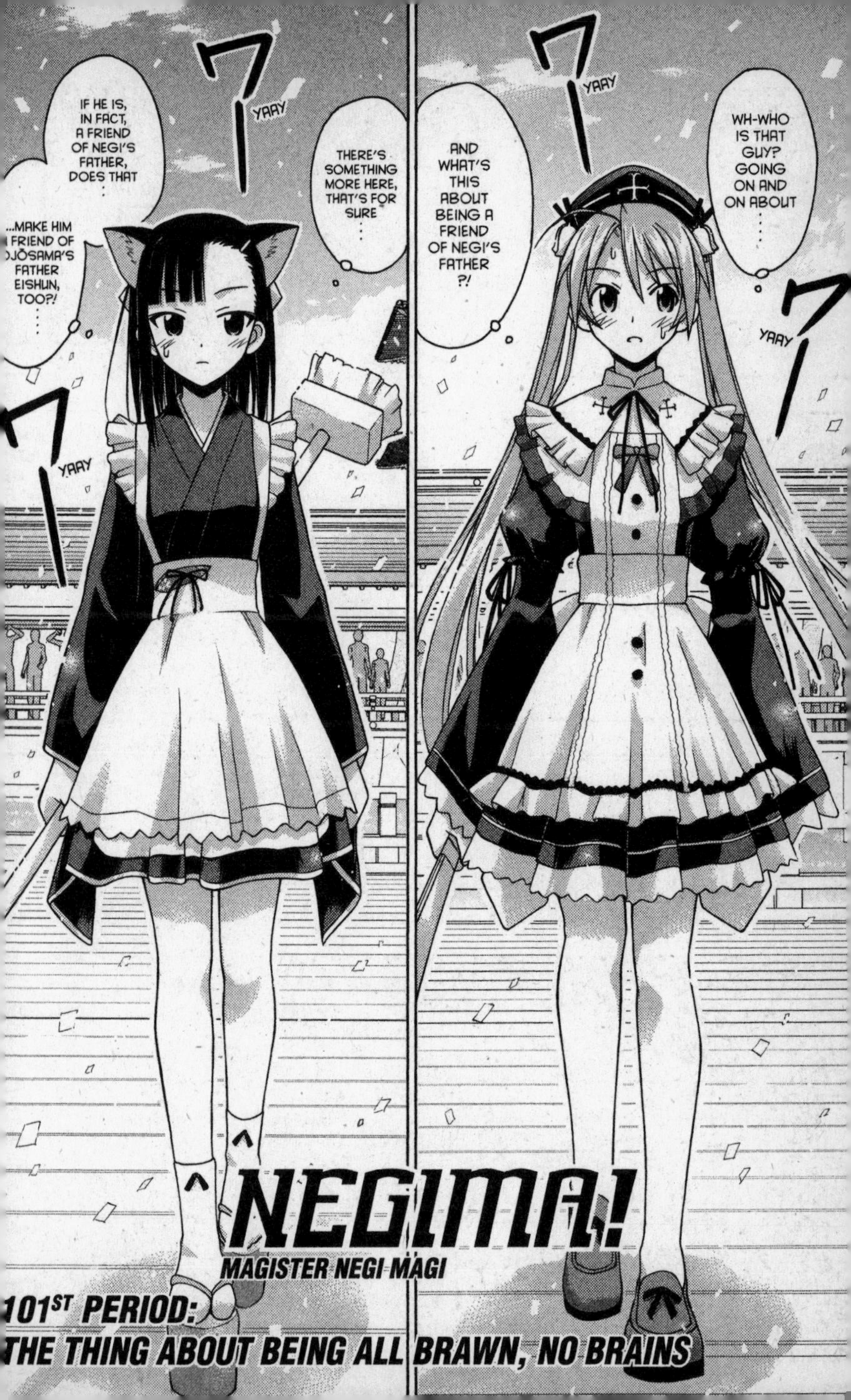
YAAY
WH-WHO IS THAT GUY? GOING ON AND ON ABOUT ....
YAAY
AND WHAT'S THIS ABOUT BEING A FRIEND OF NEGI'S FATHER ?!
THERE'S SOMETHING MORE HERE, THAT'S FOR SURE ....
YAAY
IF HE IS, IN FACT, A FRIEND OF NEGI'S FATHER, DOES THAT ...
...MAKE HIM FRIEND OF OJŌSAMA'S FATHER EISHUN, TOO?! ....
YAAY
NEGIMA!
MAGISTER NEGI MAGI
101ST PERIOD:
THE THING ABOUT BEING ALL BRAWN, NO BRAINS

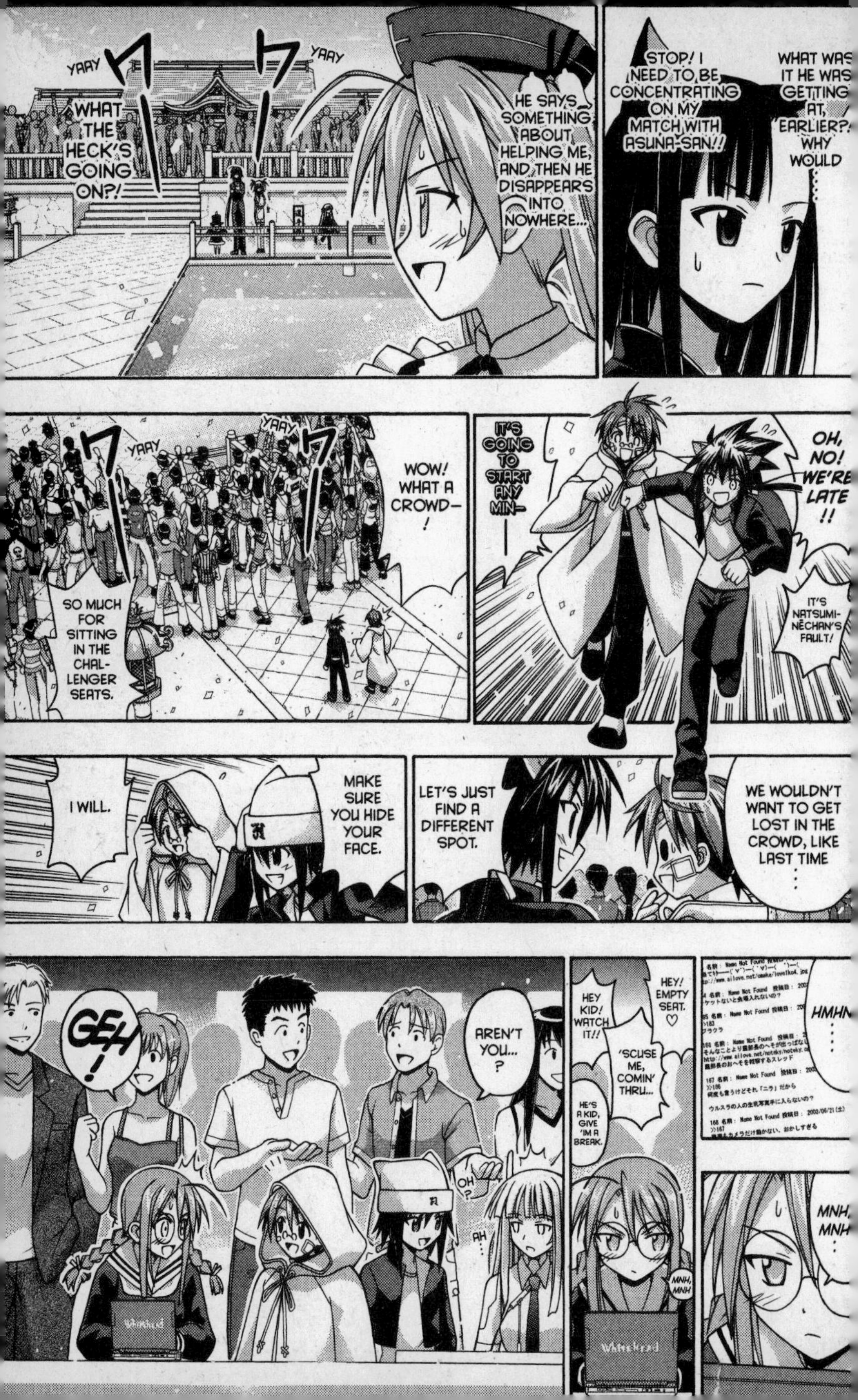
WHAT WAS IT HE WAS GETTING AT, EARLIER?! WHY WOULD...
STOP! I NEED TO BE CONCENTRATING ON MY MATCH WITH ASUNA-SAN!!
YAAY
HE SAYS SOMETHING ABOUT HELPING ME, AND THEN HE DISAPPEARS INTO NOWHERE...
YAAY
WHAT THE HECK'S GOING ON?!
OH, NO! WE'RE LATE!!
IT'S GOING TO START ANY MIN—
IT'S NATSUMI-NÊCHAN'S FAULT!
YAAY
WOW! WHAT A CROWD—!
YAAY
SO MUCH FOR SITTING IN THE CHALLENGER SEATS.
WE WOULDN'T WANT TO GET LOST IN THE CROWD, LIKE LAST TIME...
LET'S JUST FIND A DIFFERENT SPOT.
MAKE SURE YOU HIDE YOUR FACE.
I WILL.
HMHN...
MNH, MNH...
HEY! EMPTY SEAT. ♡
HEY KID! WATCH IT!!
'SCUSE ME, COMIN' THRU...
HE'S A KID, GIVE 'IM A BREAK.
MNH, MNH
AREN'T YOU...?
OH?
AH...
GEH!

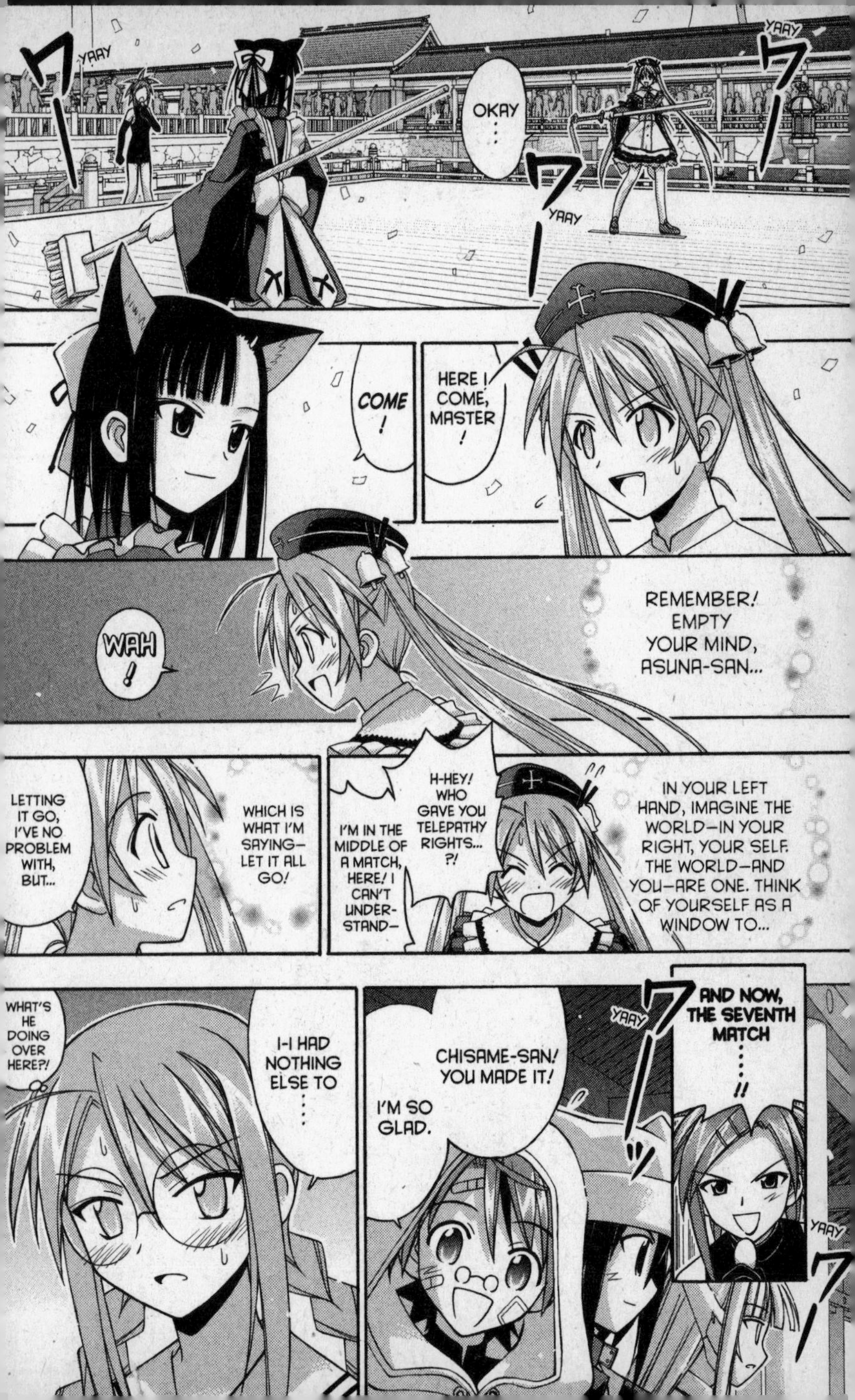
YAAY
OKAY...
YAAY
YAAY
HERE I COME, MASTER!
COME!
REMEMBER! EMPTY YOUR MIND, ASUNA-SAN...
WAH!
IN YOUR LEFT HAND, IMAGINE THE WORLD—IN YOUR RIGHT, YOUR SELF. THE WORLD—AND YOU—ARE ONE. THINK OF YOURSELF AS A WINDOW TO...
H-HEY! WHO GAVE YOU TELEPATHY RIGHTS...?!
I'M IN THE MIDDLE OF A MATCH, HERE! I CAN'T UNDER-STAND—
WHICH IS WHAT I'M SAYING—LET IT ALL GO!
LETTING IT GO, I'VE NO PROBLEM WITH, BUT...
AND NOW, THE SEVENTH MATCH.....!!
YAAY
YAAY
CHISAME-SAN! YOU MADE IT!
I'M SO GLAD.
I-I HAD NOTHING ELSE TO....
WHAT'S HE DOING OVER HERE?!

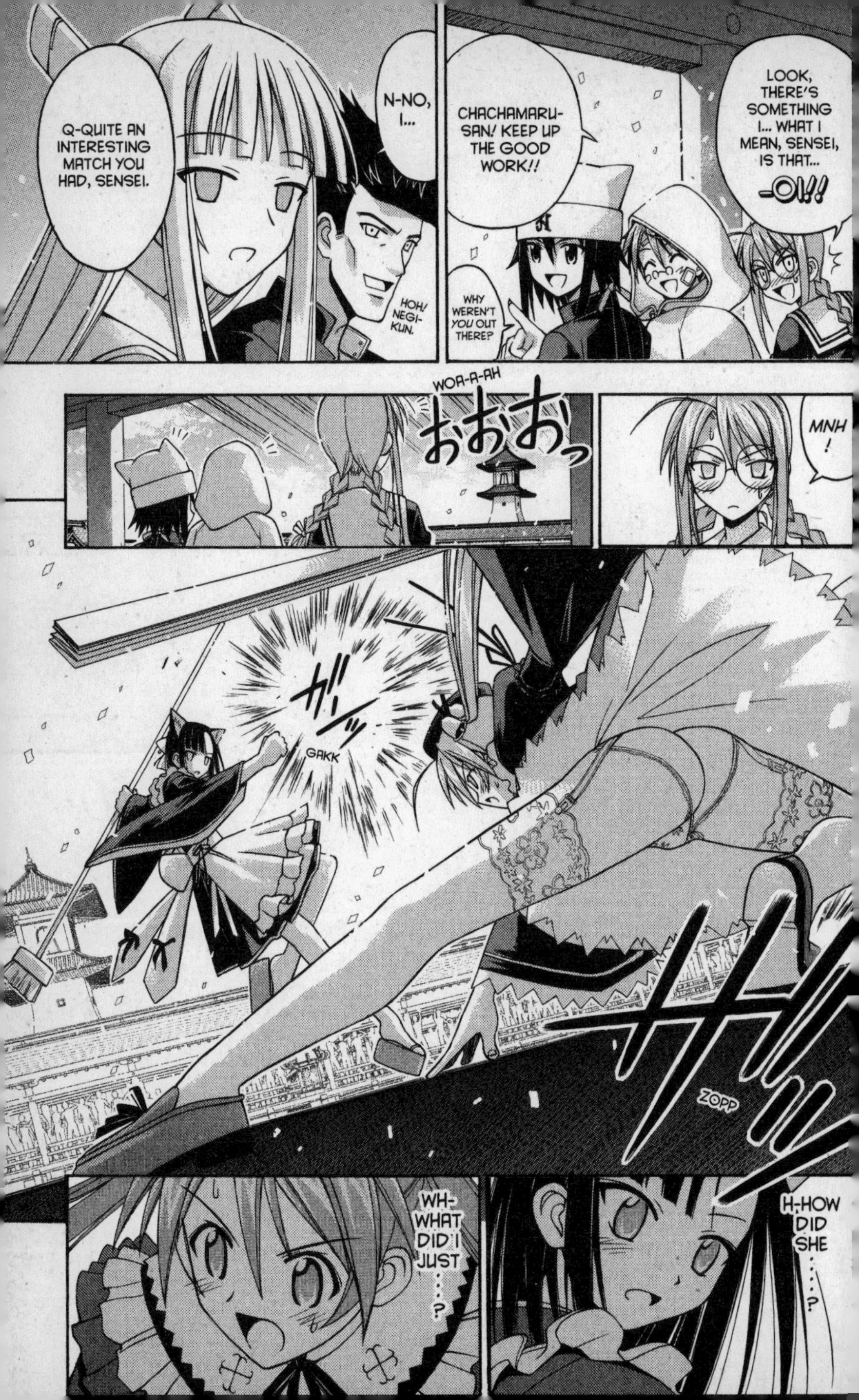

LOOK, THERE'S SOMETHING I... WHAT I MEAN, SENSEI, IS THAT...
-OH!!
CHACHAMARU-SAN! KEEP UP THE GOOD WORK!!
WHY WEREN'T YOU OUT THERE?
N-NO, I...
HOH! NEGI-KUN.
Q-QUITE AN INTERESTING MATCH YOU HAD, SENSEI.
MNH!
WOA-A-AH
おおおっ
ガッ
GAKK
ZOPP
H-HOW DID SHE......?
WH-WHAT DID I JUST......?

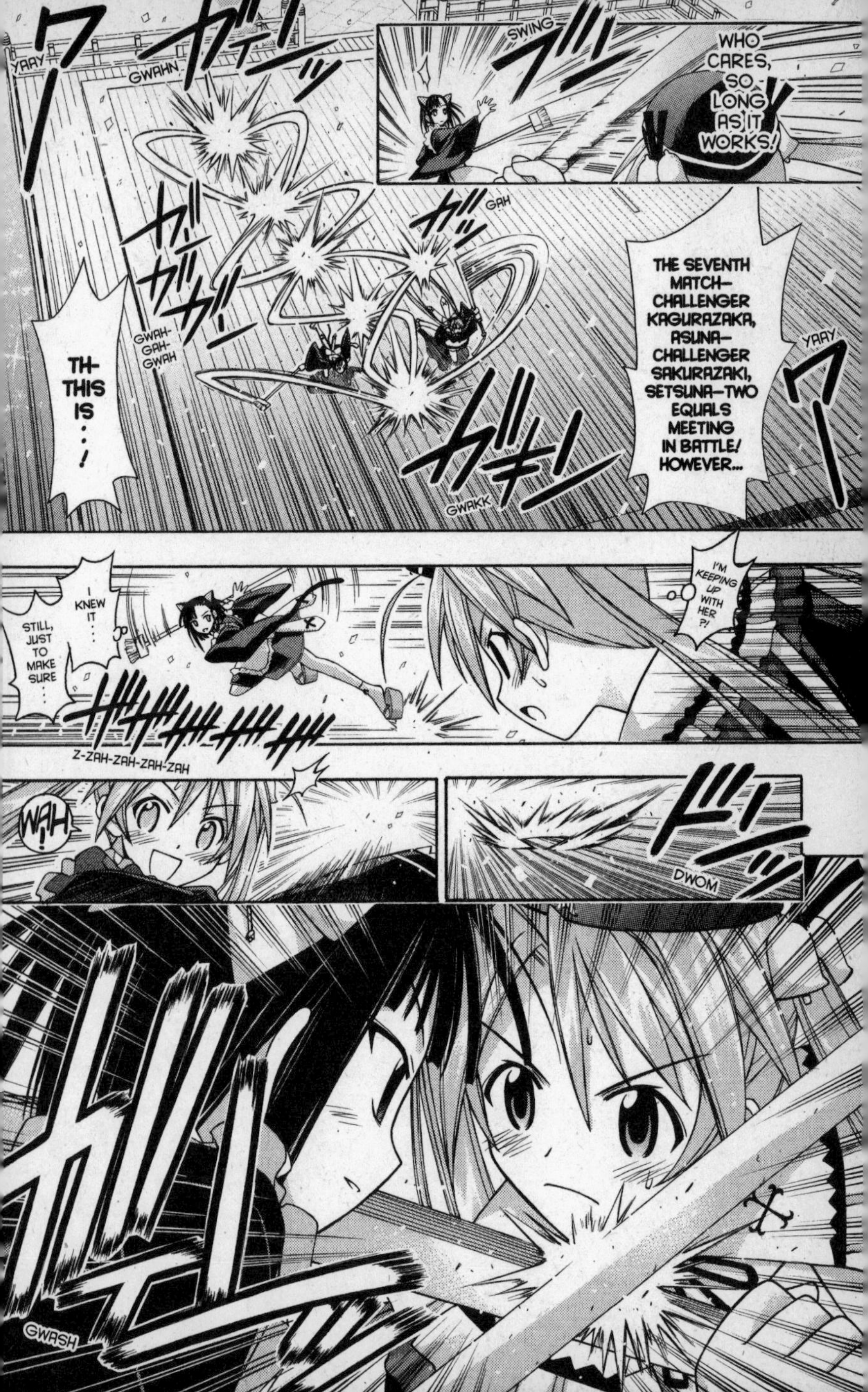
SWING
WHO CARES, SO LONG AS IT WORKS!
GWAHN
YAAY
GAH
YAAY
THE SEVENTH MATCH—CHALLENGER KAGURAZAKA, ASUNA—CHALLENGER SAKURAZAKI, SETSUNA—TWO EQUALS MEETING IN BATTLE! HOWEVER...
GWAH-GAH-GWAH
TH-THIS IS...!
GWAKK
I'M KEEPING UP WITH HER?!
I KNEW IT...
STILL, JUST TO MAKE SURE...
Z-ZAH-ZAH-ZAH-ZAH
DWOM
WAH!
GWASH

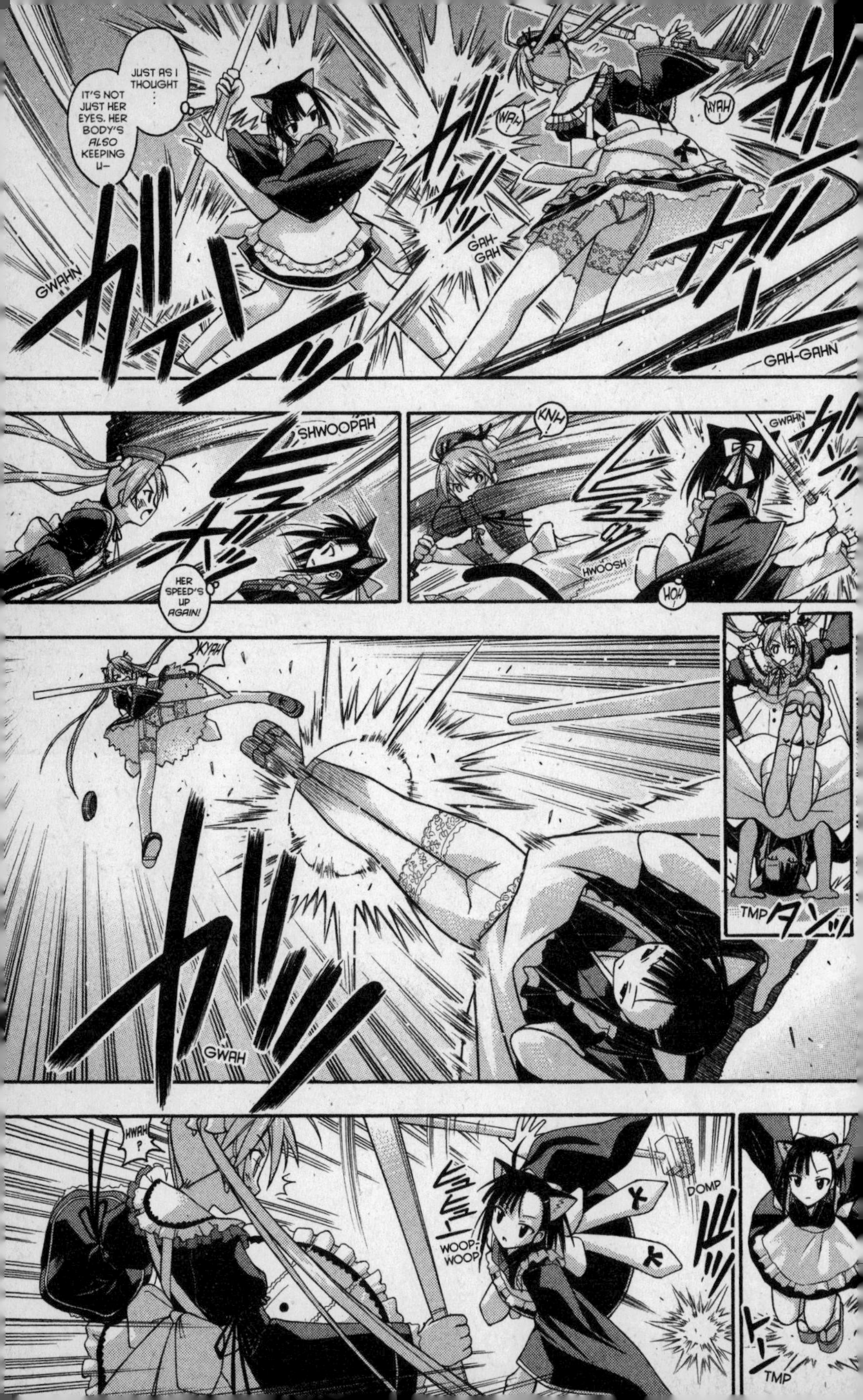

WYAH!
WAH!
GAH-GAH
GAH-GAHN
JUST AS I THOUGHT...
IT'S NOT JUST HER EYES. HER BODY'S ALSO KEEPING U—
GWAHN
GWAHN
KNH!
HWOOSH
HOH!
SHWOOPAH
HER SPEED'S UP AGAIN!
TMP
KYAH
GWAH
DOMP
TMP
WOOP-WOOP
HWAH?

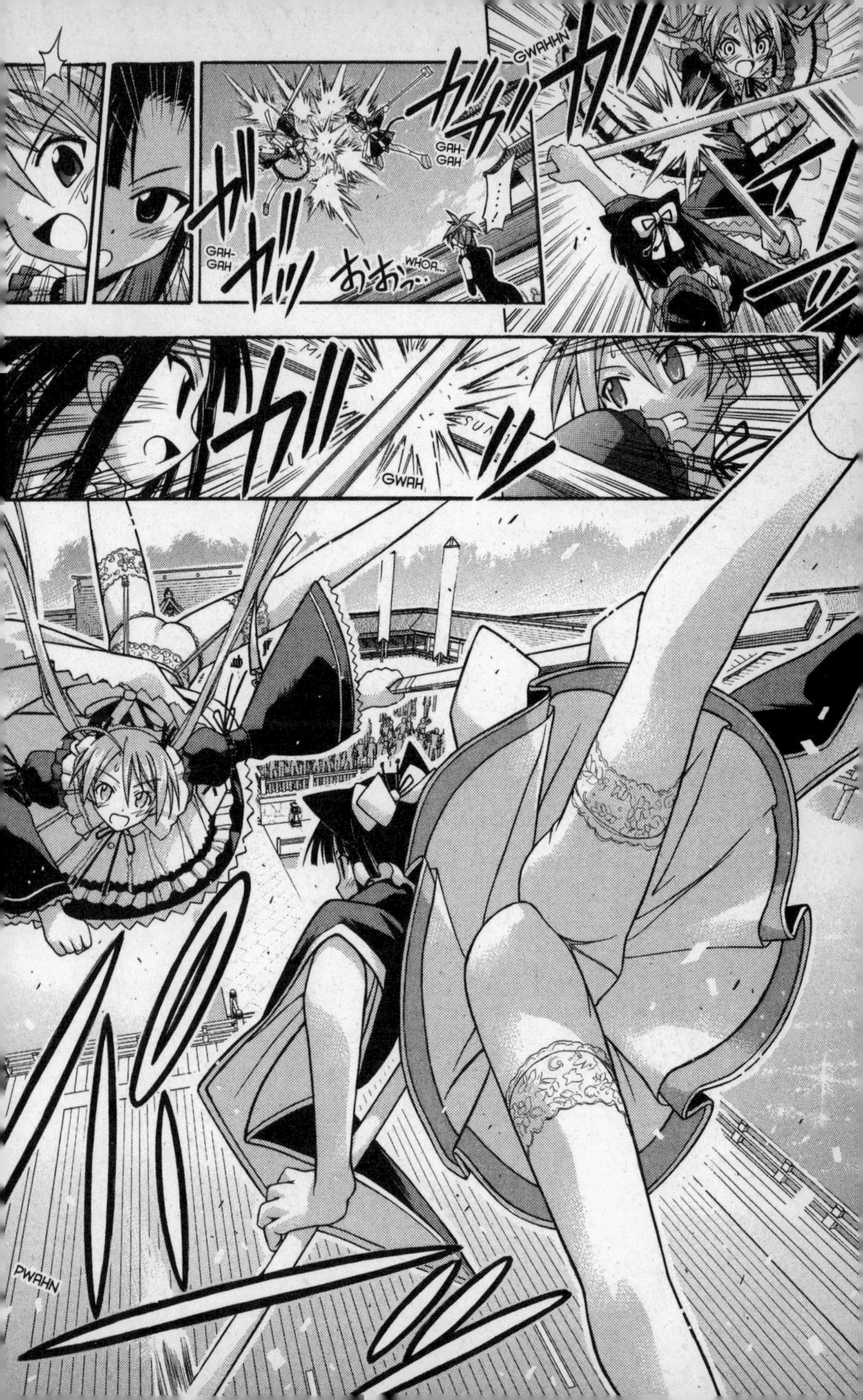
GWAHHN
GAH-GAH
WHOA...
おおっ
GAH-GAH
GWAH
PWAHN

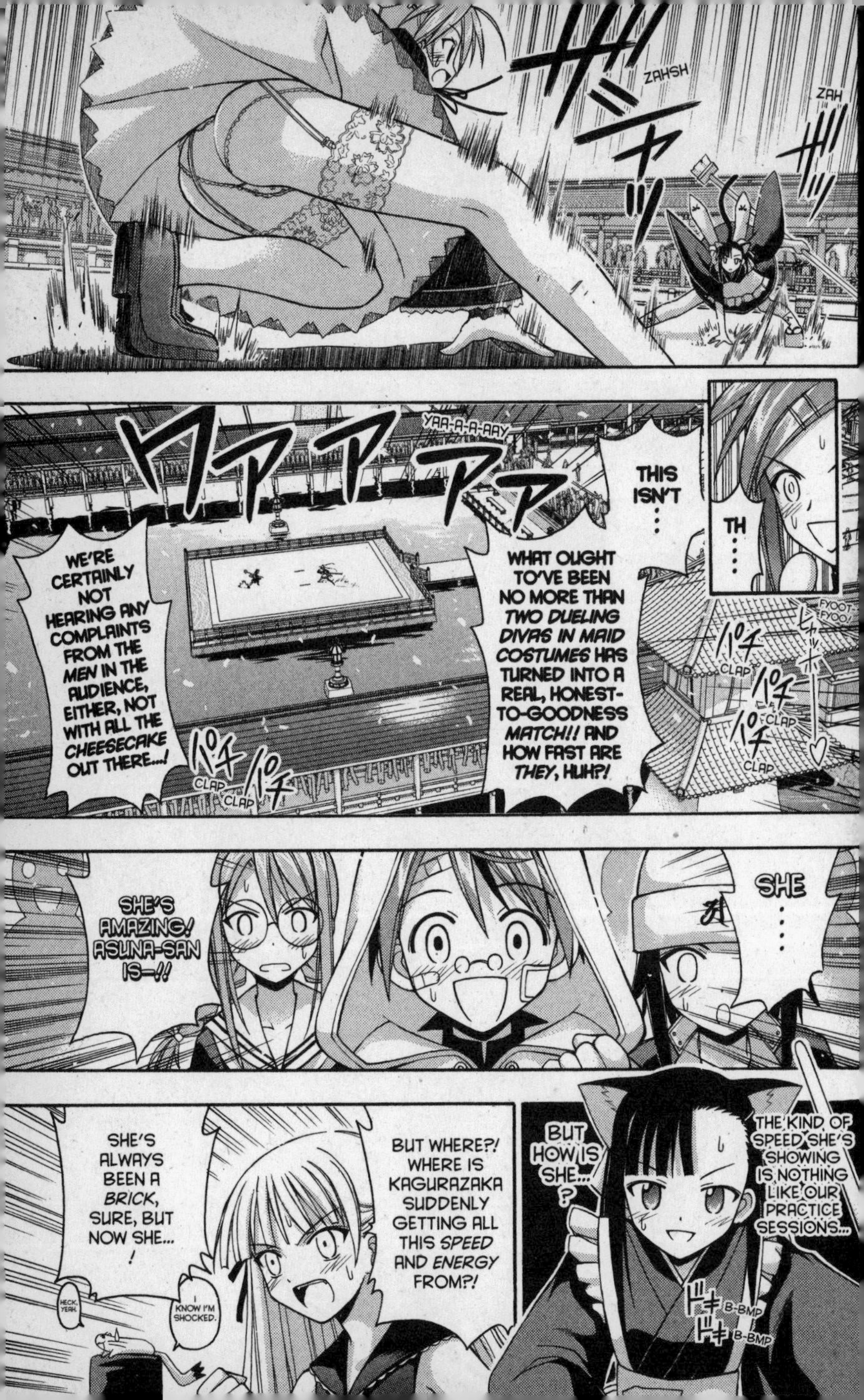
ZAHSH
ZAH
TH...
THIS ISN'T...
YAA-A-A-AAY
WHAT OUGHT TO'VE BEEN NO MORE THAN *TWO DUELING DIVAS IN MAID COSTUMES* HAS TURNED INTO A REAL, HONEST-TO-GOODNESS *MATCH!!* AND HOW FAST ARE *THEY*, HUH?!
FYOOT-FYOO!
CLAP
CLAP
CLAP
WE'RE CERTAINLY NOT HEARING ANY COMPLAINTS FROM THE *MEN* IN THE AUDIENCE, EITHER, NOT WITH ALL THE *CHEESECAKE* OUT THERE...!
CLAP
CLAP
SHE...
SHE'S AMAZING! ASUNA-SAN IS—!!
THE KIND OF SPEED SHE'S SHOWING IS NOTHING LIKE OUR PRACTICE SESSIONS...
BUT HOW IS SHE...?
B-BMP
B-BMP
BUT WHERE?! WHERE IS KAGURAZAKA SUDDENLY GETTING ALL THIS *SPEED* AND *ENERGY* FROM?!
SHE'S ALWAYS BEEN A *BRICK*, SURE, BUT NOW SHE...!
I KNOW I'M SHOCKED.
HECK, YEAH.

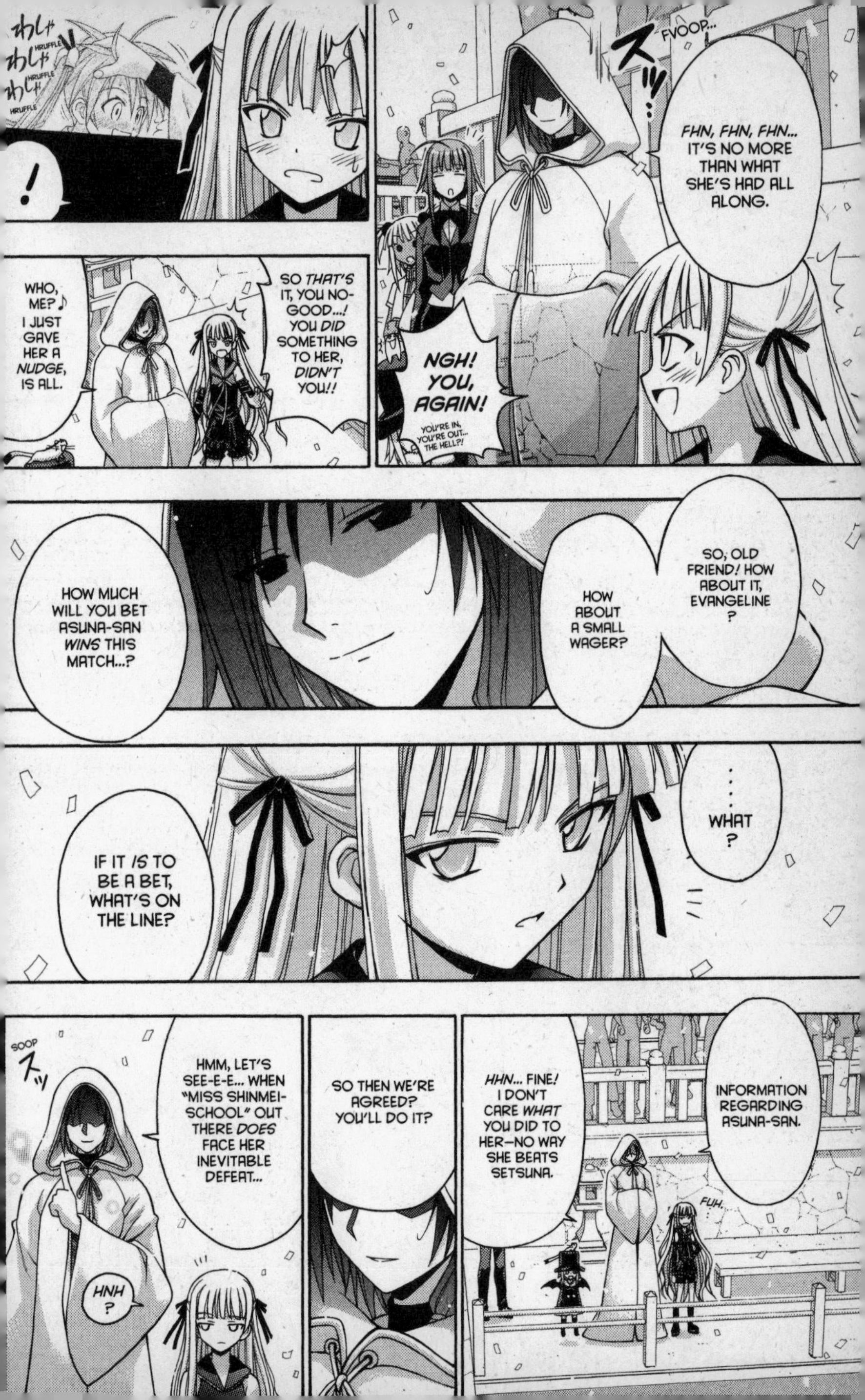
FVOOP...
FHN, FHN, FHN... IT'S NO MORE THAN WHAT SHE'S HAD ALL ALONG.
NGH! YOU, AGAIN!
YOU'RE IN, YOU'RE OUT... THE HELL?!
HRUFFLE
HRUFFLE
HRUFFLE
!
SO THAT'S IT, YOU NO-GOOD...! YOU DID SOMETHING TO HER, DIDN'T YOU!!
WHO, ME? ♪ I JUST GAVE HER A NUDGE, IS ALL.
SO, OLD FRIEND! HOW ABOUT IT, EVANGELINE?
HOW ABOUT A SMALL WAGER?
HOW MUCH WILL YOU BET ASUNA-SAN WINS THIS MATCH...?
... WHAT?
IF IT IS TO BE A BET, WHAT'S ON THE LINE?
INFORMATION REGARDING ASUNA-SAN.
FUH.
HHN... FINE! I DON'T CARE WHAT YOU DID TO HER—NO WAY SHE BEATS SETSUNA.
SO THEN WE'RE AGREED? YOU'LL DO IT?
SOOP
HMM, LET'S SEE-E-E... WHEN "MISS SHINMEI-SCHOOL" OUT THERE DOES FACE HER INEVITABLE DEFEAT...
HNH?

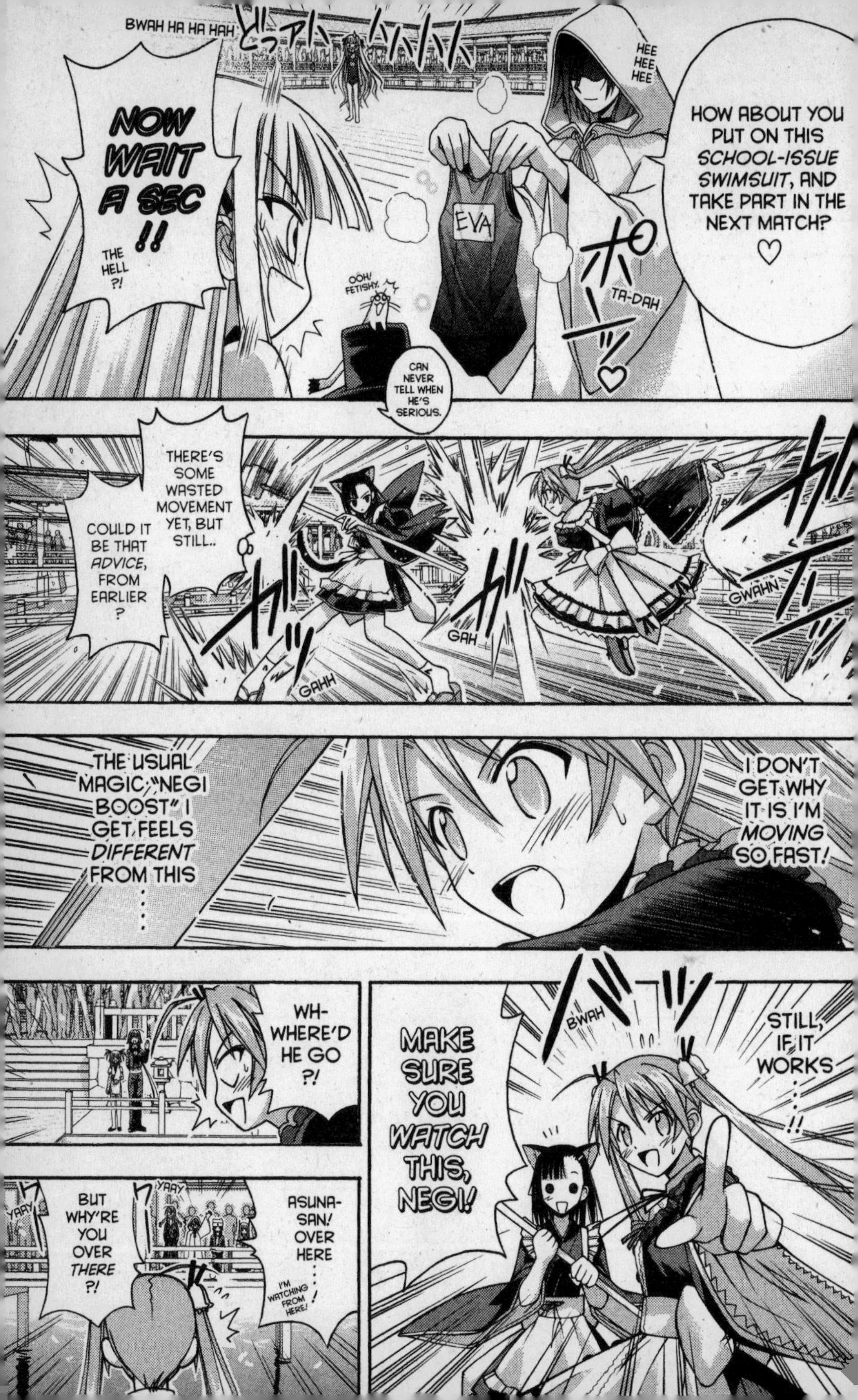
HOW ABOUT YOU PUT ON THIS SCHOOL-ISSUE SWIMSUIT, AND TAKE PART IN THE NEXT MATCH? ♡
HEE HEE HEE
TA-DAH
EVA
BWAH HA HA HAH
OOH! FETISHY.
CAN NEVER TELL WHEN HE'S SERIOUS.
NOW WAIT A SEC!!
THE HELL?!
GWAHN
THERE'S SOME WASTED MOVEMENT YET, BUT STILL..
COULD IT BE THAT ADVICE, FROM EARLIER?
GAH
GAHH
I DON'T GET WHY IT IS I'M MOVING SO FAST!
THE USUAL MAGIC "NEGI BOOST" I GET FEELS DIFFERENT FROM THIS....
BWAH
STILL, IF IT WORKS...!!
MAKE SURE YOU WATCH THIS, NEGI!
WH-WHERE'D HE GO?!
ASUNA-SAN! OVER HERE...
I'M WATCHING FROM HERE!
YAAY
YAAY
BUT WHY'RE YOU OVER THERE?!

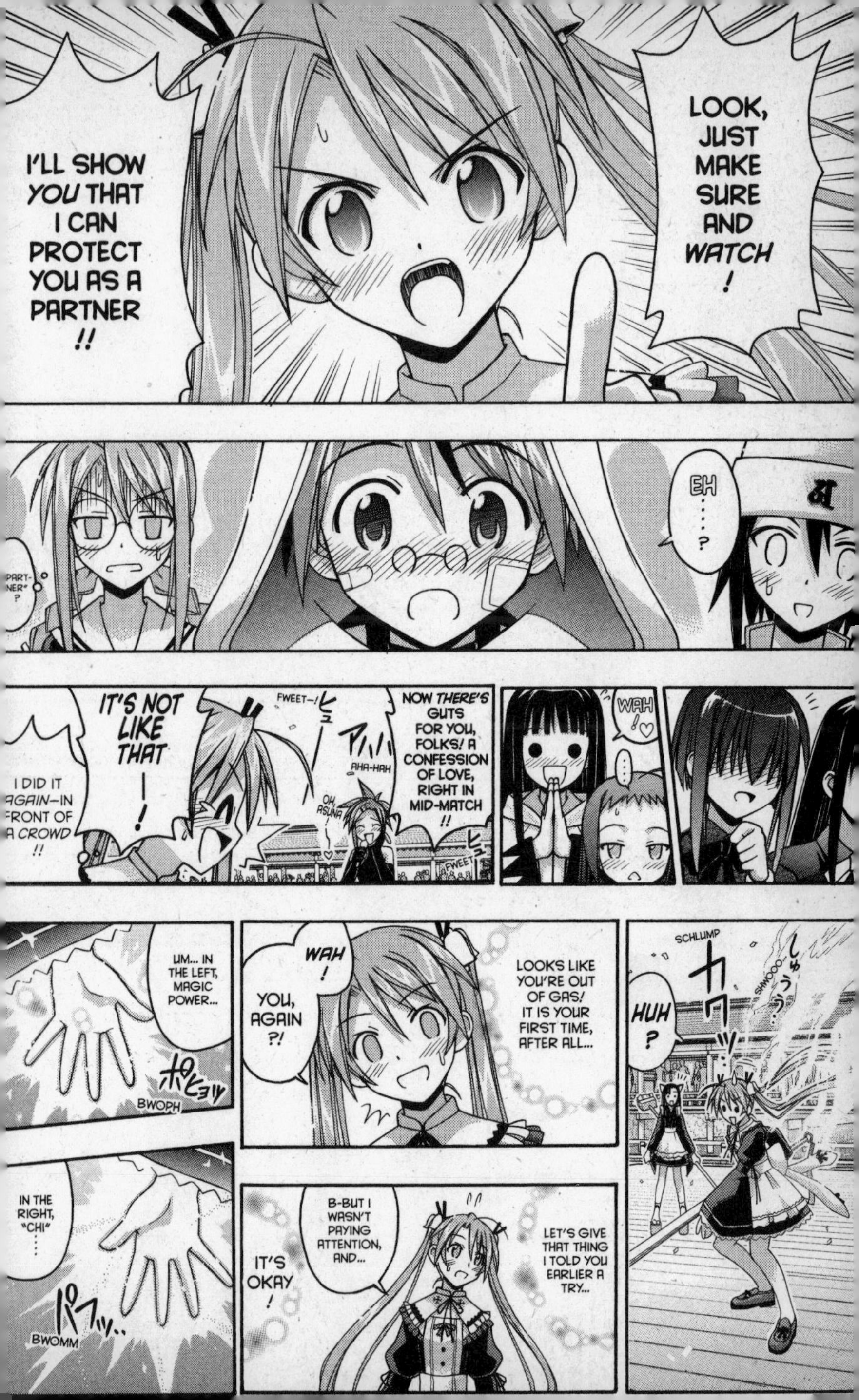
LOOK, JUST MAKE SURE AND WATCH!
I'LL SHOW YOU THAT I CAN PROTECT YOU AS A PARTNER!!
EH.....?
"PART-NER"?
WAH!♡
...
NOW THERE'S GUTS FOR YOU, FOLKS! A CONFESSION OF LOVE, RIGHT IN MID-MATCH!!
FWEET
OH, ASUNA!♡
AHA-HAH
FWEET—!
IT'S NOT LIKE THAT—!
I DID IT AGAIN—IN FRONT OF A CROWD!!
SCHLUMP
SHWOOO...
HUH?
LOOKS LIKE YOU'RE OUT OF GAS! IT IS YOUR FIRST TIME, AFTER ALL...
WAH!
YOU, AGAIN?!
UM... IN THE LEFT, MAGIC POWER...
BWOPH
LET'S GIVE THAT THING I TOLD YOU EARLIER A TRY...
B-BUT I WASN'T PAYING ATTENTION, AND...
IT'S OKAY!
IN THE RIGHT, "CHI"....
BWOMM

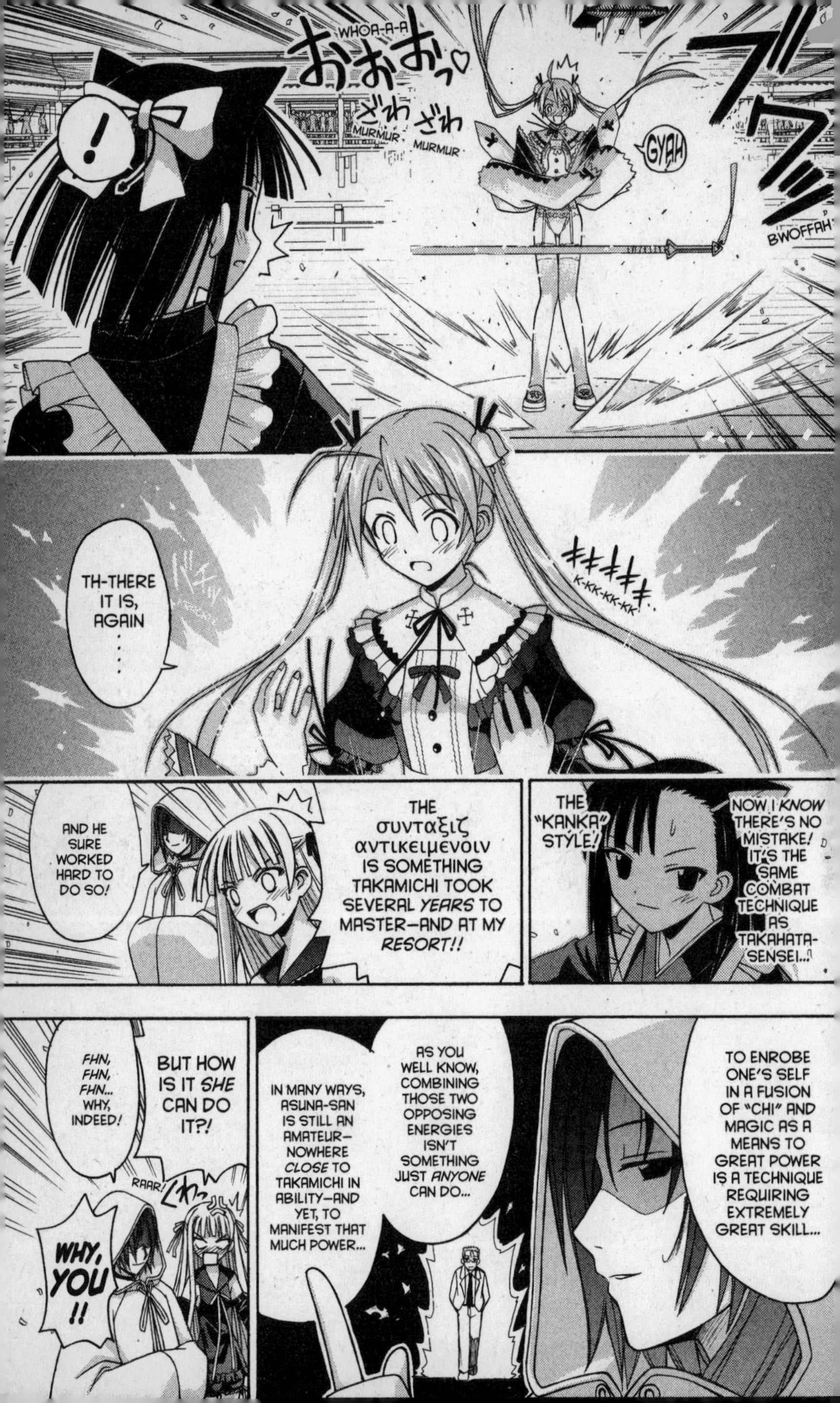
BWOFFAH
GYAH
WHOA-A-A
おおおっ♡
ざわ ざわ
MURMUR MURMUR
!
K-KK-KK-KK
TH-THERE IT IS, AGAIN ....
NOW I *KNOW* THERE'S NO MISTAKE! IT'S THE SAME COMBAT TECHNIQUE AS TAKAHATA-SENSEI...!
THE "KANKA" STYLE!
THE συνταξιζ αντικειμενοιν IS SOMETHING TAKAMICHI TOOK SEVERAL *YEARS* TO MASTER—AND AT MY *RESORT!!*
AND HE SURE WORKED HARD TO DO SO!
TO ENROBE ONE'S SELF IN A FUSION OF "CHI" AND MAGIC AS A MEANS TO GREAT POWER IS A TECHNIQUE REQUIRING EXTREMELY GREAT SKILL...
AS YOU WELL KNOW, COMBINING THOSE TWO OPPOSING ENERGIES ISN'T SOMETHING JUST *ANYONE* CAN DO...
IN MANY WAYS, ASUNA-SAN IS STILL AN AMATEUR—NOWHERE *CLOSE* TO TAKAMICHI IN ABILITY—AND YET, TO MANIFEST THAT MUCH POWER...
BUT HOW IS IT *SHE* CAN DO IT?!
FHN, FHN, FHN... WHY, INDEED!
RAAR!
WHY, YOU!!

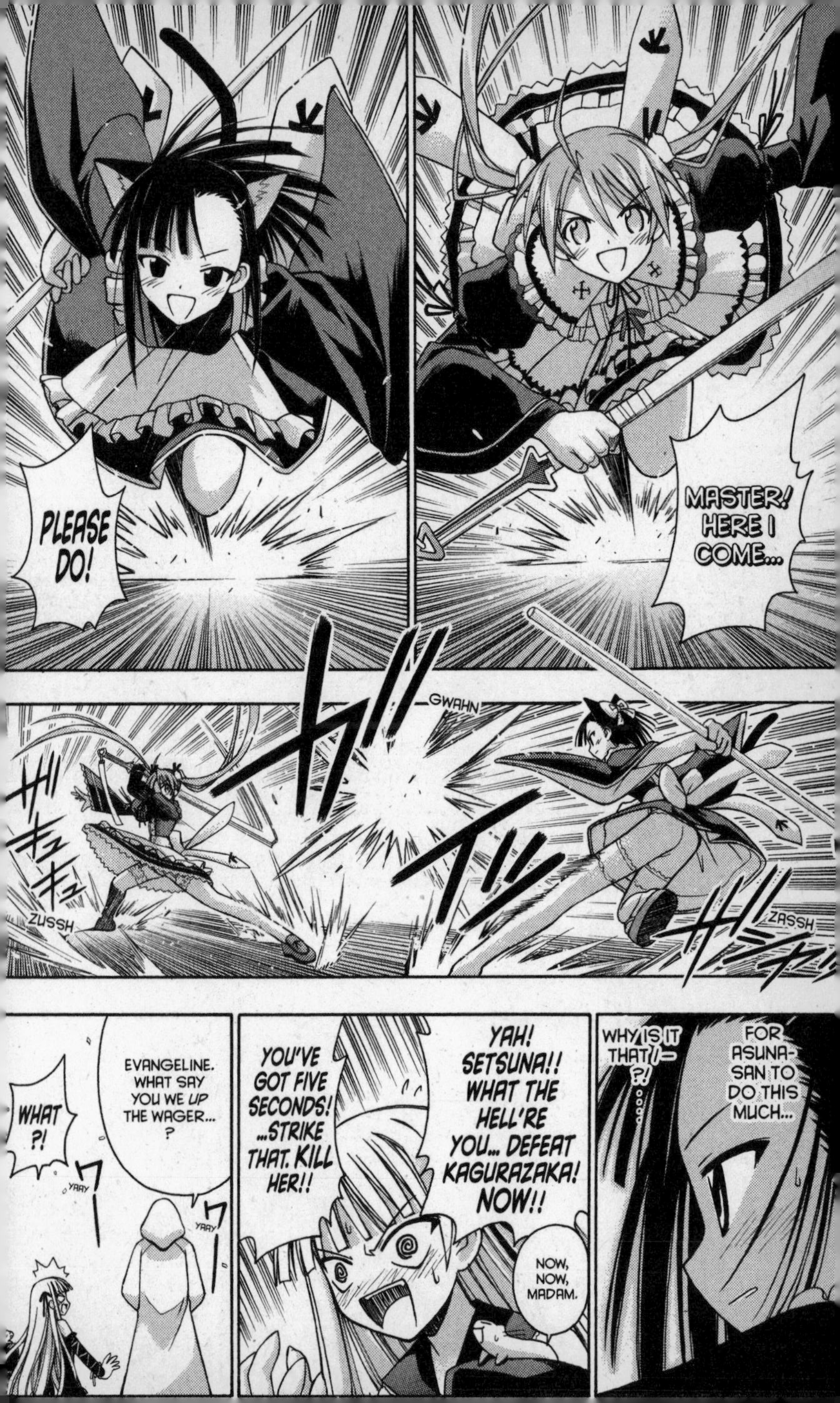
MASTER! HERE I COME...
PLEASE DO!
GWAHN
ZASSH
ZUSSH
FOR ASUNA-SAN TO DO THIS MUCH...
WHY IS IT THAT I--?!
YAH! SETSUNA!! WHAT THE HELL'RE YOU... DEFEAT KAGURAZAKA! NOW!!
YOU'VE GOT FIVE SECONDS! ...STRIKE THAT. KILL HER!!
NOW, NOW, MADAM.
EVANGELINE. WHAT SAY YOU WE UP THE WAGER...?
WHAT?!
YAAY
YAAY

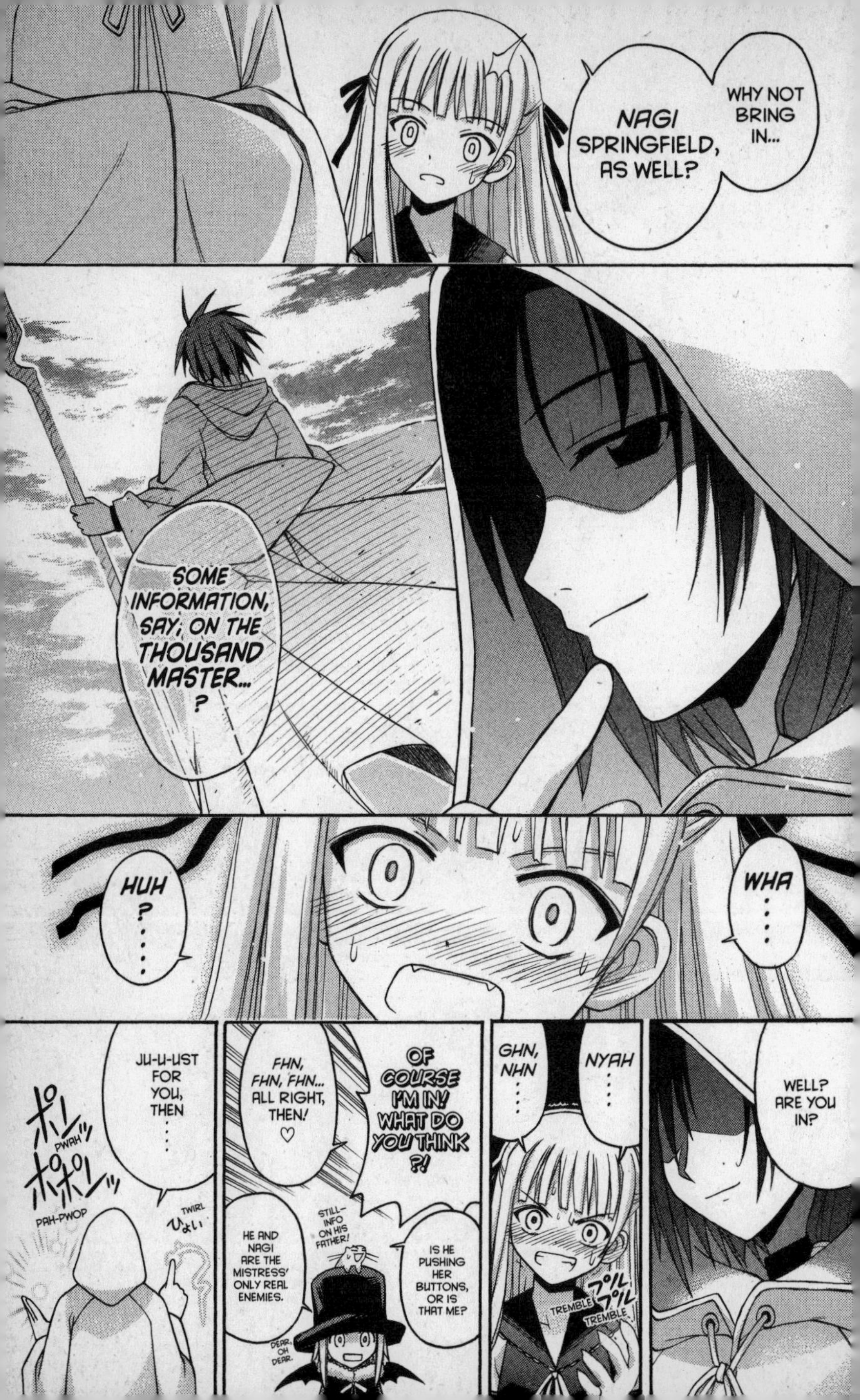
WHY NOT BRING IN...
NAGI SPRINGFIELD, AS WELL?
SOME INFORMATION, SAY, ON THE THOUSAND MASTER...?
WHA....
HUH?....
WELL? ARE YOU IN?
NYAH....
GHN, NHN....
プルプル TREMBLE TREMBLE
OF COURSE I'M IN! WHAT DO YOU THINK?!
FHN, FHN, FHN... ALL RIGHT, THEN! ♡
IS HE PUSHING HER BUTTONS, OR IS THAT ME?
STILL— INFO ON HIS FATHER!
HE AND NAGI ARE THE MISTRESS' ONLY REAL ENEMIES.
DEAR, OH DEAR.
JU-U-UST FOR YOU, THEN....
ひょい TWIRL
ポンッ PWAH
ポポンッ PAH-PWOP

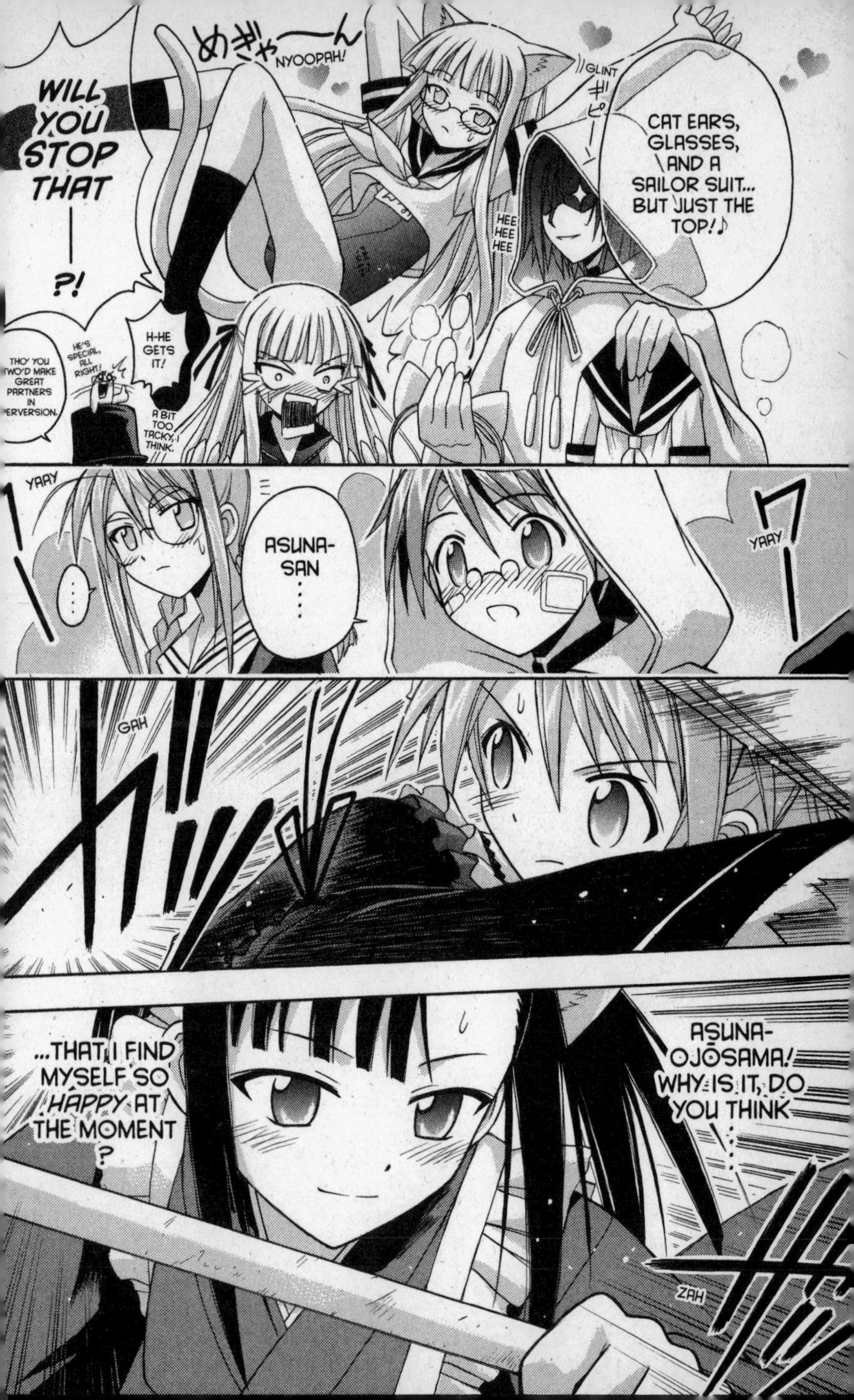
GLINT
ギピーン
CAT EARS, GLASSES, AND A SAILOR SUIT... BUT JUST THE TOP!♪
HEE HEE HEE
めぎゃーん
NYOOPAH!
WILL YOU STOP THAT——?!
H-HE GETS IT!
A BIT TOO TACKY, I THINK.
HE'S SPECIAL, ALL RIGHT!
THO' YOU TWO'D MAKE GREAT PARTNERS IN PERVERSION.
YAAY
ASUNA-SAN ....
...
YAAY
GAH
ASUNA-OJŌSAMA! WHY IS IT, DO YOU THINK...
...THAT I FIND MYSELF SO HAPPY AT THE MOMENT?
ZAH

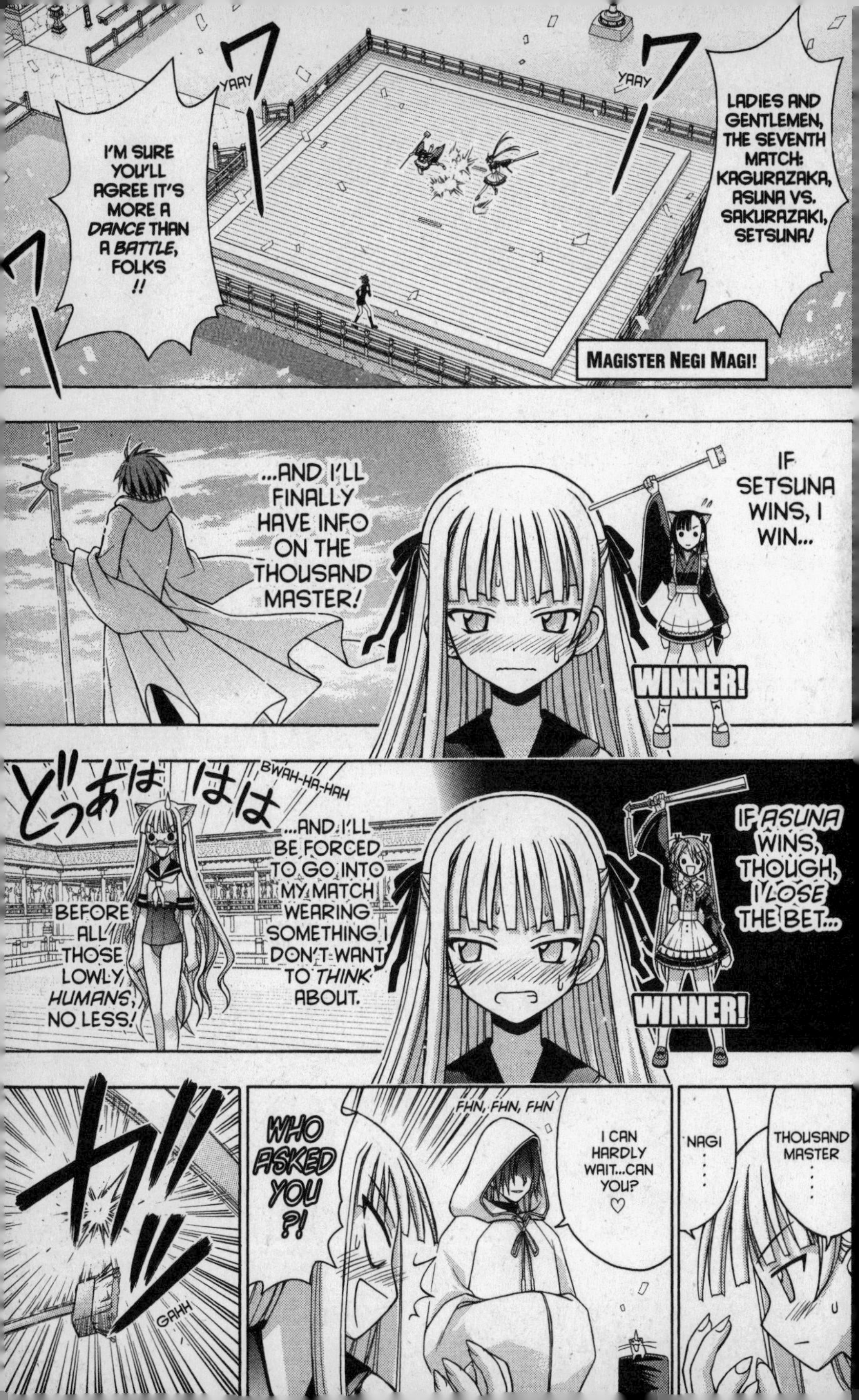
LADIES AND GENTLEMEN, THE SEVENTH MATCH: KAGURAZAKA, ASUNA VS. SAKURAZAKI, SETSUNA!
YAAY
YAAY
I'M SURE YOU'LL AGREE IT'S MORE A DANCE THAN A BATTLE, FOLKS !!
MAGISTER NEGI MAGI!
IF SETSUNA WINS, I WIN...
WINNER!
...AND I'LL FINALLY HAVE INFO ON THE THOUSAND MASTER!
IF ASUNA WINS, THOUGH, I LOSE THE BET...
WINNER!
...AND I'LL BE FORCED TO GO INTO MY MATCH WEARING SOMETHING I DON'T WANT TO THINK ABOUT.
BWAH-HA-HAH
どっあは はは
BEFORE ALL THOSE LOWLY HUMANS, NO LESS!
THOUSAND MASTER ....
NAGI ....
FHN, FHN, FHN
I CAN HARDLY WAIT...CAN YOU? ♡
WHO ASKED YOU ?!
GAHH

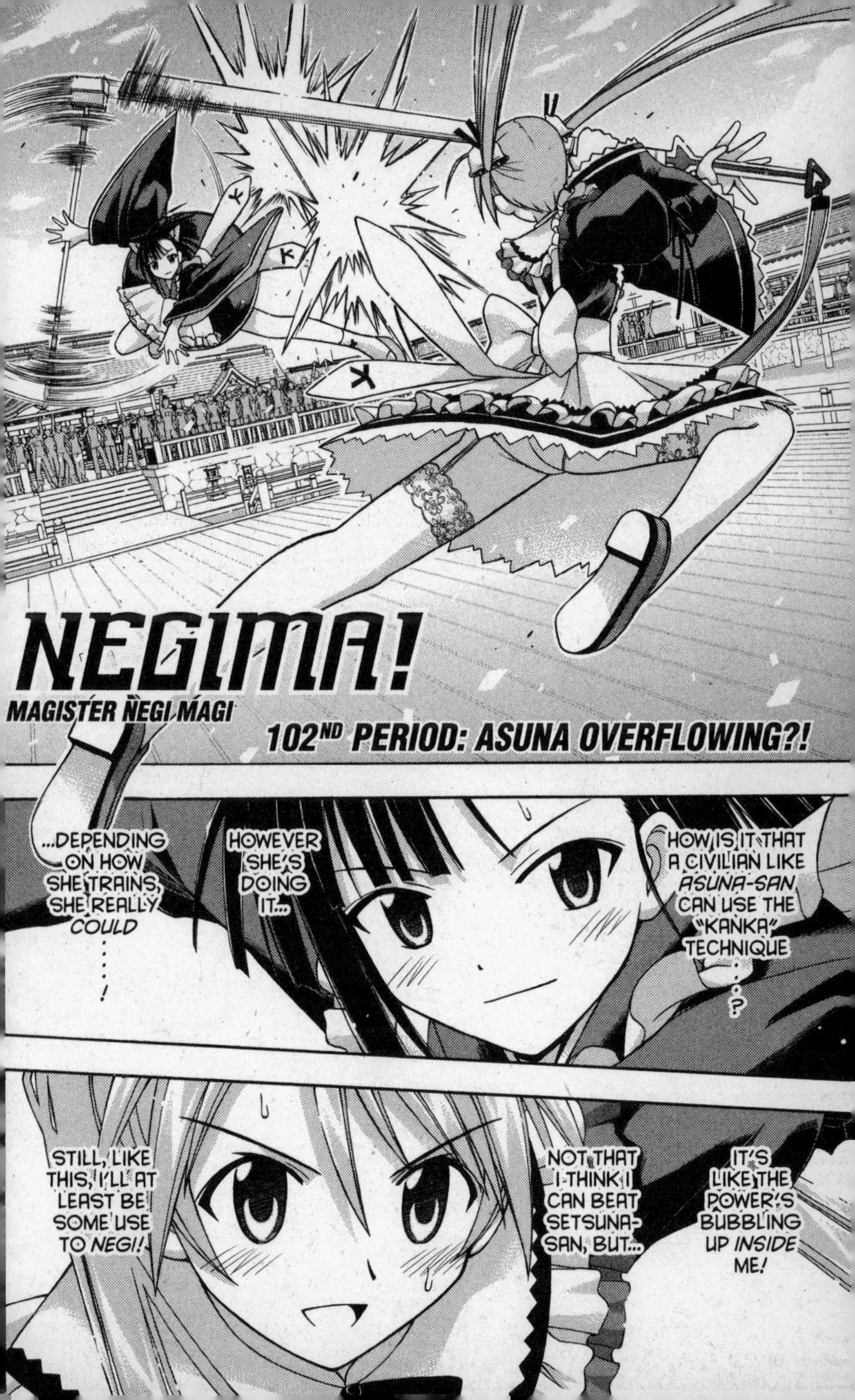
NEGIMA!
MAGISTER NEGI MAGI
102ND PERIOD: ASUNA OVERFLOWING?!
HOW IS IT THAT A CIVILIAN LIKE ASUNA-SAN CAN USE THE "KANKA" TECHNIQUE ...?
HOWEVER SHE'S DOING IT...
...DEPENDING ON HOW SHE TRAINS, SHE REALLY COULD ...!
IT'S LIKE THE POWER'S BUBBLING UP INSIDE ME!
NOT THAT I THINK I CAN BEAT SETSUNA-SAN, BUT...
STILL, LIKE THIS, I'LL AT LEAST BE SOME USE TO NEGI!

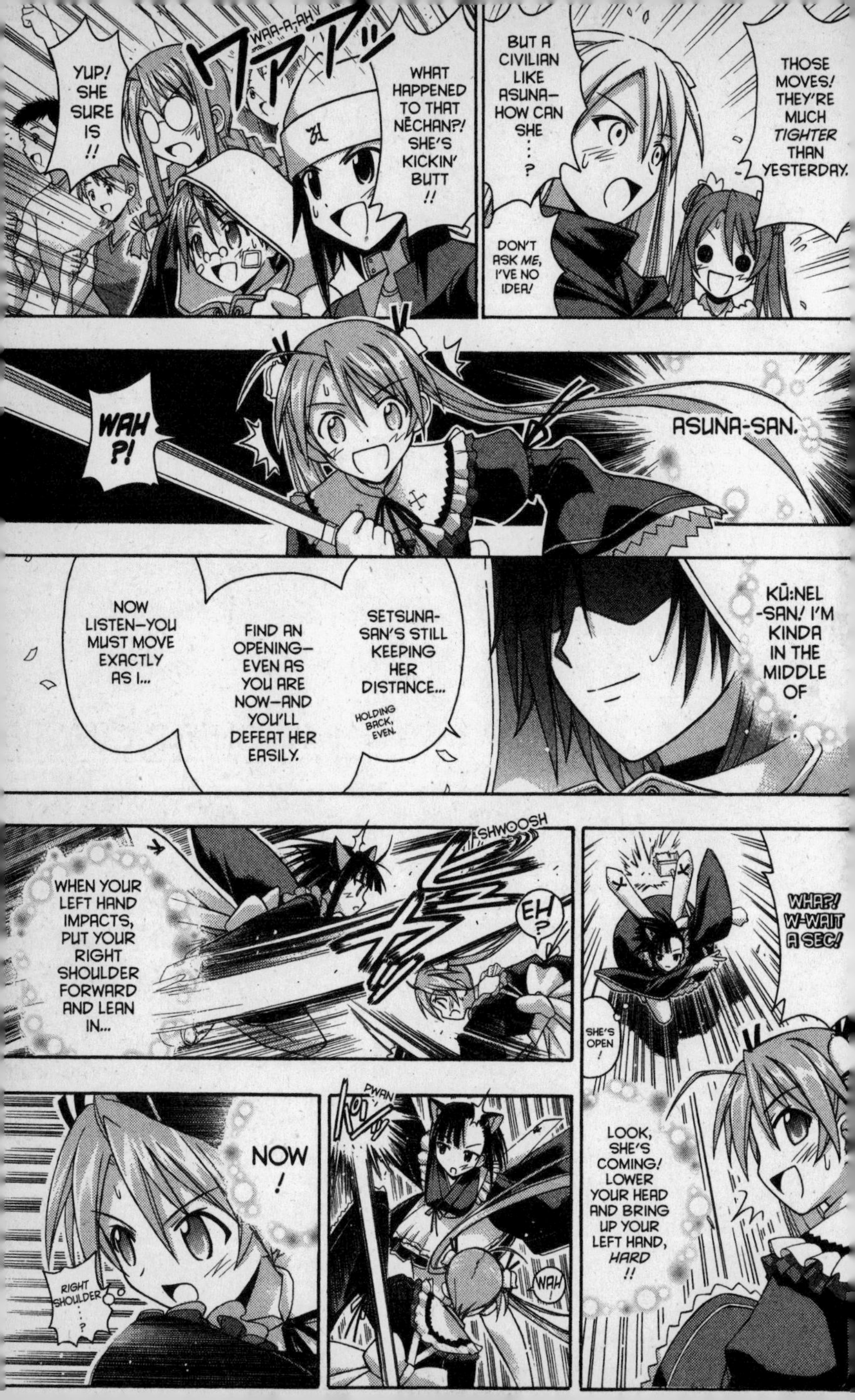
THOSE MOVES! THEY'RE MUCH *TIGHTER* THAN YESTERDAY.
BUT A CIVILIAN LIKE ASUNA—HOW CAN SHE ...?
DON'T ASK *ME*, I'VE NO IDEA!
WAA-A-AH
WHAT HAPPENED TO THAT NĒCHAN?! SHE'S KICKIN' BUTT!!
YUP! SHE SURE IS!!
ASUNA-SAN.
WAH?!
KŪ:NEL-SAN! I'M KINDA IN THE MIDDLE OF.
SETSUNA-SAN'S STILL KEEPING HER DISTANCE...
HOLDING BACK, EVEN.
FIND AN OPENING—EVEN AS YOU ARE NOW—AND YOU'LL DEFEAT HER EASILY.
NOW LISTEN—YOU MUST MOVE EXACTLY AS I...
WHAP! W-WAIT A SEC!
SHE'S OPEN!
LOOK, SHE'S COMING! LOWER YOUR HEAD AND BRING UP YOUR LEFT HAND, *HARD*!!
SHWOOSH
EH?
WHEN YOUR LEFT HAND IMPACTS, PUT YOUR RIGHT SHOULDER FORWARD AND LEAN IN...
PWAN
WAH!
NOW!
RIGHT SHOULDER...?

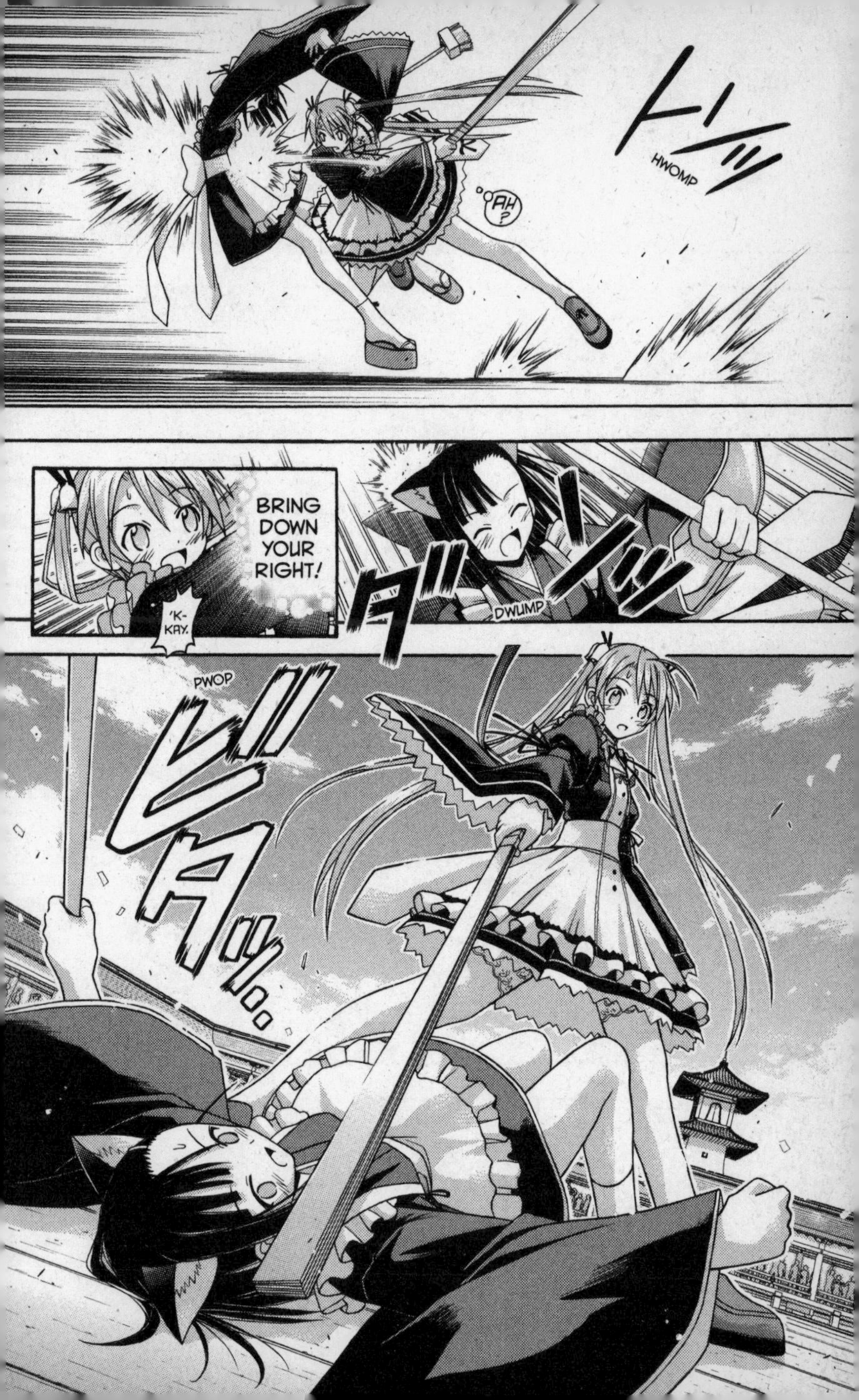
HWOMP
AH?
DWUMP
BRING DOWN YOUR RIGHT!
'K-KAY.
PWOP

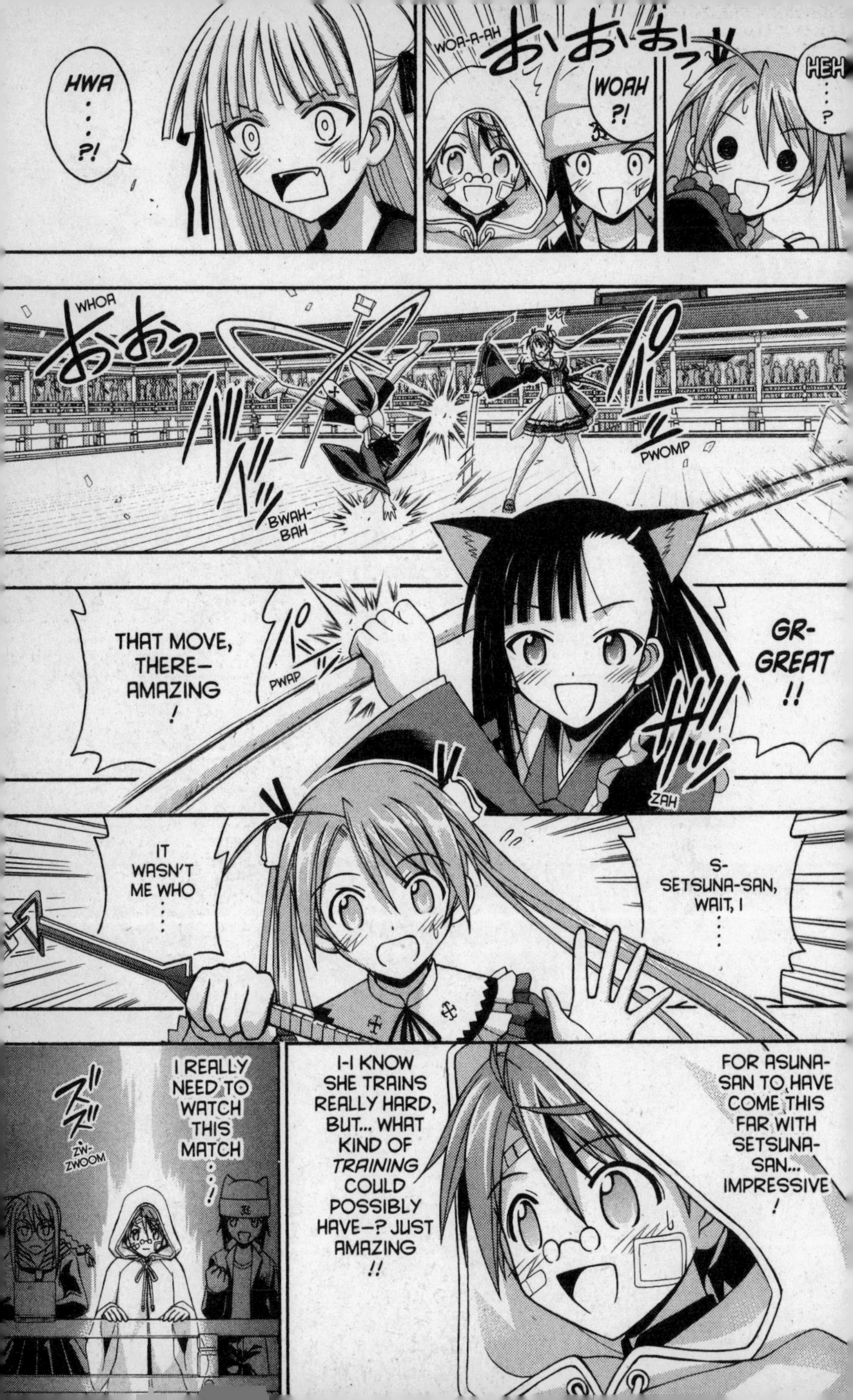
HEH . . . ?
WOAH ?!
WOA-A-AH
おおおっ
HWA . . . ?!
パ
PWOMP
ダダッ
BWAH-BAH
おおっ
WHOA
GR-GREAT !!
ザッ
ZAH
パ
PWAP
THAT MOVE, THERE—AMAZING !
S-SETSUNA-SAN, WAIT, I . . . .
IT WASN'T ME WHO . . . .
FOR ASUNA-SAN TO HAVE COME THIS FAR WITH SETSUNA-SAN... IMPRESSIVE !
I-I KNOW SHE TRAINS REALLY HARD, BUT... WHAT KIND OF *TRAINING* COULD POSSIBLY HAVE—? JUST AMAZING !!
I REALLY NEED TO WATCH THIS MATCH . . . !
ズズ
ZW-ZWOOM

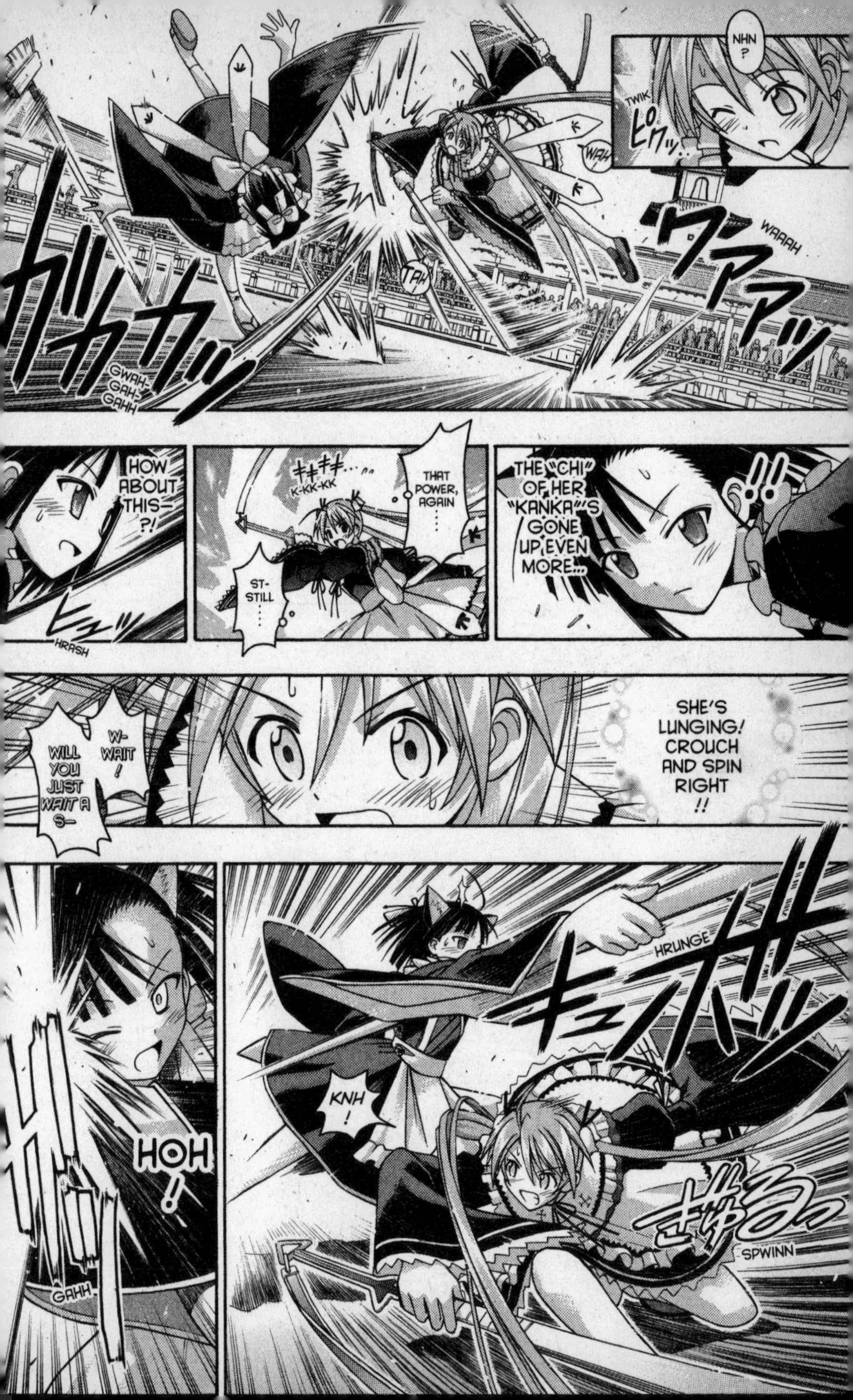
NHN ?
TWIK
WAH
WAAAH
TAH
GWAH-GAH-GAHH
THE "CHI" OF HER "KANKA"'S GONE UP EVEN MORE...
!!
THAT POWER, AGAIN ....
K-KK-KK
ST-STILL ....
HOW ABOUT THIS—?!
HRASH
SHE'S LUNGING! CROUCH AND SPIN RIGHT !!
W-WAIT!
WILL YOU JUST WAIT A S—
HRUNGE
KNH!
SPWINN
HOH!
GAHH

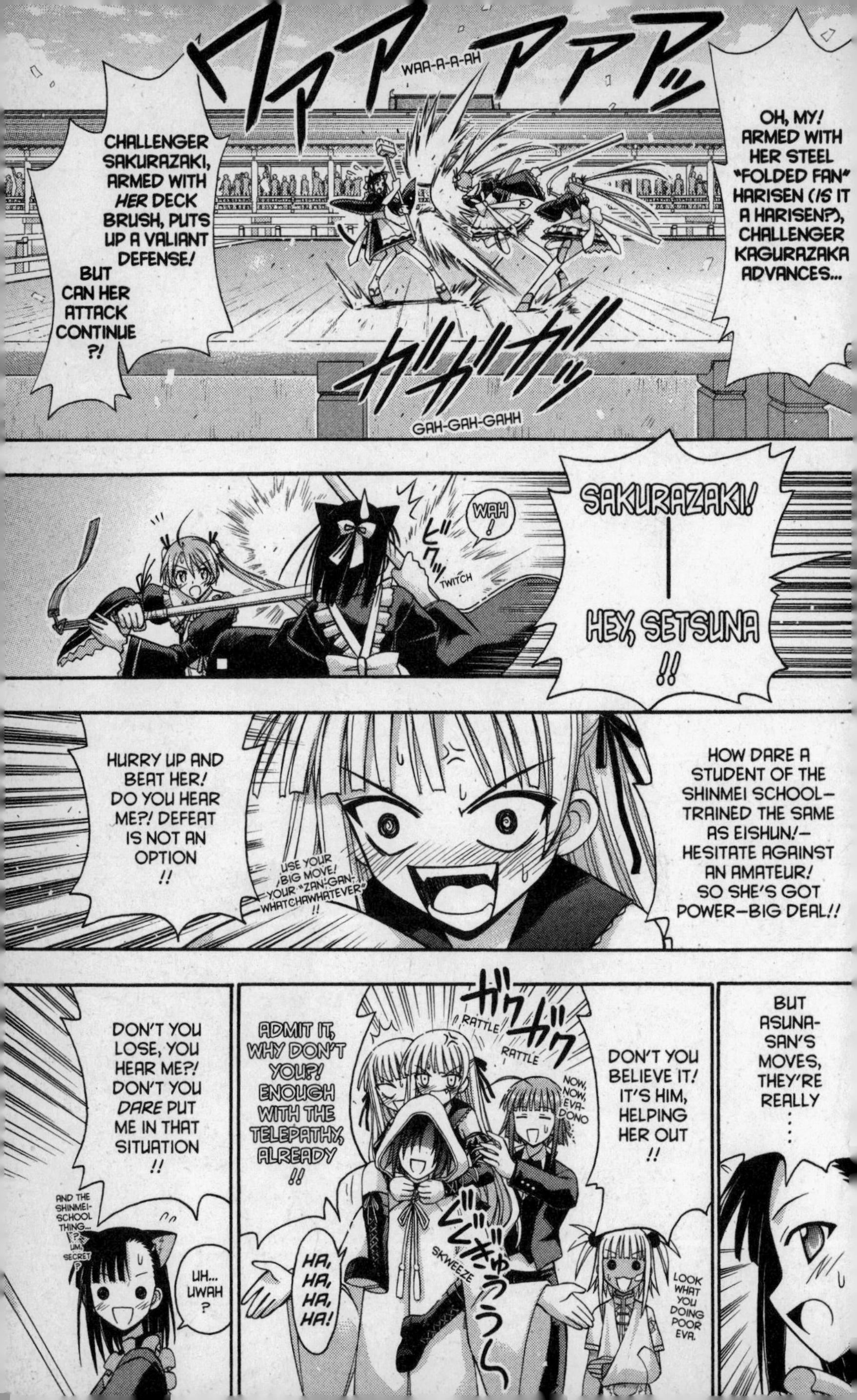
OH, MY! ARMED WITH HER STEEL "FOLDED FAN" HARISEN (IS IT A HARISEN?), CHALLENGER KAGURAZAKA ADVANCES...
WAA-A-A-AH
CHALLENGER SAKURAZAKI, ARMED WITH HER DECK BRUSH, PUTS UP A VALIANT DEFENSE!
BUT CAN HER ATTACK CONTINUE ?!
GAH-GAH-GAHH
SAKURAZAKI! — HEY, SETSUNA !!
WAH !
TWITCH
HOW DARE A STUDENT OF THE SHINMEI SCHOOL—TRAINED THE SAME AS EISHUN!—HESITATE AGAINST AN AMATEUR! SO SHE'S GOT POWER—BIG DEAL!!
HURRY UP AND BEAT HER! DO YOU HEAR ME?! DEFEAT IS NOT AN OPTION !!
USE YOUR BIG MOVE! YOUR "ZAN-GAN-WHATCHAMWHATEVER" !!
BUT ASUNA-SAN'S MOVES, THEY'RE REALLY ....
DON'T YOU BELIEVE IT! IT'S HIM, HELPING HER OUT !!
NOW, NOW, EVA-DONO...
RATTLE
RATTLE
ADMIT IT, WHY DON'T YOU?! ENOUGH WITH THE TELEPATHY, ALREADY !!
LOOK WHAT YOU DOING POOR EVA.
SKWEEZE
HA, HA, HA, HA!
DON'T YOU LOSE, YOU HEAR ME?! DON'T YOU DARE PUT ME IN THAT SITUATION !!
UH... UWAH ?
AND THE SHINMEI-SCHOOL THING...? UM, SECRET ?

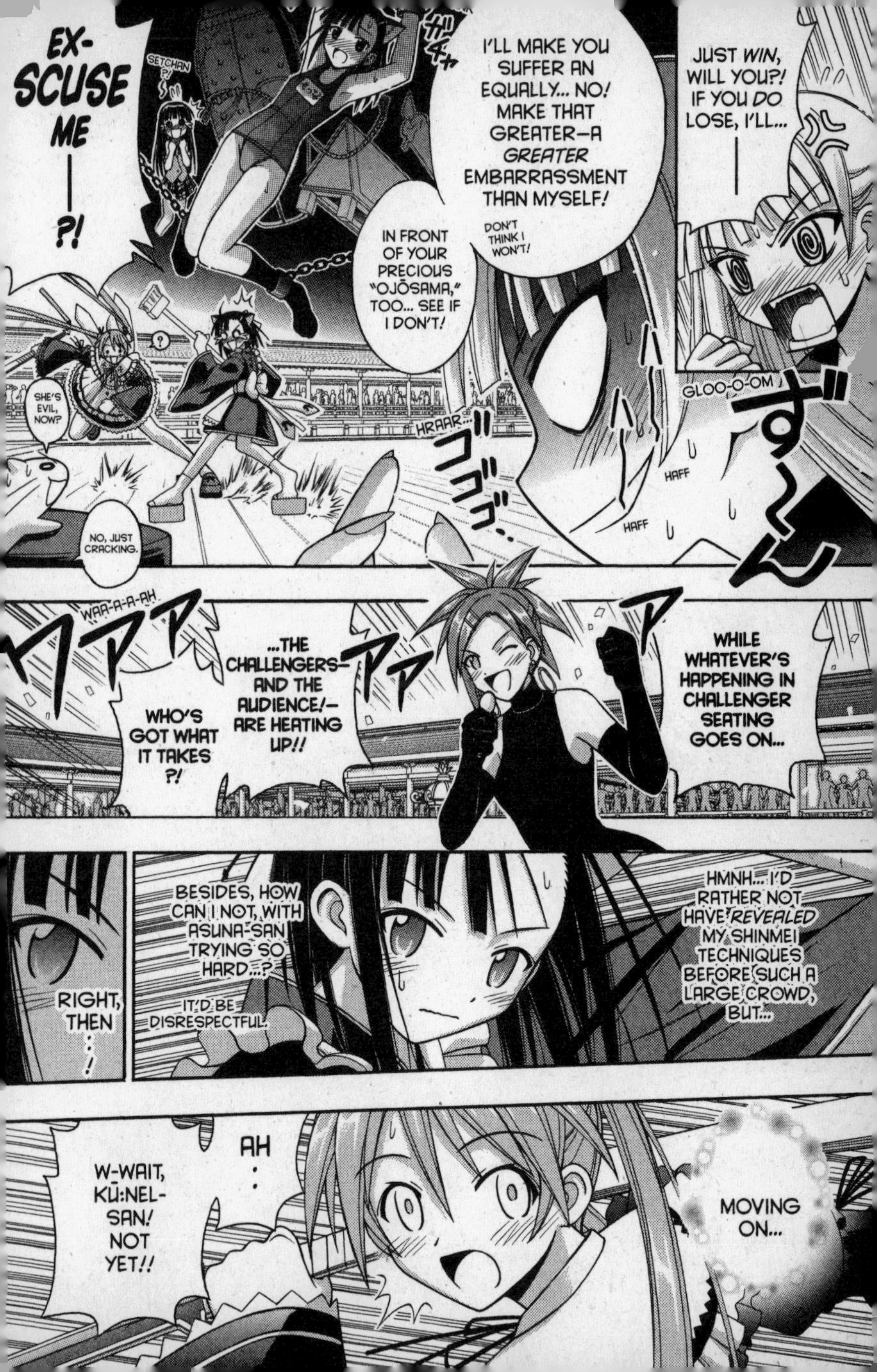
JUST WIN, WILL YOU?! IF YOU DO LOSE, I'LL... —
GLOO-O-OM
I'LL MAKE YOU SUFFER AN EQUALLY... NO! MAKE THAT GREATER—A GREATER EMBARRASSMENT THAN MYSELF!
DON'T THINK I WON'T!
IN FRONT OF YOUR PRECIOUS "OJŌSAMA," TOO... SEE IF I DON'T!
SETCHAN?!
EX-SCUSE ME—?!
HRAAR...
HAFF
HAFF
SHE'S EVIL, NOW?
NO, JUST CRACKING.
WHILE WHATEVER'S HAPPENING IN CHALLENGER SEATING GOES ON...
...THE CHALLENGERS—AND THE AUDIENCE!—ARE HEATING UP!!
WHO'S GOT WHAT IT TAKES?!
WAA-A-A-AH
HMNH... I'D RATHER NOT HAVE REVEALED MY SHINMEI TECHNIQUES BEFORE SUCH A LARGE CROWD, BUT...
BESIDES, HOW CAN I NOT, WITH ASUNA-SAN TRYING SO HARD...?
IT'D BE DISRESPECTFUL.
RIGHT, THEN...!
MOVING ON...
AH...
W-WAIT, KŪ:NEL-SAN! NOT YET!!

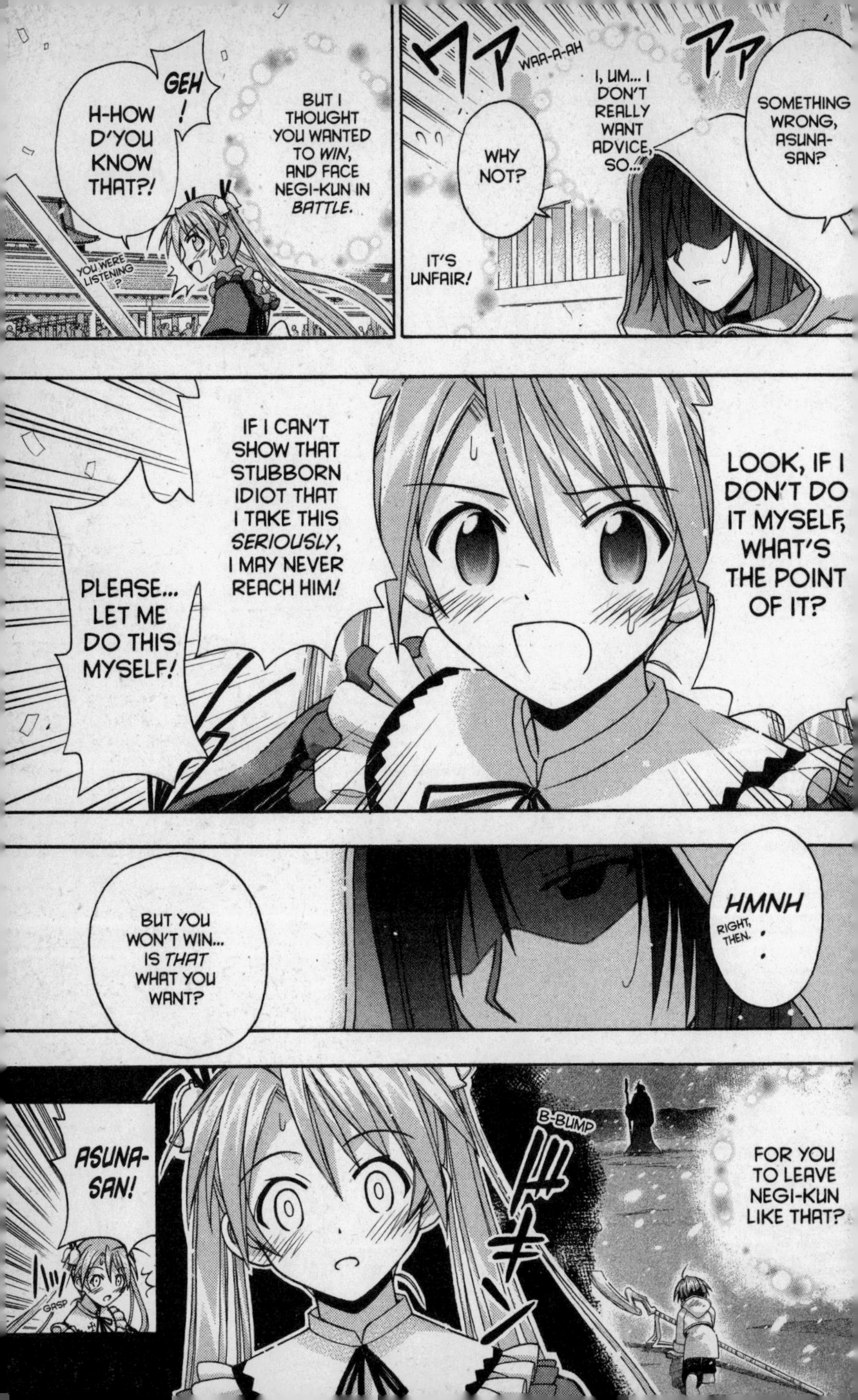
SOMETHING WRONG, ASUNA-SAN?
WAA-A-AH
I, UM... I DON'T REALLY WANT ADVICE, SO...
WHY NOT?
IT'S UNFAIR!
BUT I THOUGHT YOU WANTED TO WIN, AND FACE NEGI-KUN IN BATTLE.
GEH!
H-HOW D'YOU KNOW THAT?!
YOU WERE LISTENING?
LOOK, IF I DON'T DO IT MYSELF, WHAT'S THE POINT OF IT?
IF I CAN'T SHOW THAT STUBBORN IDIOT THAT I TAKE THIS SERIOUSLY, I MAY NEVER REACH HIM!
PLEASE... LET ME DO THIS MYSELF!
HMNH
RIGHT, THEN.
BUT YOU WON'T WIN... IS THAT WHAT YOU WANT?
FOR YOU TO LEAVE NEGI-KUN LIKE THAT?
B-BUMP
ASUNA-SAN!
GASP

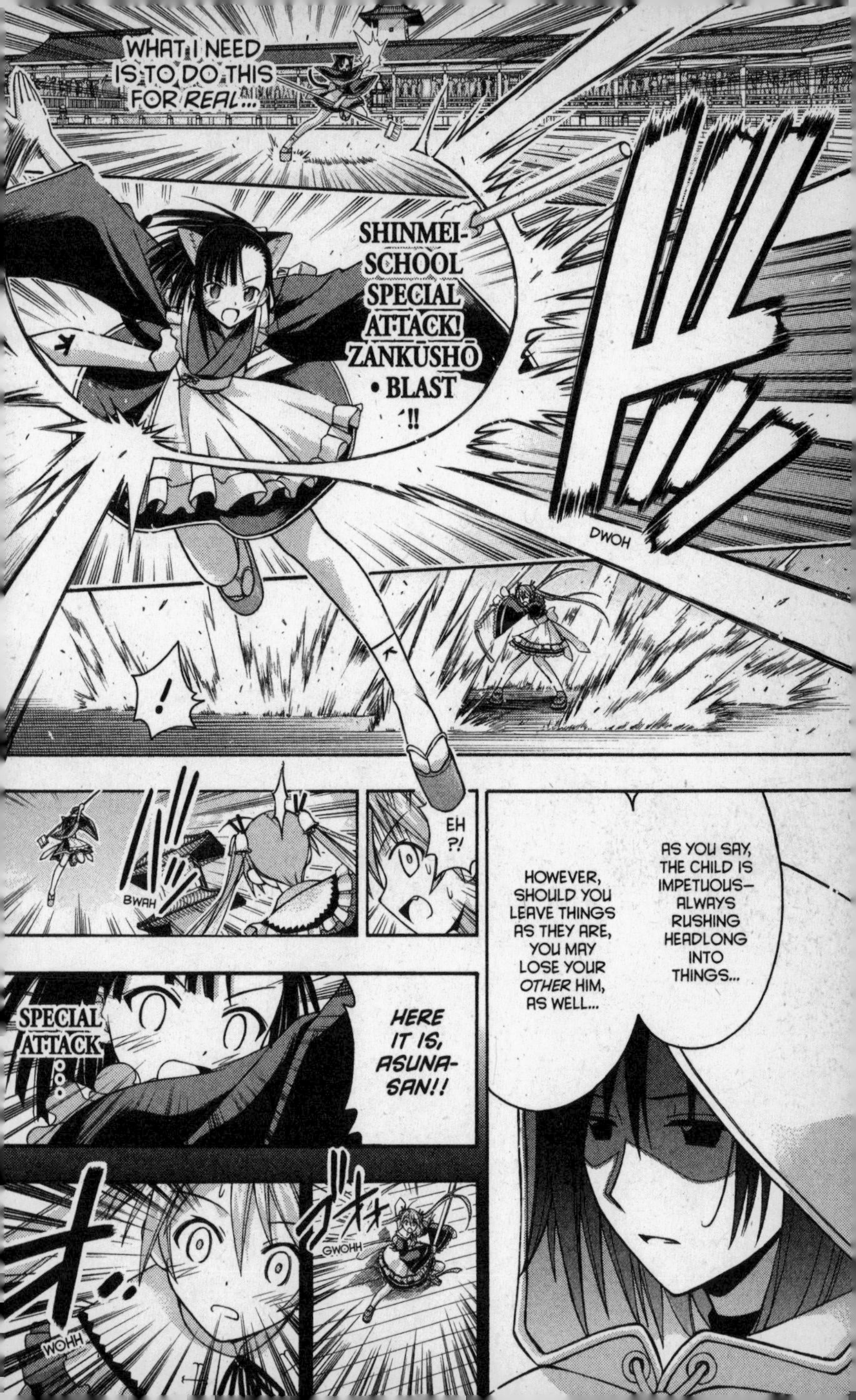
WHAT I NEED IS TO DO THIS FOR REAL...
SHINMEI-SCHOOL SPECIAL ATTACK! ZANKŪSHŌ • BLAST!!
DWOH
!
AS YOU SAY, THE CHILD IS IMPETUOUS—ALWAYS RUSHING HEADLONG INTO THINGS...
HOWEVER, SHOULD YOU LEAVE THINGS AS THEY ARE, YOU MAY LOSE YOUR OTHER HIM, AS WELL...
EH?!
BWAH
HERE IT IS, ASUNA-SAN!!
SPECIAL ATTACK...
GWOHH
WOHH

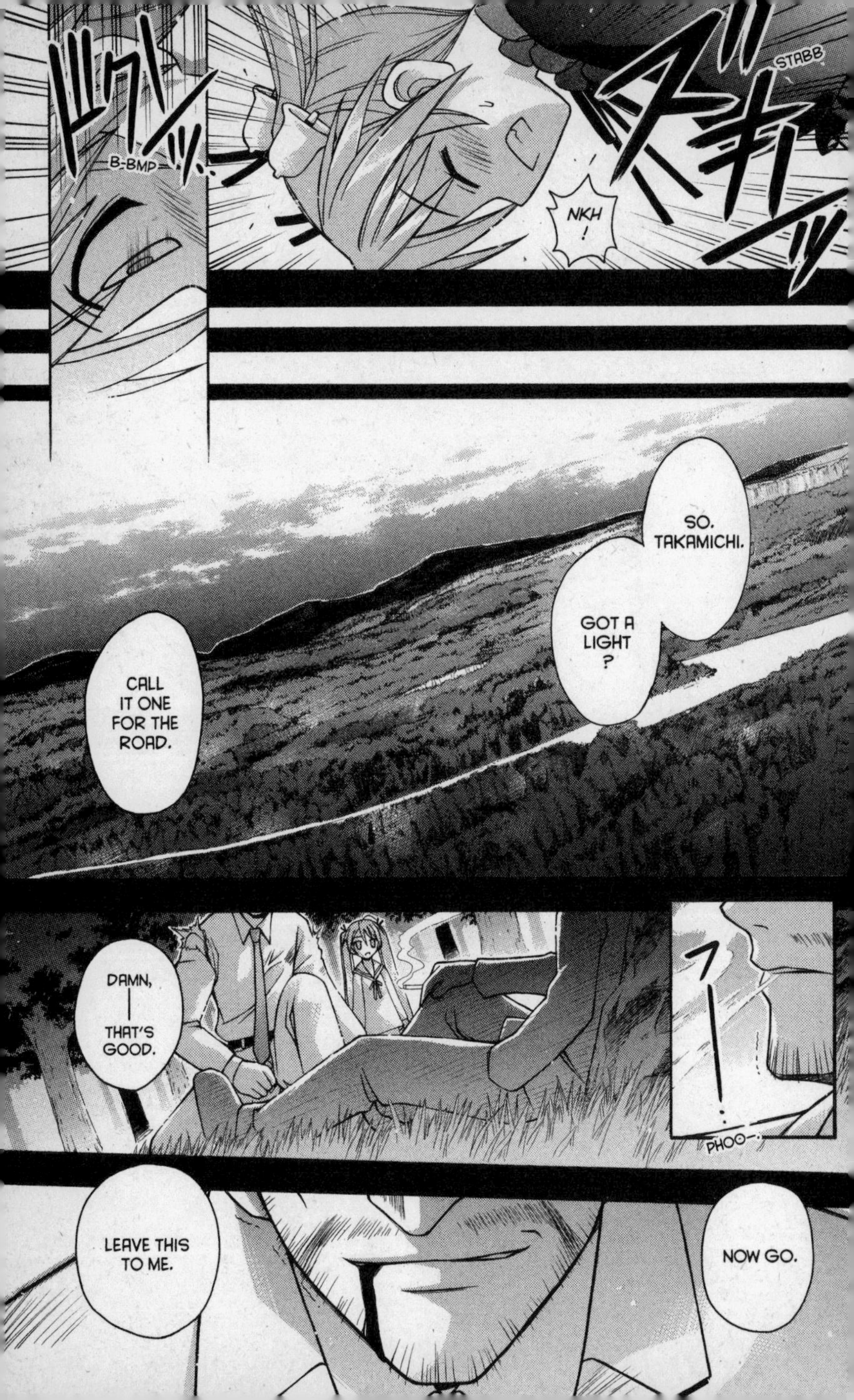
STABB
NKH!
B-BMP
SO. TAKAMICHI.
GOT A LIGHT?
CALL IT ONE FOR THE ROAD.
PHOO-
DAMN, — THAT'S GOOD.
NOW GO.
LEAVE THIS TO ME.

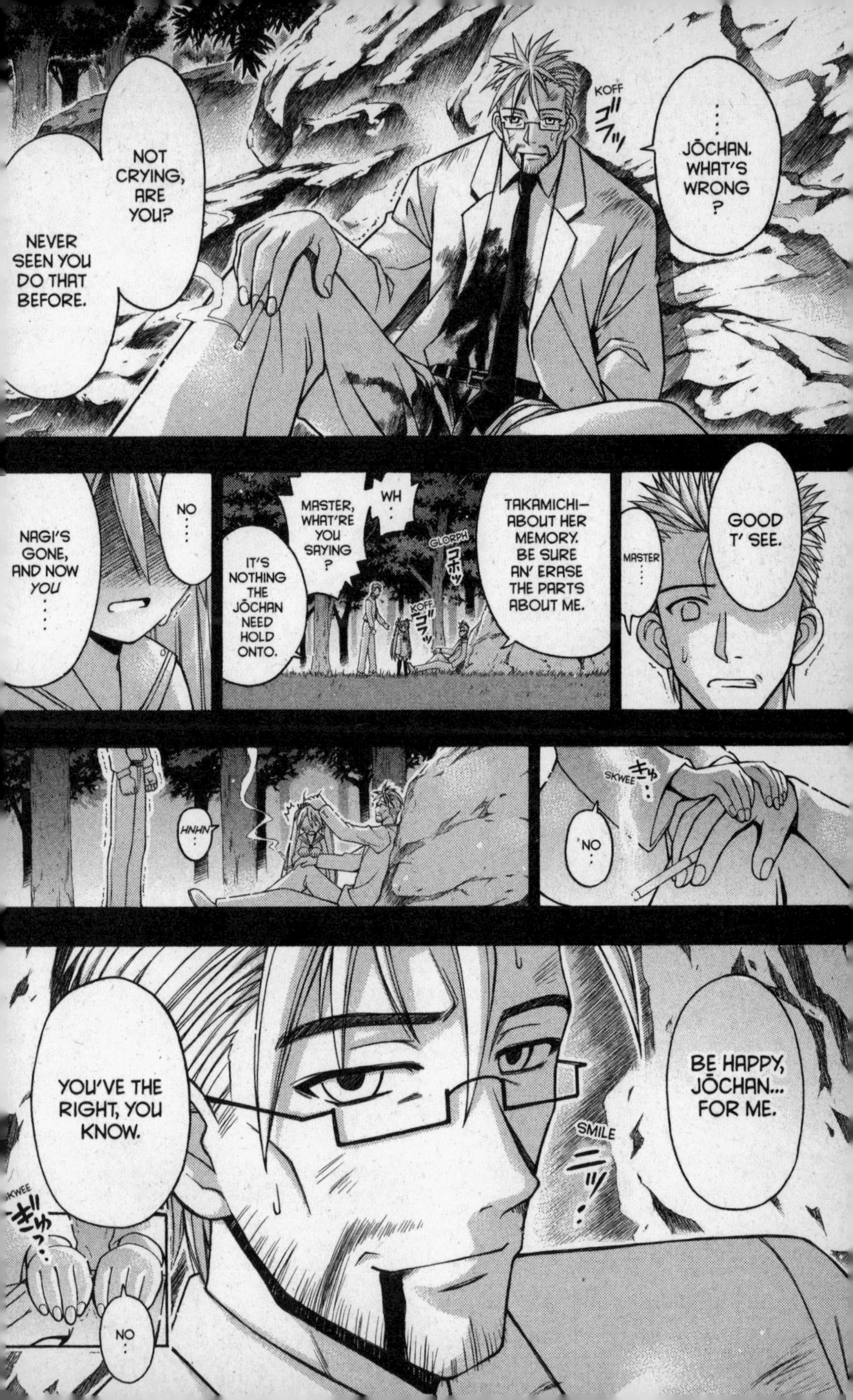
KOFF
...JŌCHAN. WHAT'S WRONG?
NOT CRYING, ARE YOU?
NEVER SEEN YOU DO THAT BEFORE.
GOOD T' SEE.
MASTER...
TAKAMICHI— ABOUT HER MEMORY. BE SURE AN' ERASE THE PARTS ABOUT ME.
GLORPH
KOFF
WH...
MASTER, WHAT'RE YOU SAYING?
IT'S NOTHING THE JŌCHAN NEED HOLD ONTO.
NO...
NAGI'S GONE, AND NOW *YOU*...
SKWEE
NO...
HNHN...
BE HAPPY, JŌCHAN... FOR ME.
SMILE
YOU'VE THE RIGHT, YOU KNOW.
SKWEE
NO...

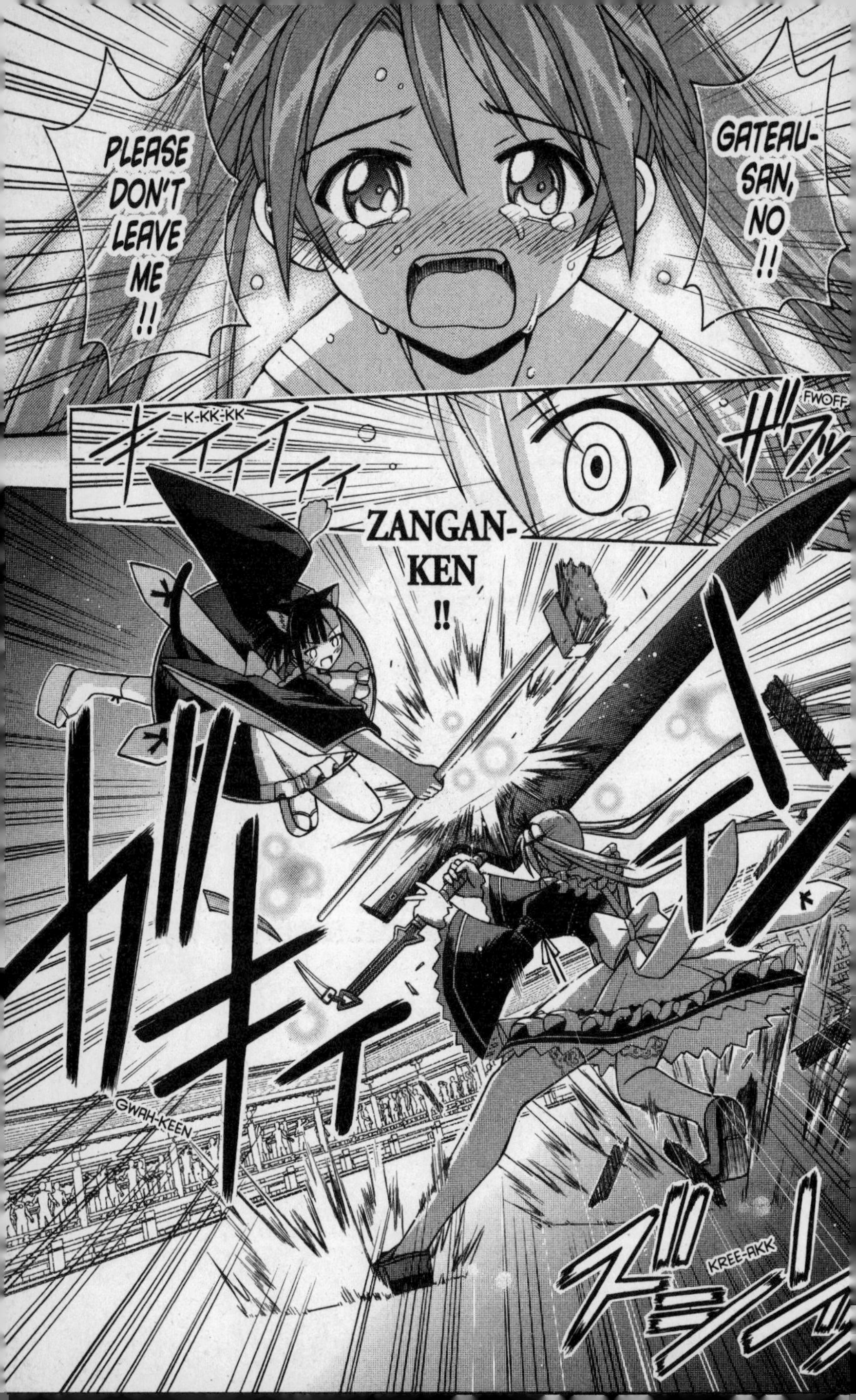
GATEAU-SAN, NO!!
PLEASE DON'T LEAVE ME!!
FWOFF
K-KK-KK
ZANGAN-KEN!!
GWAH-KEEN
KREE-AKK

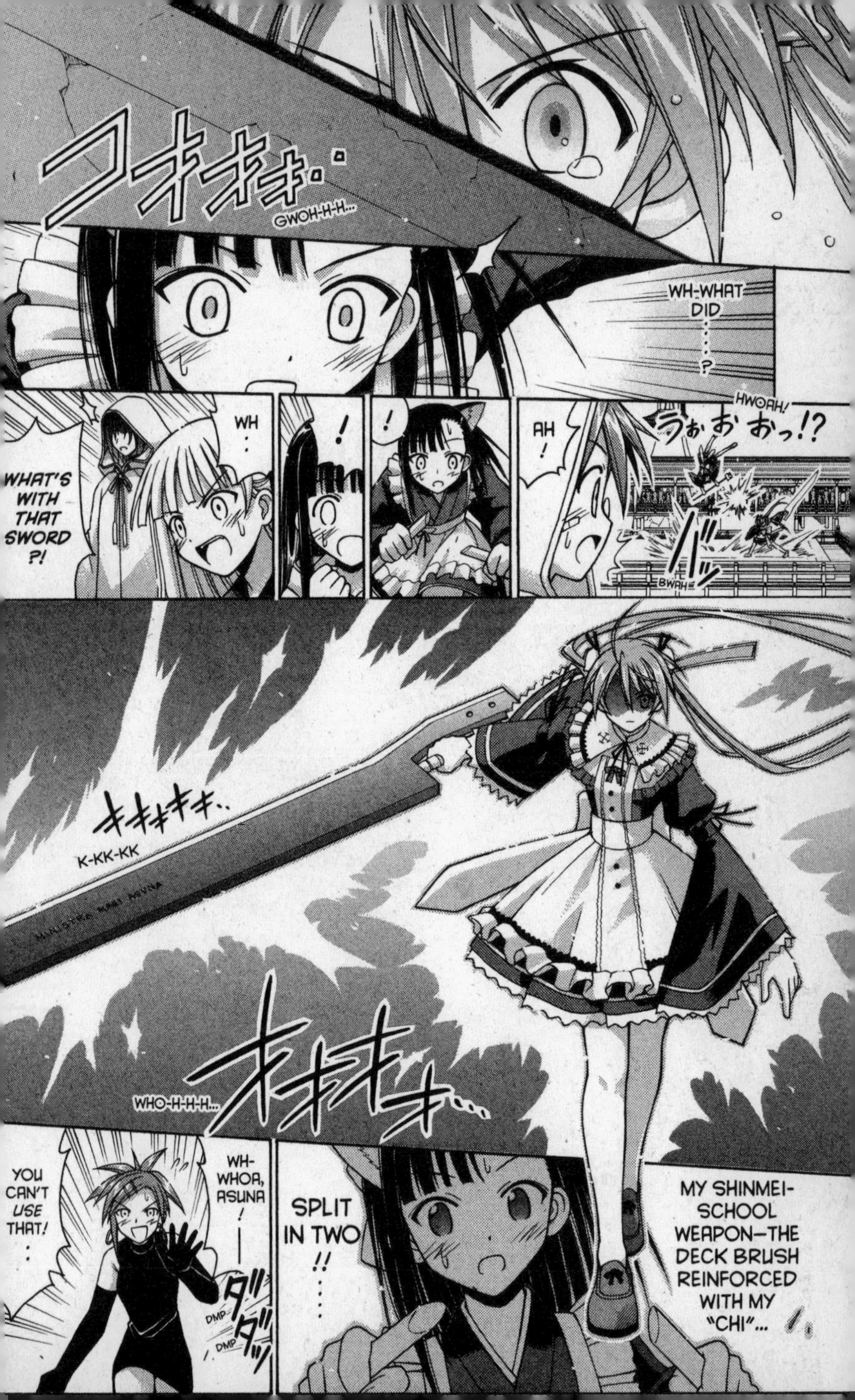
コオオォ。
GWOH-H-H...
WH-WHAT DID... ...?
HWOAH!
うぉおおっ!?
BWAH
バッ
AH!
!
!
WH...
WHAT'S WITH THAT SWORD?!
キキキキキ..
K-KK-KK
オオオオ...
WHO-H-H-H...
MY SHINMEI-SCHOOL WEAPON—THE DECK BRUSH REINFORCED WITH MY "CHI"...
SPLIT IN TWO!! ...
WH-WHOA, ASUNA! ...
ダダッ
DMP
DMP
YOU CAN'T USE THAT! ...

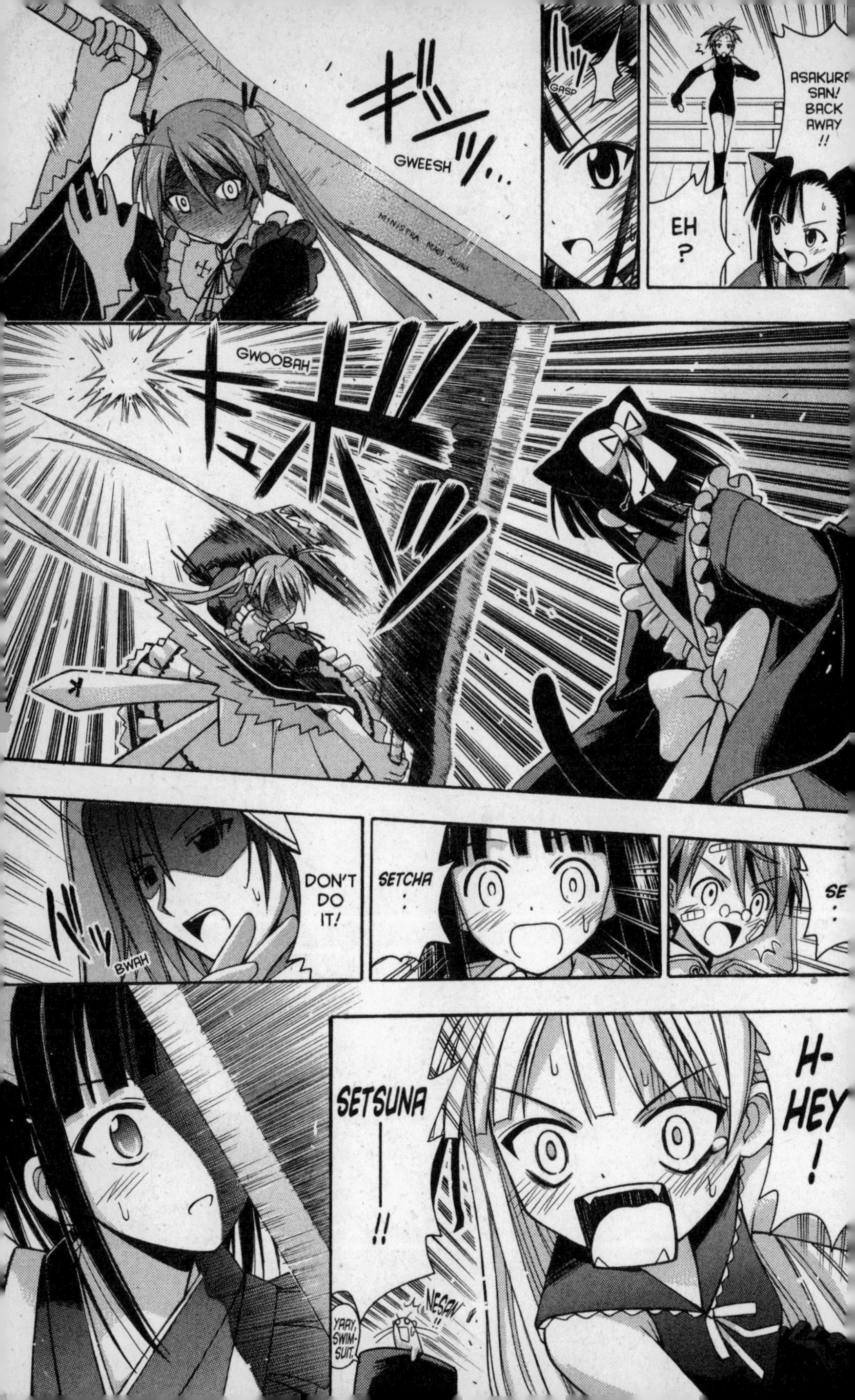
ASAKURA SAN! BACK AWAY!!
EH?
GASP
GWEESH
MINISTRA MAGI ASUNA
GWOOBAH
SE...
SETCHA...
DON'T DO IT!
BWAH
H-HEY!
SETSUNA!!
NESAN!!
YAAY, SWIM-SUIT.

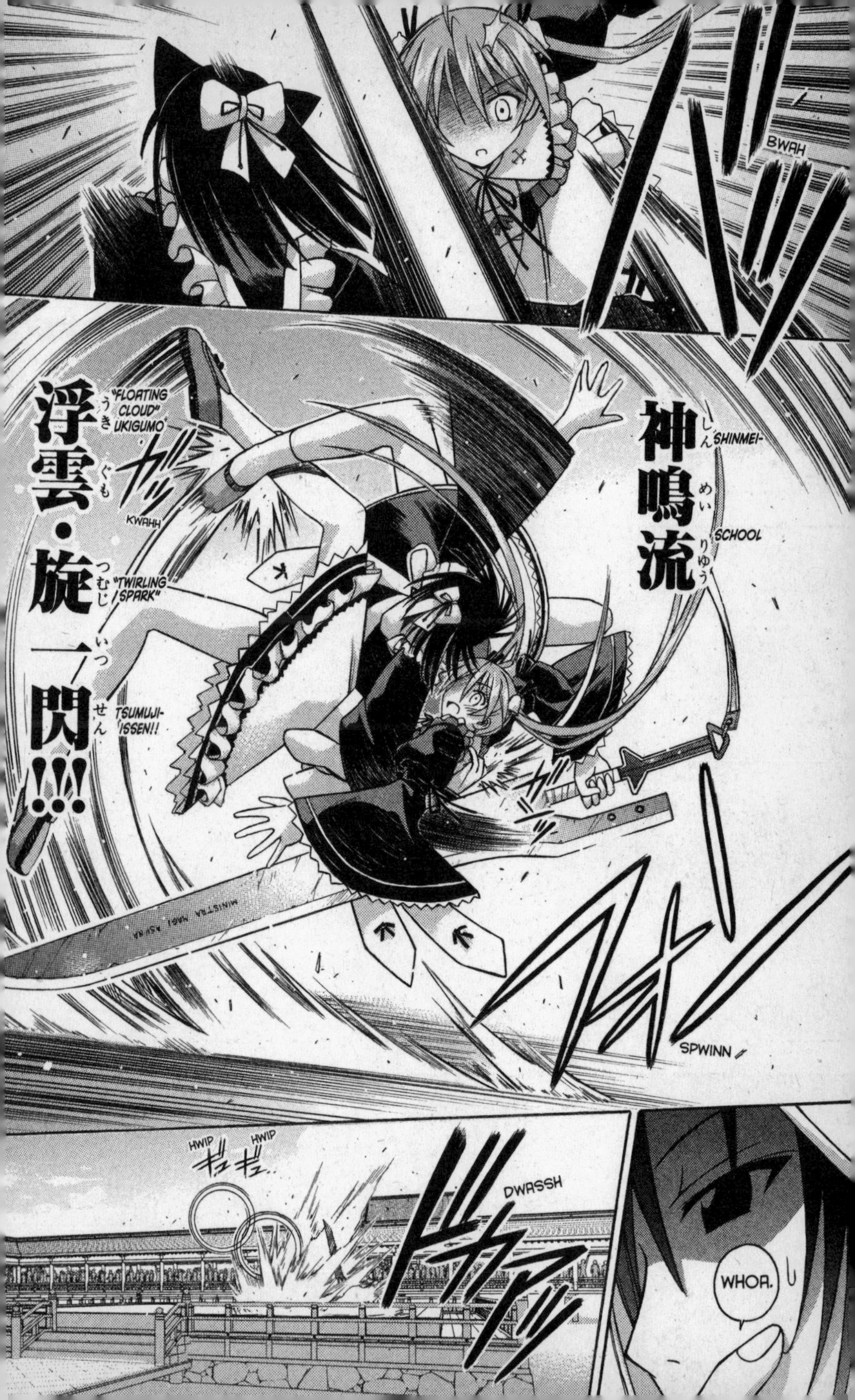
BWAH
神鳴流
SHINMEI-
SCHOOL
浮雲・旋一閃!!!
"FLOATING CLOUD" UKIGUMO
"TWIRLING SPARK" TSUMUJI-ISSEN!!
KWAHH
SPWINN
WHOA.
DWASSH
HWIP HWIP

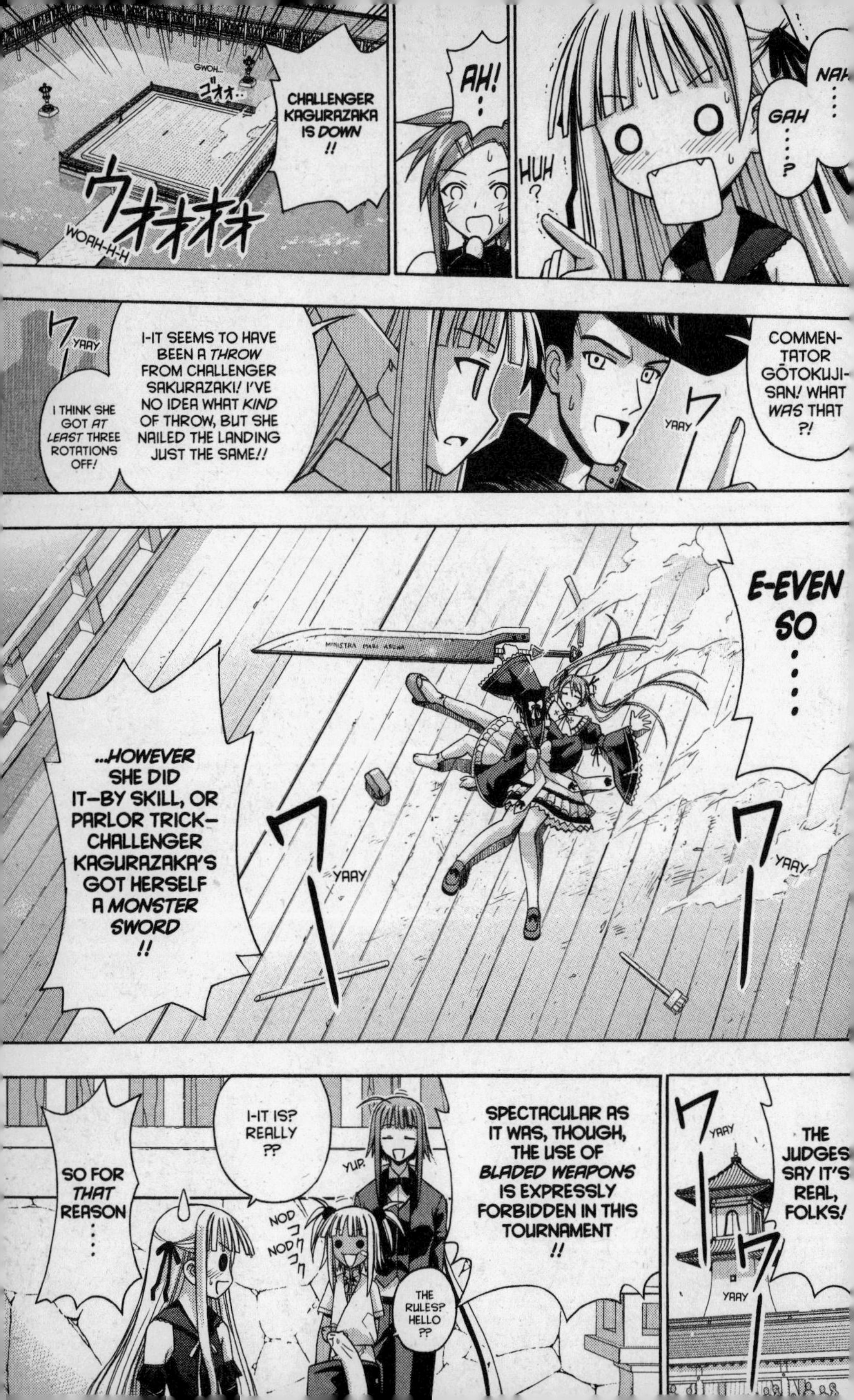
NAH...
GAH...?
HUH?
AH!...
GWOH...
ゴオオ...
CHALLENGER KAGURAZAKA IS *DOWN*!!
ウオオオオオ
WOAH-H-H
COMMENTATOR GŌTOKUJI-SAN! WHAT *WAS* THAT?!
YAAY
I-IT SEEMS TO HAVE BEEN A *THROW* FROM CHALLENGER SAKURAZAKI! I'VE NO IDEA WHAT *KIND* OF THROW, BUT SHE NAILED THE LANDING JUST THE SAME!!
I THINK SHE GOT *AT LEAST* THREE ROTATIONS OFF!
ワ
YAAY
E-EVEN SO....
YAAY
MINISTRA MAGI ASUNA
...HOWEVER SHE DID IT—BY SKILL, OR PARLOR TRICK—CHALLENGER KAGURAZAKA'S GOT HERSELF A *MONSTER SWORD*!!
YAAY
THE JUDGES SAY IT'S REAL, FOLKS!
YAAY
YAAY
SPECTACULAR AS IT WAS, THOUGH, THE USE OF *BLADED WEAPONS* IS EXPRESSLY FORBIDDEN IN THIS TOURNAMENT!!
I-IT IS? REALLY??
YUP.
SO FOR *THAT* REASON....
NOD
NOD
THE RULES? HELLO??

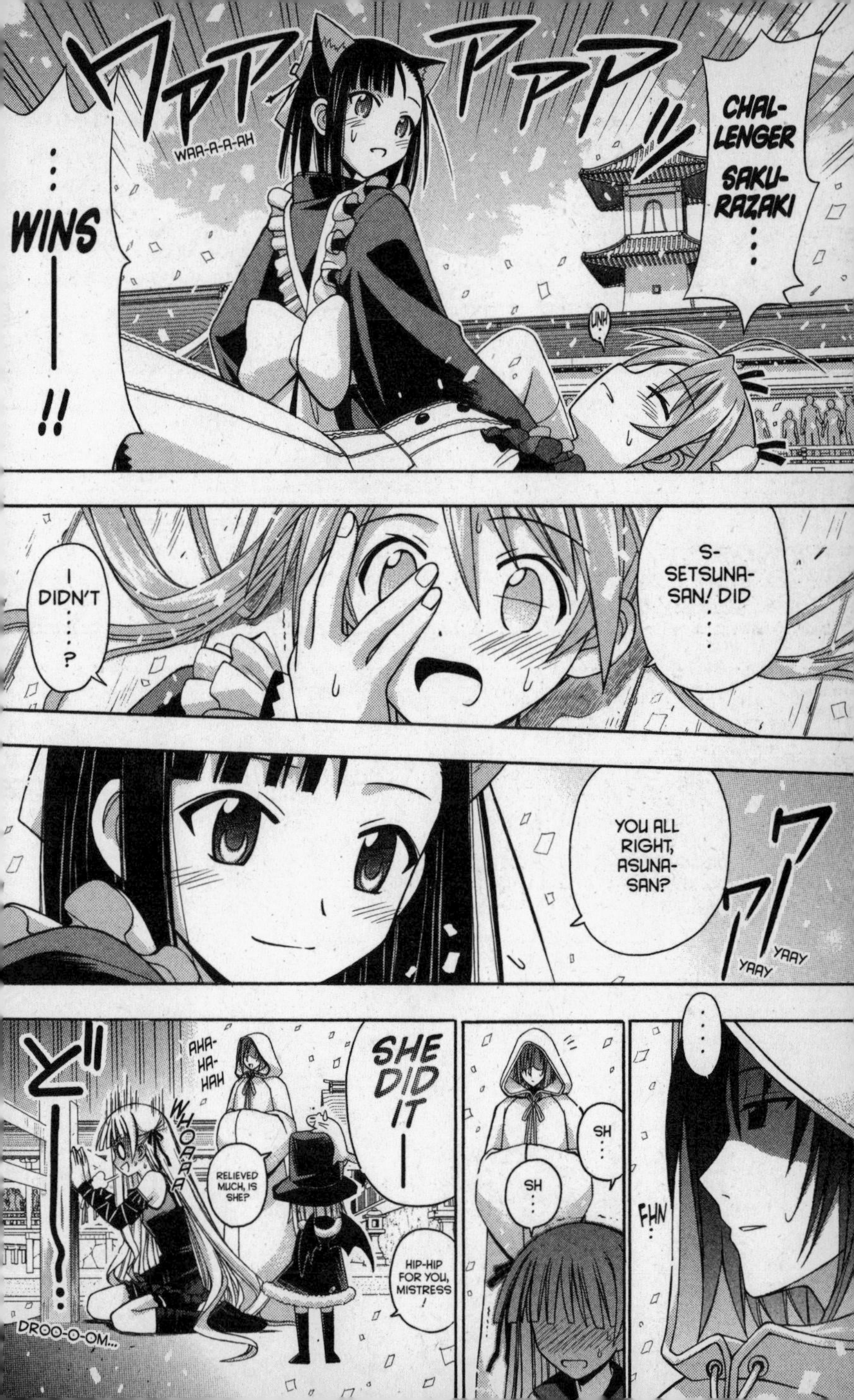
CHAL-LENGER SAKU-RAZAKI...
UNH
WAA-A-A-AH
...WINS ——!!
S-SETSUNA-SAN! DID ....
I DIDN'T ....?
YOU ALL RIGHT, ASUNA-SAN?
YAAY
YAAY
....
FHN...
SH...
SH...
SHE DID IT —
AHA-HA-HAH
RELIEVED MUCH, IS SHE?
HIP-HIP FOR YOU, MISTRESS!
WHOAAA
DROO-O-OM...

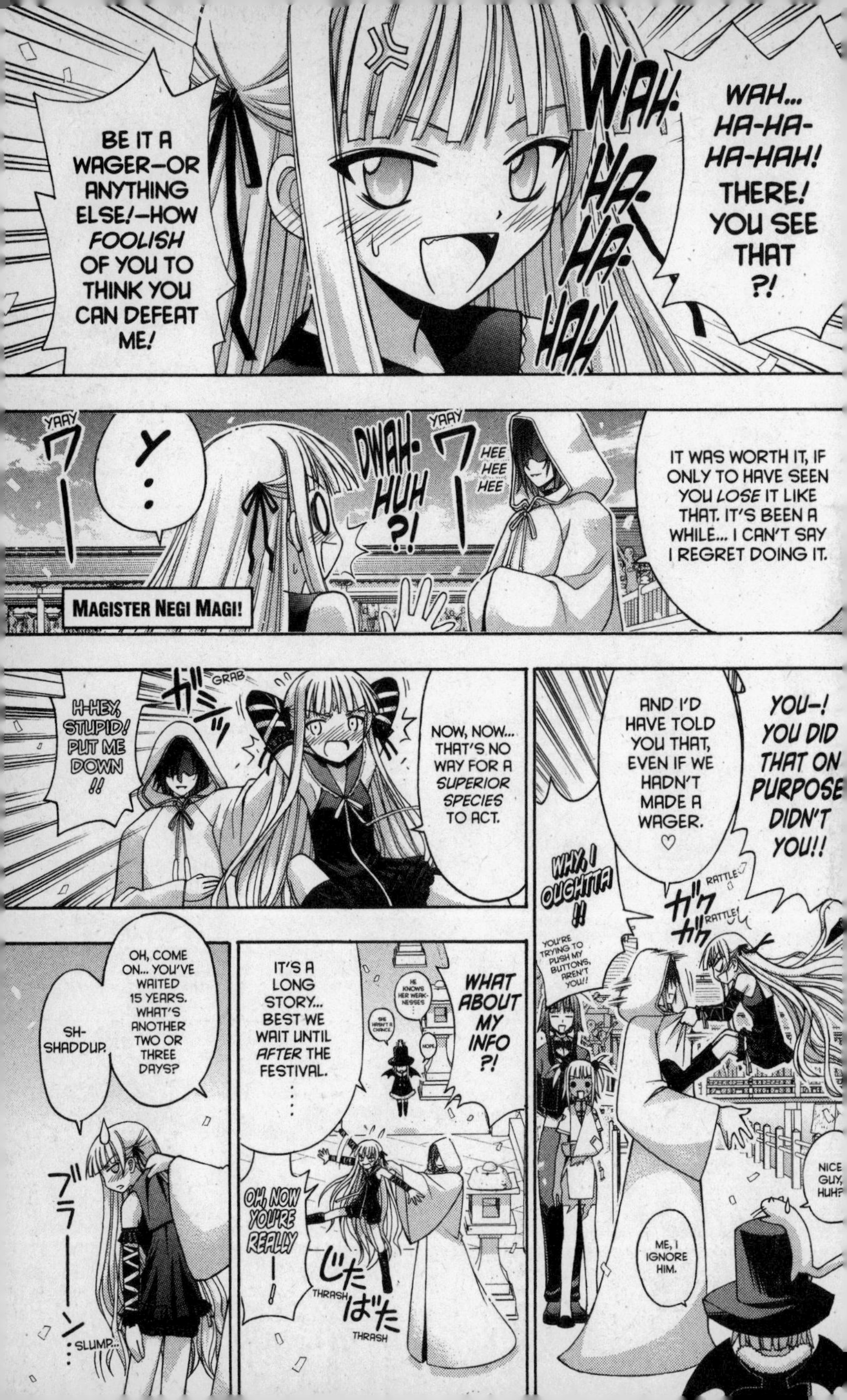
WAH... HA-HA-HA-HAH! THERE! YOU SEE THAT ?!
WAH-HA-HA-HA-HAH
BE IT A WAGER—OR ANYTHING ELSE!—HOW FOOLISH OF YOU TO THINK YOU CAN DEFEAT ME!
IT WAS WORTH IT, IF ONLY TO HAVE SEEN YOU LOSE IT LIKE THAT. IT'S BEEN A WHILE... I CAN'T SAY I REGRET DOING IT.
HEE HEE HEE
YAAY
DWAH-HUH ?!
Y...
YAAY
MAGISTER NEGI MAGI!
YOU—! YOU DID THAT ON PURPOSE DIDN'T YOU!!
AND I'D HAVE TOLD YOU THAT, EVEN IF WE HADN'T MADE A WAGER. ♡
RATTLE
RATTLE
WHY, I OUGHTTA !!
YOU'RE TRYING TO PUSH MY BUTTONS, AREN'T YOU!!
NICE GUY, HUH?
ME, I IGNORE HIM.
NOW, NOW... THAT'S NO WAY FOR A SUPERIOR SPECIES TO ACT.
GRAB
H-HEY, STUPID! PUT ME DOWN !!
WHAT ABOUT MY INFO ?!
IT'S A LONG STORY... BEST WE WAIT UNTIL AFTER THE FESTIVAL. ...
HE KNOWS HER WEAKNESSES...
SHE HASN'T A CHANCE
NOPE.
OH, NOW YOU'RE REALLY—!
THRASH
THRASH
OH, COME ON... YOU'VE WAITED 15 YEARS. WHAT'S ANOTHER TWO OR THREE DAYS?
SH-SHADDUP.
SLUMP...

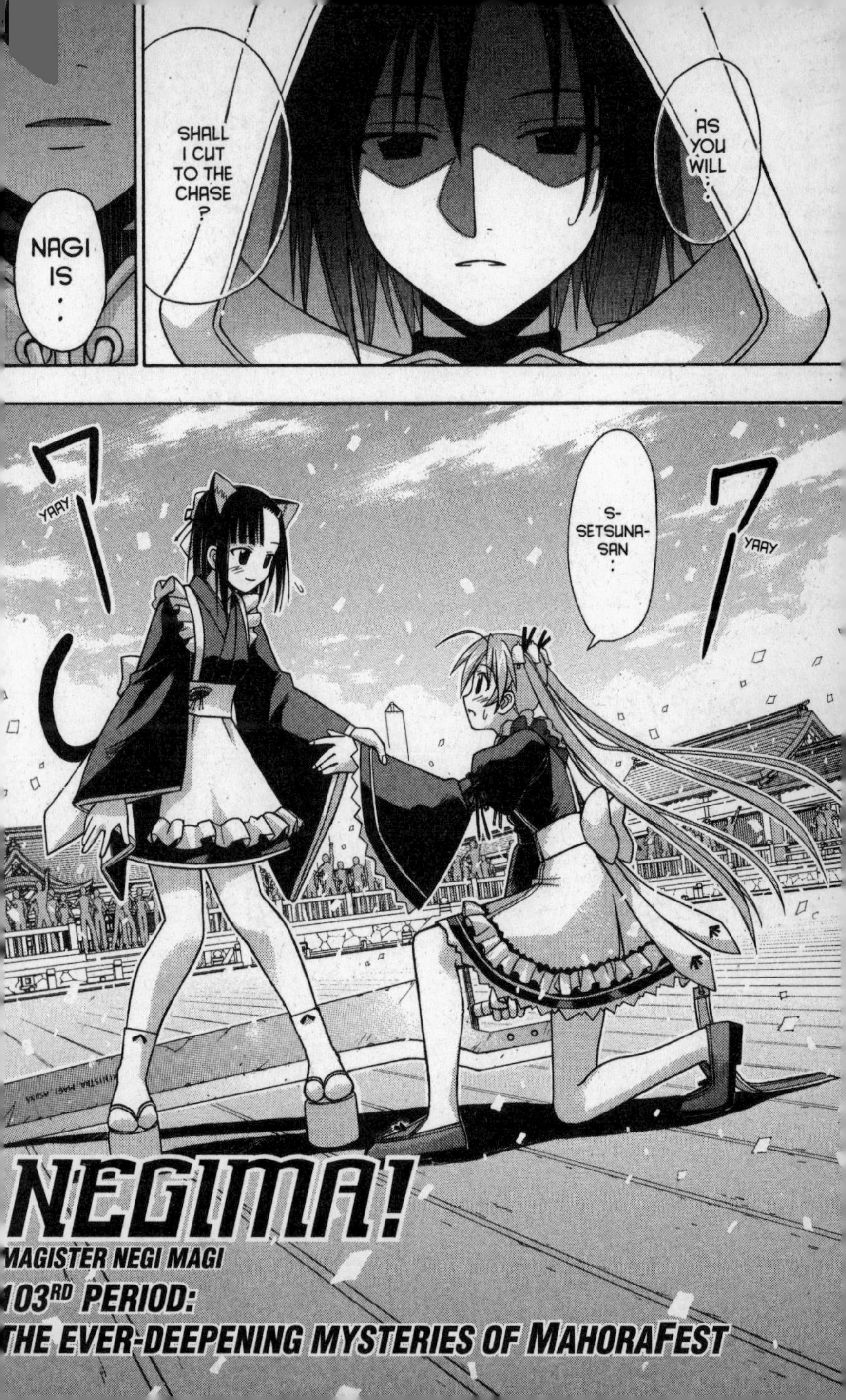
AS YOU WILL...
SHALL I CUT TO THE CHASE?
NAGI IS...
YAAY
S-SETSUNA-SAN...
YAAY
NEGIMA!
MAGISTER NEGI MAGI
103RD PERIOD:
THE EVER-DEEPENING MYSTERIES OF MAHORAFEST

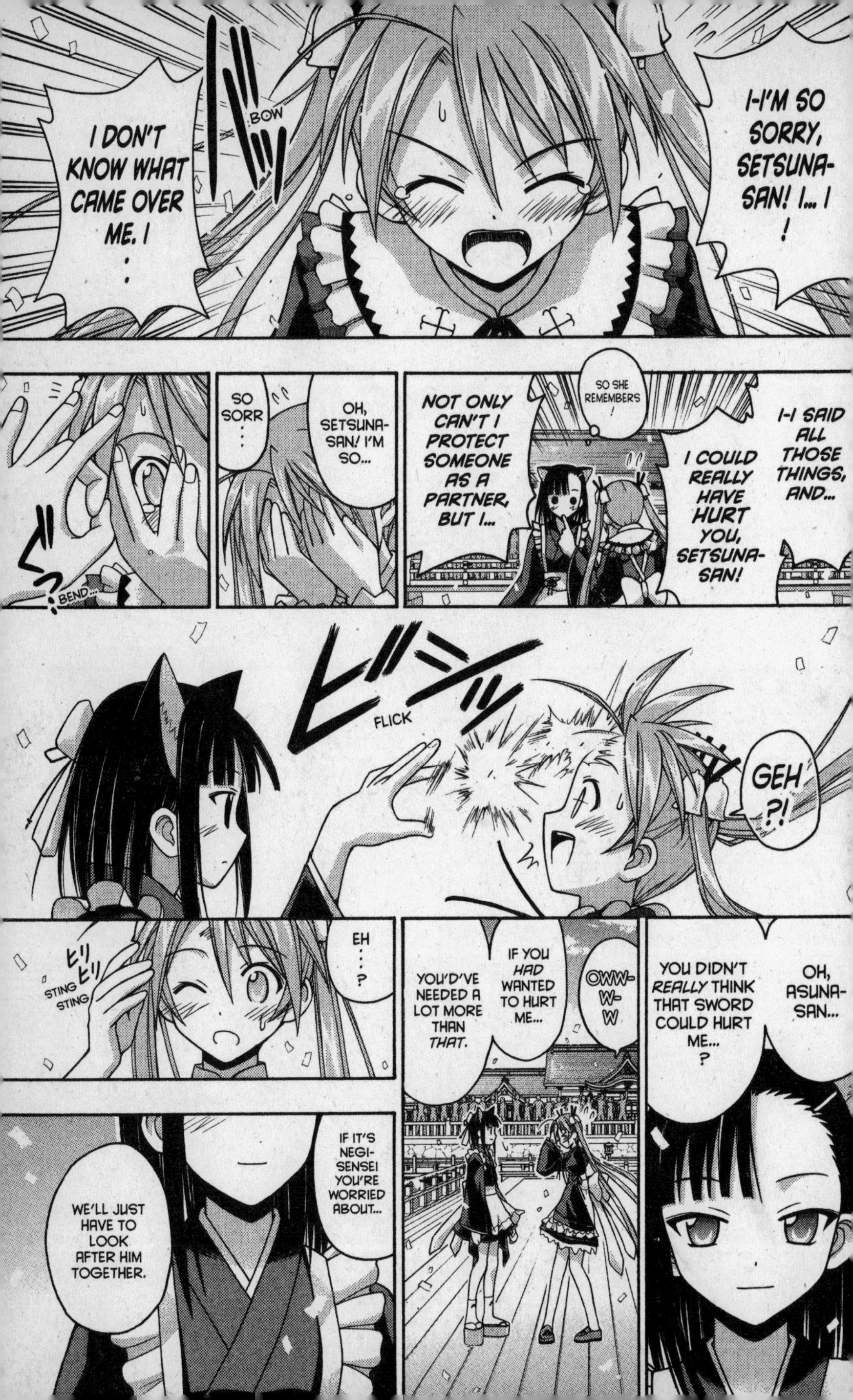

I-I'M SO SORRY, SETSUNA-SAN! I... I!
BOW
I DON'T KNOW WHAT CAME OVER ME. I...
I-I SAID ALL THOSE THINGS, AND...
I COULD REALLY HAVE HURT YOU, SETSUNA-SAN!
SO SHE REMEMBERS!
NOT ONLY CAN'T I PROTECT SOMEONE AS A PARTNER, BUT I...
OH, SETSUNA-SAN! I'M SO...
SO SORR...
BEND...
GEH?!
FLICK
OH, ASUNA-SAN...
YOU DIDN'T REALLY THINK THAT SWORD COULD HURT ME...?
OWW-W-W
IF YOU HAD WANTED TO HURT ME...
YOU'D'VE NEEDED A LOT MORE THAN THAT.
EH...?
STING STING
IF IT'S NEGI-SENSEI YOU'RE WORRIED ABOUT...
WE'LL JUST HAVE TO LOOK AFTER HIM TOGETHER.

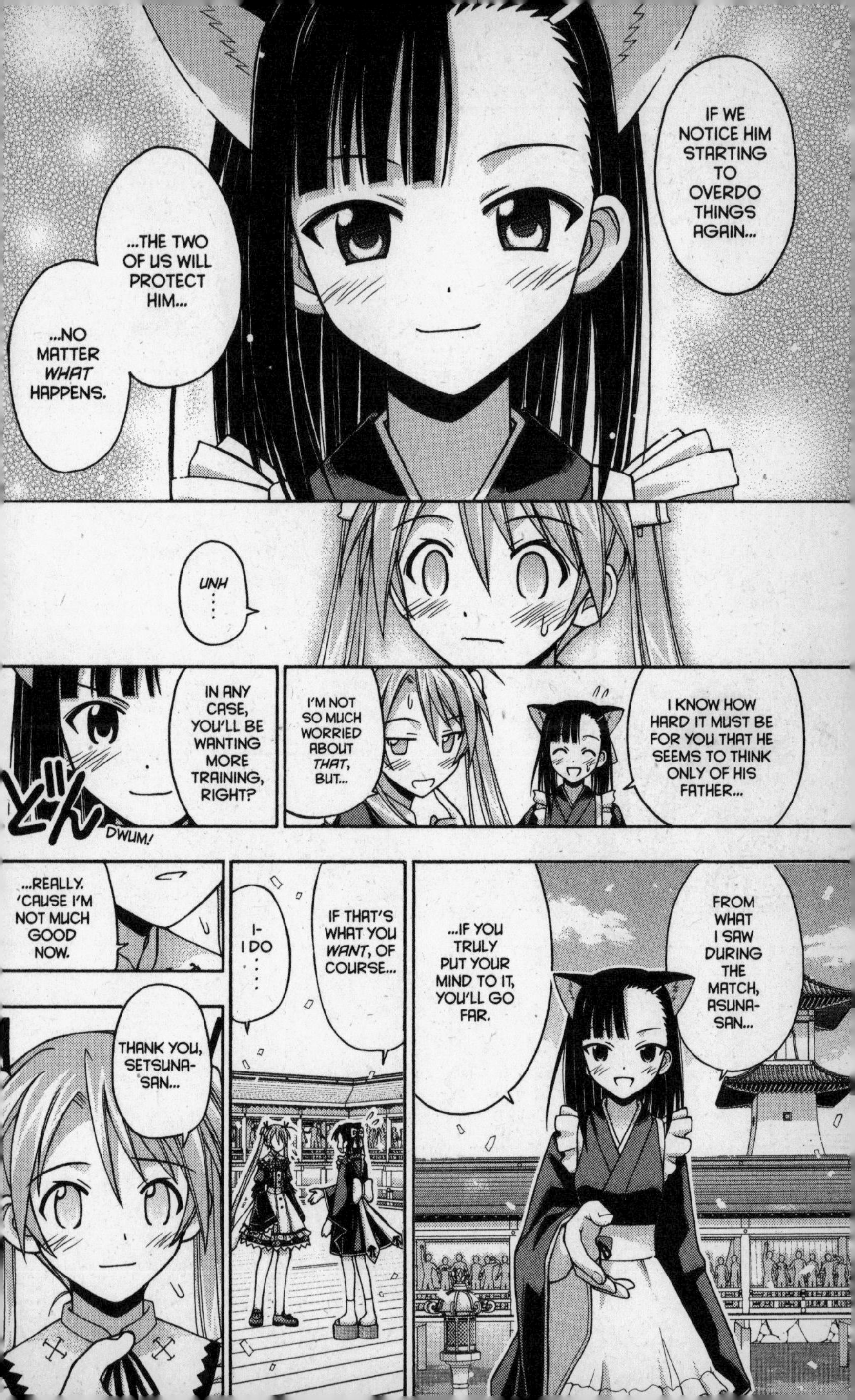

IF WE NOTICE HIM STARTING TO OVERDO THINGS AGAIN...
...THE TWO OF US WILL PROTECT HIM...
...NO MATTER *WHAT* HAPPENS.
UNH .....
I KNOW HOW HARD IT MUST BE FOR YOU THAT HE SEEMS TO THINK ONLY OF HIS FATHER...
I'M NOT SO MUCH WORRIED ABOUT *THAT*, BUT...
IN ANY CASE, YOU'LL BE WANTING MORE TRAINING, RIGHT?
どん
DWUM!
FROM WHAT I SAW DURING THE MATCH, ASUNA-SAN...
...IF YOU TRULY PUT YOUR MIND TO IT, YOU'LL GO FAR.
IF THAT'S WHAT YOU *WANT*, OF COURSE...
I- I DO.....
...REALLY. 'CAUSE I'M NOT MUCH GOOD NOW.
THANK YOU, SETSUNA-SAN...

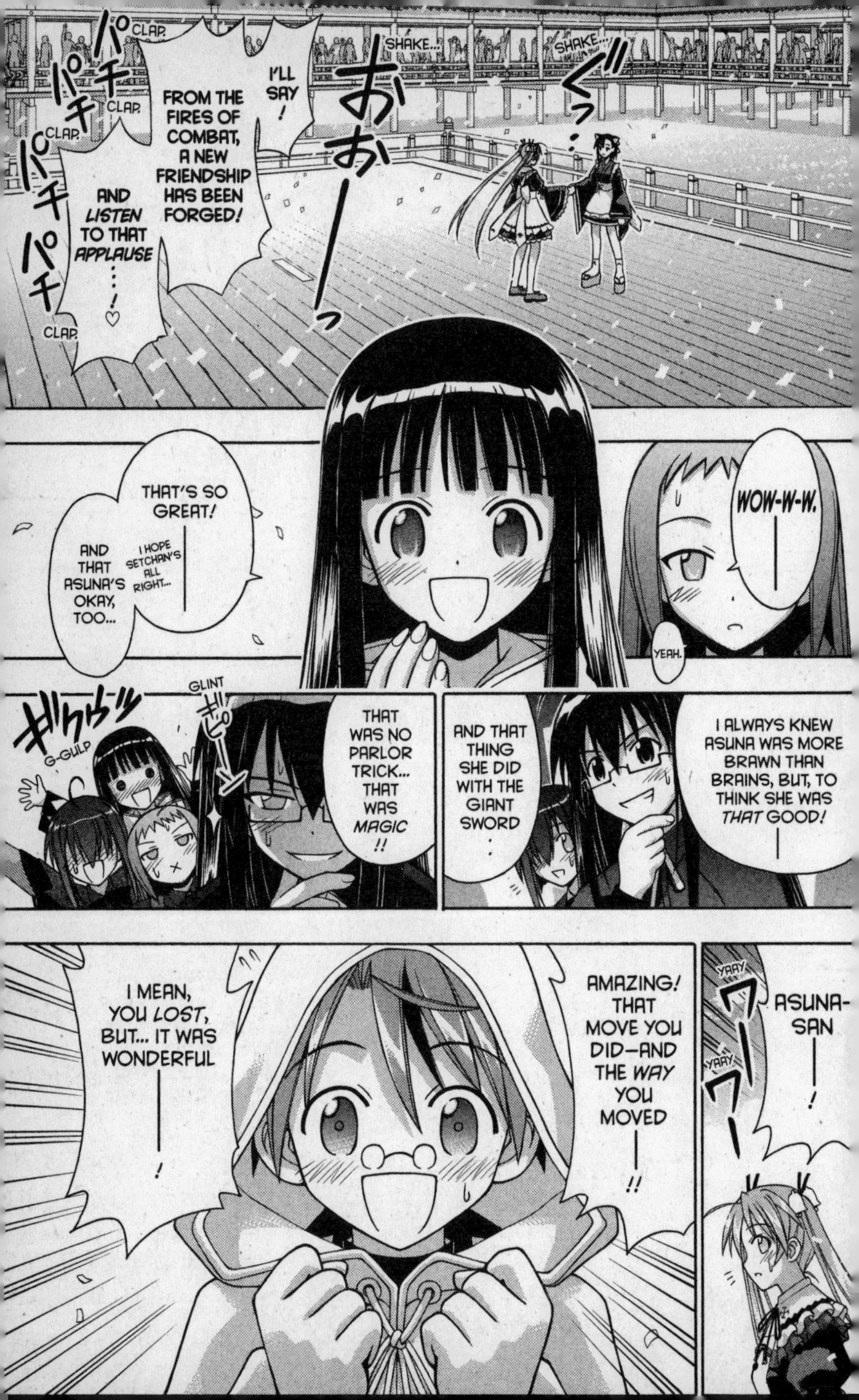
ぐっ…
SHAKE…
SHAKE…
おおーーっ
I'LL SAY!
FROM THE FIRES OF COMBAT, A NEW FRIENDSHIP HAS BEEN FORGED!
AND *LISTEN* TO THAT *APPLAUSE*…!♡
パチ CLAP.
パチ CLAP.
パチ CLAP.
パチ CLAP.
WOW-W-W.—
YEAH.
THAT'S SO GREAT!—
AND THAT ASUNA'S OKAY, TOO…
I HOPE SETCHAN'S ALL RIGHT…—
I ALWAYS KNEW ASUNA WAS MORE BRAWN THAN BRAINS, BUT, TO THINK SHE WAS *THAT* GOOD!—
AND THAT THING SHE DID WITH THE GIANT SWORD…
THAT WAS NO PARLOR TRICK… THAT WAS *MAGIC*!!
ギラッ GLINT
ギクッ G-GULP
ASUNA-SAN—!
ワー YAAY
ワー YAAY
AMAZING! THAT MOVE YOU DID—AND THE *WAY* YOU MOVED—!!
I MEAN, YOU *LOST*, BUT… IT WAS WONDERFUL—!

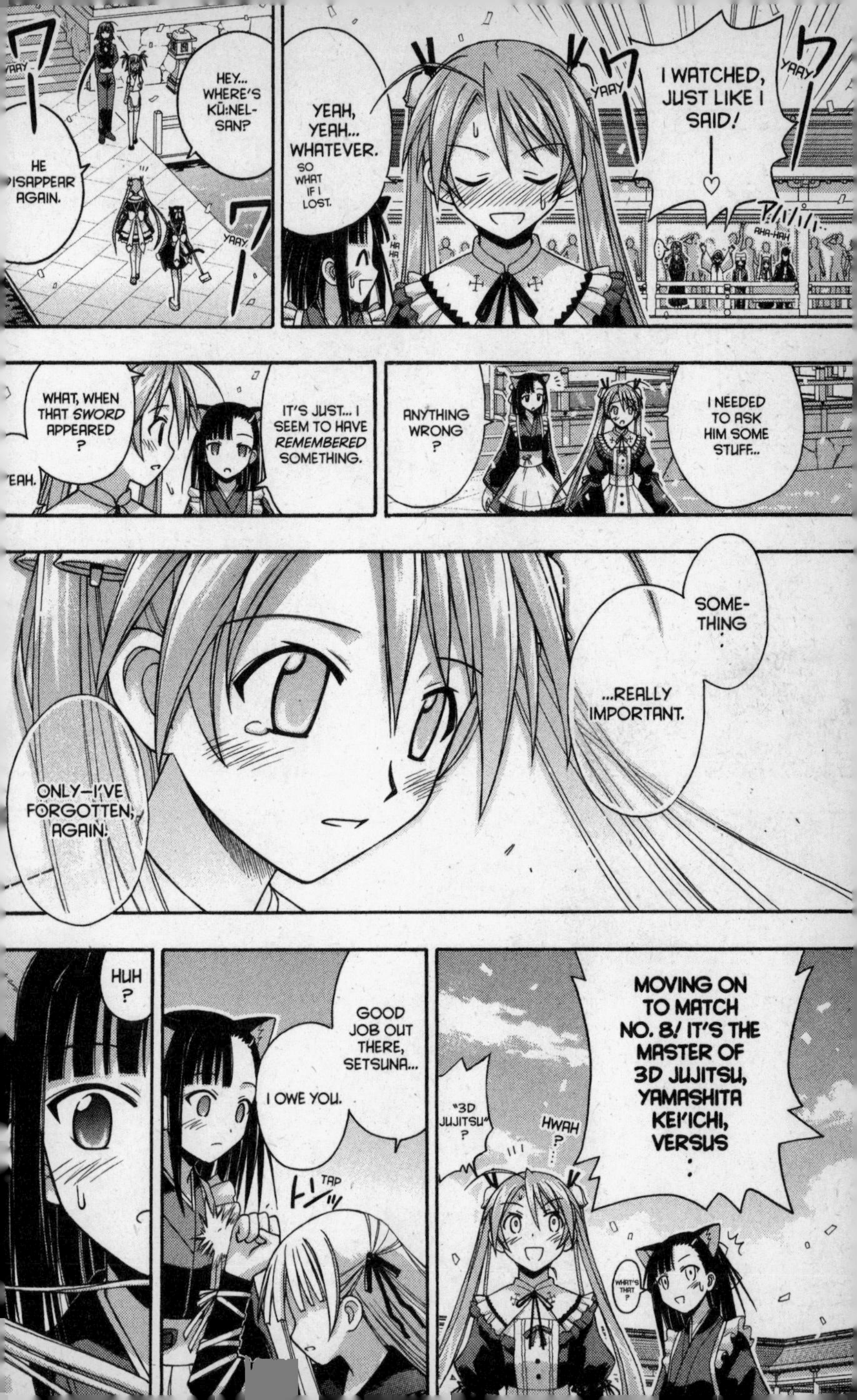
YAAY
I WATCHED, JUST LIKE I SAID! ♡
YAAY
YAAY
AHA-HAH
YEAH, YEAH... WHATEVER.
SO WHAT IF I LOST.
HA HA
HEY... WHERE'S KŪ:NEL-SAN?
YAAY
HE DISAPPEAR AGAIN.
YAAY
I NEEDED TO ASK HIM SOME STUFF...
ANYTHING WRONG?
IT'S JUST... I SEEM TO HAVE *REMEMBERED* SOMETHING.
WHAT, WHEN THAT *SWORD* APPEARED?
YEAH.
SOMETHING...
...REALLY IMPORTANT.
ONLY—I'VE FORGOTTEN, AGAIN.
MOVING ON TO MATCH NO. 8! IT'S THE MASTER OF 3D JUJITSU, YAMASHITA KEI'ICHI, VERSUS...
HWAH?
"3D JUJITSU"?
WHAT'S THAT?
GOOD JOB OUT THERE, SETSUNA...
I OWE YOU.
TAP
HUH?

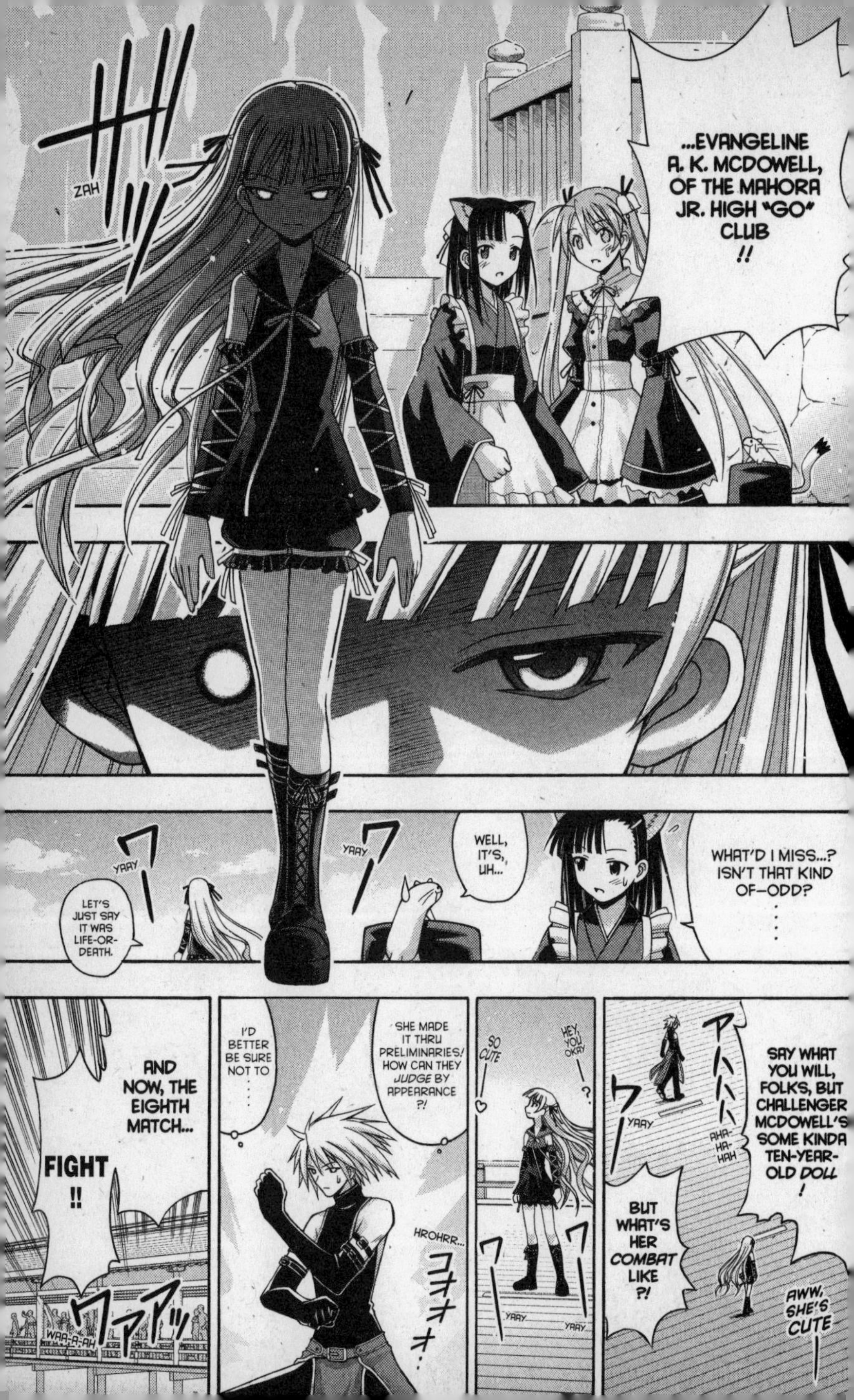
...EVANGELINE A. K. MCDOWELL, OF THE MAHORA JR. HIGH "GO" CLUB !!
ZAH
WHAT'D I MISS...? ISN'T THAT KIND OF—ODD? . . .
WELL, IT'S, UH...
YAAY
YAAY
LET'S JUST SAY IT WAS LIFE-OR-DEATH.
SAY WHAT YOU WILL, FOLKS, BUT CHALLENGER MCDOWELL'S SOME KINDA TEN-YEAR-OLD *DOLL* !
AHA-HA-HAH
YAAY
BUT WHAT'S HER *COMBAT* LIKE ?!
AWW, SHE'S CUTE—
HEY, YOU OKAY—?
SO CUTE—♡
YAAY
YAAY
SHE MADE IT THRU PRELIMINARIES! HOW CAN THEY *JUDGE* BY APPEARANCE ?!
I'D BETTER BE SURE NOT TO . . .
HROHRR...
AND NOW, THE EIGHTH MATCH...
FIGHT !!
WAA-A-AH

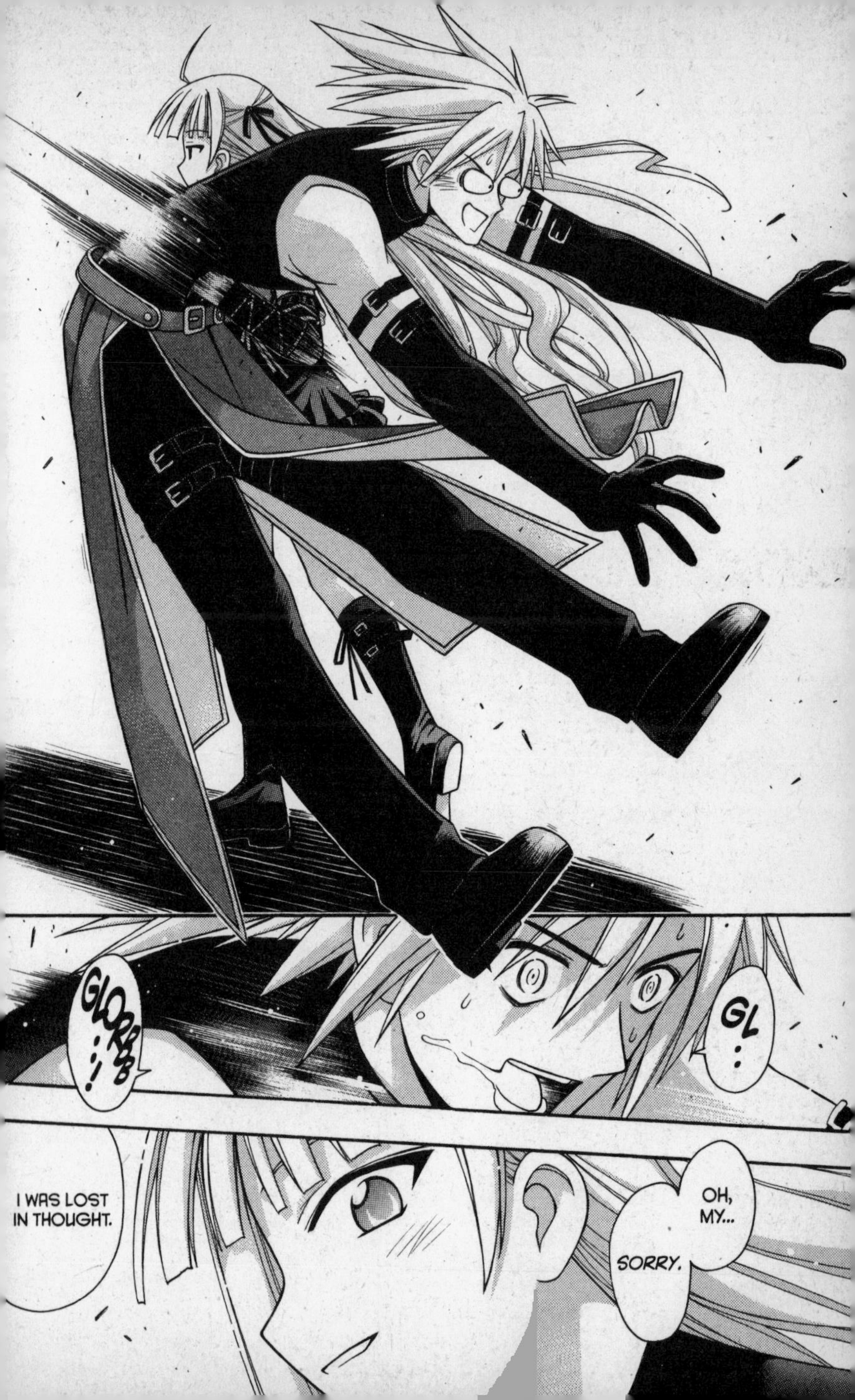
GL..
GLORRB..!
OH, MY...
SORRY.
I WAS LOST IN THOUGHT.

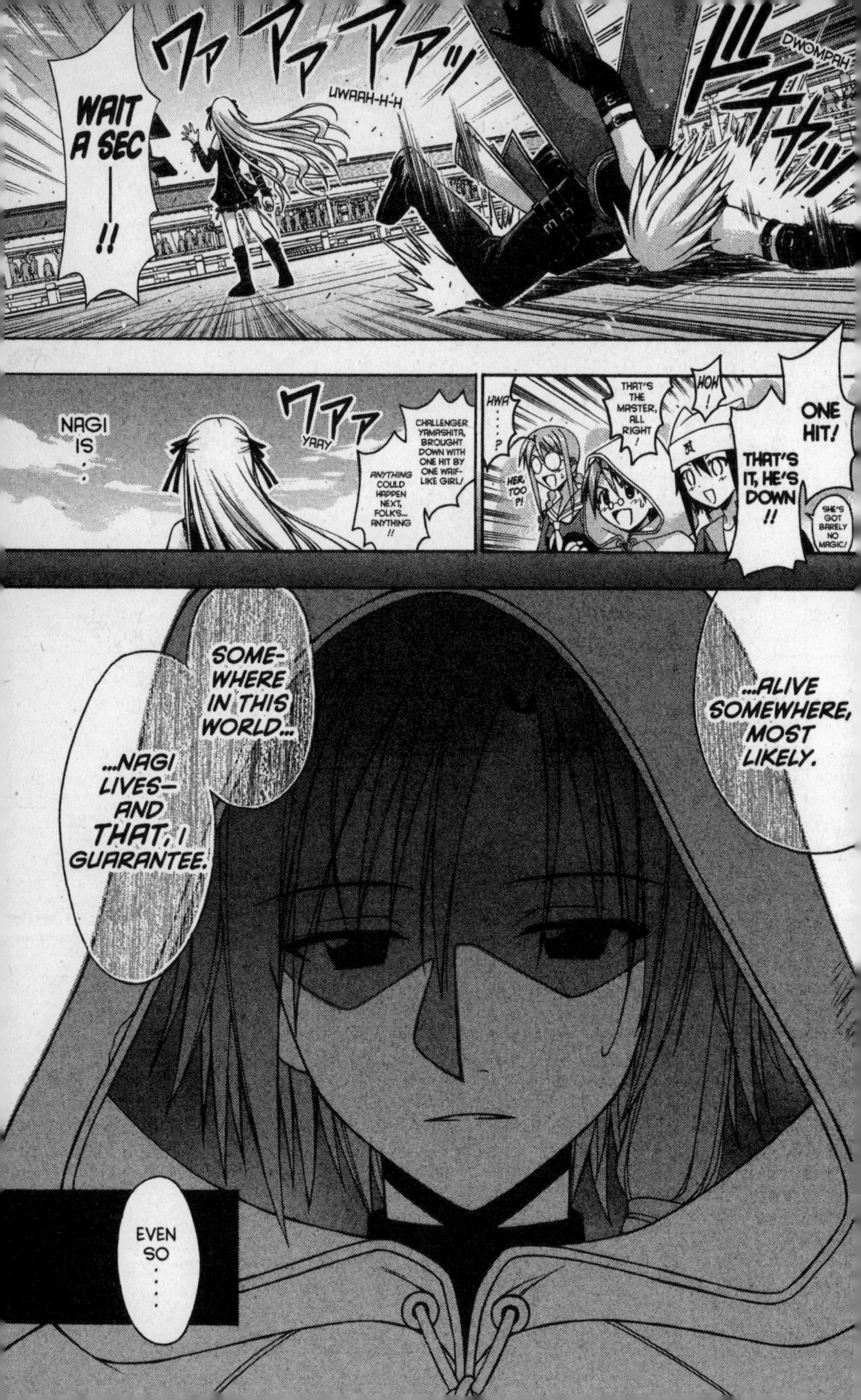
DWOMPAH
UWAAH-H-H
WAIT A SEC—!!
ONE HIT!
THAT'S IT, HE'S DOWN!!
SHE'S GOT BARELY NO MAGIC!
HOH!
THAT'S THE MASTER, ALL RIGHT!
HWA...?
HER, TOO?!
CHALLENGER YAMASHITA, BROUGHT DOWN WITH ONE HIT BY ONE WAIF-LIKE GIRL!
ANYTHING COULD HAPPEN NEXT, FOLKS... ANYTHING!!
YAAY
NAGI IS...
...ALIVE SOMEWHERE, MOST LIKELY.
SOMEWHERE IN THIS WORLD...
...NAGI LIVES—AND THAT, I GUARANTEE.
EVEN SO....

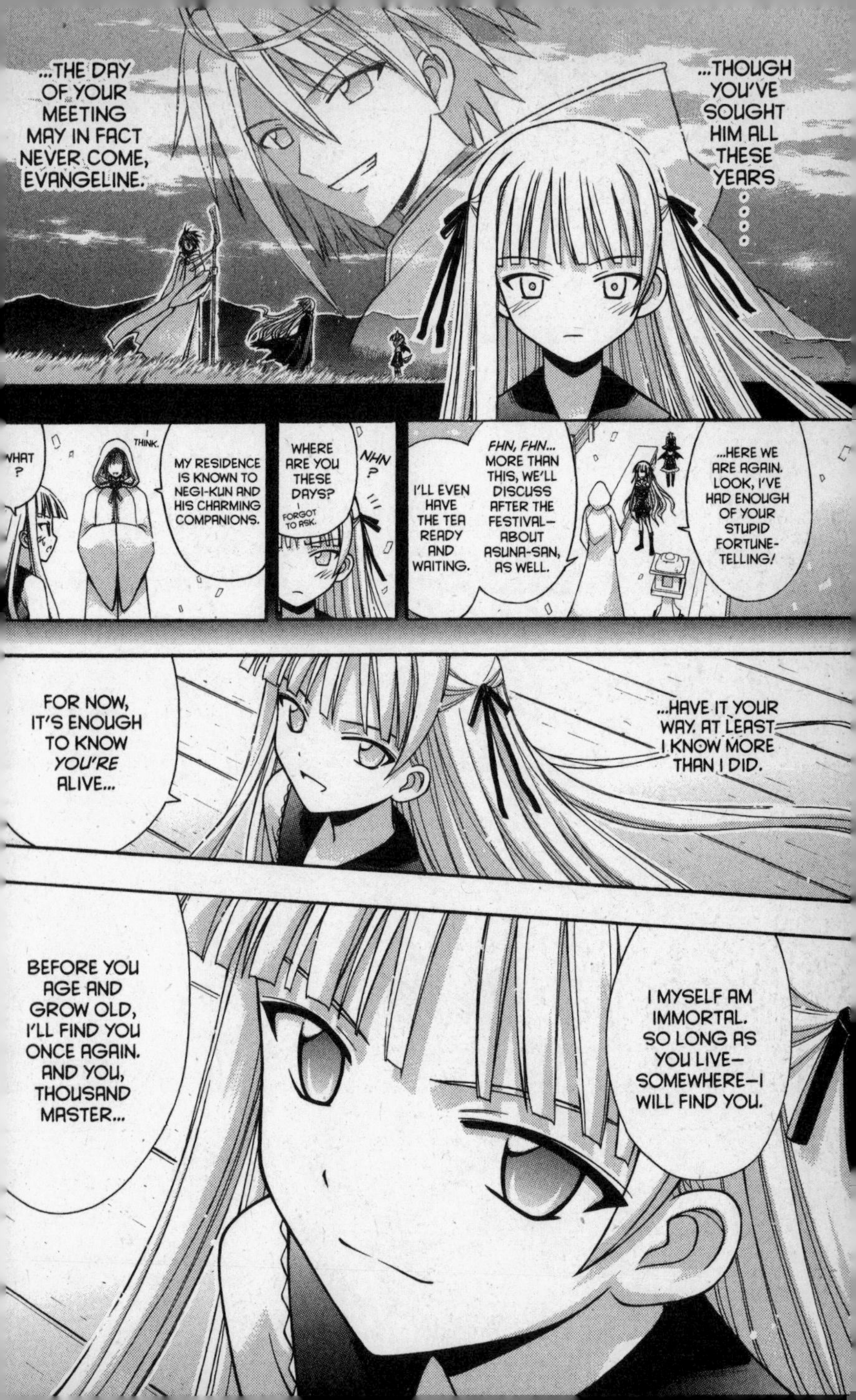
...THOUGH YOU'VE SOUGHT HIM ALL THESE YEARS....
...THE DAY OF YOUR MEETING MAY IN FACT NEVER COME, EVANGELINE.
...HERE WE ARE AGAIN. LOOK, I'VE HAD ENOUGH OF YOUR STUPID FORTUNE-TELLING!
FHN, FHN... MORE THAN THIS, WE'LL DISCUSS AFTER THE FESTIVAL—ABOUT ASUNA-SAN, AS WELL.
I'LL EVEN HAVE THE TEA READY AND WAITING.
NHN?
WHERE ARE YOU THESE DAYS?
I FORGOT TO ASK.
MY RESIDENCE IS KNOWN TO NEGI-KUN AND HIS CHARMING COMPANIONS.
I THINK.
WHAT?
...HAVE IT YOUR WAY. AT LEAST I KNOW MORE THAN I DID.
FOR NOW, IT'S ENOUGH TO KNOW *YOU'RE* ALIVE...
I MYSELF AM IMMORTAL. SO LONG AS YOU LIVE—SOMEWHERE—I WILL FIND YOU.
BEFORE YOU AGE AND GROW OLD, I'LL FIND YOU ONCE AGAIN. AND YOU, THOUSAND MASTER...

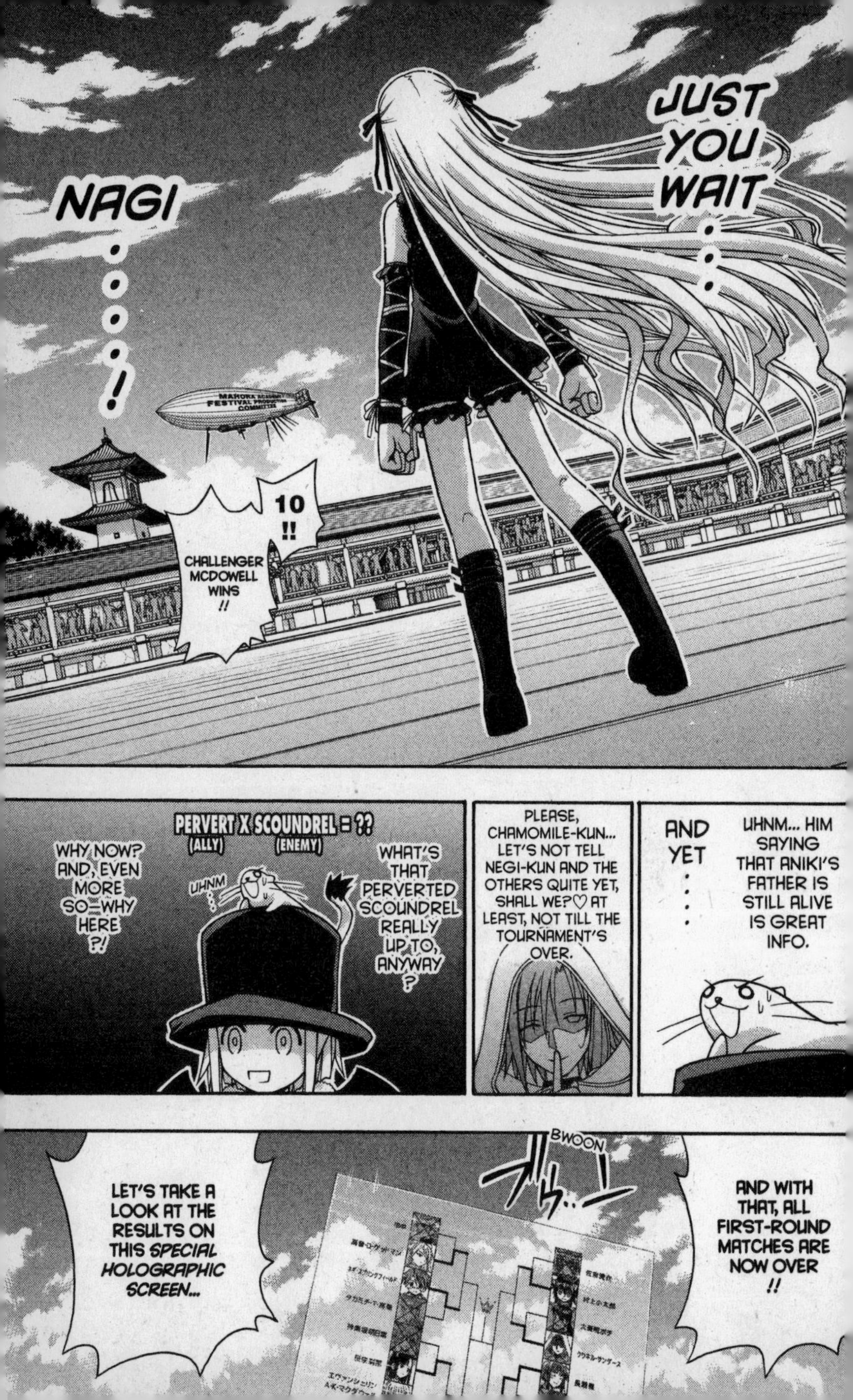

JUST YOU WAIT...
NAGI.....!
10!!
CHALLENGER MCDOWELL WINS!!
UHNM... HIM SAYING THAT ANIKI'S FATHER IS STILL ALIVE IS GREAT INFO.
AND YET....
PLEASE, CHAMOMILE-KUN... LET'S NOT TELL NEGI-KUN AND THE OTHERS QUITE YET, SHALL WE?♡ AT LEAST, NOT TILL THE TOURNAMENT'S OVER.
PERVERT X SCOUNDREL = ??
(ALLY) (ENEMY)
WHAT'S THAT PERVERTED SCOUNDREL REALLY UP TO, ANYWAY?
UHNM...
WHY NOW? AND, EVEN MORE SO—WHY HERE?!
AND WITH THAT, ALL FIRST-ROUND MATCHES ARE NOW OVER!!
BWOON
LET'S TAKE A LOOK AT THE RESULTS ON THIS SPECIAL HOLOGRAPHIC SCREEN...

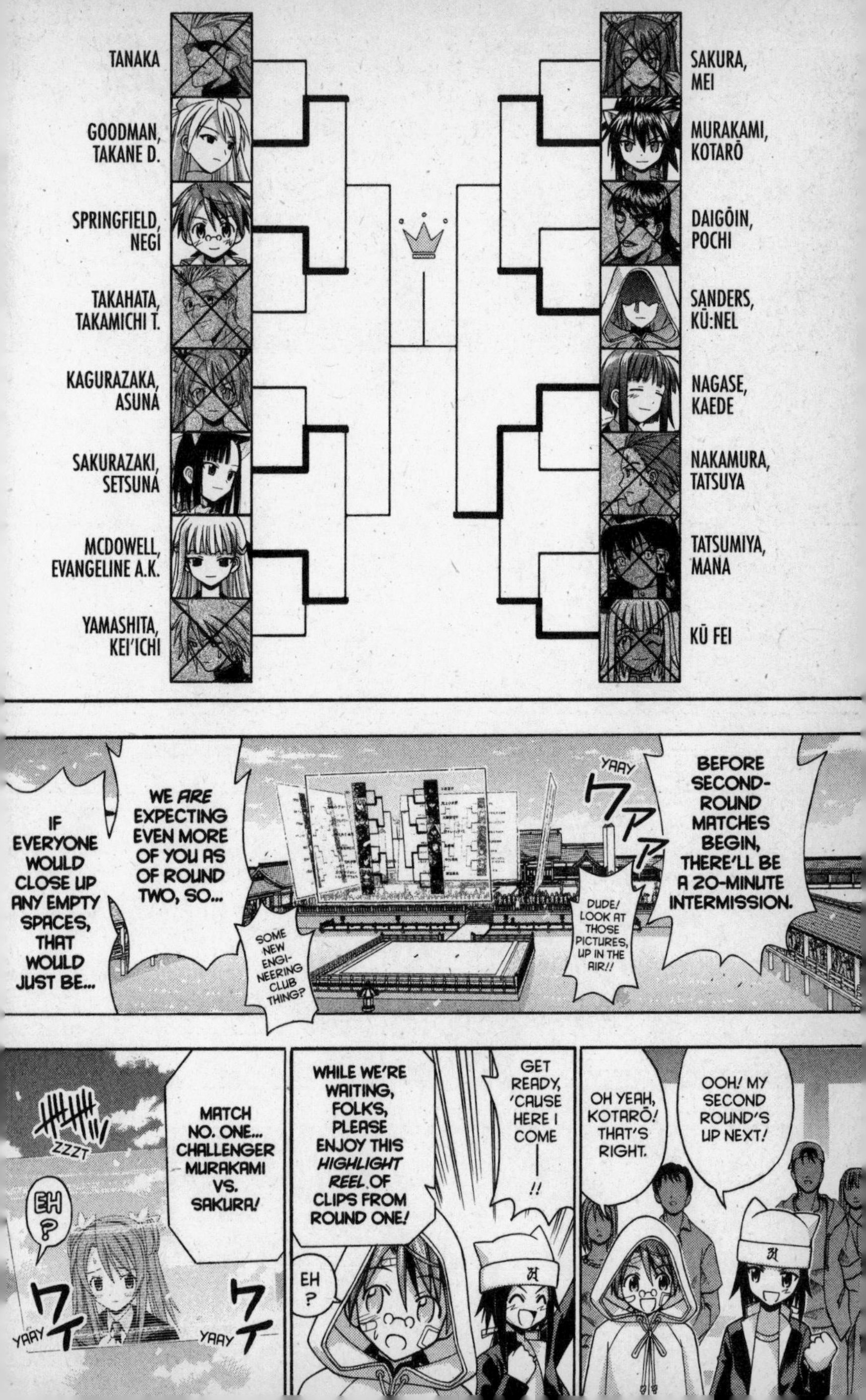

TANAKA
GOODMAN, TAKANE D.
SPRINGFIELD, NEGI
TAKAHATA, TAKAMICHI T.
KAGURAZAKA, ASUNA
SAKURAZAKI, SETSUNA
MCDOWELL, EVANGELINE A.K.
YAMASHITA, KEI'ICHI
SAKURA, MEI
MURAKAMI, KOTARŌ
DAIGŌIN, POCHI
SANDERS, KŪ:NEL
NAGASE, KAEDE
NAKAMURA, TATSUYA
TATSUMIYA, MANA
KŪ FEI
YAAY
BEFORE SECOND-ROUND MATCHES BEGIN, THERE'LL BE A 20-MINUTE INTERMISSION.
DUDE! LOOK AT THOSE PICTURES, UP IN THE AIR!!
SOME NEW ENGINEERING CLUB THING?
WE *ARE* EXPECTING EVEN MORE OF YOU AS OF ROUND TWO, SO...
IF EVERYONE WOULD CLOSE UP ANY EMPTY SPACES, THAT WOULD JUST BE...
OOH! MY SECOND ROUND'S UP NEXT!
OH YEAH, KOTARŌ! THAT'S RIGHT.
GET READY, 'CAUSE HERE I COME——!!
WHILE WE'RE WAITING, FOLKS, PLEASE ENJOY THIS *HIGHLIGHT REEL* OF CLIPS FROM ROUND ONE!
EH?
MATCH NO. ONE... CHALLENGER MURAKAMI VS. SAKURA!
ZZZT
EH?
YAAY
YAAY

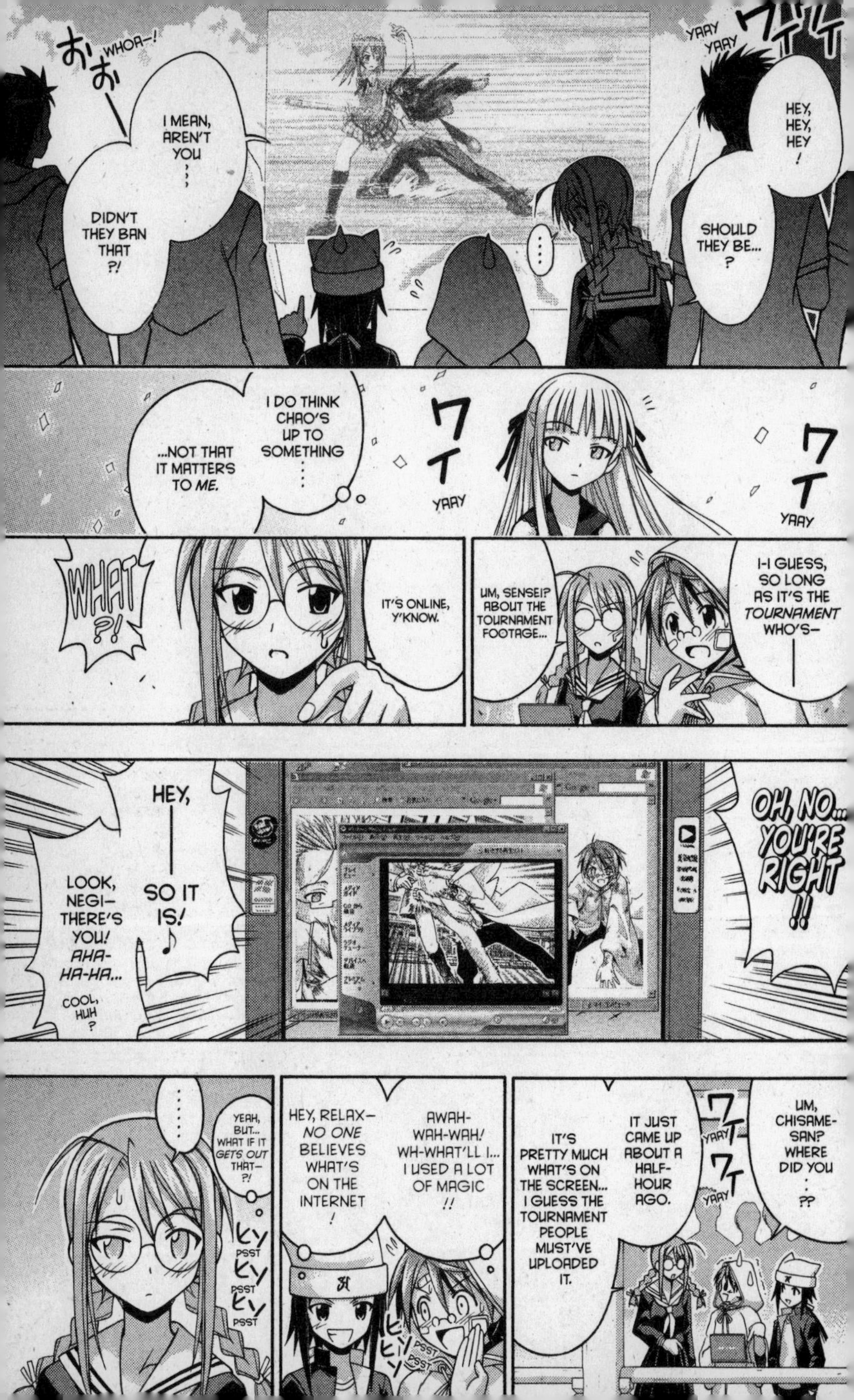
ワイワイ YAAY YAAY
HEY, HEY, HEY!
SHOULD THEY BE...?
....
I MEAN, AREN'T YOU...
DIDN'T THEY BAN THAT?!
おお WHOA—!
ワイ YAAY
ワイ YAAY
I DO THINK CHAO'S UP TO SOMETHING...
...NOT THAT IT MATTERS TO *ME.*
I-I GUESS, SO LONG AS IT'S THE *TOURNAMENT* WHO'S—
UM, SENSEI? ABOUT THE TOURNAMENT FOOTAGE...
IT'S ONLINE, Y'KNOW.
WHAT?!
OH, NO... YOU'RE RIGHT!!
HEY, — SO IT IS! ♪
LOOK, NEGI—THERE'S YOU! *AHA-HA-HA...*
COOL, HUH?
UM, CHISAME-SAN? WHERE DID YOU...??
ワイ YAAY ワイ YAAY
IT JUST CAME UP ABOUT A HALF-HOUR AGO.
IT'S PRETTY MUCH WHAT'S ON THE SCREEN... I GUESS THE TOURNAMENT PEOPLE MUST'VE UPLOADED IT.
AWAH-WAH-WAH! WH-WHAT'LL I... I USED A LOT OF MAGIC!!
HEY, RELAX—*NO ONE* BELIEVES WHAT'S ON THE INTERNET!
ヒソ PSST ヒソ PSST
YEAH, BUT... WHAT IF IT *GETS OUT* THAT—?!
......
ヒソ PSST ヒソ PSST ヒソ PSST

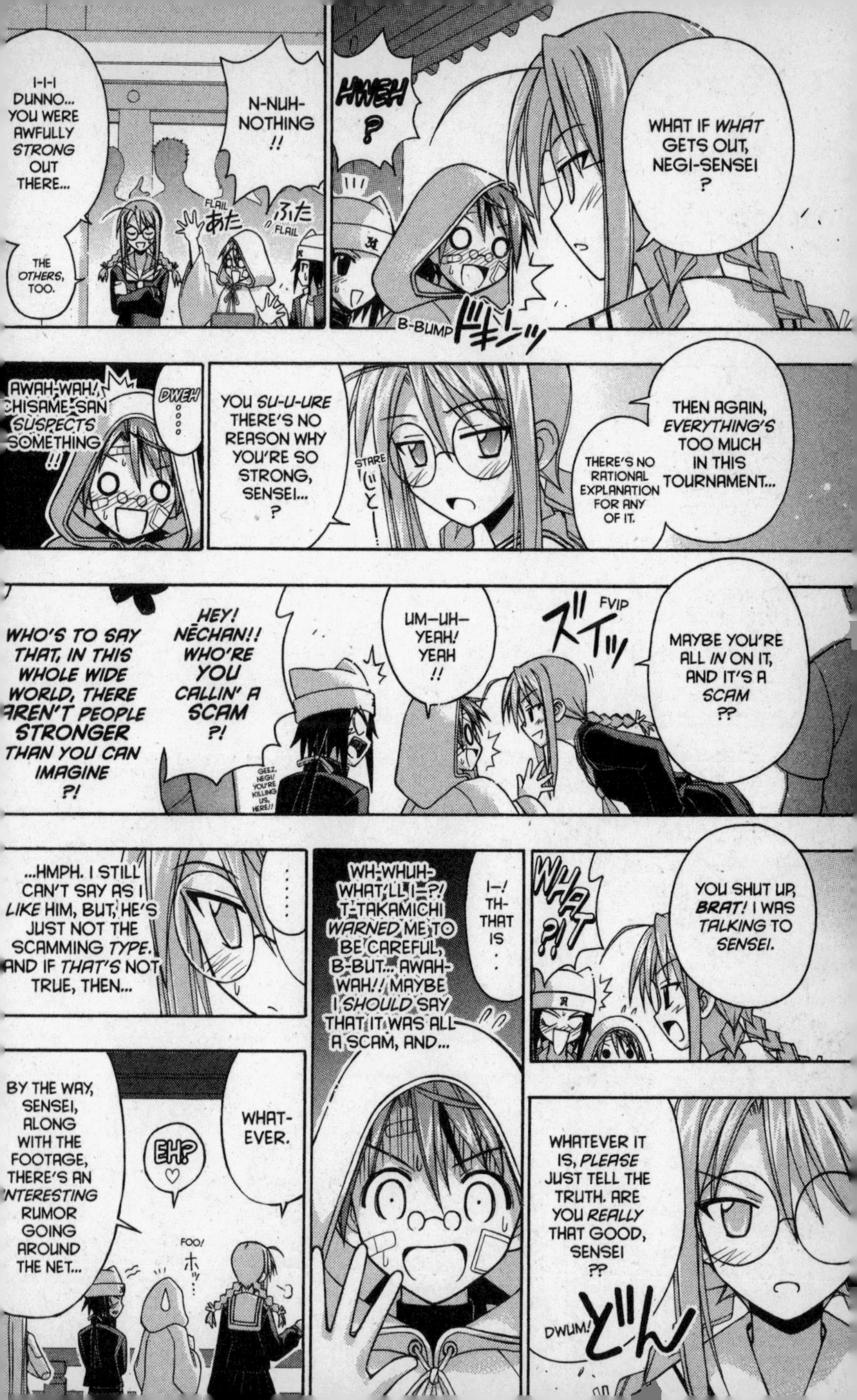
WHAT IF WHAT GETS OUT, NEGI-SENSEI?
HWEH?
B-BUMP ドキッ
N-NUH-NOTHING!!
FLAIL あた
ふた FLAIL
I-I-I DUNNO... YOU WERE AWFULLY STRONG OUT THERE...
THE OTHERS, TOO.
THEN AGAIN, EVERYTHING'S TOO MUCH IN THIS TOURNAMENT...
THERE'S NO RATIONAL EXPLANATION FOR ANY OF IT.
YOU SU-U-URE THERE'S NO REASON WHY YOU'RE SO STRONG, SENSEI...?
STARE じとー
DWEH ....
AWAH-WAH! CHISAME-SAN SUSPECTS SOMETHING!!
MAYBE YOU'RE ALL IN ON IT, AND IT'S A SCAM??
FVIP ズイッ
UM—UH—YEAH! YEAH!!
HEY! NECHAN!! WHO'RE YOU CALLIN' A SCAM?!
GEEZ, NEGI! YOU'RE KILLING US, HERE!!
WHO'S TO SAY THAT, IN THIS WHOLE WIDE WORLD, THERE AREN'T PEOPLE STRONGER THAN YOU CAN IMAGINE?!
YOU SHUT UP, BRAT! I WAS TALKING TO SENSEI.
WHAT?!
I—! TH-THAT IS . . .
WH-WHUH-WHAT'LL I—?! T-TAKAMICHI WARNED ME TO BE CAREFUL, B-BUT... AWAH-WAH!! MAYBE I SHOULD SAY THAT IT WAS ALL A SCAM, AND...
......
...HMPH. I STILL CAN'T SAY AS I LIKE HIM, BUT, HE'S JUST NOT THE SCAMMING TYPE. AND IF THAT'S NOT TRUE, THEN...
WHATEVER IT IS, PLEASE JUST TELL THE TRUTH. ARE YOU REALLY THAT GOOD, SENSEI??
DWUM! どん
WHAT-EVER.
EH? ♡
BY THE WAY, SENSEI, ALONG WITH THE FOOTAGE, THERE'S AN INTERESTING RUMOR GOING AROUND THE NET...
FOO! ホッ...

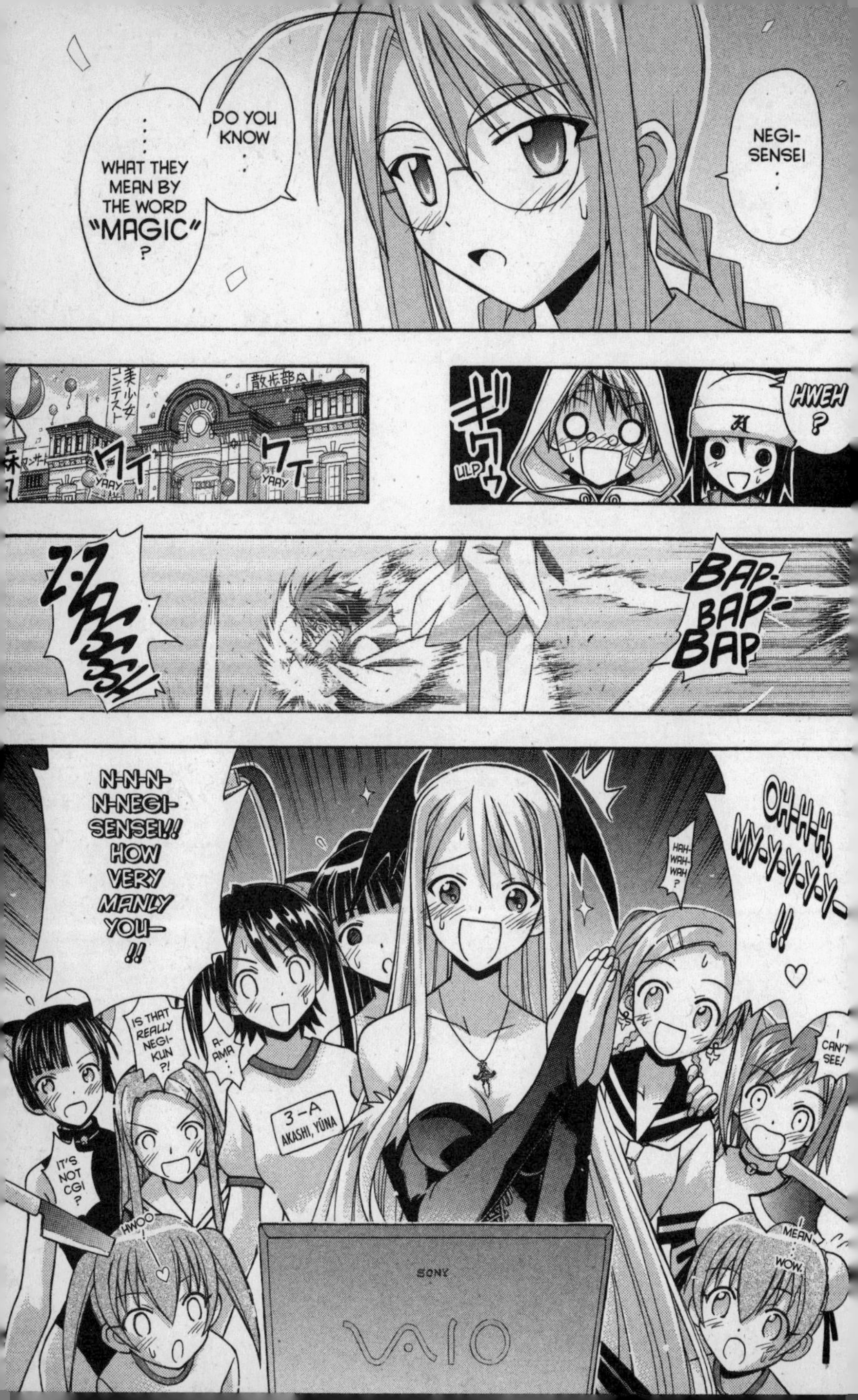
NEGI-SENSEI . . .
DO YOU KNOW . . .
. . . WHAT THEY MEAN BY THE WORD "MAGIC" ?
HWEH ?
ギクゥ
ULP
散歩部
美少女コンテスト
ワイ
YAAY
ワイ
YAAY
BAP-BAP-BAP
OH-H-H-H, MY-Y-Y-Y-Y-Y-!!
HAH-WAH-WAH ?
N-N-N-N-NEGI-SENSEI!! HOW VERY MANLY YOU—!!
I CAN'T SEE!
I MEAN . . . WOW.
A-AMA . . .
3-A AKASHI, YŪNA
IS THAT REALLY NEGI-KUN ?!
IT'S NOT CGI ?
HWOO !
SONY
VAIO

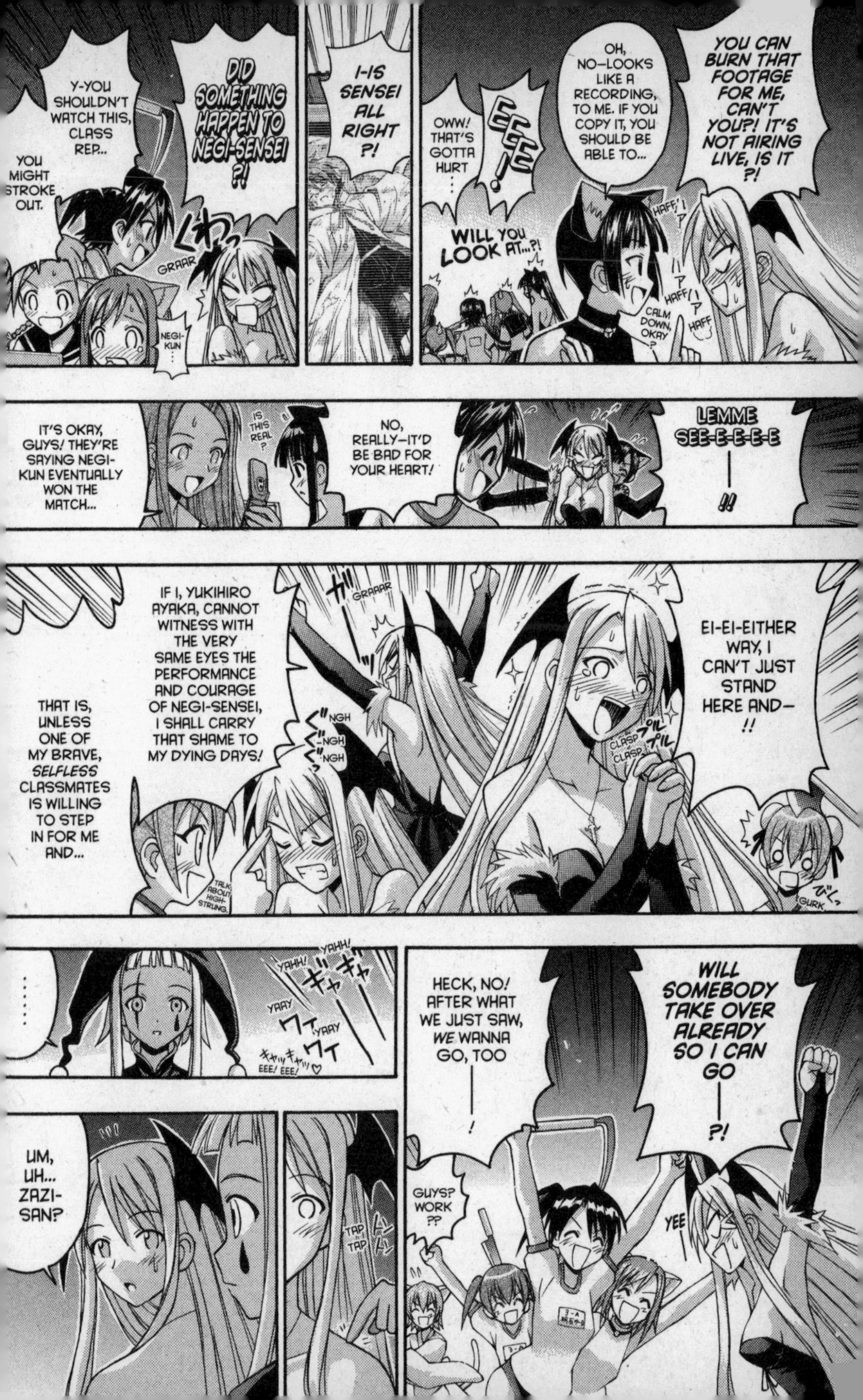
YOU CAN BURN THAT FOOTAGE FOR ME, CAN'T YOU?! IT'S NOT AIRING LIVE, IS IT?!
OH, NO—LOOKS LIKE A RECORDING, TO ME. IF YOU COPY IT, YOU SHOULD BE ABLE TO...
EEE!
OWW! THAT'S GOTTA HURT...
HAFF HAFF HAFF
CALM DOWN, OKAY?
WILL YOU LOOK AT...?!
I-IS SENSEI ALL RIGHT?!
DID SOMETHING HAPPEN TO NEGI-SENSEI?!
Y-YOU SHOULDN'T WATCH THIS, CLASS REP...
YOU MIGHT STROKE OUT.
GRAAR
NEGI-KUN...
LEMME SEE-E-E-E-E—!!
NO, REALLY—IT'D BE BAD FOR YOUR HEART!
IS THIS REAL?
IT'S OKAY, GUYS! THEY'RE SAYING NEGI-KUN EVENTUALLY WON THE MATCH...
EI-EI-EITHER WAY, I CAN'T JUST STAND HERE AND—!!
CLASP CLASP
GURK
GRAAAR
NGH NGH NGH
IF I, YUKIHIRO AYAKA, CANNOT WITNESS WITH THE VERY SAME EYES THE PERFORMANCE AND COURAGE OF NEGI-SENSEI, I SHALL CARRY THAT SHAME TO MY DYING DAYS!
THAT IS, UNLESS ONE OF MY BRAVE, *SELFLESS* CLASSMATES IS WILLING TO STEP IN FOR ME AND...
TALK ABOUT HIGH-STRUNG.
WILL SOMEBODY TAKE OVER ALREADY SO I CAN GO—?!
HECK, NO! AFTER WHAT WE JUST SAW, *WE* WANNA GO, TOO—!
GUYS? WORK??
YEE
YAHH! YAHH!
YAAY YAAY
EEE! EEE!
......
TAP TAP
UM, UH... ZAZI-SAN?

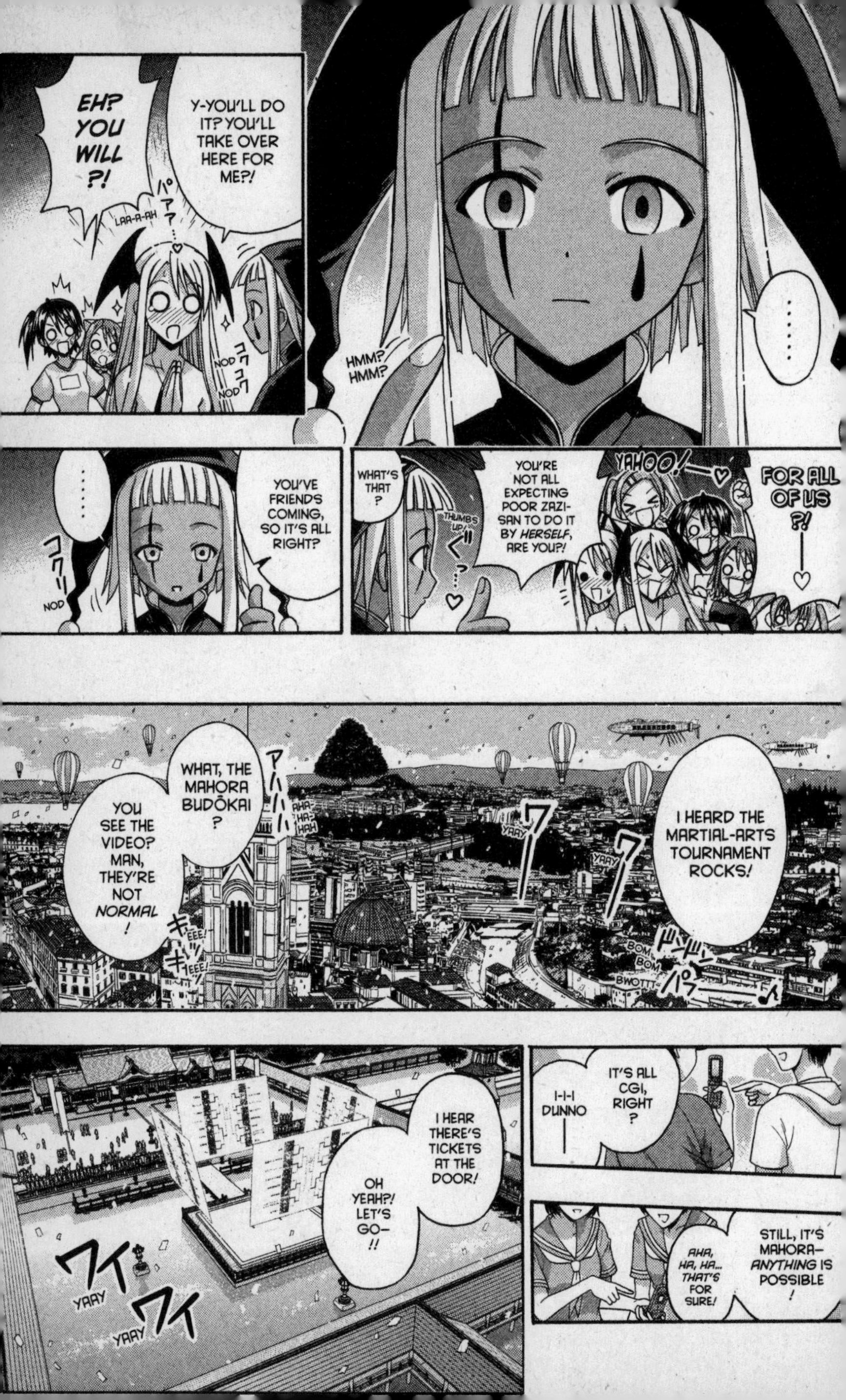

HMM? HMM?
......
Y-YOU'LL DO IT? YOU'LL TAKE OVER HERE FOR ME?!
EH? YOU WILL?!
LAA-A-AH
NOD
NOD
FOR ALL OF US?!
YAHOO!
YOU'RE NOT ALL EXPECTING POOR ZAZI-SAN TO DO IT BY *HERSELF*, ARE YOU?!
THUMBS UP!
WHAT'S THAT?
YOU'VE FRIENDS COMING, SO IT'S ALL RIGHT?
......
NOD
I HEARD THE MARTIAL-ARTS TOURNAMENT ROCKS!
YAAY
YAAY
BOM
BOM
BWOTTT
AHA HA HAH
WHAT, THE MAHORA BUDŌKAI?
YOU SEE THE VIDEO? MAN, THEY'RE NOT *NORMAL*!
EEE!
EEE!
IT'S ALL CGI, RIGHT?
I-I-I DUNNO—
STILL, IT'S MAHORA— *ANYTHING* IS POSSIBLE!
AHA, HA, HA... THAT'S FOR SURE!
I HEAR THERE'S TICKETS AT THE DOOR!
OH YEAH?! LET'S GO—!!
YAAY
YAAY

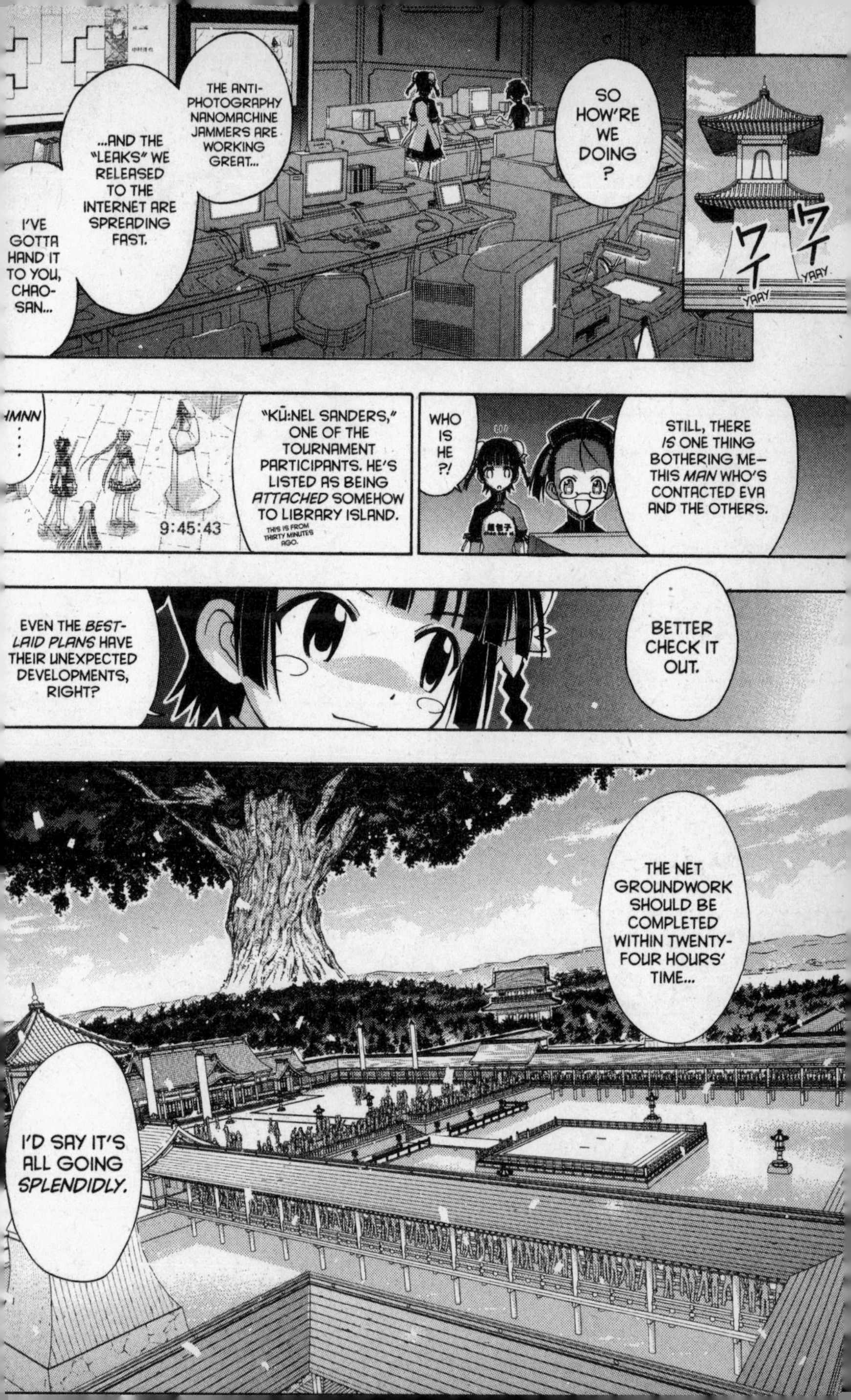
ワイ
YAAY
ワイ
YAAY
SO HOW'RE WE DOING?
THE ANTI-PHOTOGRAPHY NANOMACHINE JAMMERS ARE WORKING GREAT...
...AND THE "LEAKS" WE RELEASED TO THE INTERNET ARE SPREADING FAST.
I'VE GOTTA HAND IT TO YOU, CHAO-SAN...
STILL, THERE *IS* ONE THING BOTHERING ME—THIS *MAN* WHO'S CONTACTED EVA AND THE OTHERS.
WHO IS HE?!
"KŪ:NEL SANDERS," ONE OF THE TOURNAMENT PARTICIPANTS. HE'S LISTED AS BEING *ATTACHED* SOMEHOW TO LIBRARY ISLAND.
THIS IS FROM THIRTY MINUTES AGO.
9:45:43
HMNN.....
BETTER CHECK IT OUT.
EVEN THE *BEST-LAID PLANS* HAVE THEIR UNEXPECTED DEVELOPMENTS, RIGHT?
THE NET GROUNDWORK SHOULD BE COMPLETED WITHIN TWENTY-FOUR HOURS' TIME...
I'D SAY IT'S ALL GOING *SPLENDIDLY*.

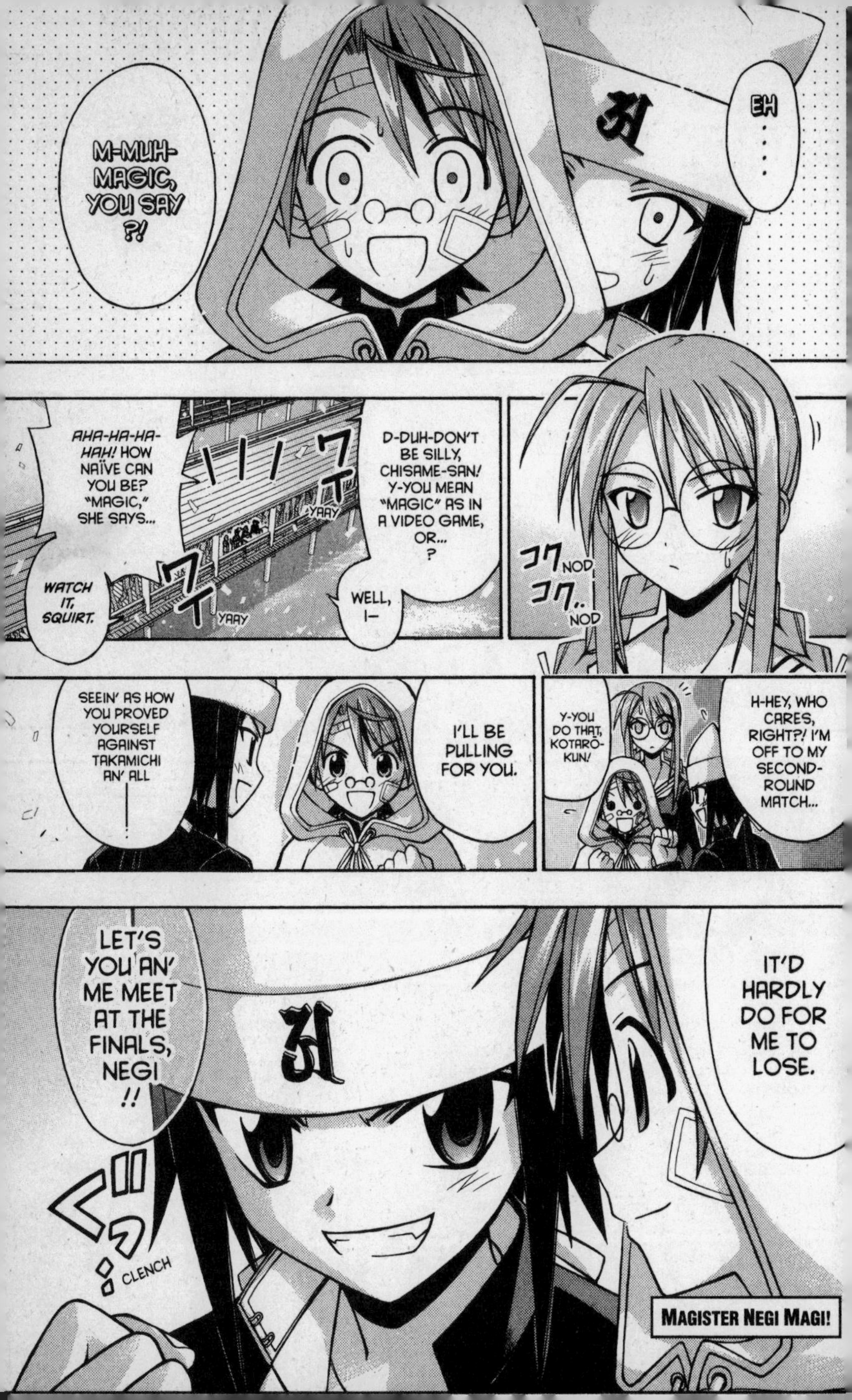
EH......
M-MUH-MAGIC, YOU SAY ?!
コク NOD コク.. NOD
D-DUH-DON'T BE SILLY, CHISAME-SAN! Y-YOU MEAN "MAGIC" AS IN A VIDEO GAME, OR... ?
AHA-HA-HA-HAH! HOW NAÏVE CAN YOU BE? "MAGIC," SHE SAYS...
YAAY
WELL, I—
WATCH IT, SQUIRT.
YAAY
H-HEY, WHO CARES, RIGHT?! I'M OFF TO MY SECOND-ROUND MATCH...
Y-YOU DO THAT, KOTARŌ-KUN!
I'LL BE PULLING FOR YOU.
SEEIN' AS HOW YOU PROVED YOURSELF AGAINST TAKAMICHI AN' ALL —
IT'D HARDLY DO FOR ME TO LOSE.
LET'S YOU AN' ME MEET AT THE FINALS, NEGI !!
CLENCH
MAGISTER NEGI MAGI!

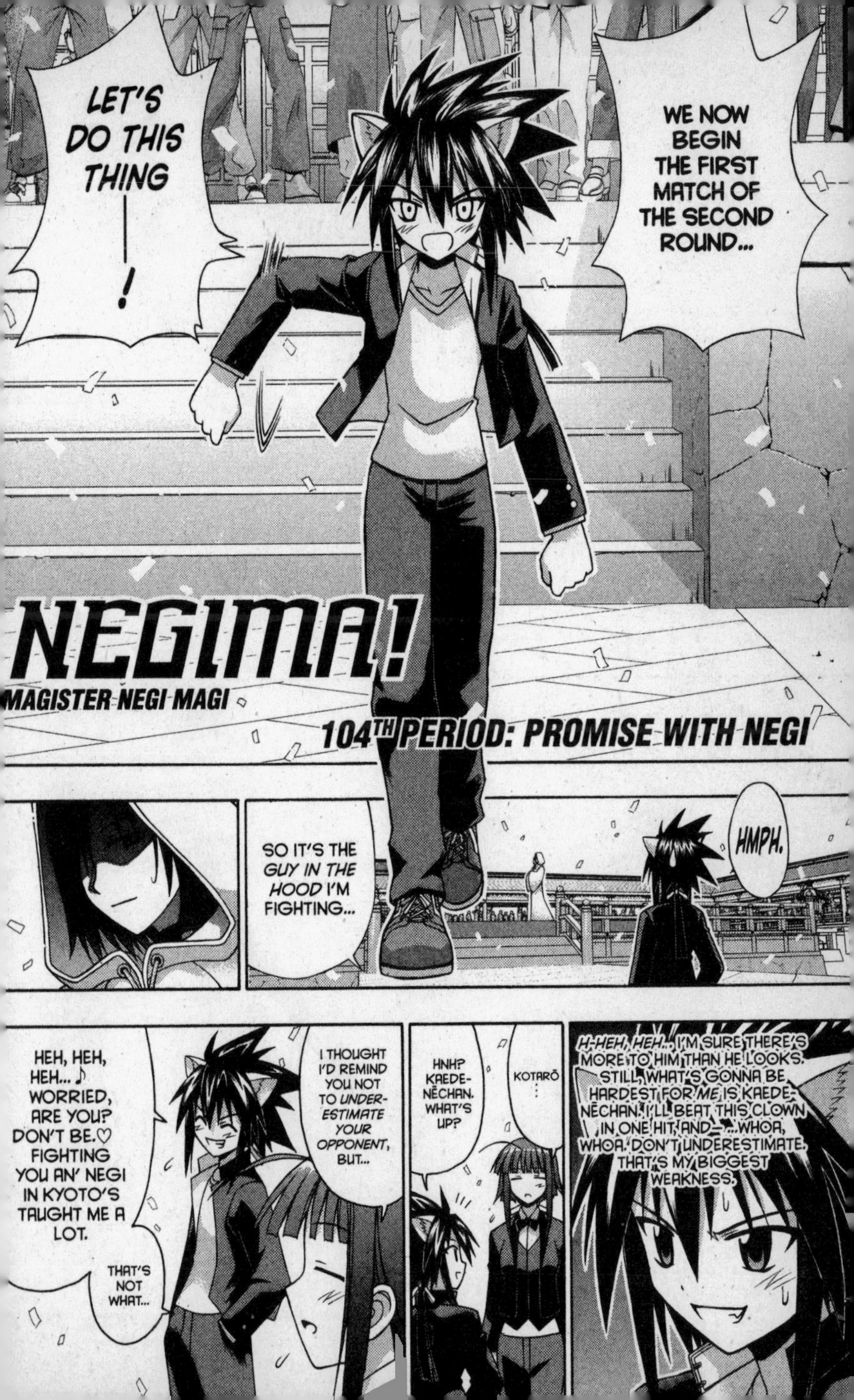
WE NOW BEGIN THE FIRST MATCH OF THE SECOND ROUND...
LET'S DO THIS THING—!
NEGIMA!
MAGISTER NEGI MAGI
104TH PERIOD: PROMISE WITH NEGI
HMPH.
SO IT'S THE *GUY IN THE HOOD* I'M FIGHTING...
H-HEH, HEH... I'M SURE THERE'S MORE TO HIM THAN HE LOOKS. STILL, WHAT'S GONNA BE HARDEST FOR *ME* IS KAEDE-NĒCHAN. I'LL BEAT THIS CLOWN IN ONE HIT, AND— ...WHOA, WHOA. DON'T UNDERESTIMATE. THAT'S MY BIGGEST WEAKNESS.
KOTARŌ...
HNH? KAEDE-NĒCHAN. WHAT'S UP?
I THOUGHT I'D REMIND YOU NOT TO *UNDER-ESTIMATE YOUR OPPONENT*, BUT...
HEH, HEH, HEH...♪ WORRIED, ARE YOU? DON'T BE.♡ FIGHTING YOU AN' NEGI IN KYOTO'S TAUGHT ME A LOT.
THAT'S NOT WHAT...

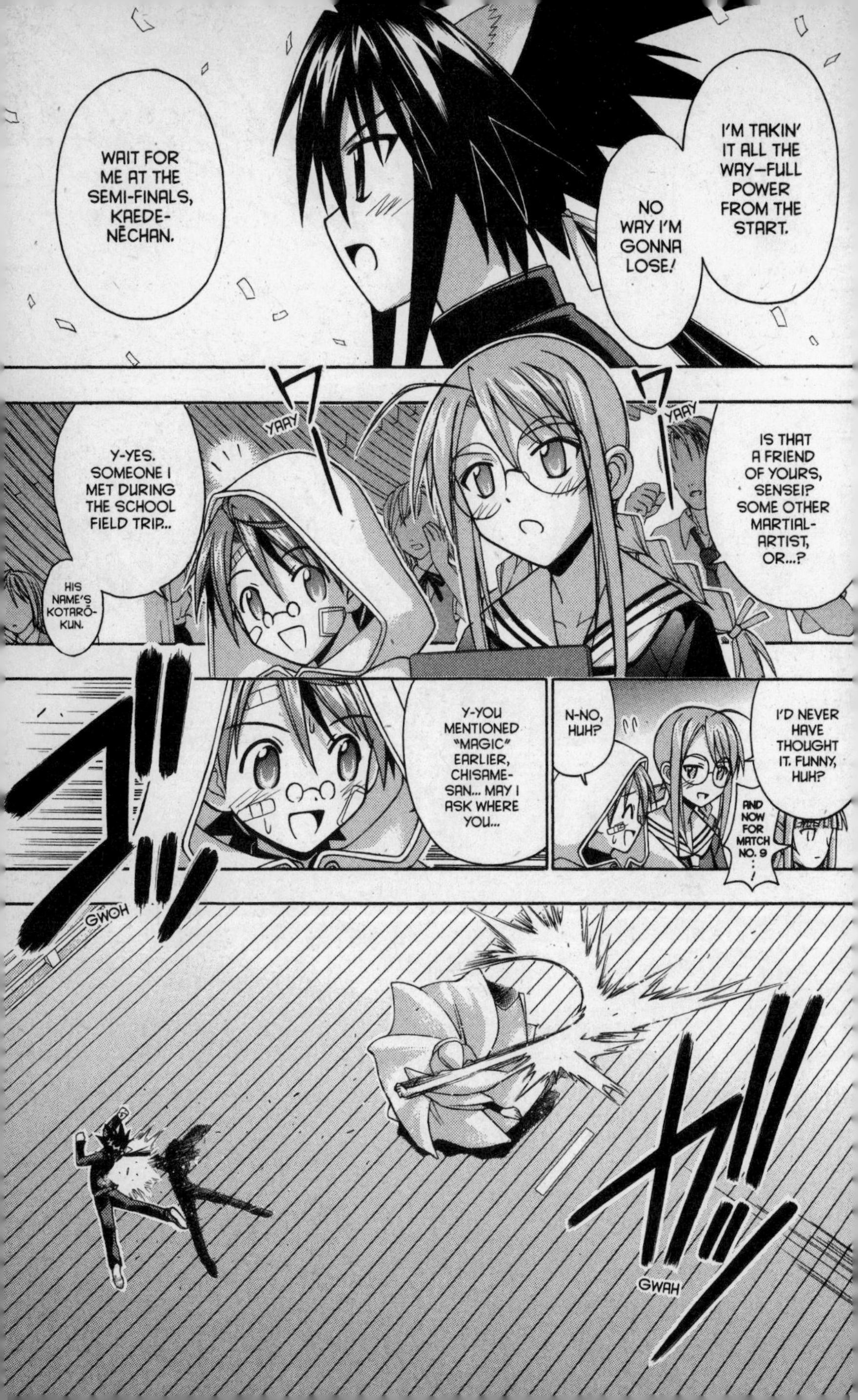
I'M TAKIN' IT ALL THE WAY—FULL POWER FROM THE START.
NO WAY I'M GONNA LOSE!
WAIT FOR ME AT THE SEMI-FINALS, KAEDE-NĒCHAN.
YAAY
YAAY
IS THAT A FRIEND OF YOURS, SENSEI? SOME OTHER MARTIAL-ARTIST, OR...?
Y-YES. SOMEONE I MET DURING THE SCHOOL FIELD TRIP...
HIS NAME'S KOTARŌ-KUN.
I'D NEVER HAVE THOUGHT IT. FUNNY, HUH?
N-NO, HUH?
AND NOW FOR MATCH NO. 9 . . . !
Y-YOU MENTIONED "MAGIC" EARLIER, CHISAME-SAN... MAY I ASK WHERE YOU...
GWOH
GWAH

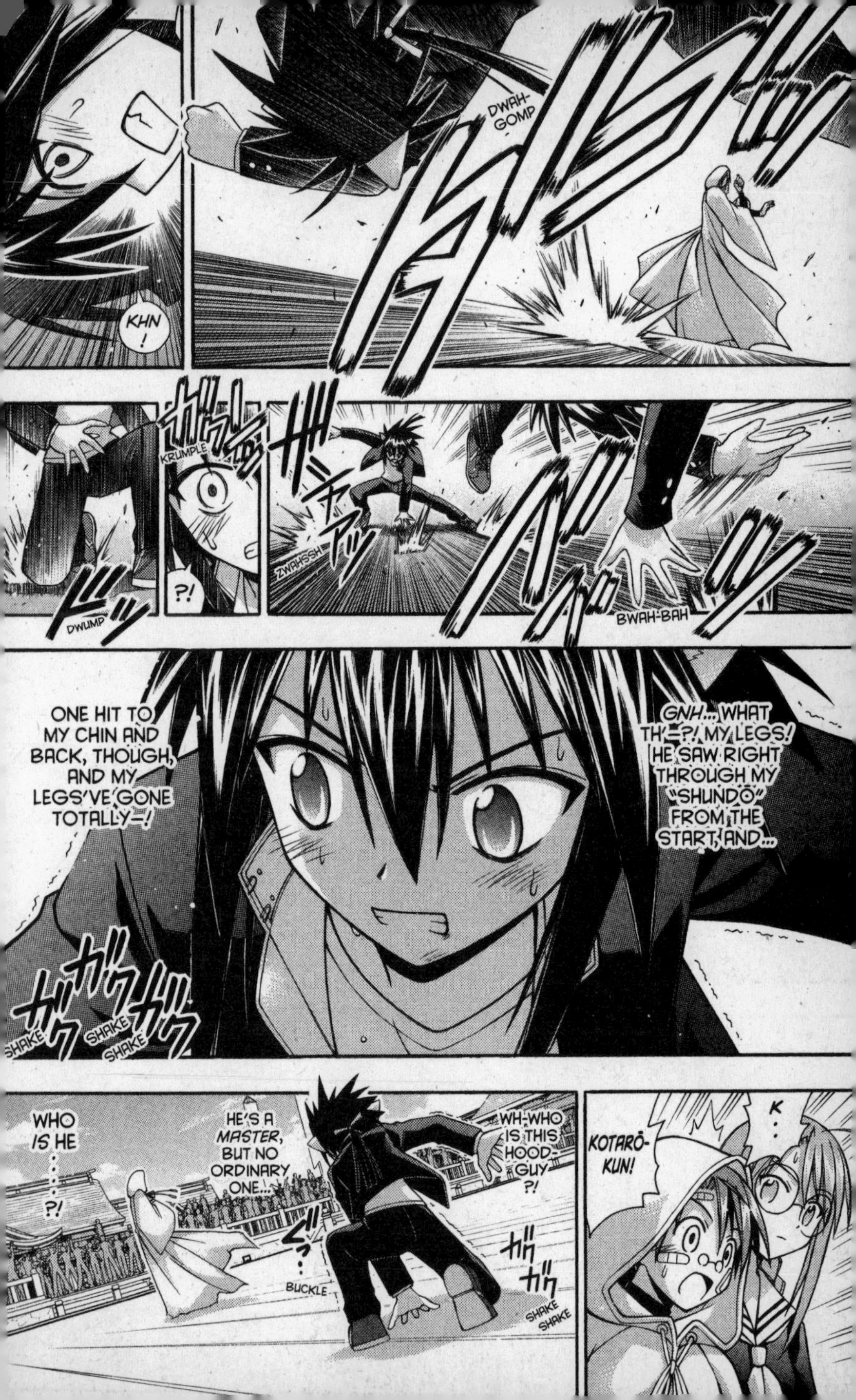
DWAH-GOMP
KHN!
BWAH-BAH
ZWAHSSH
KRUMPLE
?!
DWUMP
GNH... WHAT TH—?! MY LEGS! HE SAW RIGHT THROUGH MY "SHUNDŌ" FROM THE START, AND...
ONE HIT TO MY CHIN AND BACK, THOUGH, AND MY LEGS'VE GONE TOTALLY—!
SHAKE SHAKE SHAKE
K...
KOTARŌ-KUN!
WH-WHO IS THIS HOOD GUY?!
HE'S A MASTER, BUT NO ORDINARY ONE...
WHO IS HE.....?!
BUCKLE
SHAKE SHAKE

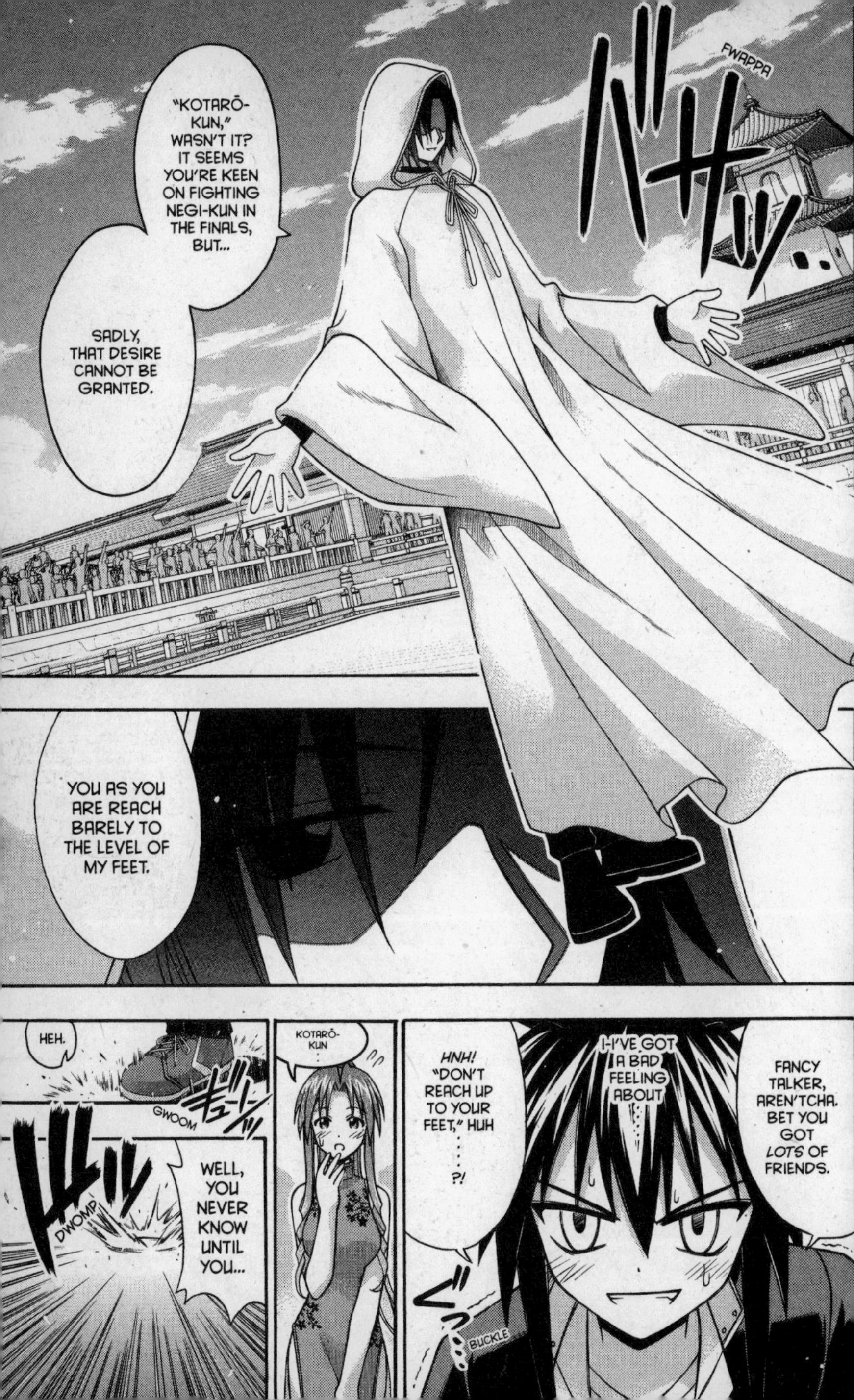
FWAPPA
"KOTARŌ-KUN," WASN'T IT? IT SEEMS YOU'RE KEEN ON FIGHTING NEGI-KUN IN THE FINALS, BUT...
SADLY, THAT DESIRE CANNOT BE GRANTED.
YOU AS YOU ARE REACH BARELY TO THE LEVEL OF MY FEET.
FANCY TALKER, AREN'TCHA. BET YOU GOT *LOTS* OF FRIENDS.
I-I'VE GOT A BAD FEELING ABOUT
HNH! "DON'T REACH UP TO YOUR FEET," HUH ...?!
BUCKLE
KOTARŌ-KUN ...
HEH.
GWOOM
WELL, YOU NEVER KNOW UNTIL YOU...
DWOMP

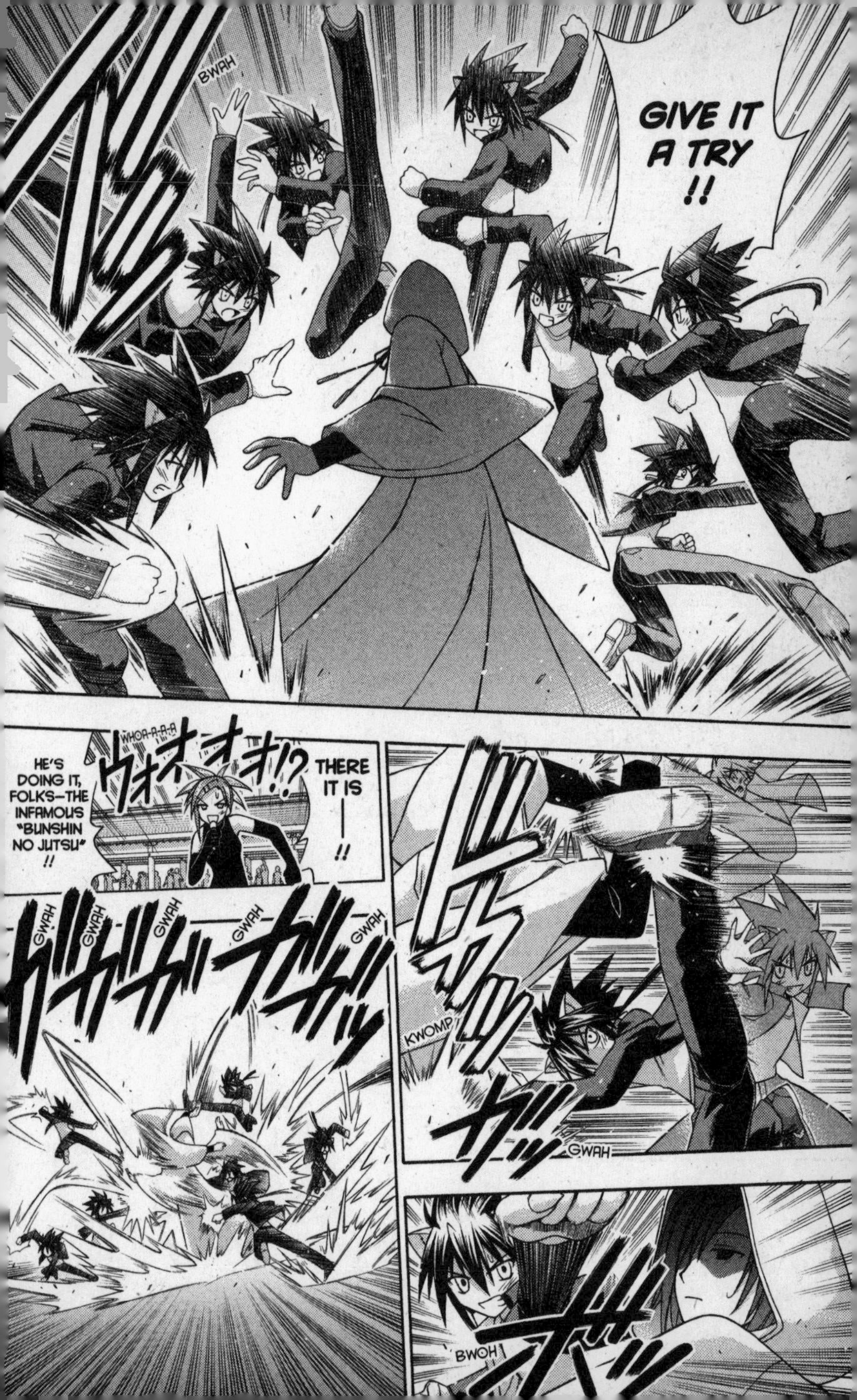

GIVE IT A TRY !!
BWAH
THERE IT IS — !!
WHOA-A-A-A
HE'S DOING IT, FOLKS—THE INFAMOUS "BUNSHIN NO JUTSU" !!
KWOMP
GWAH
GWAH
GWAH
GWAH
GWAH
GWAH
BWOH

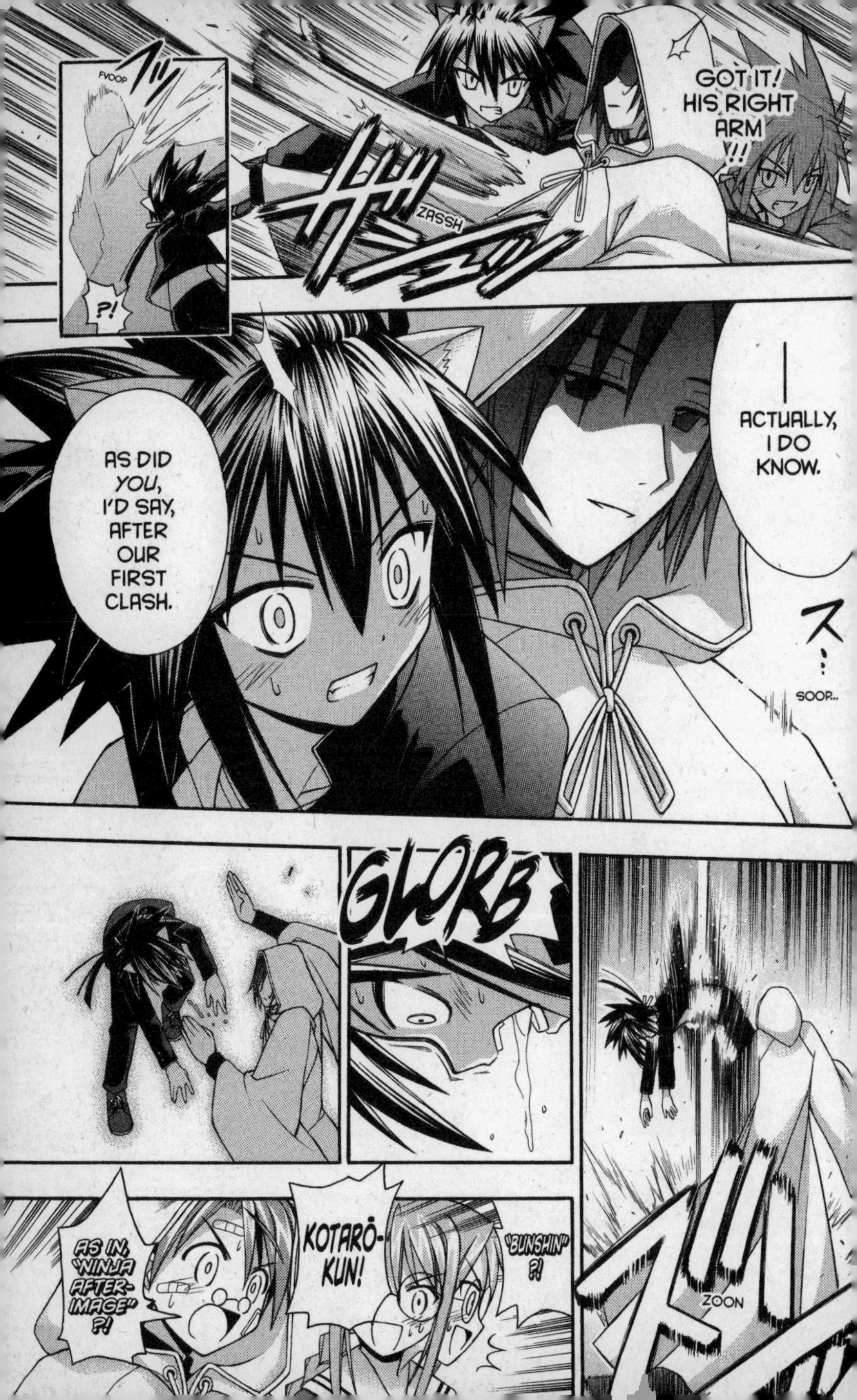
GOT IT! HIS RIGHT ARM!!
ZASSH
FVOOP
?!
ACTUALLY, I DO KNOW.
AS DID YOU, I'D SAY, AFTER OUR FIRST CLASH.
SOOP...
ZOON
GLORB
KOTARŌ-KUN!
"BUNSHIN"?!
AS IN, "NINJA AFTER-IMAGE"?!

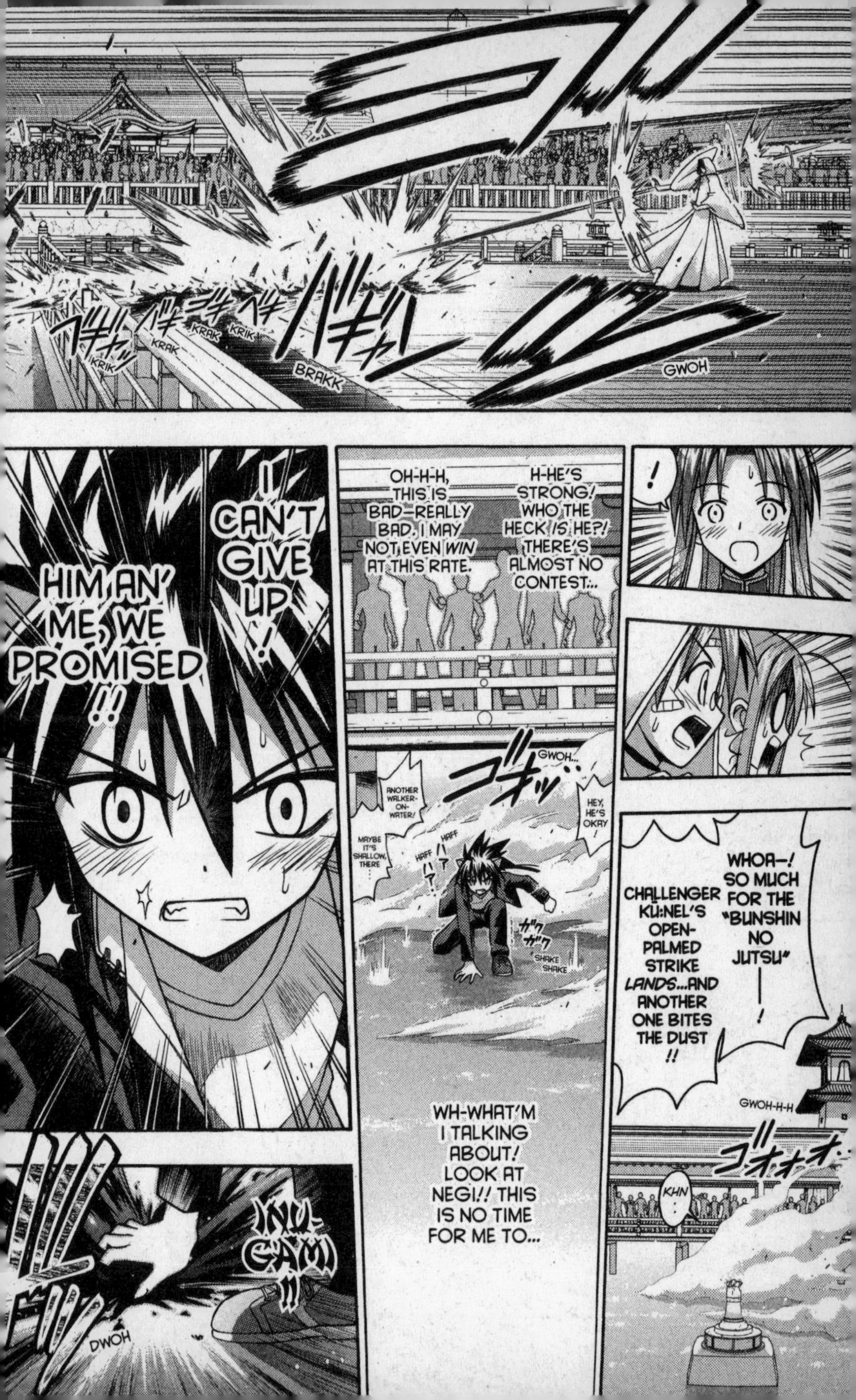
KRIK
KRAK
KRAK
KRIK
BRAKK
GWOH
!
WHOA—! SO MUCH FOR THE "BUNSHIN NO JUTSU"—!
CHALLENGER KU:NEL'S OPEN-PALMED STRIKE LANDS...AND ANOTHER ONE BITES THE DUST!!
GWOH-H-H
KHN...
H-HE'S STRONG! WHO THE HECK IS HE?! THERE'S ALMOST NO CONTEST...
OH-H-H, THIS IS BAD—REALLY BAD. I MAY NOT EVEN WIN AT THIS RATE.
GWOH...
HEY, HE'S OKAY!
ANOTHER WALKER-ON-WATER!
MAYBE IT'S SHALLOW THERE...
HAFF HAFF
SHAKE SHAKE
WH-WHAT'M I TALKING ABOUT! LOOK AT NEGI!! THIS IS NO TIME FOR ME TO...
I CAN'T GIVE UP...!
HIM AN' ME, WE PROMISED!!
INU-GAMI!!
DWOH

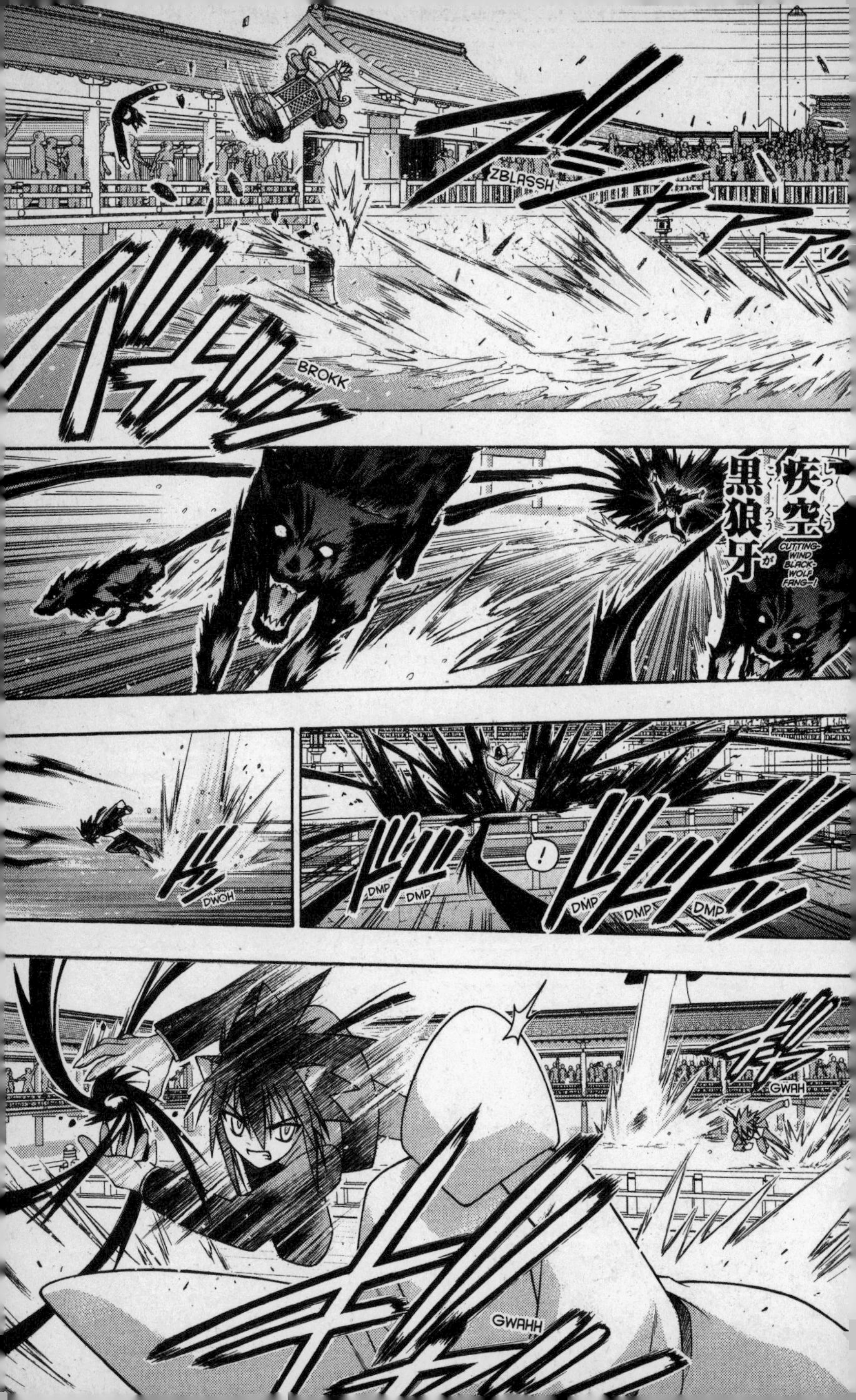
ZBLASSH
BROKK
疾空黒狼牙が
CUTTING-WIND BLACK-WOLF FANG—!
!
DMP
DMP
DMP
DMP
DMP
DWOH
GWAH
GWAHH

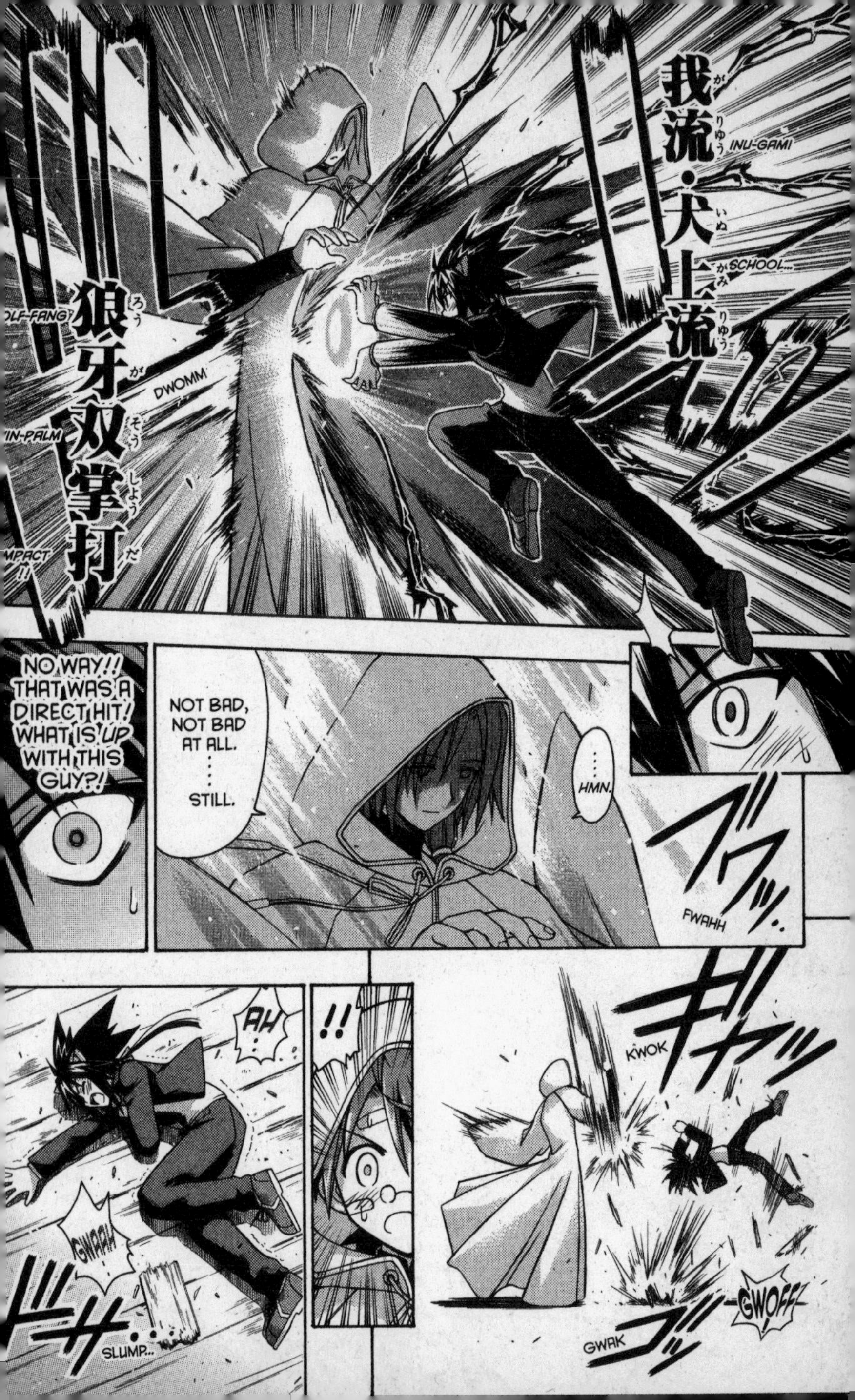

我流・犬上流
INU-GAMI SCHOOL...
狼牙双掌打
OLF-FANG IN-PALM MPACT!!
DWOMM
..... HMN.
NOT BAD, NOT BAD AT ALL. ..... STILL.
FWAHH
NO WAY!! THAT WAS A DIRECT HIT! WHAT IS UP WITH THIS GUY?!
KWOK
GWOFF!
GWAK
!!
AH...
GWAAH
SLUMP...

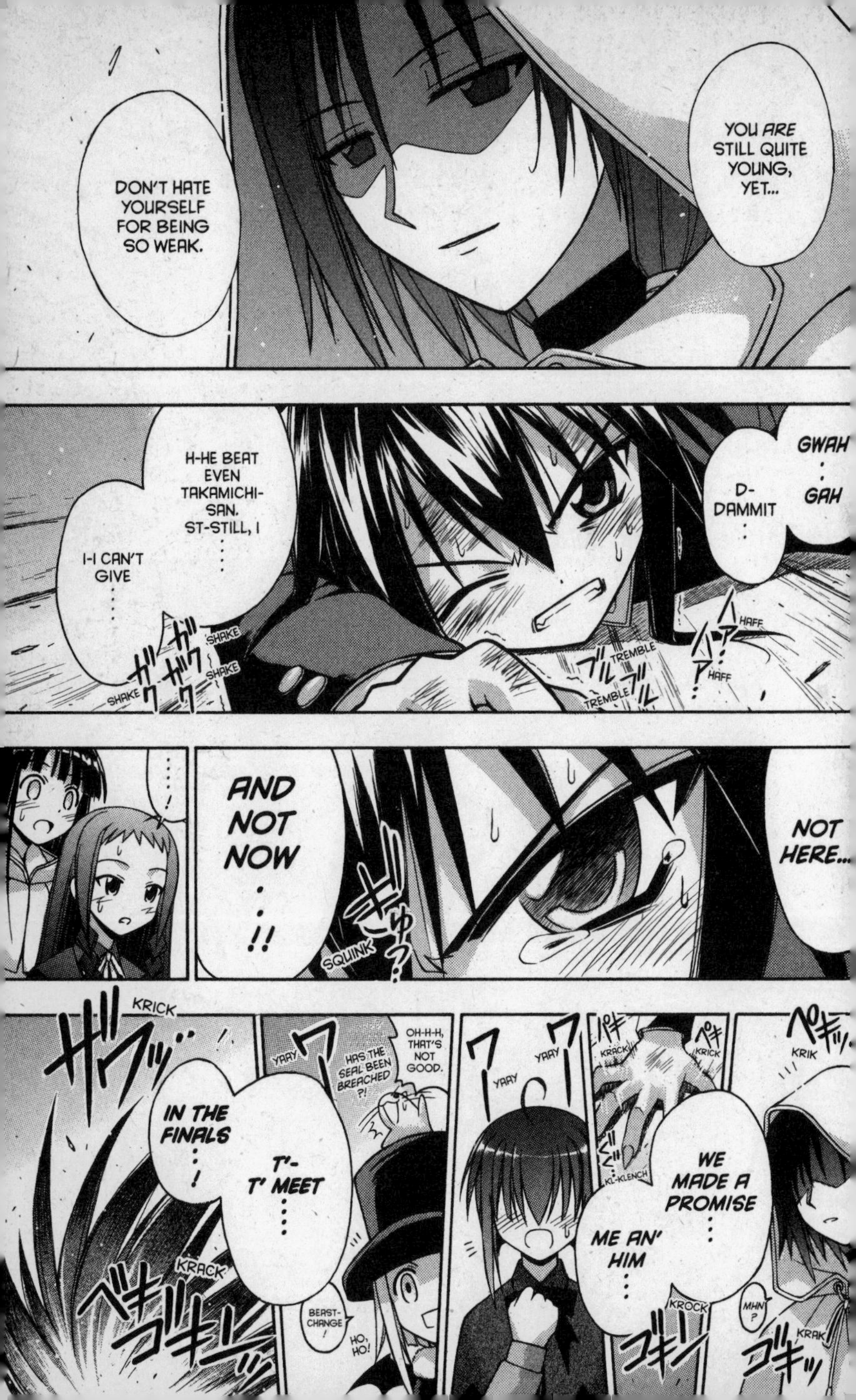
YOU ARE STILL QUITE YOUNG, YET...
DON'T HATE YOURSELF FOR BEING SO WEAK.
GWAH : GAH
D-DAMMIT : :
HAFF
HAFF
TREMBLE
TREMBLE
H-HE BEAT EVEN TAKAMICHI-SAN. ST-STILL, I ....
I-I CAN'T GIVE ....
SHAKE
SHAKE
SHAKE
NOT HERE...
SQUINK
AND NOT NOW ..!!
....!
KRIK
MHN?
KRAK
KRICK
KRACK
KL-KLENCH
WE MADE A PROMISE ..
ME AN' HIM ..
KROCK
YAAY
YAAY
OH-H-H, THAT'S NOT GOOD.
HAS THE SEAL BEEN BREACHED?!
YAAY
BEAST-CHANGE!
HO, HO!
KRICK
T'- T' MEET ....
IN THE FINALS ..!
KRACK

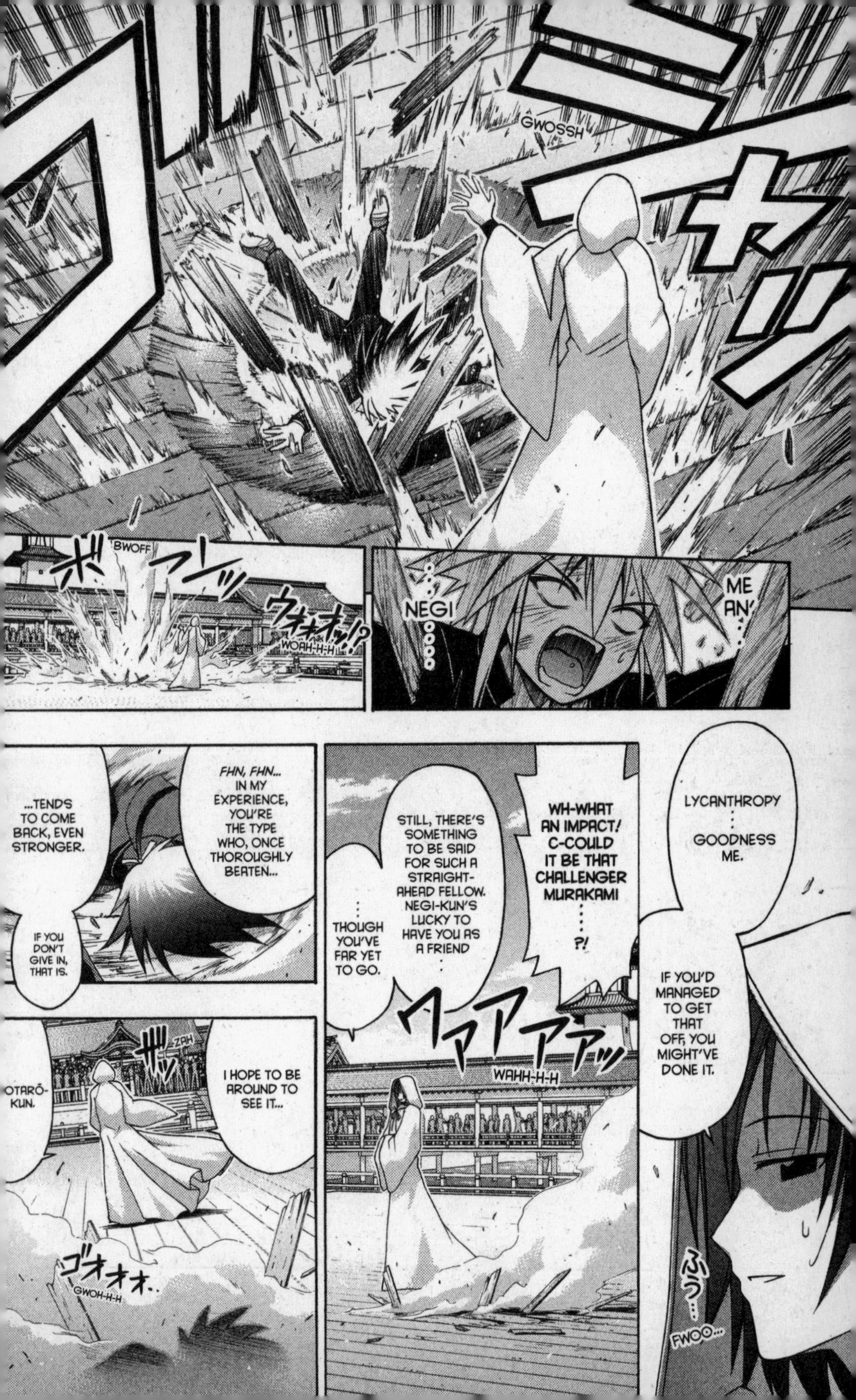

GWOSSH
ME AN'...
NEGI.....
BWOFF
WOAH-H-H
LYCANTHROPY... GOODNESS ME.
IF YOU'D MANAGED TO GET THAT OFF, YOU MIGHT'VE DONE IT.
FWOO...
WH-WHAT AN IMPACT! C-COULD IT BE THAT CHALLENGER MURAKAMI.....?!
STILL, THERE'S SOMETHING TO BE SAID FOR SUCH A STRAIGHT-AHEAD FELLOW. NEGI-KUN'S LUCKY TO HAVE YOU AS A FRIEND...
...THOUGH YOU'VE FAR YET TO GO.
WAHH-H-H
FHN, FHN... IN MY EXPERIENCE, YOU'RE THE TYPE WHO, ONCE THOROUGHLY BEATEN...
...TENDS TO COME BACK, EVEN STRONGER.
IF YOU DON'T GIVE IN, THAT IS.
I HOPE TO BE AROUND TO SEE IT...
OTARŌ-KUN.
ZAH
GWOH-H-H

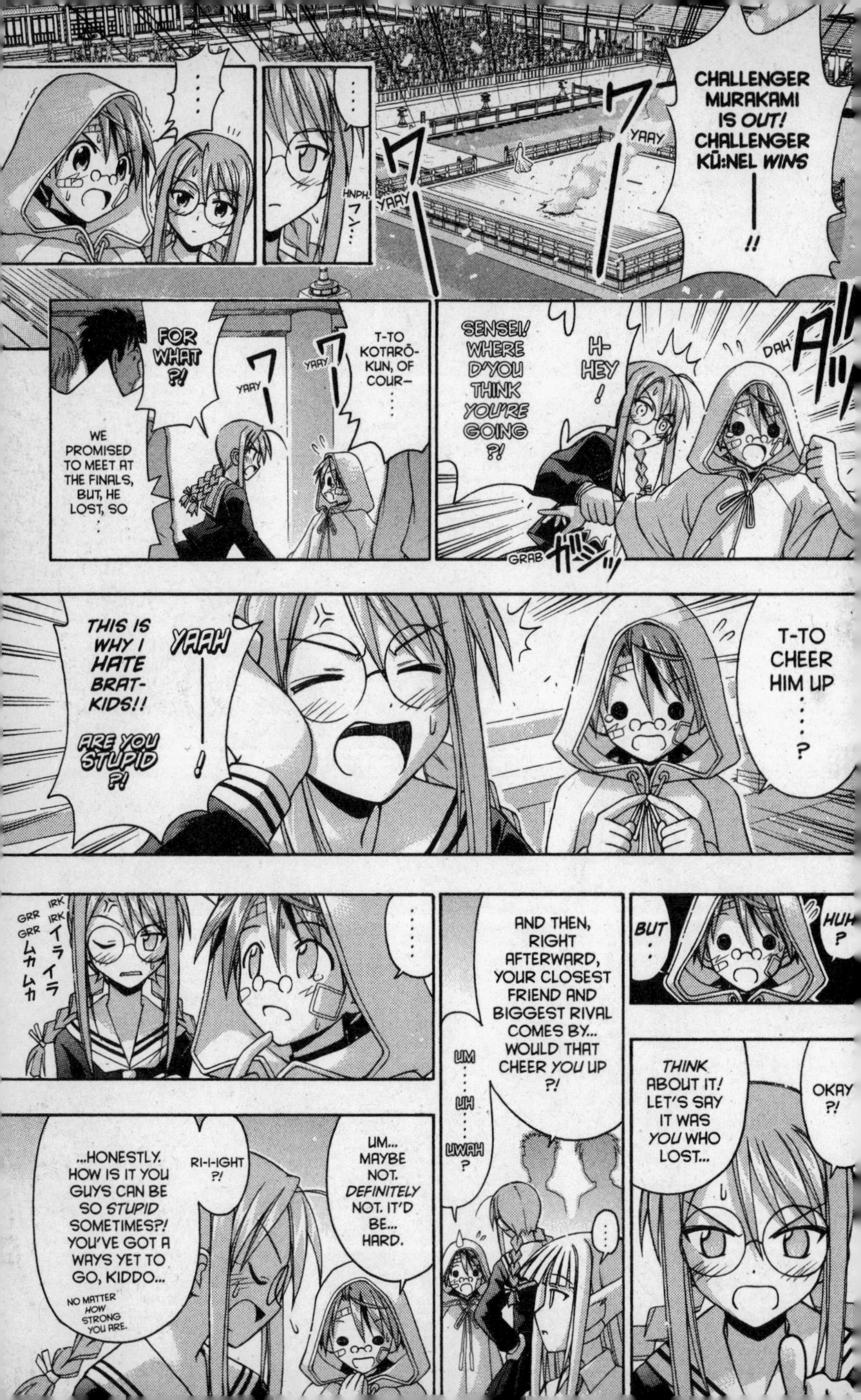
CHALLENGER MURAKAMI IS *OUT!* CHALLENGER KŪ:NEL *WINS* — !!
YAAY ワー
YAAY ワー
HNPH. フン…
....
....
DAH ダッ
H-HEY!
SENSEI! WHERE D'YOU THINK *YOU'RE* GOING?!
GRAB ガシッ
T-TO KOTARŌ-KUN, OF COUR— ....
YAAY ワー
YAAY ワー
FOR WHAT?!
WE PROMISED TO MEET AT THE FINALS, BUT, HE LOST, SO...
T-TO CHEER HIM UP....?
YAAAH — !
THIS IS WHY I HATE BRAT-KIDS!!
ARE YOU STUPID?!
HUH?
BUT..
OKAY?!
THINK ABOUT IT! LET'S SAY IT WAS *YOU* WHO LOST...
AND THEN, RIGHT AFTERWARD, YOUR CLOSEST FRIEND AND BIGGEST RIVAL COMES BY... WOULD THAT CHEER *YOU* UP?!
UM.... UH.... UWAH?
....
GRR GRR ムカムカ
IRK IRK イライラ
....
UM... MAYBE NOT. *DEFINITELY* NOT. IT'D BE... HARD.
RI-I-IGHT?!
...HONESTLY. HOW IS IT YOU GUYS CAN BE SO *STUPID* SOMETIMES?! YOU'VE GOT A WAYS YET TO GO, KIDDO...
NO MATTER *HOW* STRONG YOU ARE.

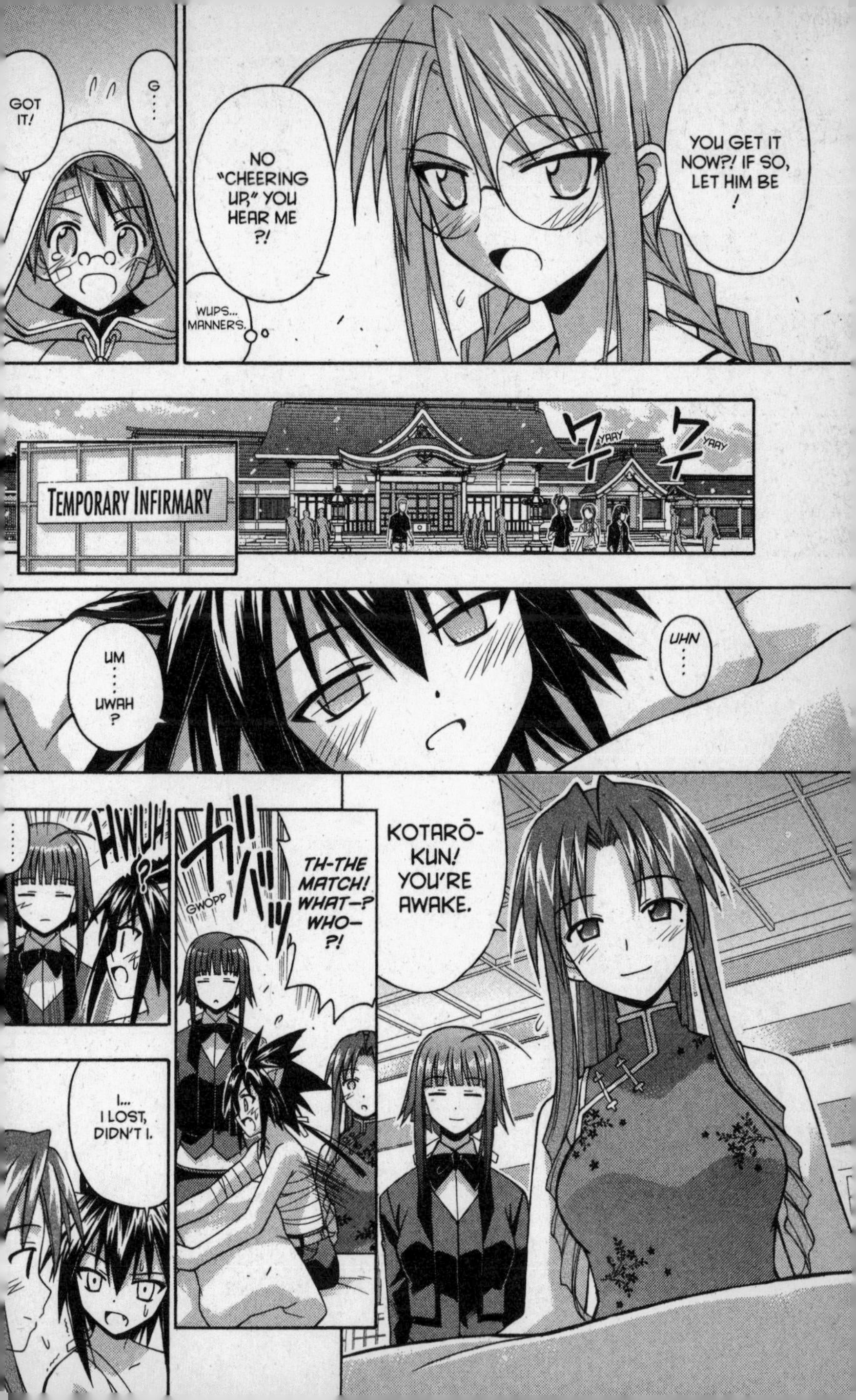
YOU GET IT NOW?! IF SO, LET HIM BE!
NO "CHEERING UP," YOU HEAR ME?!
WUPS... MANNERS.
G....
GOT IT!
TEMPORARY INFIRMARY
ワイ
YAAY
ワイ
YAAY
UHN....
UM.... UWAH?
KOTARŌ-KUN! YOU'RE AWAKE.
TH-THE MATCH! WHAT—? WHO—?!
ガバッ
GWOPP
HWUH?!
....
I... I LOST, DIDN'T I.

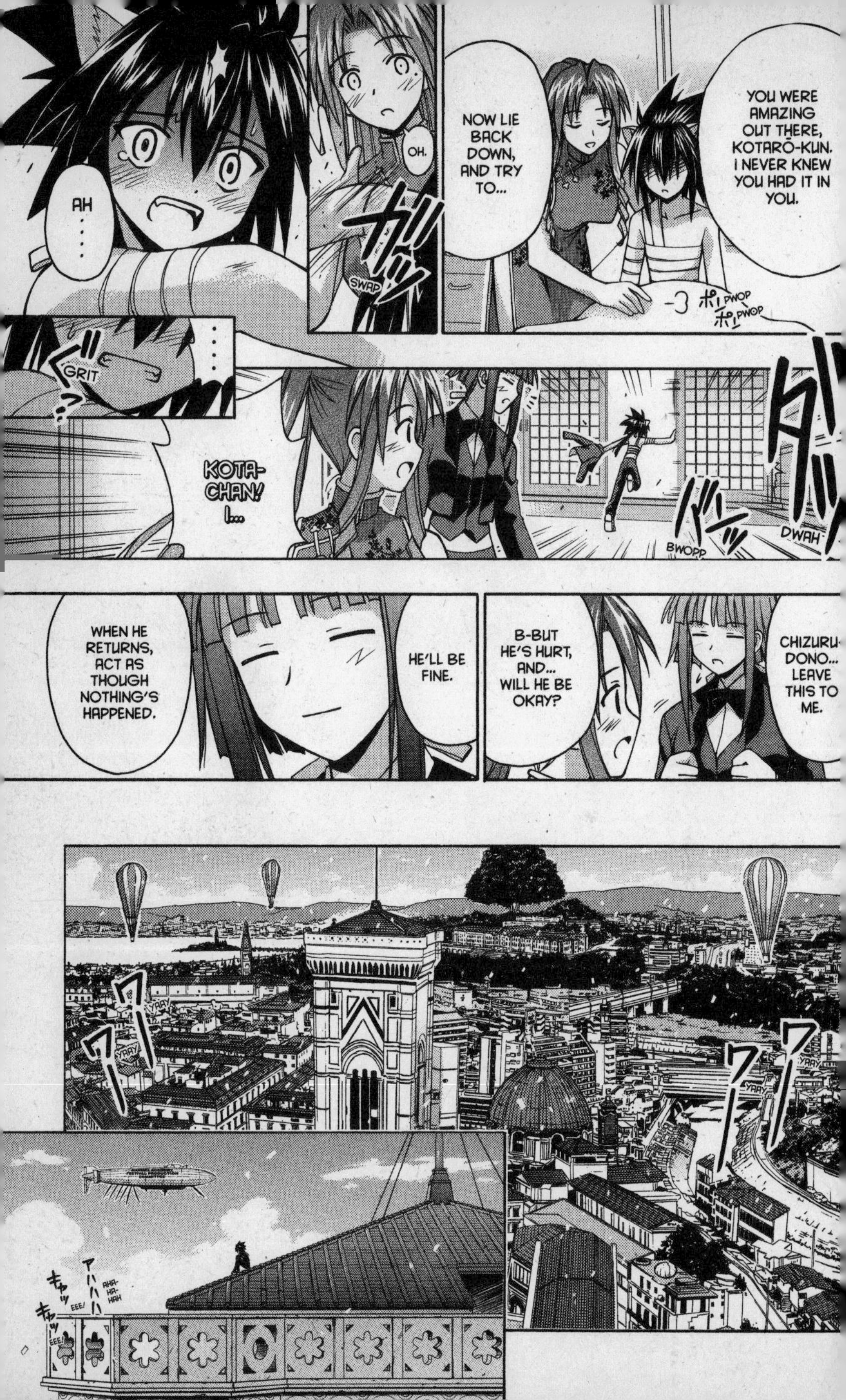
YOU WERE AMAZING OUT THERE, KOTARŌ-KUN. I NEVER KNEW YOU HAD IT IN YOU.
NOW LIE BACK DOWN, AND TRY TO...
PWOP
PWOP
OH.
SWAP
AH ....
...
GRIT
DWAH
BWOPP
KOTA-CHAN! I...
CHIZURU-DONO... LEAVE THIS TO ME.
B-BUT HE'S HURT, AND... WILL HE BE OKAY?
HE'LL BE FINE.
WHEN HE RETURNS, ACT AS THOUGH NOTHING'S HAPPENED.
YAAY
YAAY
YAAY
YAAY
AHA-HA-HAH
EEE!
EEE!

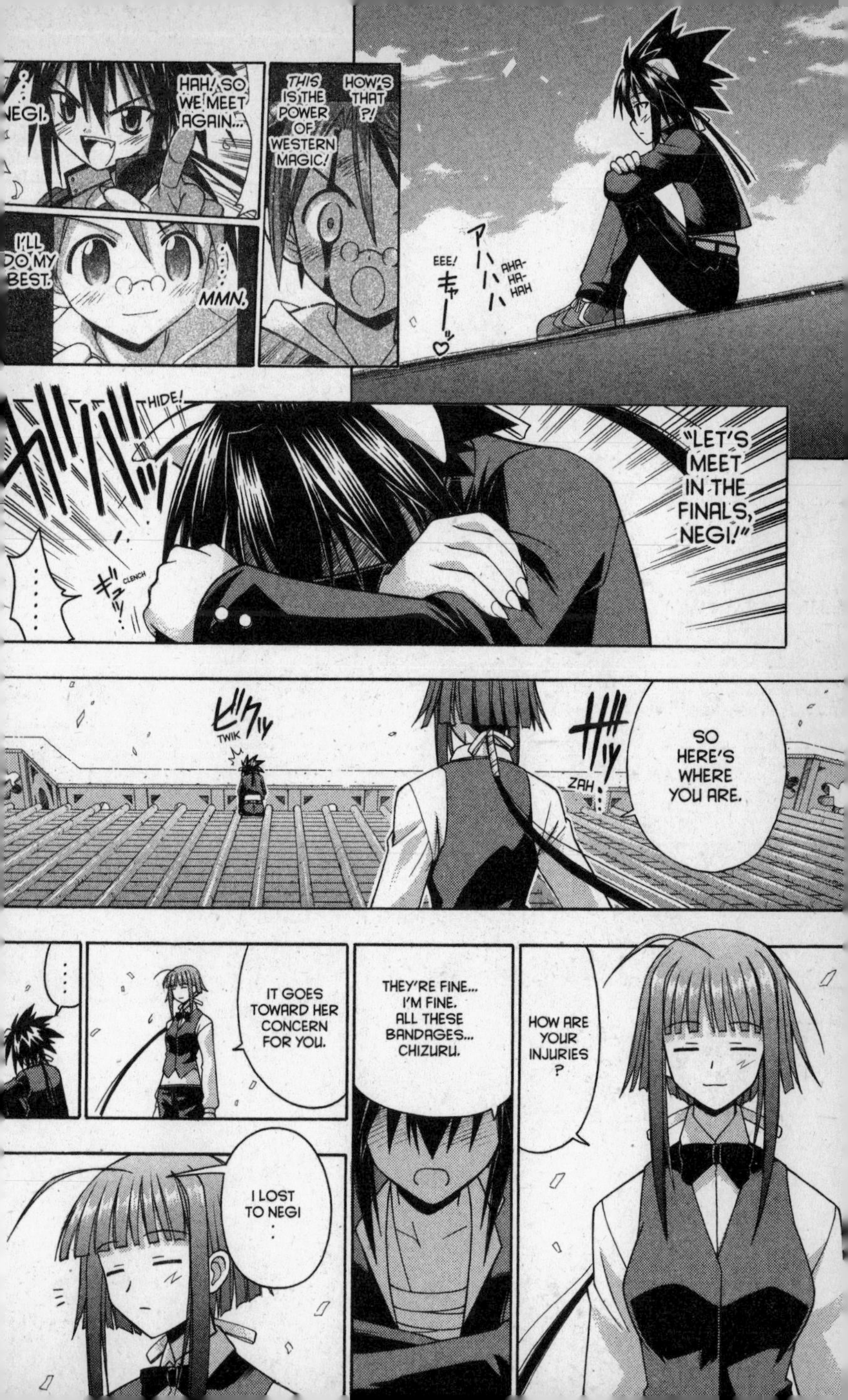
EEE!
キャーッ
AHA-HA-HAH
アハハハ
HOW'S THAT?!
THIS IS THE POWER OF WESTERN MAGIC!
HAH! SO WE MEET AGAIN...
...NEGI.
...MMN.
I'LL DO MY BEST.
"LET'S MEET IN THE FINALS, NEGI!"
ガバッ
HIDE!
ギュッ
CLENCH
......
SO HERE'S WHERE YOU ARE.
ザッ
ZAH
ビクッ
TWIK
HOW ARE YOUR INJURIES?
THEY'RE FINE... I'M FINE. ALL THESE BANDAGES... CHIZURU.
IT GOES TOWARD HER CONCERN FOR YOU.
....
I LOST TO NEGI
:

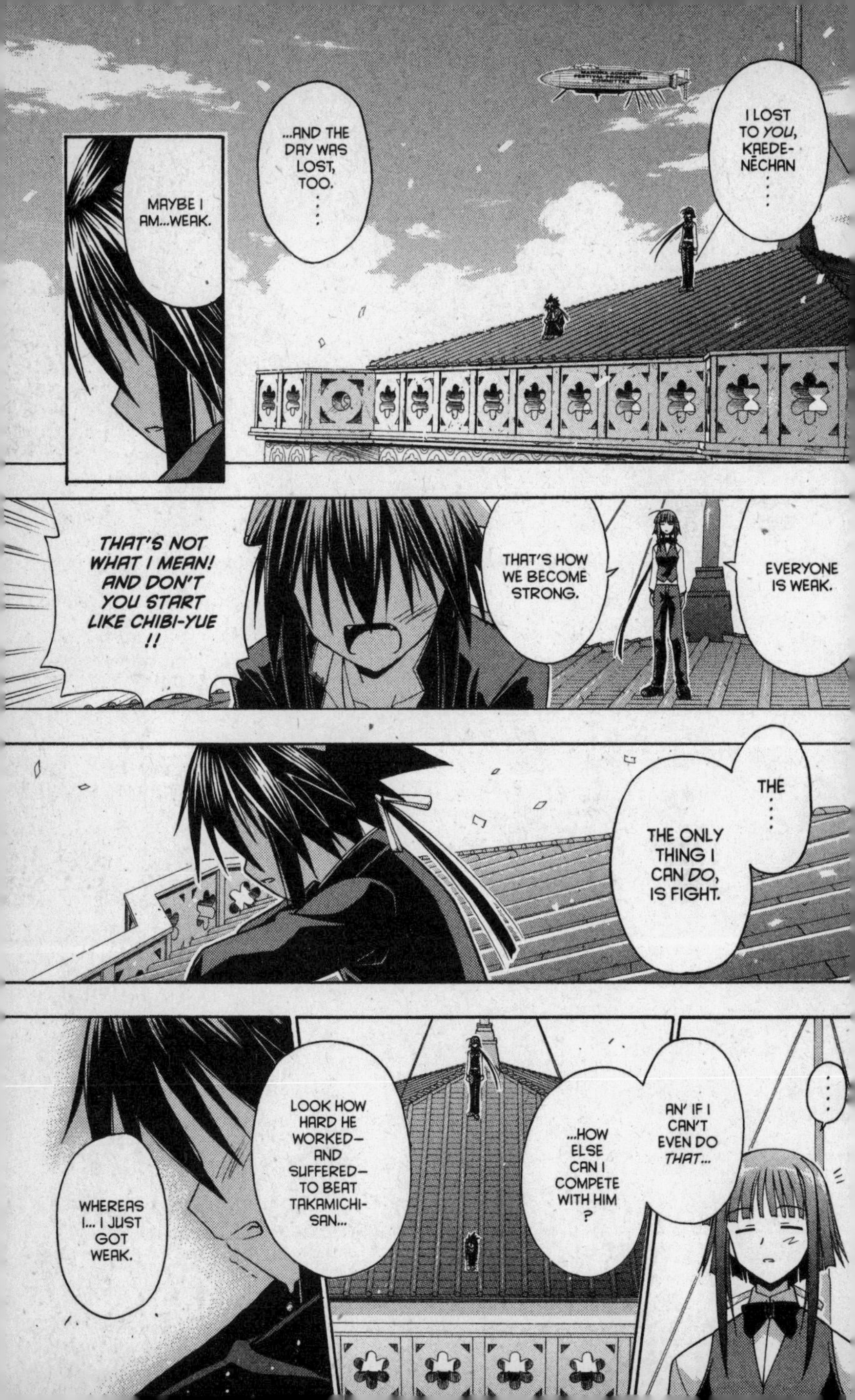
I LOST TO *YOU*, KAEDE-NĒCHAN ....
...AND THE DAY WAS LOST, TOO. ....
MAYBE I AM...WEAK.
EVERYONE IS WEAK.
THAT'S HOW WE BECOME STRONG.
THAT'S NOT WHAT I MEAN! AND DON'T YOU START LIKE CHIBI-YUE !!
THE ....
THE ONLY THING I CAN *DO*, IS FIGHT.
....
AN' IF I CAN'T EVEN DO *THAT*...
...HOW ELSE CAN I COMPETE WITH HIM ?
LOOK HOW HARD HE WORKED— AND SUFFERED— TO BEAT TAKAMICHI-SAN...
WHEREAS I... I JUST GOT WEAK.

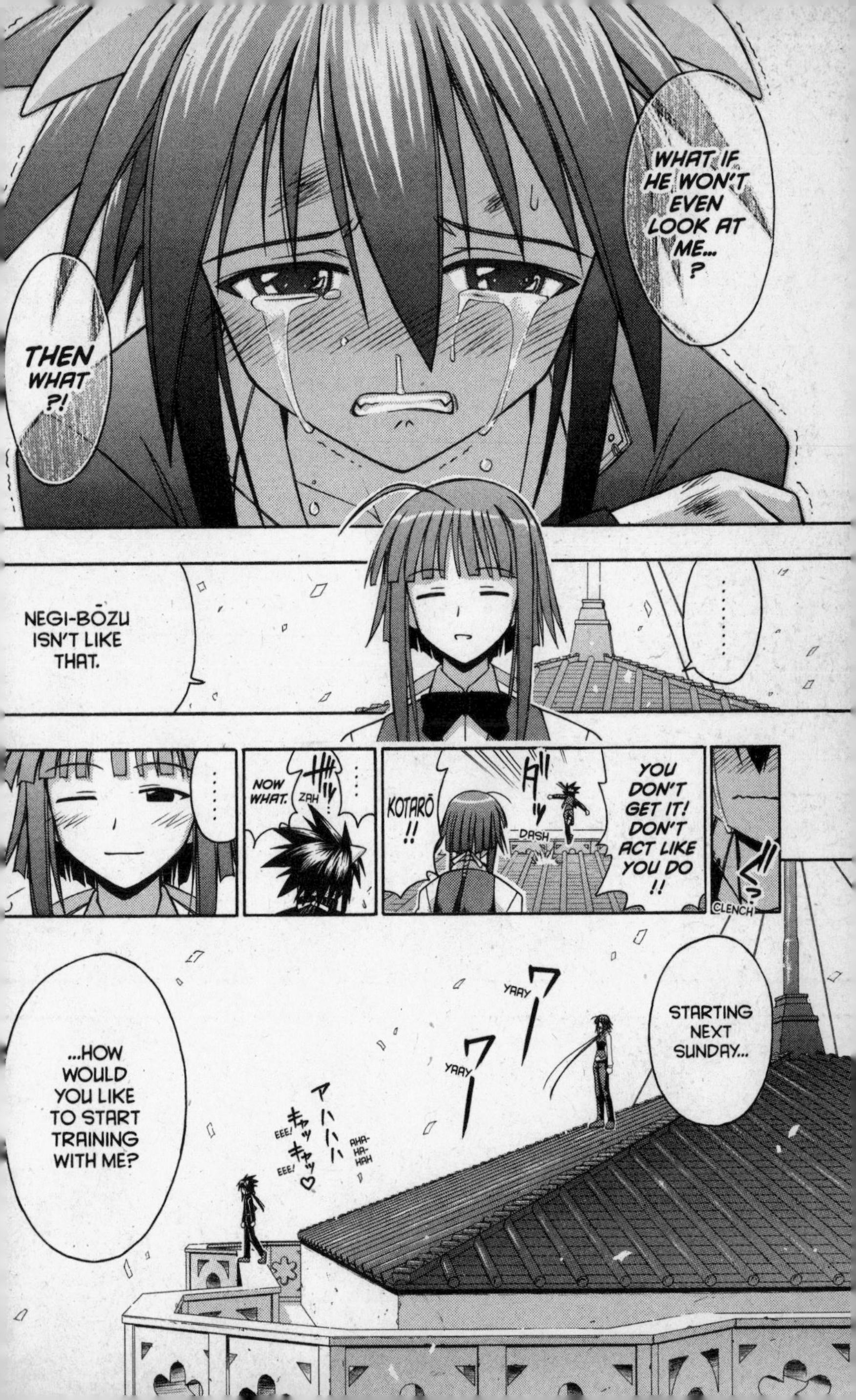
WHAT IF HE WON'T EVEN LOOK AT ME... ?
THEN WHAT ?!
......
NEGI-BŌZU ISN'T LIKE THAT.
CLENCH
YOU DON'T GET IT! DON'T ACT LIKE YOU DO !!
DASH
KOTARŌ !!
......
ZAH
NOW WHAT.
......
STARTING NEXT SUNDAY...
YAAY
YAAY
AHA-HA-HAH
EEE!
EEE!
...HOW WOULD YOU LIKE TO START TRAINING WITH ME?

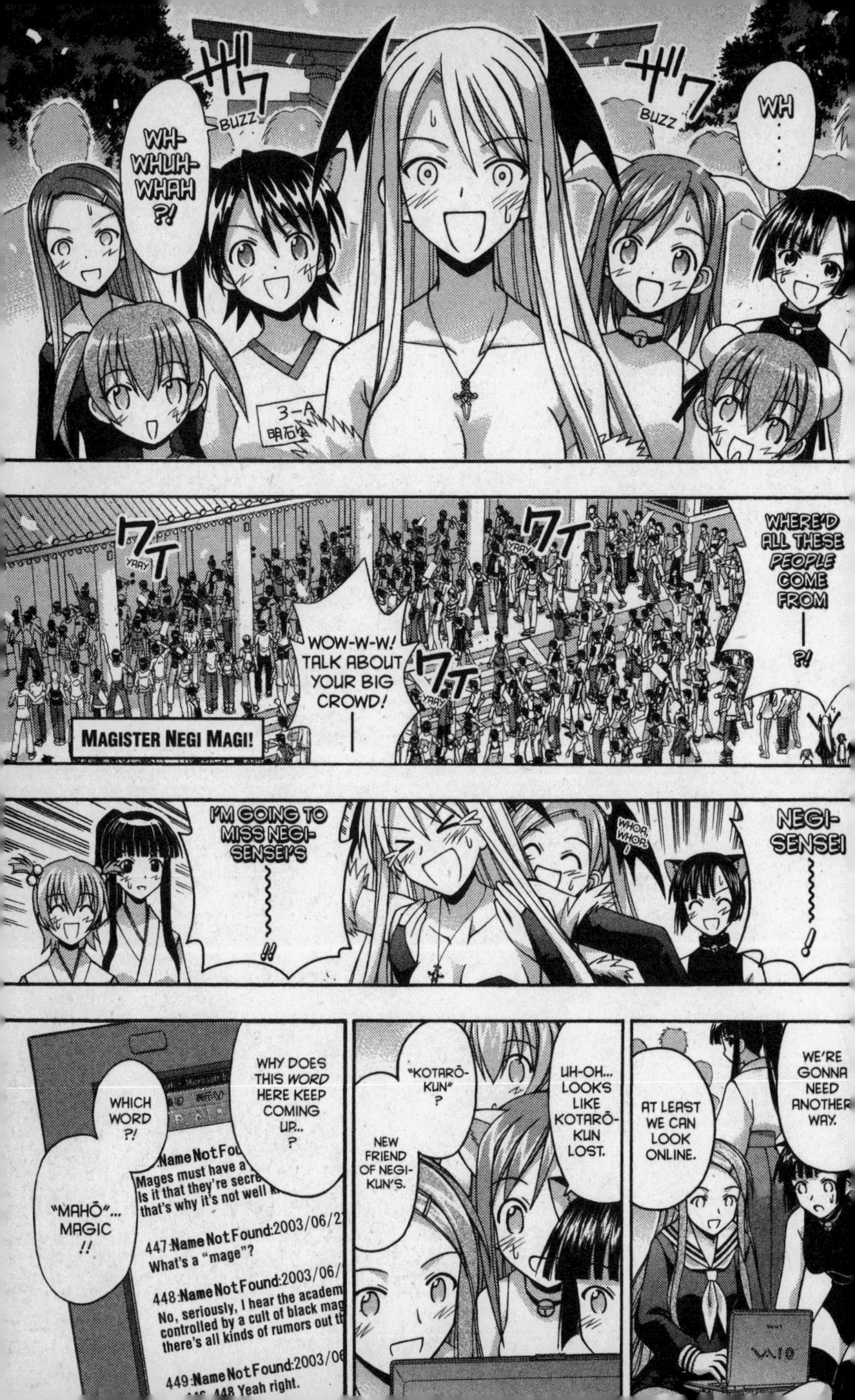

WH . . .
BUZZ
BUZZ
WH-WHUH-WHAH?!
3-A
WHERE'D ALL THESE PEOPLE COME FROM —?!
YAAY
YAAY
WOW-W-W! TALK ABOUT YOUR BIG CROWD! —
YAAY
MAGISTER NEGI MAGI!
NEGI-SENSEI ~~~!
WHOA, WHOA!
I'M GOING TO MISS NEGI-SENSEI'S ~~~!!
WE'RE GONNA NEED ANOTHER WAY.
AT LEAST WE CAN LOOK ONLINE.
UH-OH... LOOKS LIKE KOTARŌ-KUN LOST.
"KOTARŌ-KUN"?
NEW FRIEND OF NEGI-KUN'S.
WHY DOES THIS WORD HERE KEEP COMING UP...?
WHICH WORD?!
"MAHŌ"... MAGIC!!
447:Name Not Found:2003/06/2
What's a "mage"?
448:Name Not Found:2003/06/
No, seriously, I hear the academ
449:Name Not Found:2003/06
Yeah right.

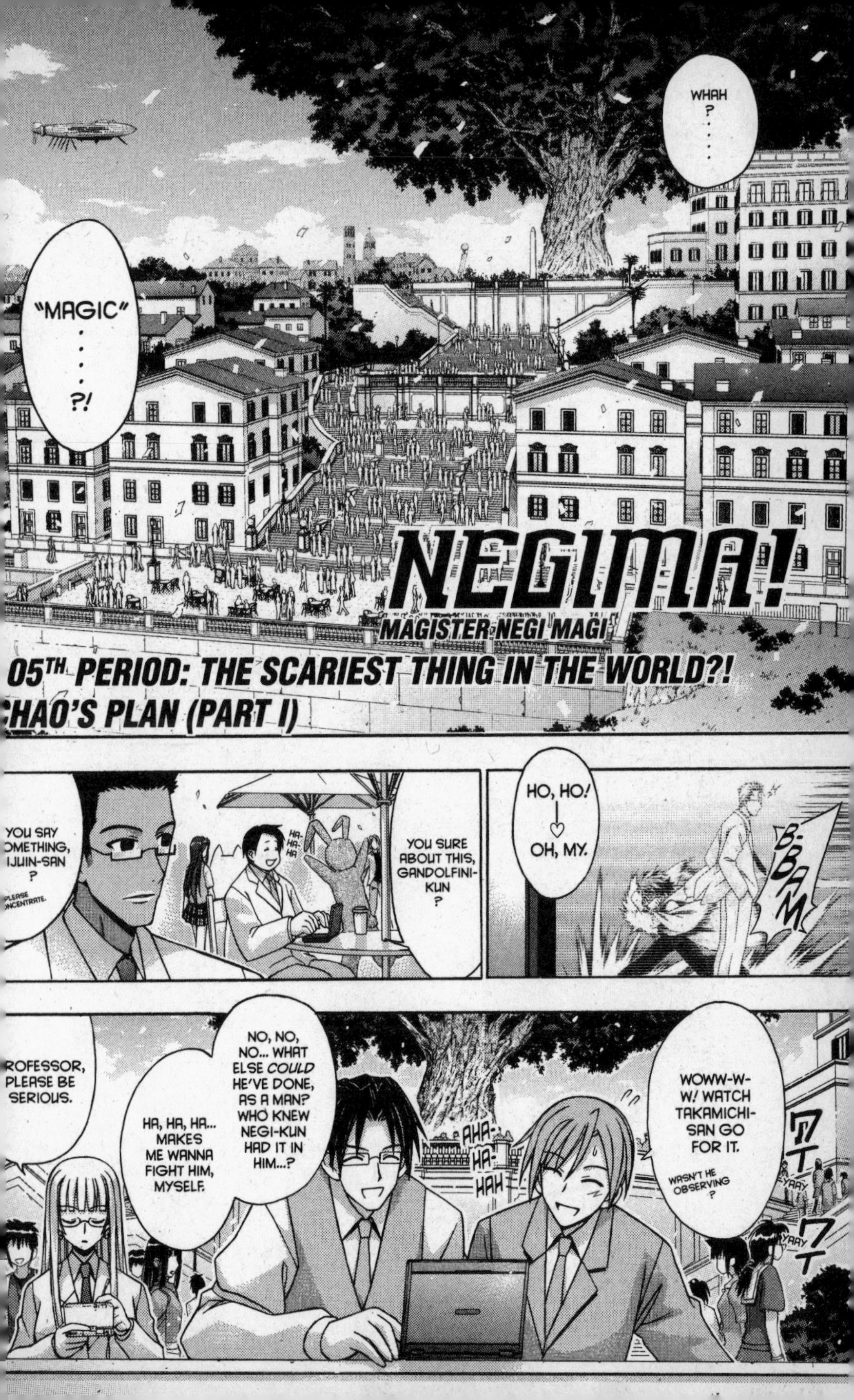
WHAH ?......
"MAGIC".....?!
NEGIMA!
MAGISTER NEGI MAGI
05TH PERIOD: THE SCARIEST THING IN THE WORLD?!
CHAO'S PLAN (PART I)
HO, HO! ↓ ♡ OH, MY.
B-BAM
YOU SURE ABOUT THIS, GANDOLFINI-KUN ?
HA-HA-HA
YOU SAY OMETHING, IJUIN-SAN ?
PLEASE ONCENTRATE.
WOWW-W-W! WATCH TAKAMICHI-SAN GO FOR IT.
WASN'T HE OBSERVING ?
YAAY
YAAY
AHA-HA-HAH
NO, NO, NO... WHAT ELSE *COULD* HE'VE DONE, AS A MAN? WHO KNEW NEGI-KUN HAD IT IN HIM...?
HA, HA, HA... MAKES ME WANNA FIGHT HIM, MYSELF.
ROFESSOR, PLEASE BE SERIOUS.

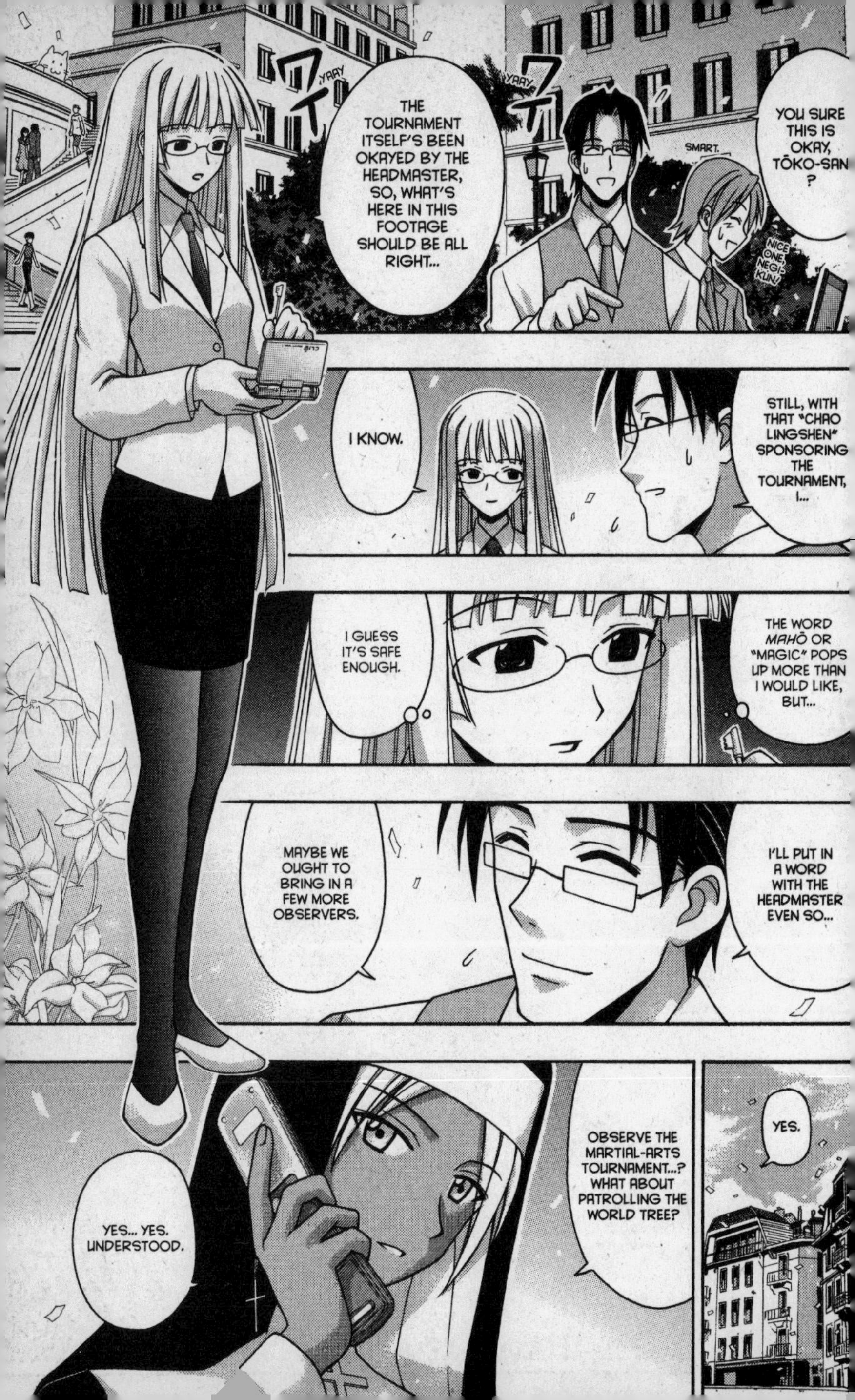
YOU SURE THIS IS OKAY, TŌKO-SAN?
NICE ONE, NEGI-KUN!
SMART.
YAAY
THE TOURNAMENT ITSELF'S BEEN OKAYED BY THE HEADMASTER, SO, WHAT'S HERE IN THIS FOOTAGE SHOULD BE ALL RIGHT...
YAAY
STILL, WITH THAT "CHAO LINGSHEN" SPONSORING THE TOURNAMENT, I...
I KNOW.
THE WORD *MAHŌ* OR "MAGIC" POPS UP MORE THAN I WOULD LIKE, BUT...
I GUESS IT'S SAFE ENOUGH.
I'LL PUT IN A WORD WITH THE HEADMASTER EVEN SO...
MAYBE WE OUGHT TO BRING IN A FEW MORE OBSERVERS.
YES.
OBSERVE THE MARTIAL-ARTS TOURNAMENT...? WHAT ABOUT PATROLLING THE WORLD TREE?
YES... YES. UNDERSTOOD.

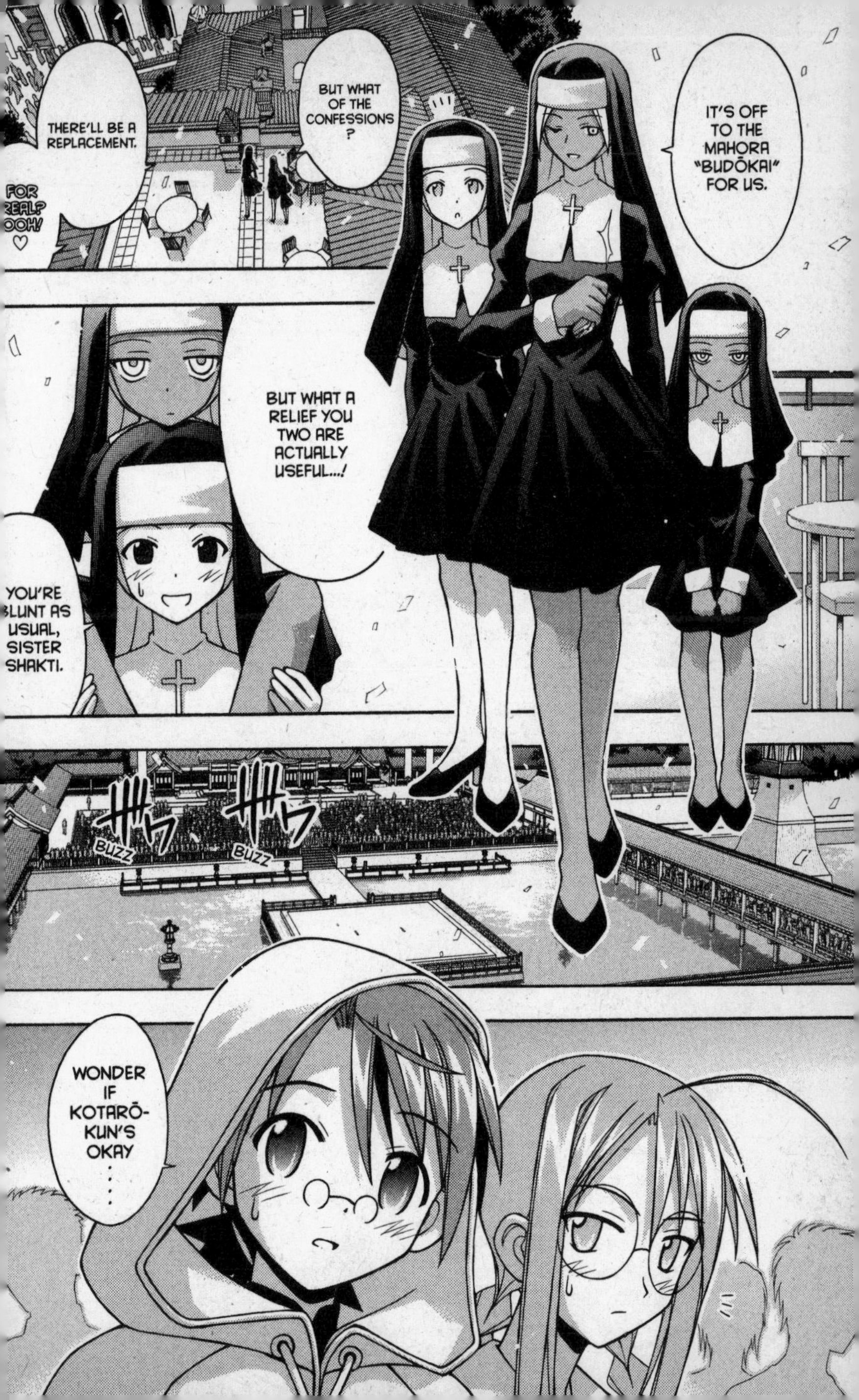
IT'S OFF TO THE MAHORA "BUDŌKAI" FOR US.
BUT WHAT OF THE CONFESSIONS ?
THERE'LL BE A REPLACEMENT.
FOR REAL? OOH! ♡
BUT WHAT A RELIEF YOU TWO ARE ACTUALLY USEFUL...!
YOU'RE BLUNT AS USUAL, SISTER SHAKTI.
BUZZ
BUZZ
WONDER IF KOTARŌ-KUN'S OKAY ....

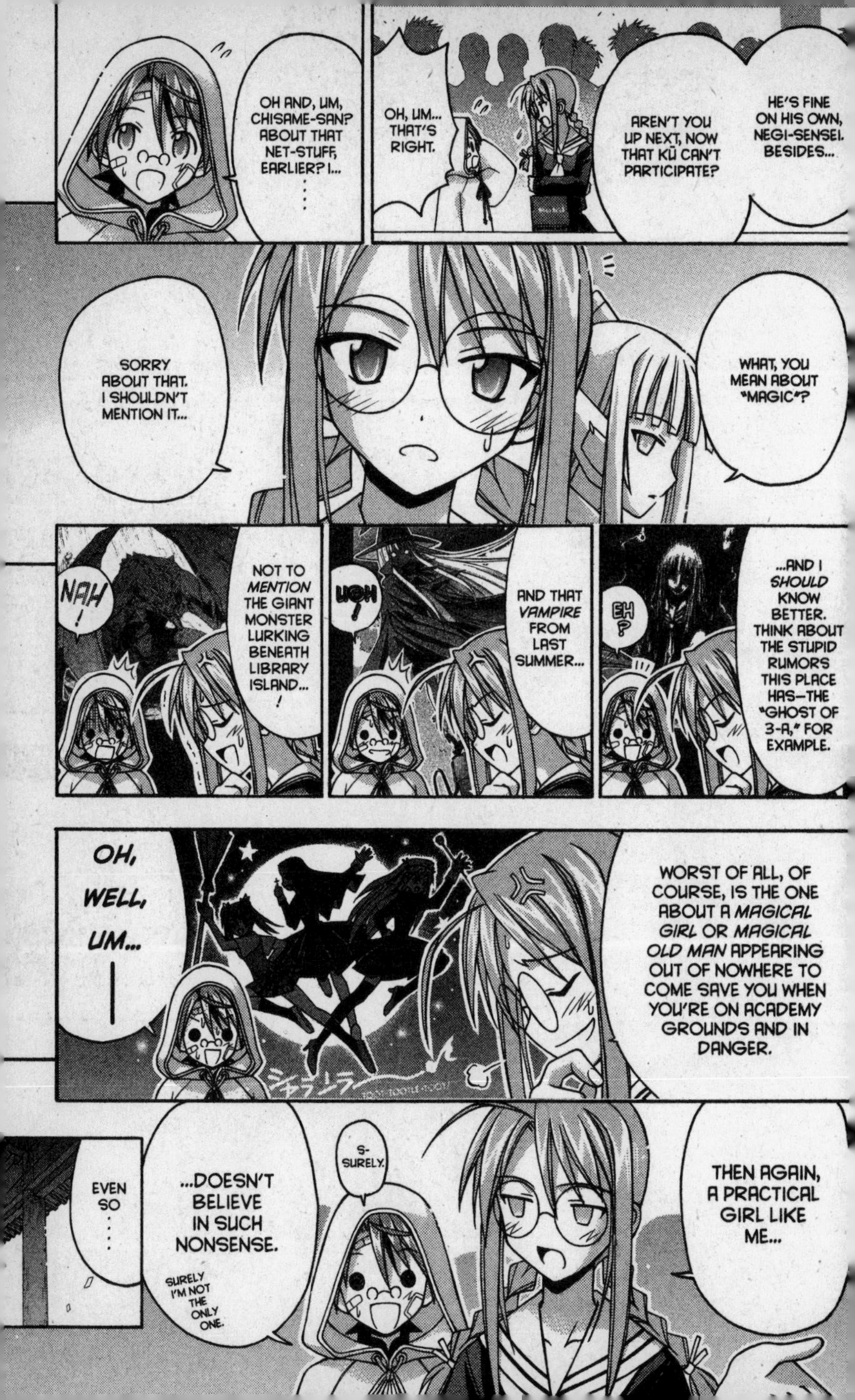
HE'S FINE ON HIS OWN, NEGI-SENSEI. BESIDES...
AREN'T YOU UP NEXT, NOW THAT KŪ CAN'T PARTICIPATE?
OH, UM... THAT'S RIGHT.
OH AND, UM, CHISAME-SAN? ABOUT THAT NET-STUFF, EARLIER? I... . . .
WHAT, YOU MEAN ABOUT "MAGIC"?
SORRY ABOUT THAT. I SHOULDN'T MENTION IT...
...AND I *SHOULD* KNOW BETTER. THINK ABOUT THE STUPID RUMORS THIS PLACE HAS—THE "GHOST OF 3-A," FOR EXAMPLE.
EH?
AND THAT *VAMPIRE* FROM LAST SUMMER...
UGH!
NOT TO *MENTION* THE GIANT MONSTER LURKING BENEATH LIBRARY ISLAND...!
NAH!
WORST OF ALL, OF COURSE, IS THE ONE ABOUT A *MAGICAL GIRL* OR *MAGICAL OLD MAN* APPEARING OUT OF NOWHERE TO COME SAVE YOU WHEN YOU'RE ON ACADEMY GROUNDS AND IN DANGER.
OH, WELL, UM... |
THEN AGAIN, A PRACTICAL GIRL LIKE ME...
S-SURELY.
...DOESN'T BELIEVE IN SUCH NONSENSE.
SURELY I'M NOT THE ONLY ONE.
EVEN SO . . .

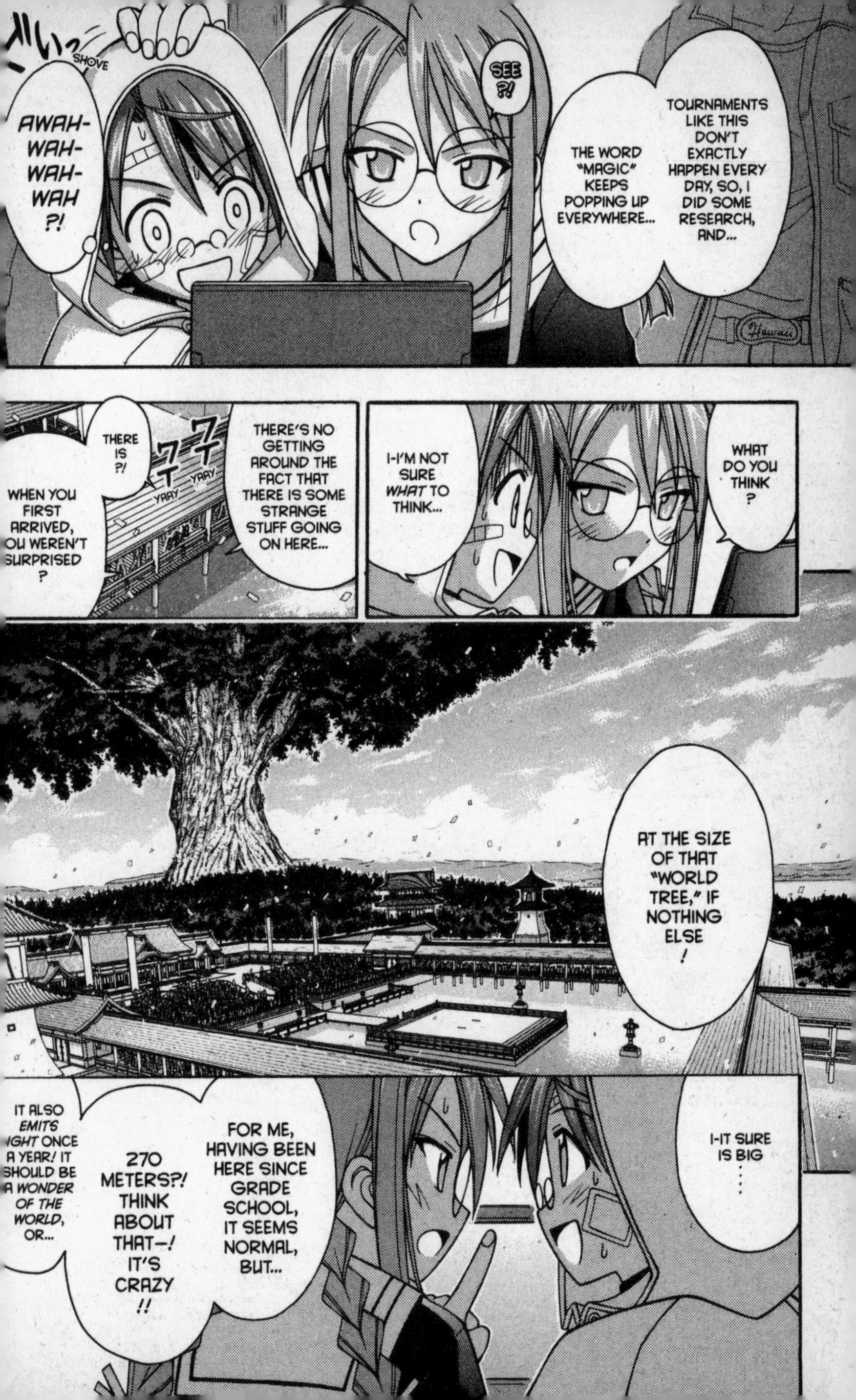
TOURNAMENTS LIKE THIS DON'T EXACTLY HAPPEN EVERY DAY, SO, I DID SOME RESEARCH, AND...
THE WORD "MAGIC" KEEPS POPPING UP EVERYWHERE...
SEE ?!
SHOVE
AWAH-WAH-WAH-WAH ?!
WHAT DO YOU THINK ?
I-I'M NOT SURE *WHAT* TO THINK...
THERE'S NO GETTING AROUND THE FACT THAT THERE IS SOME STRANGE STUFF GOING ON HERE...
YAAY
YAAY
THERE IS ?!
WHEN YOU FIRST ARRIVED, OU WEREN'T SURPRISED ?
AT THE SIZE OF THAT "WORLD TREE," IF NOTHING ELSE !
I-IT SURE IS BIG ....
FOR ME, HAVING BEEN HERE SINCE GRADE SCHOOL, IT SEEMS NORMAL, BUT...
270 METERS?! THINK ABOUT THAT—! IT'S CRAZY !!
IT ALSO *EMITS IGHT* ONCE A YEAR! IT SHOULD BE A *WONDER OF THE WORLD*, OR...

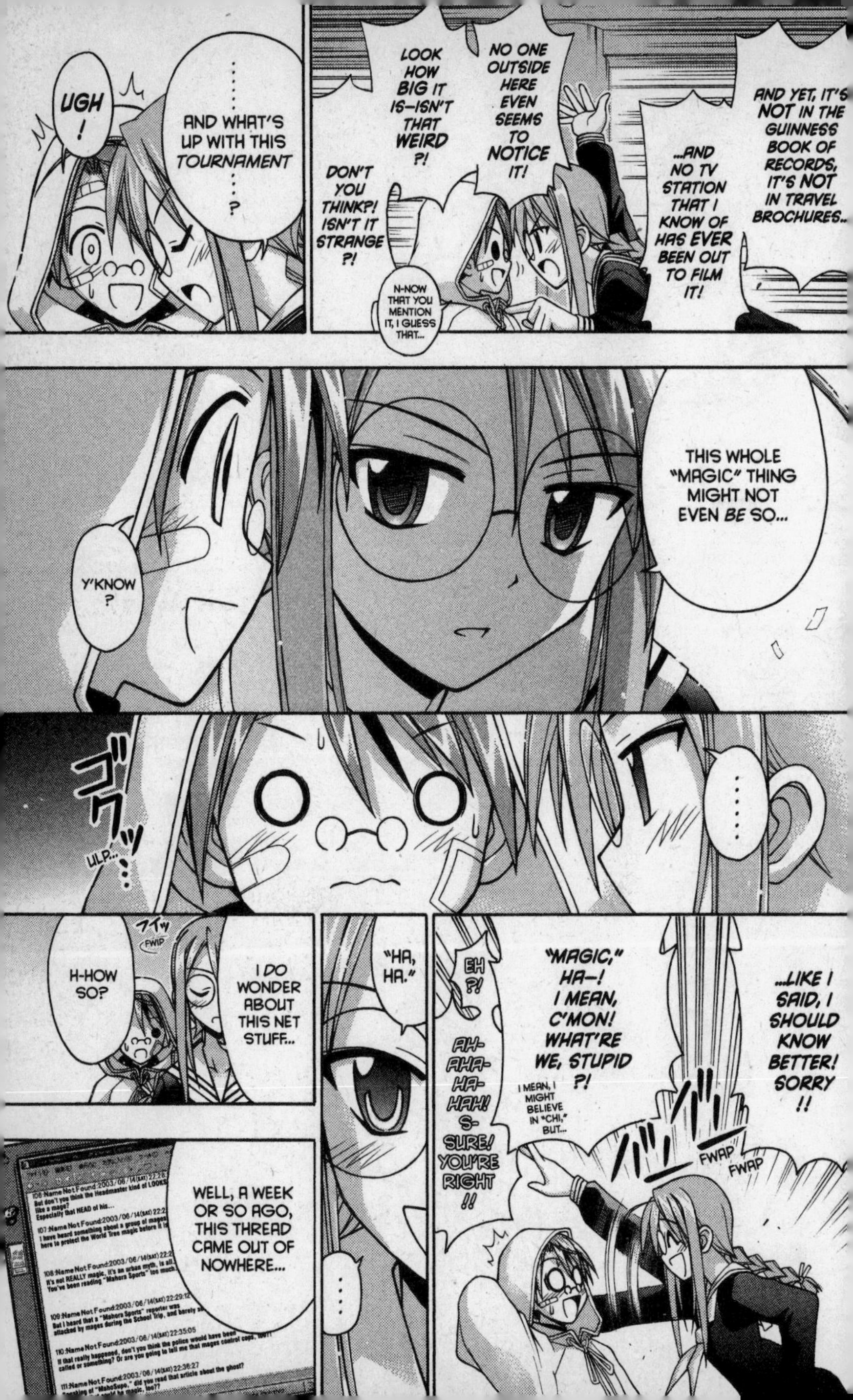

AND YET, IT'S NOT IN THE GUINNESS BOOK OF RECORDS, IT'S NOT IN TRAVEL BROCHURES...
...AND NO TV STATION THAT I KNOW OF HAS EVER BEEN OUT TO FILM IT!
NO ONE OUTSIDE HERE EVEN SEEMS TO NOTICE IT!
LOOK HOW BIG IT IS—ISN'T THAT WEIRD?!
DON'T YOU THINK?! ISN'T IT STRANGE?!
N-NOW THAT YOU MENTION IT, I GUESS THAT...
......AND WHAT'S UP WITH THIS TOURNAMENT......?
UGH!
THIS WHOLE "MAGIC" THING MIGHT NOT EVEN BE SO...
Y'KNOW?
......
ULP...
...LIKE I SAID, I SHOULD KNOW BETTER! SORRY!!
"MAGIC," HA—! I MEAN, C'MON! WHAT'RE WE, STUPID?!
I MEAN, I MIGHT BELIEVE IN "CHI," BUT...
FWAP
FWAP
EH?!
AH-AHA-HA-HAH! S-SURE! YOU'RE RIGHT!!
"HA, HA."
......
I DO WONDER ABOUT THIS NET STUFF...
FWIP
H-HOW SO?
WELL, A WEEK OR SO AGO, THIS THREAD CAME OUT OF NOWHERE...
106:Name Not Found:2003/06/14(SAT) 22:28
But don't you think the Headmaster kind of LOOKS like a mage?
Especially that HEAD of his...
107:Name Not Found:2003/06/14(SAT) 22:2
I have heard something about a group of mages here to protect the World Tree magic before
108:Name Not Found:2003/06/14(SAT) 22:2
It's not REALLY magic, it's an urban myth, is all.
You've been reading "Mahora Sports" too much.
109:Name Not Found:2003/06/14(SAT) 22:29:12
But I heard that a "Mahora Sports" reporter was attacked by mages during the School Trip, and barely
110:Name Not Found:2003/06/14(SAT) 22:35:05
If that really happened, don't you think the police would have been called or something? Or are you going to tell me that mages control cops, too?!
111:Name Not Found:2003/06/14(SAT) 22:36:27
Speaking of "MahoSupo," did you read that article about the ghost?

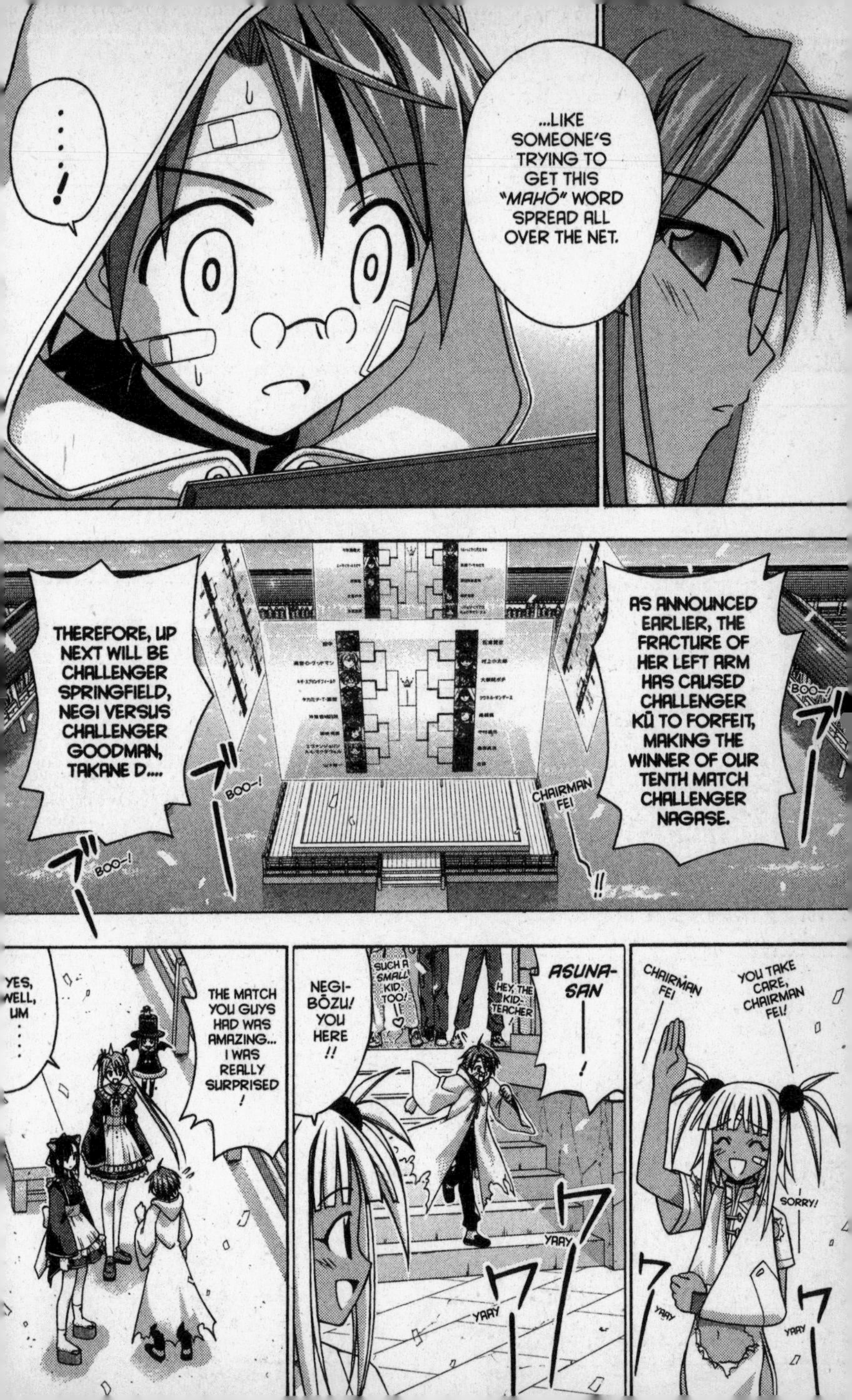
...LIKE SOMEONE'S TRYING TO GET THIS "MAHŌ" WORD SPREAD ALL OVER THE NET.
....!
AS ANNOUNCED EARLIER, THE FRACTURE OF HER LEFT ARM HAS CAUSED CHALLENGER KŪ TO FORFEIT, MAKING THE WINNER OF OUR TENTH MATCH CHALLENGER NAGASE.
BOO-!
CHAIRMAN FEI
!!
THEREFORE, UP NEXT WILL BE CHALLENGER SPRINGFIELD, NEGI VERSUS CHALLENGER GOODMAN, TAKANE D....
BOO-!
BOO-!
CHAIRMAN FEI
YOU TAKE CARE, CHAIRMAN FEI!
SORRY!
YAAY
YAAY
ASUNA-SAN!
HEY, THE KID-TEACHER!
SUCH A SMALL KID, TOO!
NEGI-BŌZU! YOU HERE!!
YAAY
YAAY
THE MATCH YOU GUYS HAD WAS AMAZING... I WAS REALLY SURPRISED!
YES, WELL, UM.....

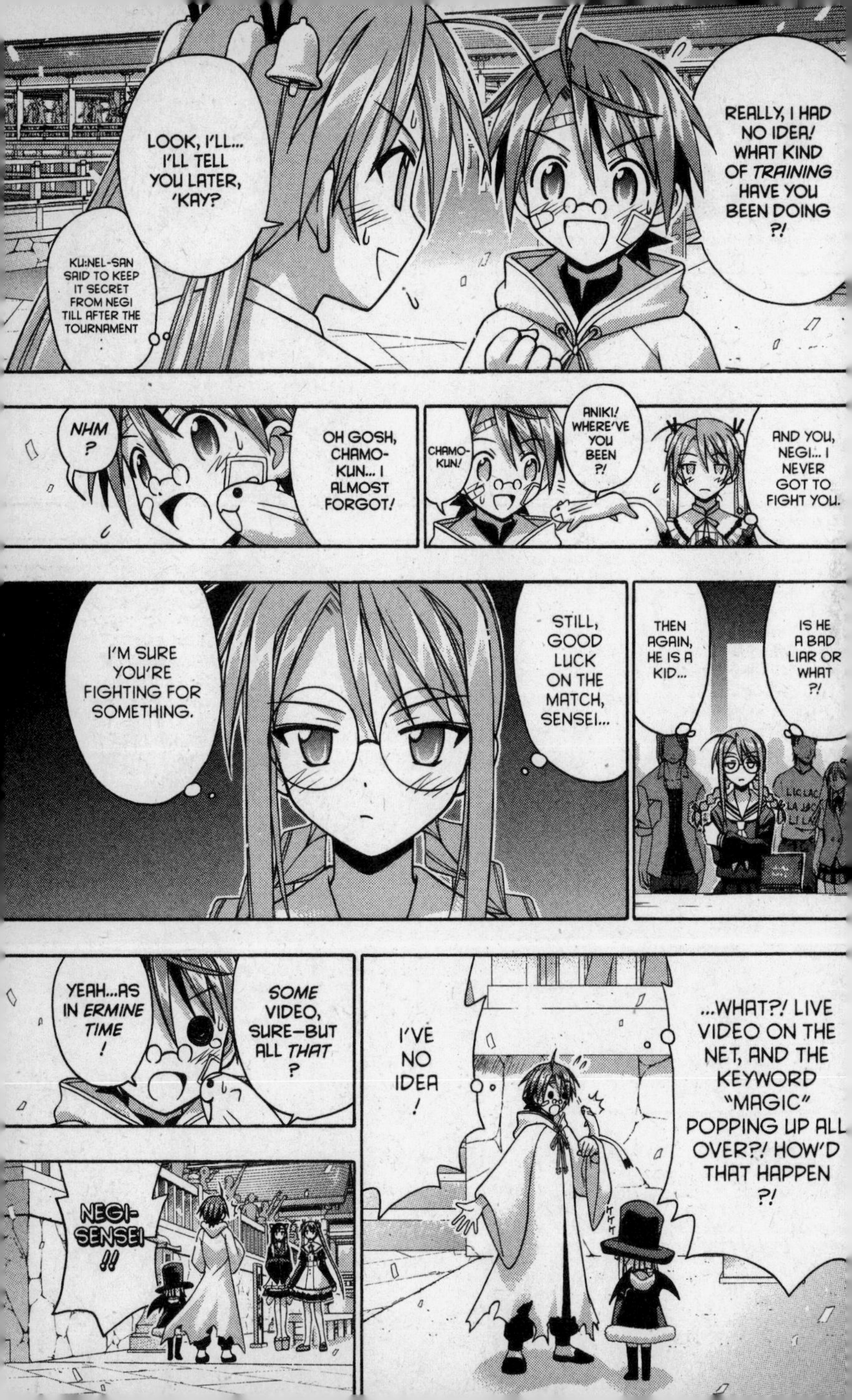
REALLY, I HAD NO IDEA! WHAT KIND OF *TRAINING* HAVE YOU BEEN DOING ?!
LOOK, I'LL... I'LL TELL YOU LATER, 'KAY?
KU:NEL-SAN SAID TO KEEP IT SECRET FROM NEGI TILL AFTER THE TOURNAMENT
AND YOU, NEGI... I NEVER GOT TO FIGHT YOU.
ANIKI! WHERE'VE YOU BEEN ?!
CHAMO-KUN!
OH GOSH, CHAMO-KUN... I ALMOST FORGOT!
NHM ?
IS HE A BAD LIAR OR WHAT ?!
THEN AGAIN, HE IS A KID...
STILL, GOOD LUCK ON THE MATCH, SENSEI...
I'M SURE YOU'RE FIGHTING FOR SOMETHING.
...WHAT?! LIVE VIDEO ON THE NET, AND THE KEYWORD "MAGIC" POPPING UP ALL OVER?! HOW'D THAT HAPPEN ?!
I'VE NO IDEA !
SOME VIDEO, SURE—BUT ALL *THAT* ?
YEAH...AS IN *ERMINE TIME* !
NEGI-SENSEI !!

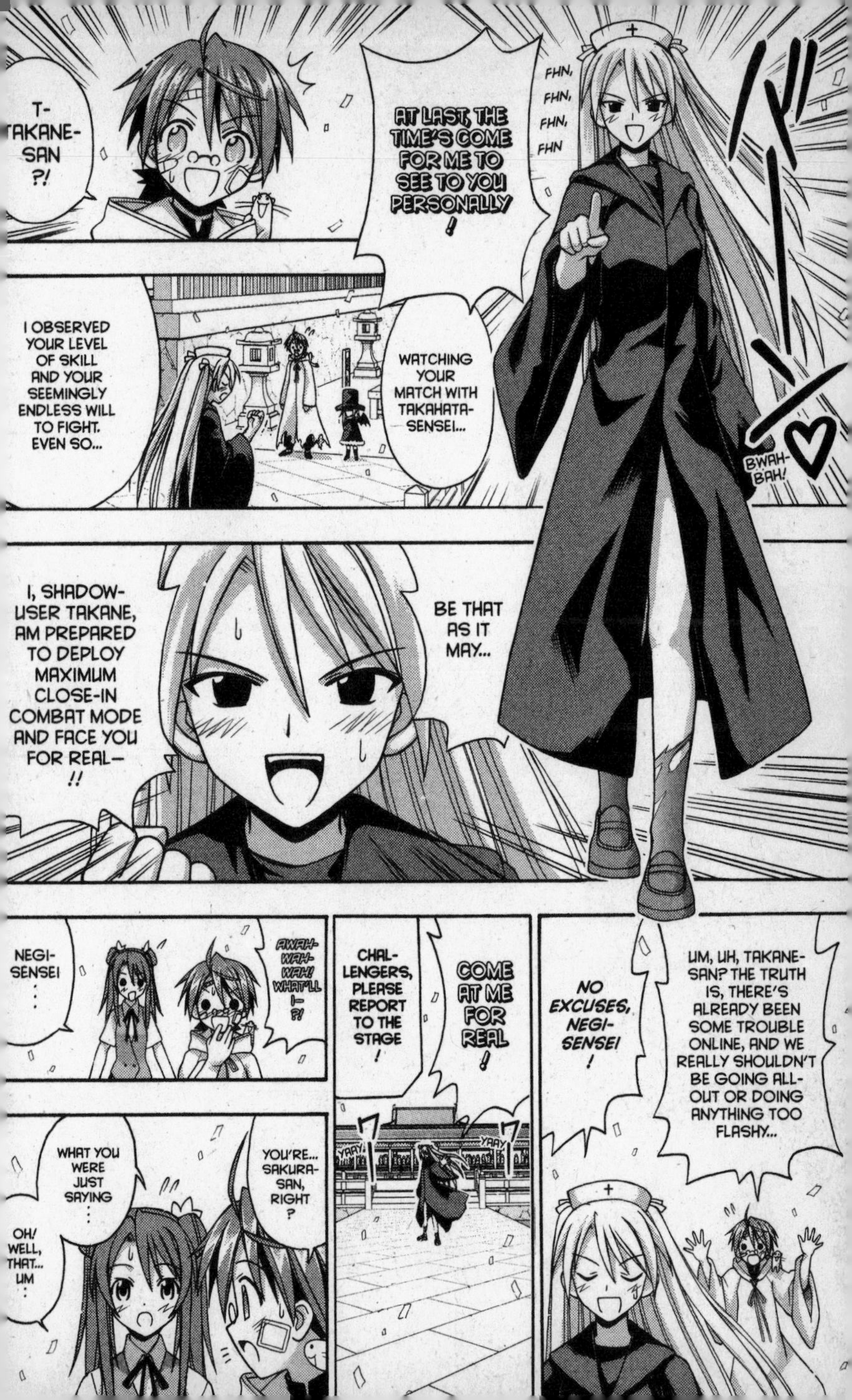

FHN, FHN, FHN, FHN
AT LAST, THE TIME'S COME FOR ME TO SEE TO YOU PERSONALLY!
BWAH-BAH!
T-TAKANE-SAN?!
WATCHING YOUR MATCH WITH TAKAHATA-SENSEI...
I OBSERVED YOUR LEVEL OF SKILL AND YOUR SEEMINGLY ENDLESS WILL TO FIGHT. EVEN SO...
BE THAT AS IT MAY...
I, SHADOW-USER TAKANE, AM PREPARED TO DEPLOY MAXIMUM CLOSE-IN COMBAT MODE AND FACE YOU FOR REAL—!!
UM, UH, TAKANE-SAN? THE TRUTH IS, THERE'S ALREADY BEEN SOME TROUBLE ONLINE, AND WE REALLY SHOULDN'T BE GOING ALL-OUT OR DOING ANYTHING TOO FLASHY...
NO EXCUSES, NEGI-SENSEI!
COME AT ME FOR REAL!
CHALLENGERS, PLEASE REPORT TO THE STAGE!
YAAY
YAAY
AWAH-WAH-WAH! WHAT'LL I-?!
NEGI-SENSEI...
YOU'RE... SAKURA-SAN, RIGHT?
WHAT YOU WERE JUST SAYING...
OH! WELL, THAT... UM...

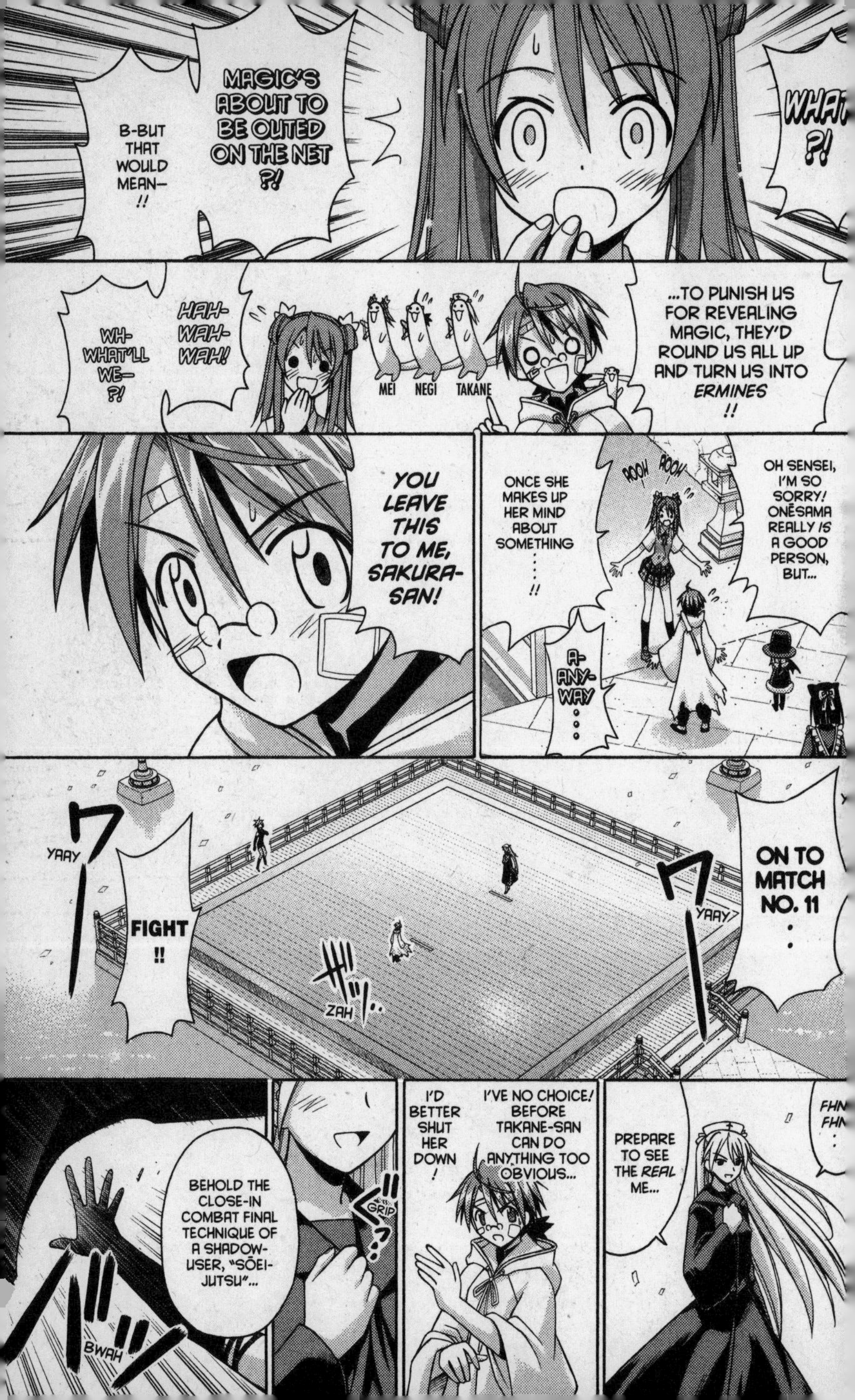
WHAT ?!
MAGIC'S ABOUT TO BE OUTED ON THE NET ?!
B-BUT THAT WOULD MEAN—!!
...TO PUNISH US FOR REVEALING MAGIC, THEY'D ROUND US ALL UP AND TURN US INTO ERMINES !!
TAKANE
NEGI
MEI
HAH-WAH-WAH!
WH-WHAT'LL WE— ?!
OH SENSEI, I'M SO SORRY! ONĒSAMA REALLY IS A GOOD PERSON, BUT...
ROOH ROOH
ONCE SHE MAKES UP HER MIND ABOUT SOMETHING .....!!
A-ANYWAY...
YOU LEAVE THIS TO ME, SAKURA-SAN!
ON TO MATCH NO. 11 ..
YAAY
FIGHT !!
ZAH
YAAY
FHN FHN ..
PREPARE TO SEE THE REAL ME...
I'VE NO CHOICE! BEFORE TAKANE-SAN CAN DO ANYTHING TOO OBVIOUS...
I'D BETTER SHUT HER DOWN !
GRIP
?
BEHOLD THE CLOSE-IN COMBAT FINAL TECHNIQUE OF A SHADOW-USER, "SŌEI-JUTSU"...
BWAH

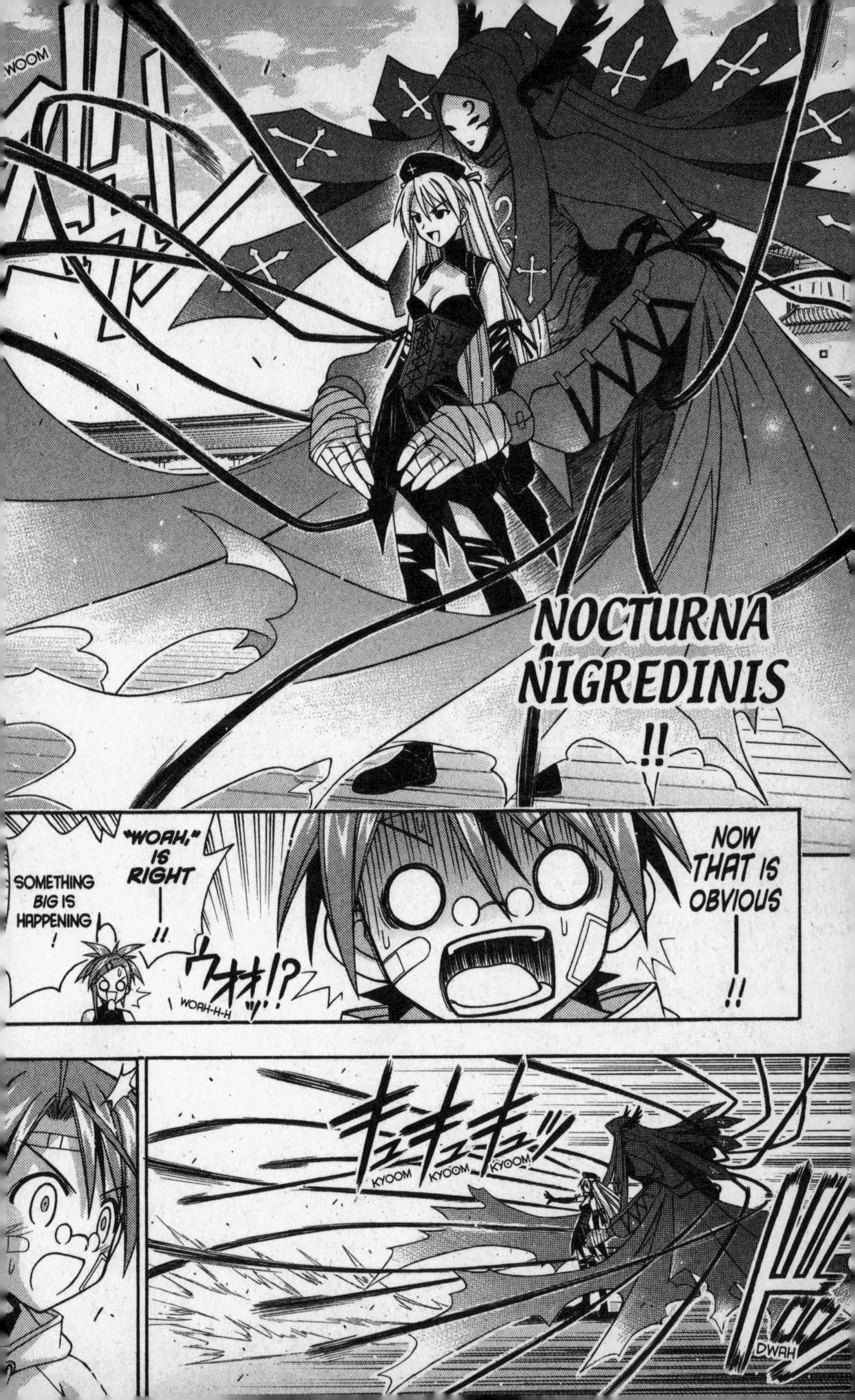
WOOM
NOCTURNA NIGREDINIS !!
NOW THAT IS OBVIOUS — !!
ウオオッ!? WOAH-H-H
"WOAH," IS RIGHT — !!
SOMETHING BIG IS HAPPENING!
DWAH
キュキュキュッ KYOOM KYOOM KYOOM

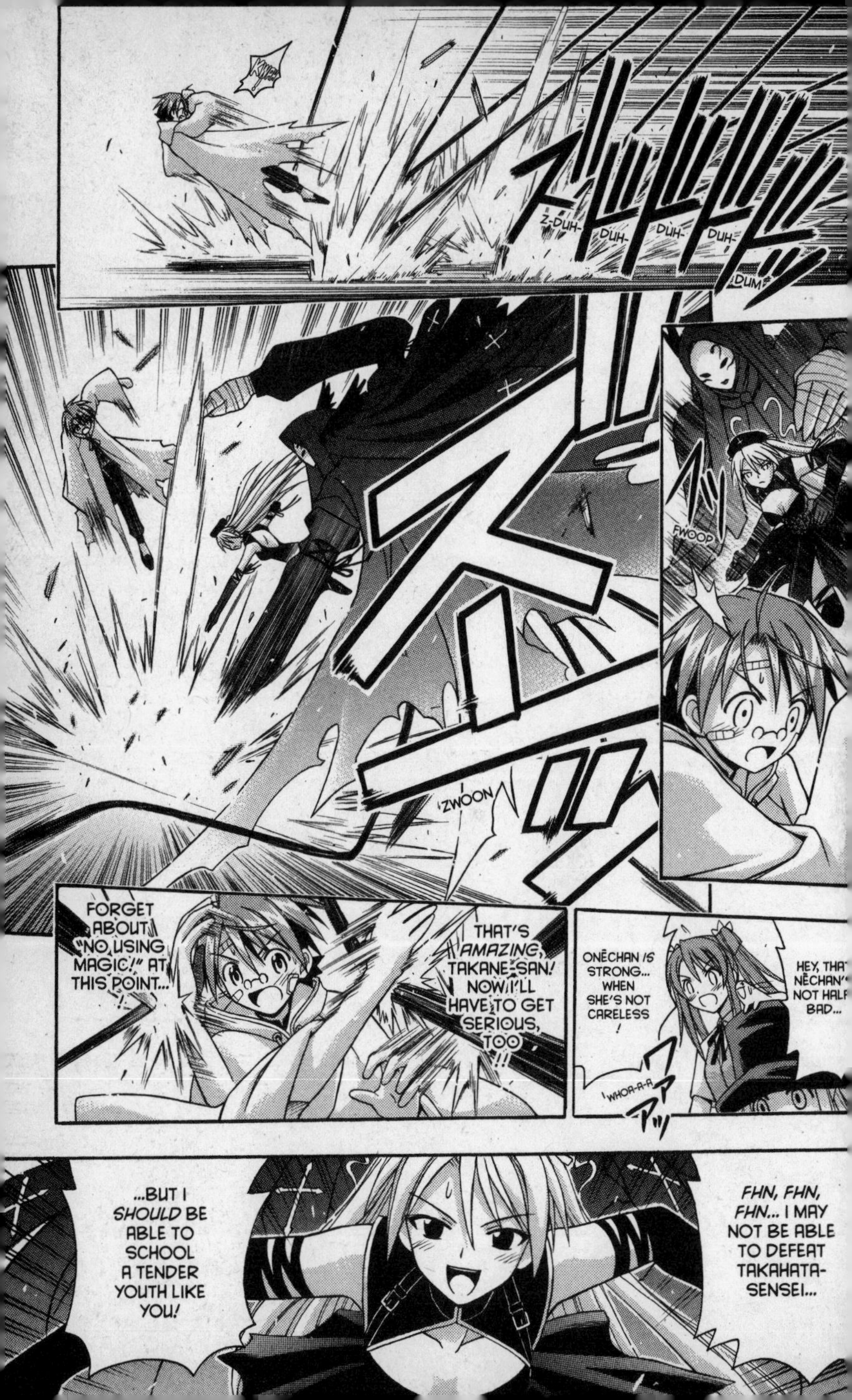
Z-DUH-DUH-DUH-DUH-DUM
FWOOD
ZWOON
HEY, THAT NĒCHAN' NOT HALF BAD...
ONĒCHAN IS STRONG... WHEN SHE'S NOT CARELESS!
WHOA-A-A
THAT'S AMAZING, TAKANE-SAN! NOW I'LL HAVE TO GET SERIOUS, TOO!!
FORGET ABOUT "NO USING MAGIC!" AT THIS POINT...
FHN, FHN, FHN... I MAY NOT BE ABLE TO DEFEAT TAKAHATA-SENSEI...
...BUT I SHOULD BE ABLE TO SCHOOL A TENDER YOUTH LIKE YOU!

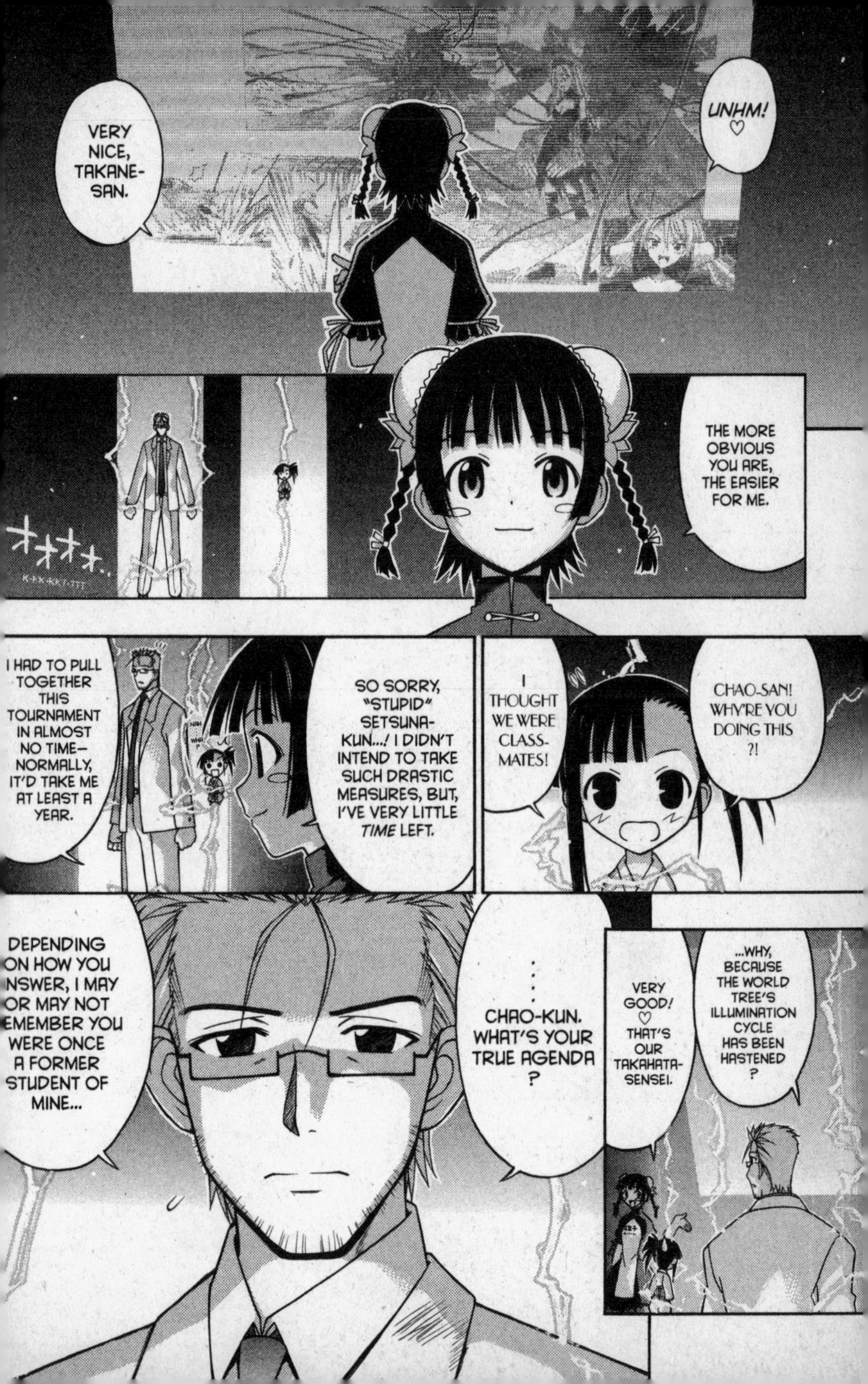
UNHM! ♡
VERY NICE, TAKANE-SAN.
THE MORE OBVIOUS YOU ARE, THE EASIER FOR ME.
CHAO-SAN! WHY'RE YOU DOING THIS ?!
I THOUGHT WE WERE CLASS-MATES!
SO SORRY, "STUPID" SETSUNA-KUN...! I DIDN'T INTEND TO TAKE SUCH DRASTIC MEASURES, BUT, I'VE VERY LITTLE TIME LEFT.
I HAD TO PULL TOGETHER THIS TOURNAMENT IN ALMOST NO TIME— NORMALLY, IT'D TAKE ME AT LEAST A YEAR.
...WHY, BECAUSE THE WORLD TREE'S ILLUMINATION CYCLE HAS BEEN HASTENED ?
VERY GOOD! ♡ THAT'S OUR TAKAHATA-SENSEI.
... CHAO-KUN. WHAT'S YOUR TRUE AGENDA ?
DEPENDING ON HOW YOU NSWER, I MAY OR MAY NOT EMEMBER YOU WERE ONCE A FORMER STUDENT OF MINE...

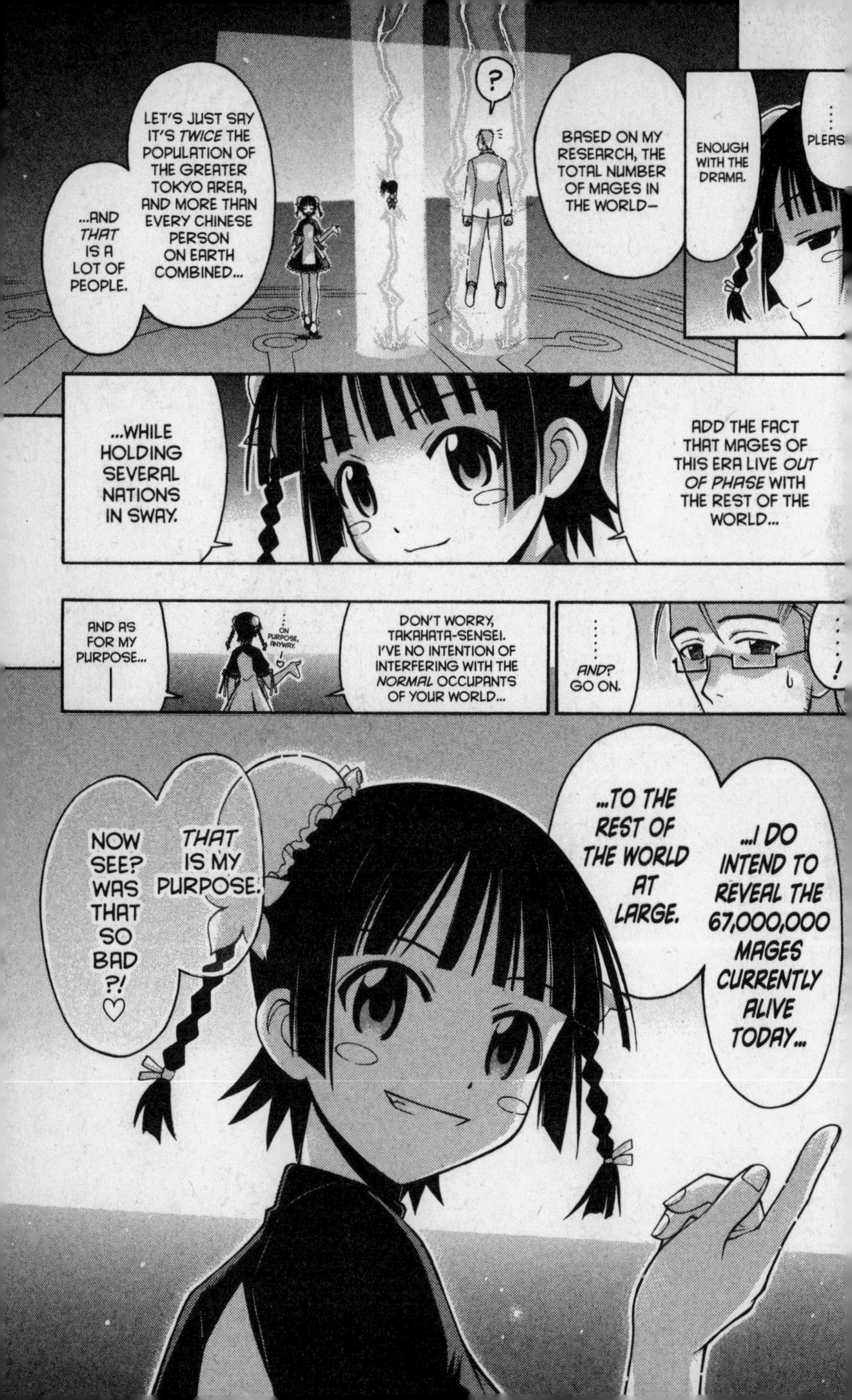

...PLEAS
ENOUGH WITH THE DRAMA.
?
BASED ON MY RESEARCH, THE TOTAL NUMBER OF MAGES IN THE WORLD—
LET'S JUST SAY IT'S *TWICE* THE POPULATION OF THE GREATER TOKYO AREA, AND MORE THAN EVERY CHINESE PERSON ON EARTH COMBINED...
...AND *THAT* IS A LOT OF PEOPLE.
ADD THE FACT THAT MAGES OF THIS ERA LIVE *OUT OF PHASE* WITH THE REST OF THE WORLD...
...WHILE HOLDING SEVERAL NATIONS IN SWAY.
......!
...... *AND?* GO ON.
DON'T WORRY, TAKAHATA-SENSEI. I'VE NO INTENTION OF INTERFERING WITH THE *NORMAL* OCCUPANTS OF YOUR WORLD...
...ON PURPOSE, ANYWAY. ♡
AND AS FOR MY PURPOSE...
...I DO INTEND TO REVEAL THE 67,000,000 MAGES CURRENTLY ALIVE TODAY...
...TO THE REST OF THE WORLD AT LARGE.
THAT IS MY PURPOSE.
NOW SEE? WAS THAT SO BAD?! ♡

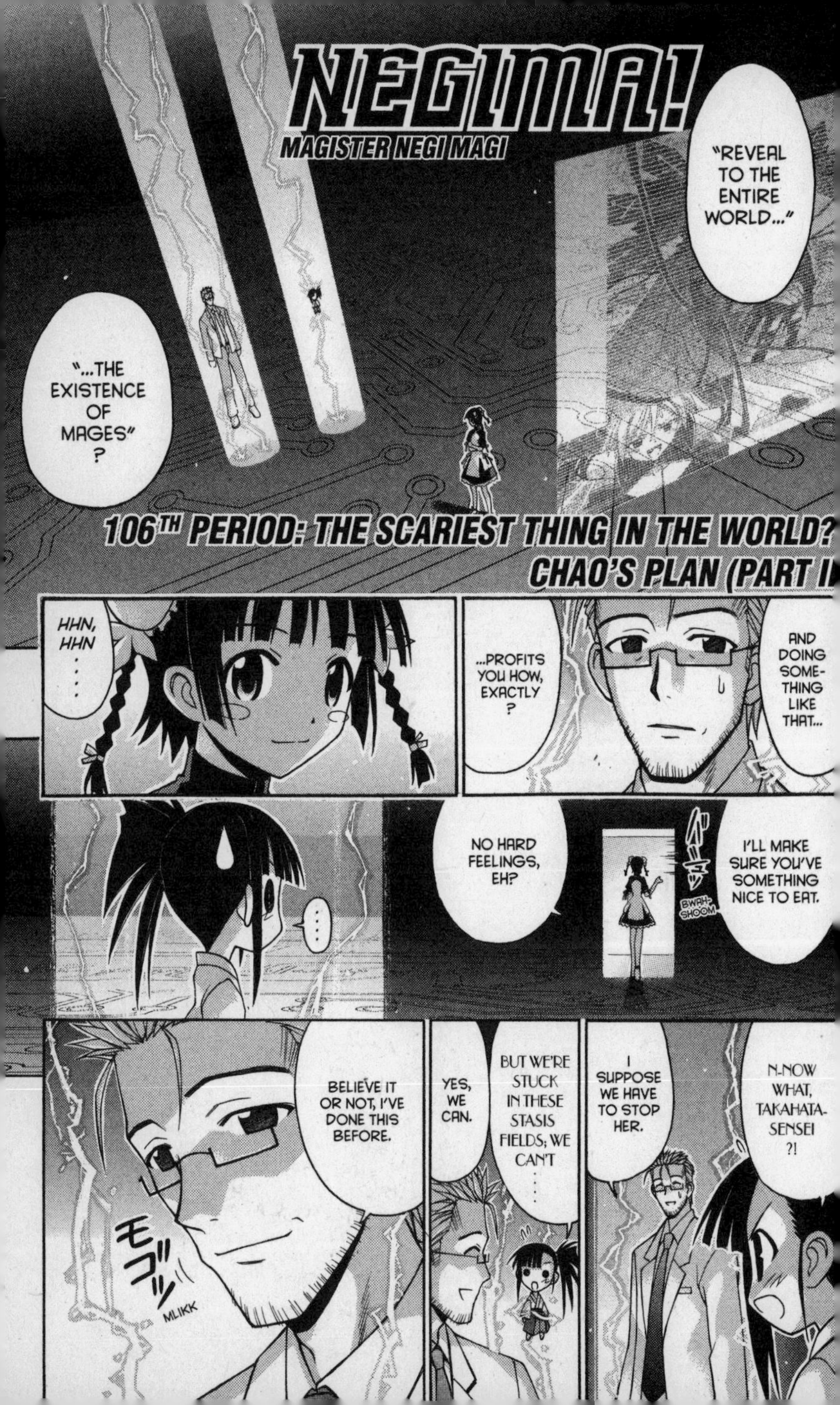
NEGIMA!
MAGISTER NEGI MAGI
"REVEAL TO THE ENTIRE WORLD..."
"...THE EXISTENCE OF MAGES" ?
106TH PERIOD: THE SCARIEST THING IN THE WORLD?
CHAO'S PLAN (PART I
AND DOING SOMETHING LIKE THAT...
...PROFITS YOU HOW, EXACTLY ?
HHN, HHN ....
I'LL MAKE SURE YOU'VE SOMETHING NICE TO EAT.
BWAH-SHOOM
NO HARD FEELINGS, EH?
....
N-NOW WHAT, TAKAHATA-SENSEI ?!
I SUPPOSE WE HAVE TO STOP HER.
BUT WE'RE STUCK IN THESE STASIS FIELDS; WE CAN'T ...
YES, WE CAN.
BELIEVE IT OR NOT, I'VE DONE THIS BEFORE.
MLIKK

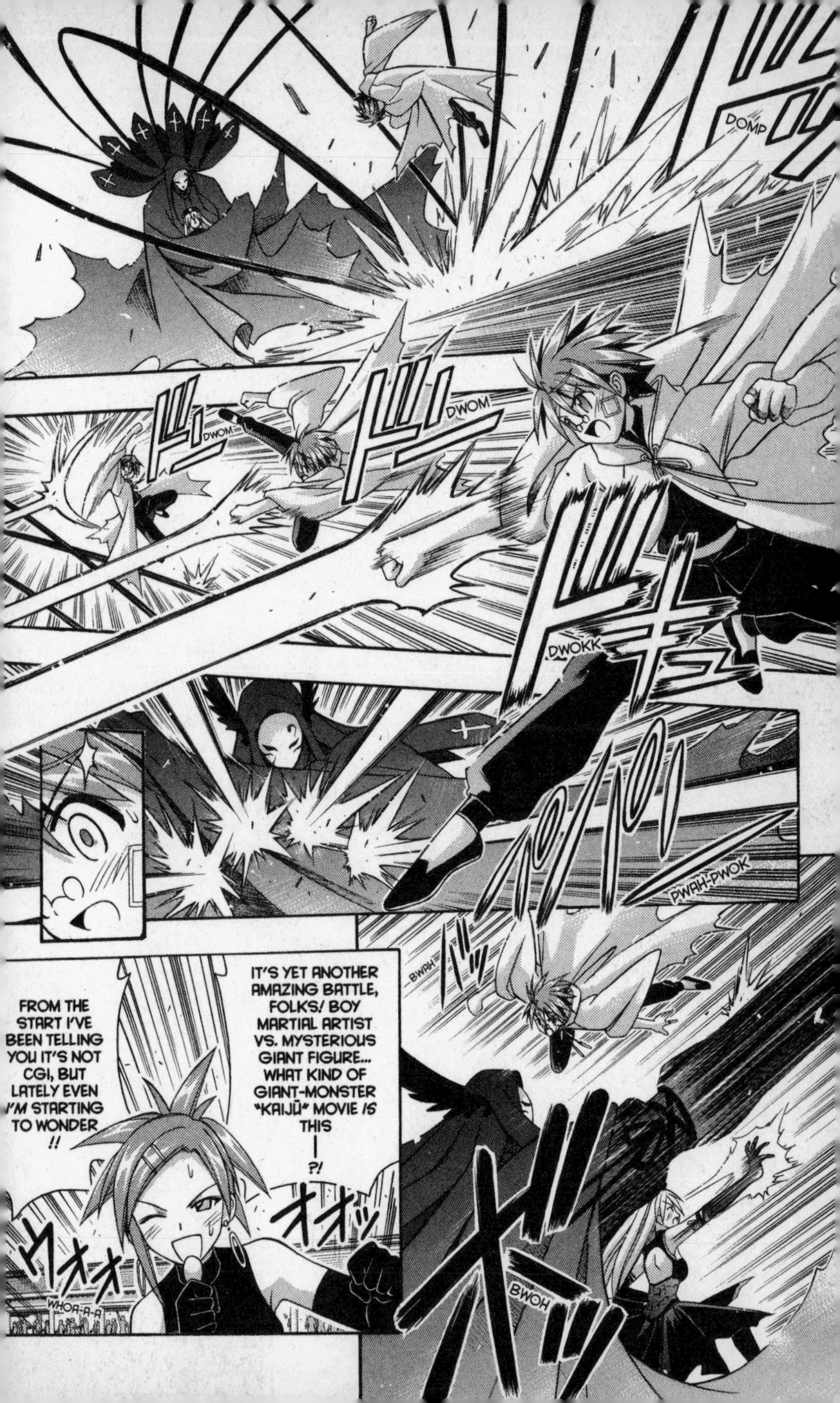
DOMP
DWOM
DWOM
DWOKK
PWAH-PWOK
BWAH
BWOH
IT'S YET ANOTHER AMAZING BATTLE, FOLKS! BOY MARTIAL ARTIST VS. MYSTERIOUS GIANT FIGURE... WHAT KIND OF GIANT-MONSTER "KAIJŪ" MOVIE *IS* THIS —?!
FROM THE START I'VE BEEN TELLING YOU IT'S NOT CGI, BUT LATELY EVEN *I'M* STARTING TO WONDER !!
オオッ
ウオオ
WHOA-A-A

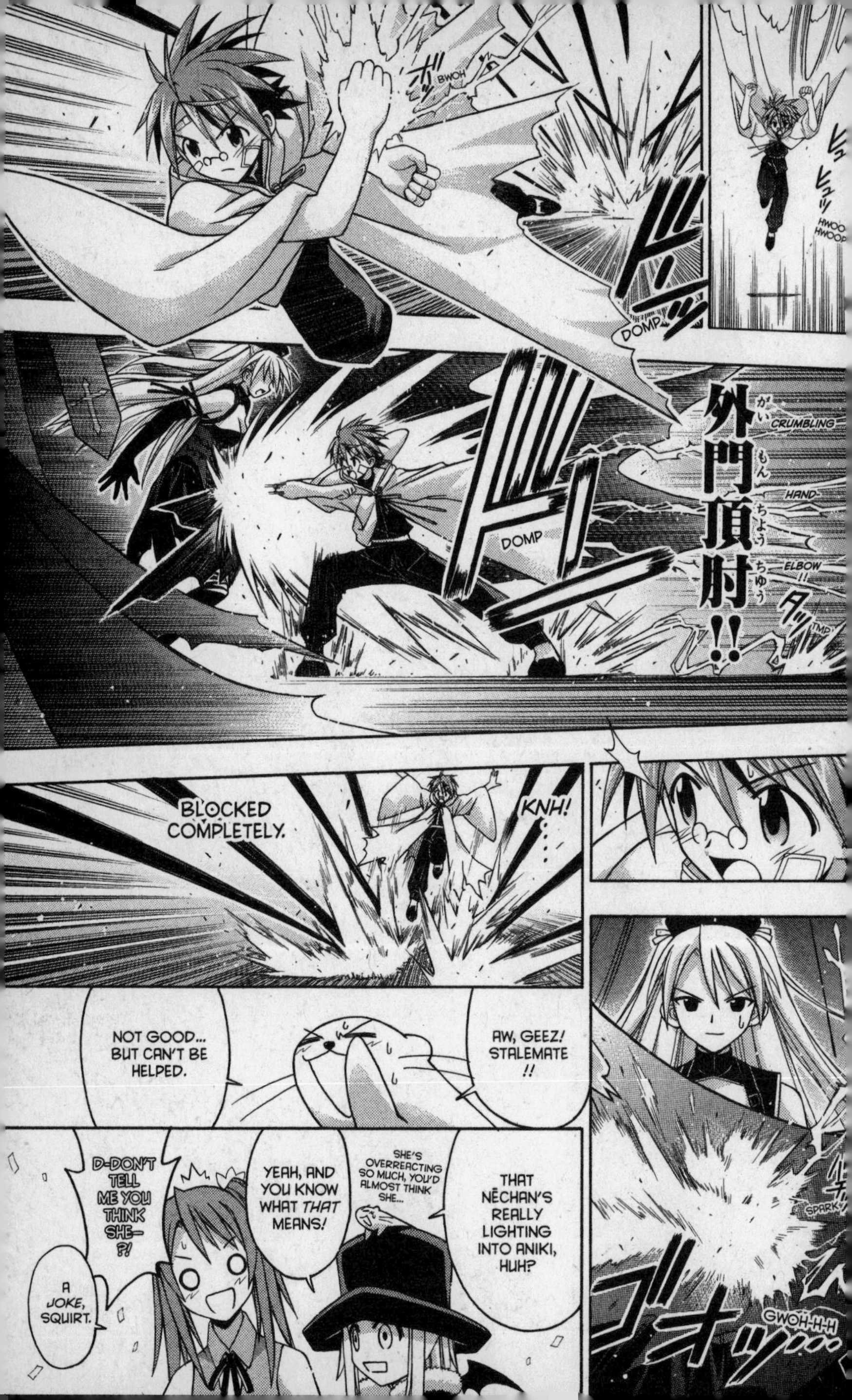
HWOOP HWOOP
BWOH
DOMP
外門頂肘!!
CRUMBLING HAND ELBOW!!
TMP
DOMP
KNH!
BLOCKED COMPLETELY.
SPARK
GWOH-H-H
AW, GEEZ! STALEMATE!!
NOT GOOD... BUT CAN'T BE HELPED.
THAT NĒCHAN'S REALLY LIGHTING INTO ANIKI, HUH?
SHE'S OVERREACTING SO MUCH, YOU'D ALMOST THINK SHE...
YEAH, AND YOU KNOW WHAT *THAT* MEANS!
D-DON'T TELL ME YOU THINK SHE—?!
A JOKE, SQUIRT.

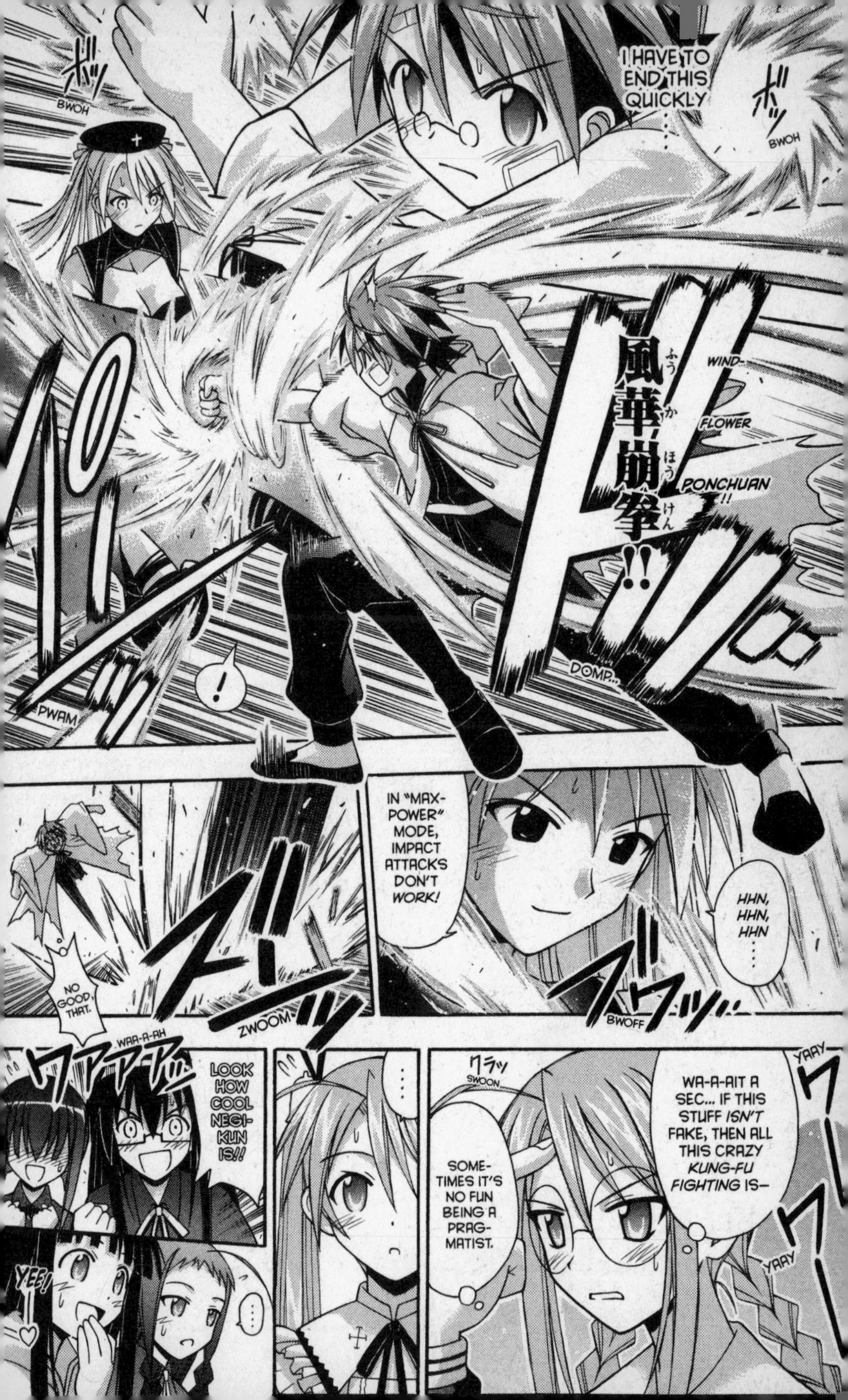
BWOH
I HAVE TO END THIS QUICKLY...
BWOH
風華崩拳!!
WIND-FLOWER PONCHUAN!!
DOMP...
!
PWAM
IN "MAX-POWER" MODE, IMPACT ATTACKS DON'T WORK!
HHN, HHN, HHN.....
BWOFF
ZWOOM
NO GOOD, THAT.
YAAY
WA-A-AIT A SEC... IF THIS STUFF ISN'T FAKE, THEN ALL THIS CRAZY KUNG-FU FIGHTING IS—
SWOON
YAAY
....
SOMETIMES IT'S NO FUN BEING A PRAGMATIST.
WAA-A-AH
LOOK HOW COOL NEGI-KUN IS!!
YEE! ♥
....

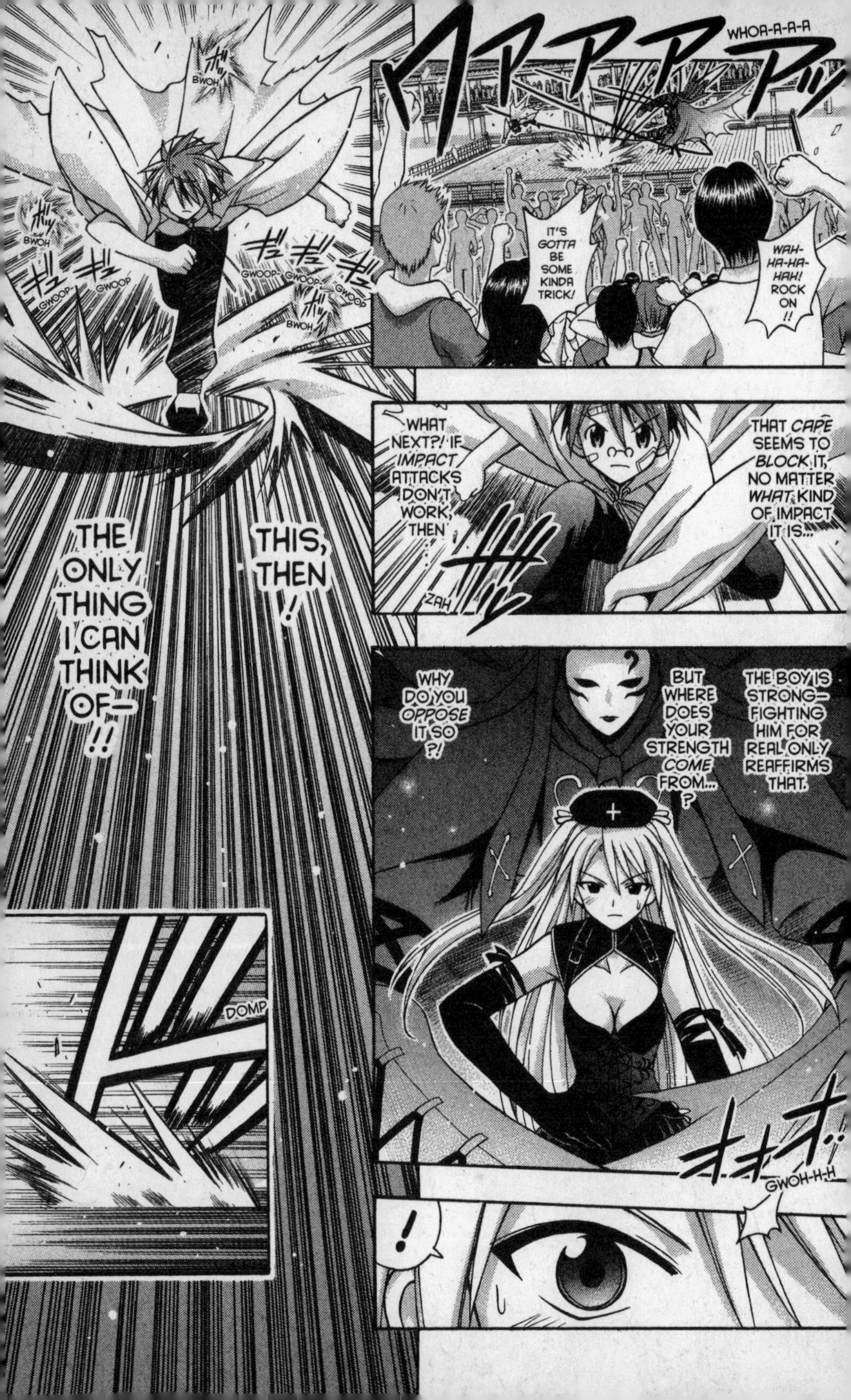
WHOA-A-A-A
WAH-HA-HA-HAH! ROCK ON!!
IT'S GOTTA BE SOME KINDA TRICK!
THAT CAPE SEEMS TO BLOCK IT, NO MATTER WHAT KIND OF IMPACT IT IS...
WHAT NEXT?! IF IMPACT ATTACKS DON'T WORK, THEN
ZAH
THE BOY IS STRONG—FIGHTING HIM FOR REAL ONLY REAFFIRMS THAT.
BUT WHERE DOES YOUR STRENGTH COME FROM...?
WHY DO YOU OPPOSE IT SO?!
GWOH-H-H
BWOH
BWOH
GWOOP GWOOP GWOOP GWOOP GWOOP
BWOH
THIS, THEN!
THE ONLY THING I CAN THINK OF—!!
!
DOMP

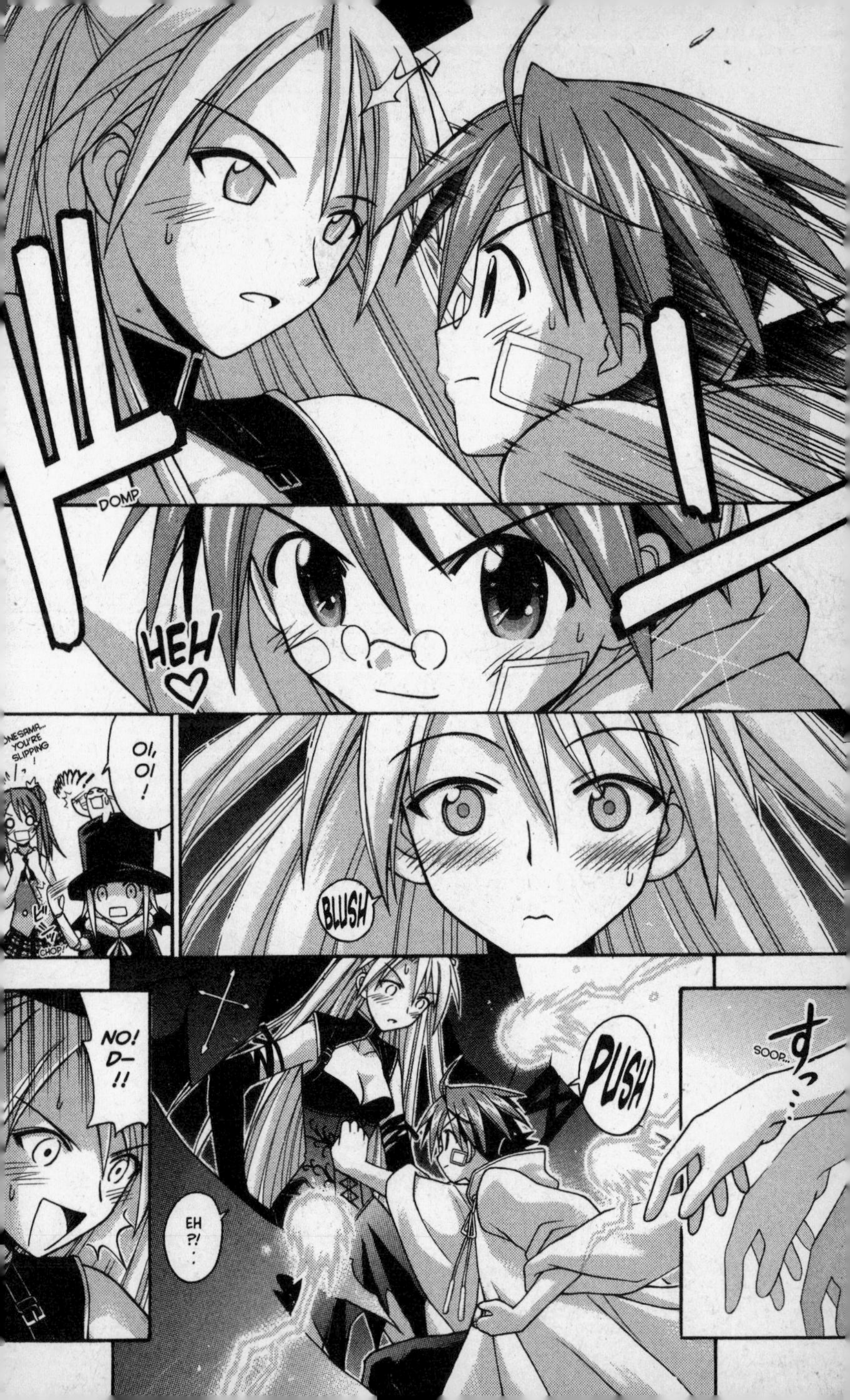
DOMP
HEH ♥
BLUSH
OI, OI!
ONESAMA... YOU'RE SLIPPING
CHOP!
SOOP...
す…
PUSH
EH ?!..
NO! D—!!

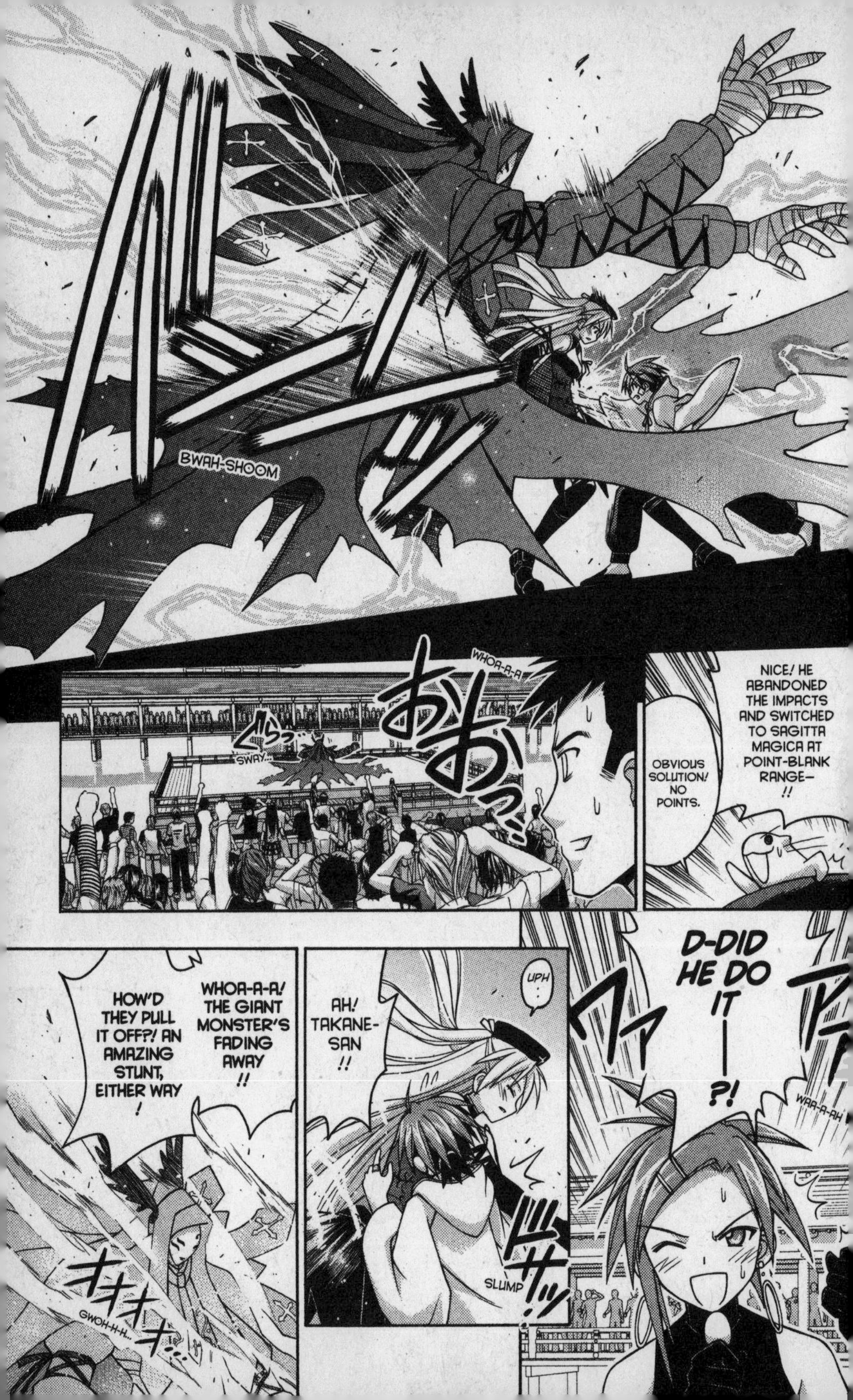
BWAH-SHOOM
NICE! HE ABANDONED THE IMPACTS AND SWITCHED TO SAGITTA MAGICA AT POINT-BLANK RANGE—!!
OBVIOUS SOLUTION! NO POINTS.
WHOA-A-A
SWAY...
D-DID HE DO IT—?!
WAA-A-AH
UPH
AH! TAKANE-SAN!!
SLUMP
WHOA-A-A! THE GIANT MONSTER'S FADING AWAY!!
HOW'D THEY PULL IT OFF?! AN AMAZING STUNT, EITHER WAY!
GWOH-H-H...

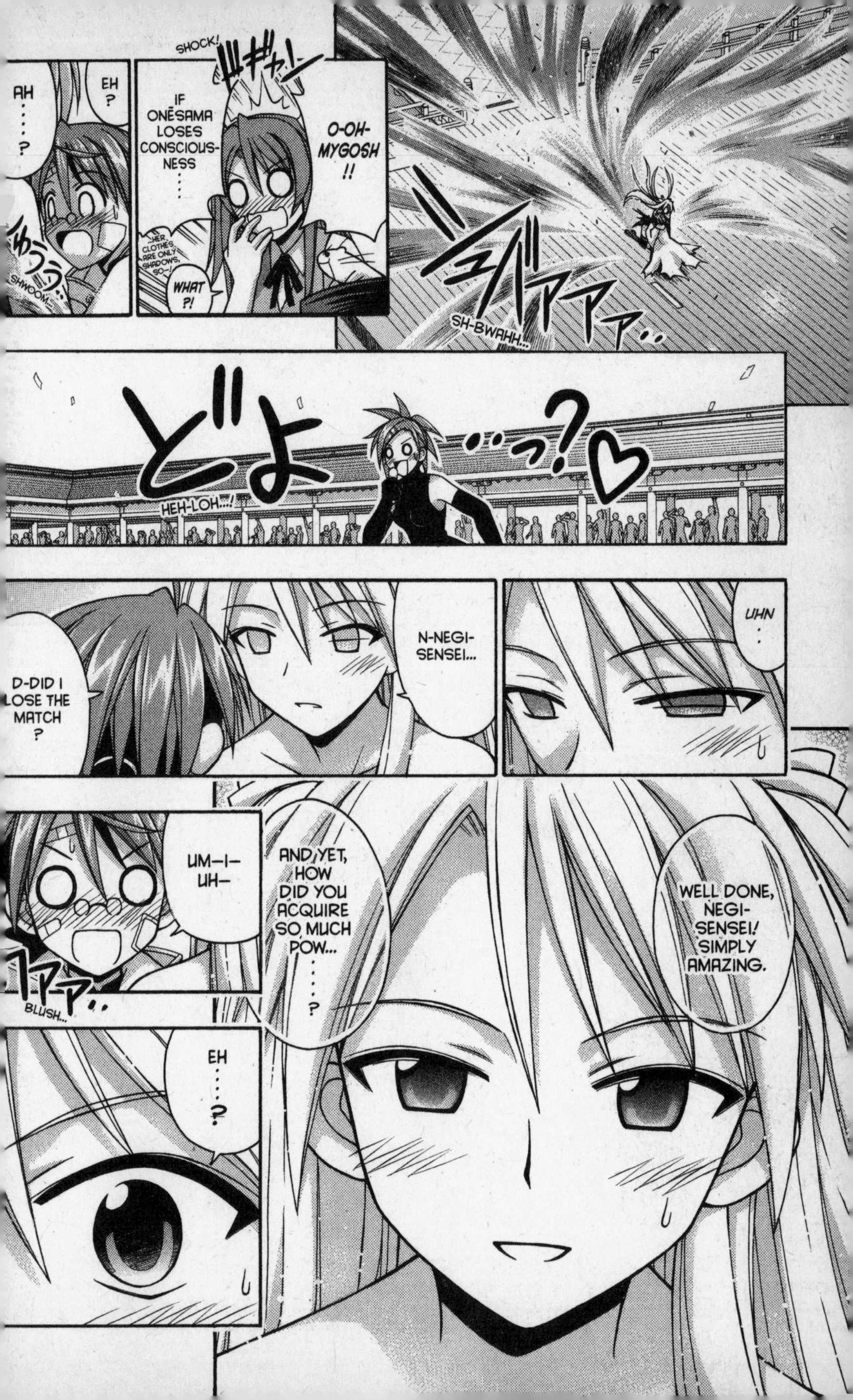
SH-BWAHH...
SHOCK!
IF ONĒSAMA LOSES CONSCIOUSNESS....
O-OH-MYGOSH!!
...HER CLOTHES ARE ONLY SHADOWS, SO—!
WHAT?!
EH?
AH....?
SHWOOM...
どよっ?
HEH-LOH...!
UHN..
N-NEGI-SENSEI...
D-DID I LOSE THE MATCH?
WELL DONE, NEGI-SENSEI! SIMPLY AMAZING.
AND YET, HOW DID YOU ACQUIRE SO MUCH POW.....?
UM—I—UH—
BLUSH...
EH....?

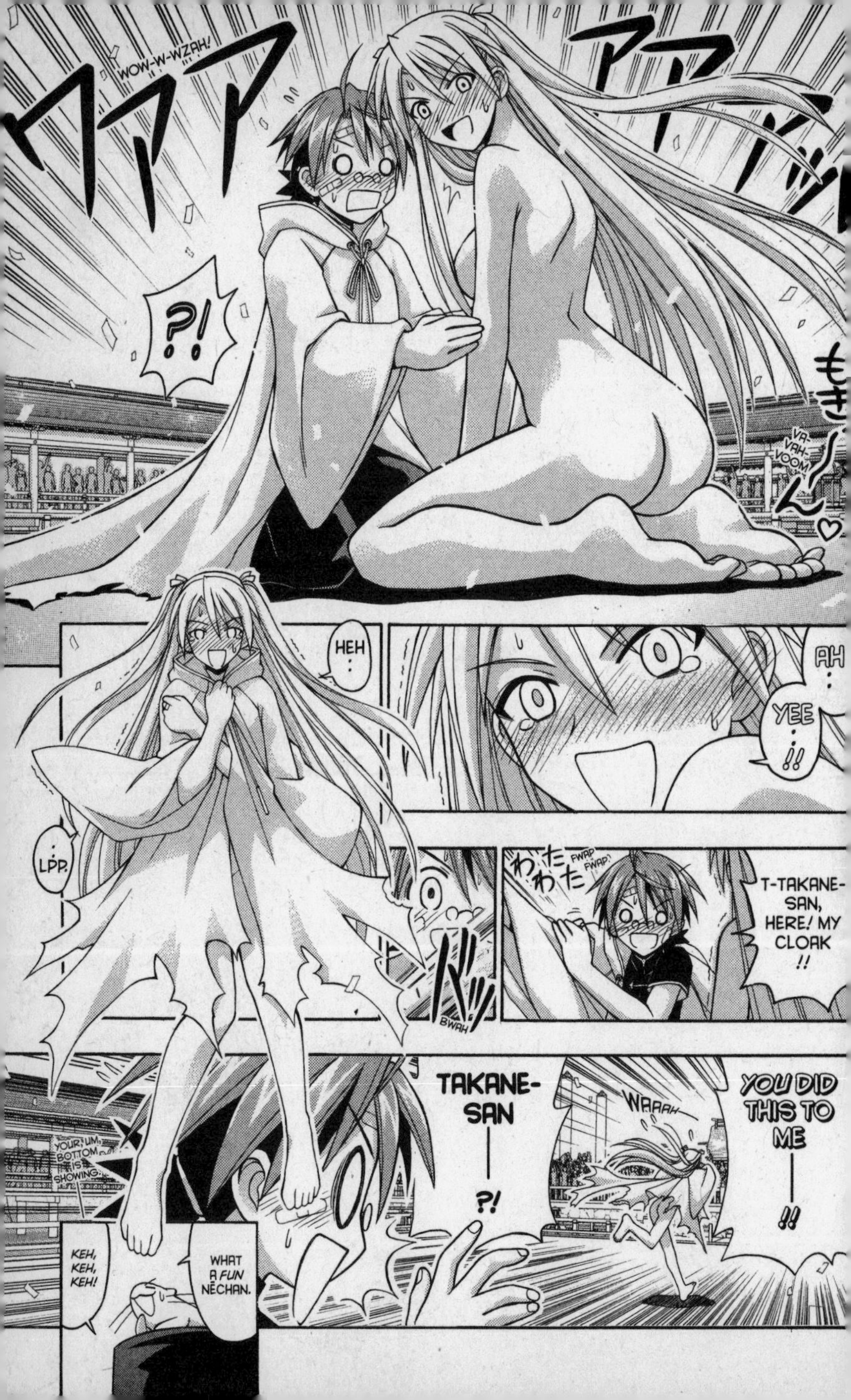

WOW-W-WZAH!
?!
VA-VAH-VOOM
AH... YEE...!!
HEH...
...LPP.
T-TAKANE-SAN, HERE! MY CLOAK!!
FWAP FWAP
BWAH
YOU DID THIS TO ME—!!
WAAAH
TAKANE-SAN—?!
YOUR, UM, BOTTOM IS SHOWING.
WHAT A FUN NÊCHAN.
KEH, KEH, KEH!

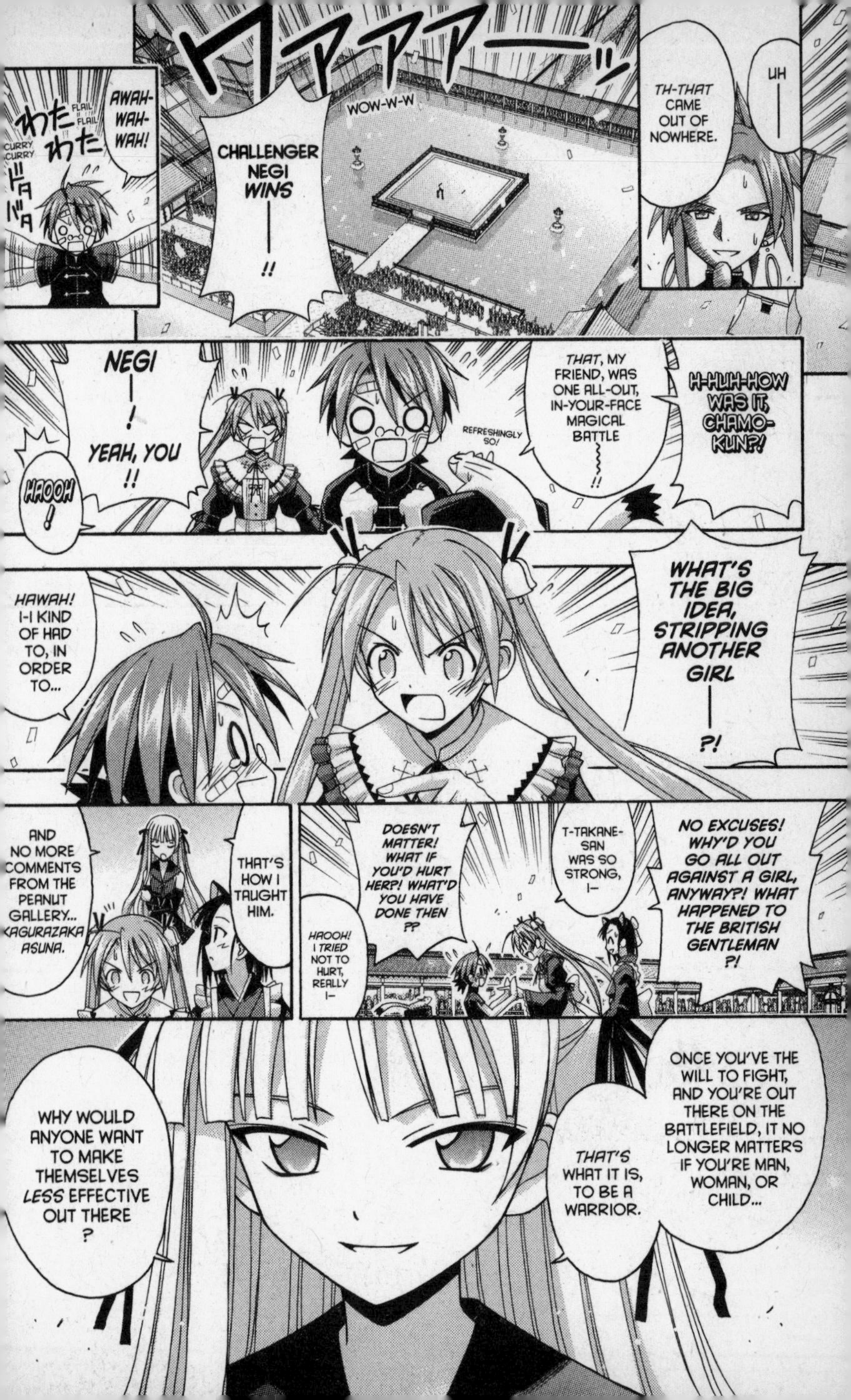
UH—
TH-THAT CAME OUT OF NOWHERE.
ワァァァーッ
WOW-W-W
CHALLENGER NEGI WINS—!!
AWAH-WAH-WAH!
わたわた
FLAIL FLAIL
ドタバタ
SCURRY SCURRY
H-HUH-HOW WAS IT, CHAMO-KUN?!
THAT, MY FRIEND, WAS ONE ALL-OUT, IN-YOUR-FACE MAGICAL BATTLE~!!
REFRESHINGLY SO!
NEGI—! YEAH, YOU!!
HAOOH!
WHAT'S THE BIG IDEA, STRIPPING ANOTHER GIRL—?!
HAWAH! I-I KIND OF HAD TO, IN ORDER TO...
NO EXCUSES! WHY'D YOU GO ALL OUT AGAINST A GIRL, ANYWAY?! WHAT HAPPENED TO THE BRITISH GENTLEMAN?!
T-TAKANE-SAN WAS SO STRONG, I—
DOESN'T MATTER! WHAT IF YOU'D HURT HER?! WHAT'D YOU HAVE DONE THEN??
HAOOH! I TRIED NOT TO HURT, REALLY I—
THAT'S HOW I TAUGHT HIM.
AND NO MORE COMMENTS FROM THE PEANUT GALLERY... KAGURAZAKA ASUNA.
ONCE YOU'VE THE WILL TO FIGHT, AND YOU'RE OUT THERE ON THE BATTLEFIELD, IT NO LONGER MATTERS IF YOU'RE MAN, WOMAN, OR CHILD...
THAT'S WHAT IT IS, TO BE A WARRIOR.
WHY WOULD ANYONE WANT TO MAKE THEMSELVES LESS EFFECTIVE OUT THERE?

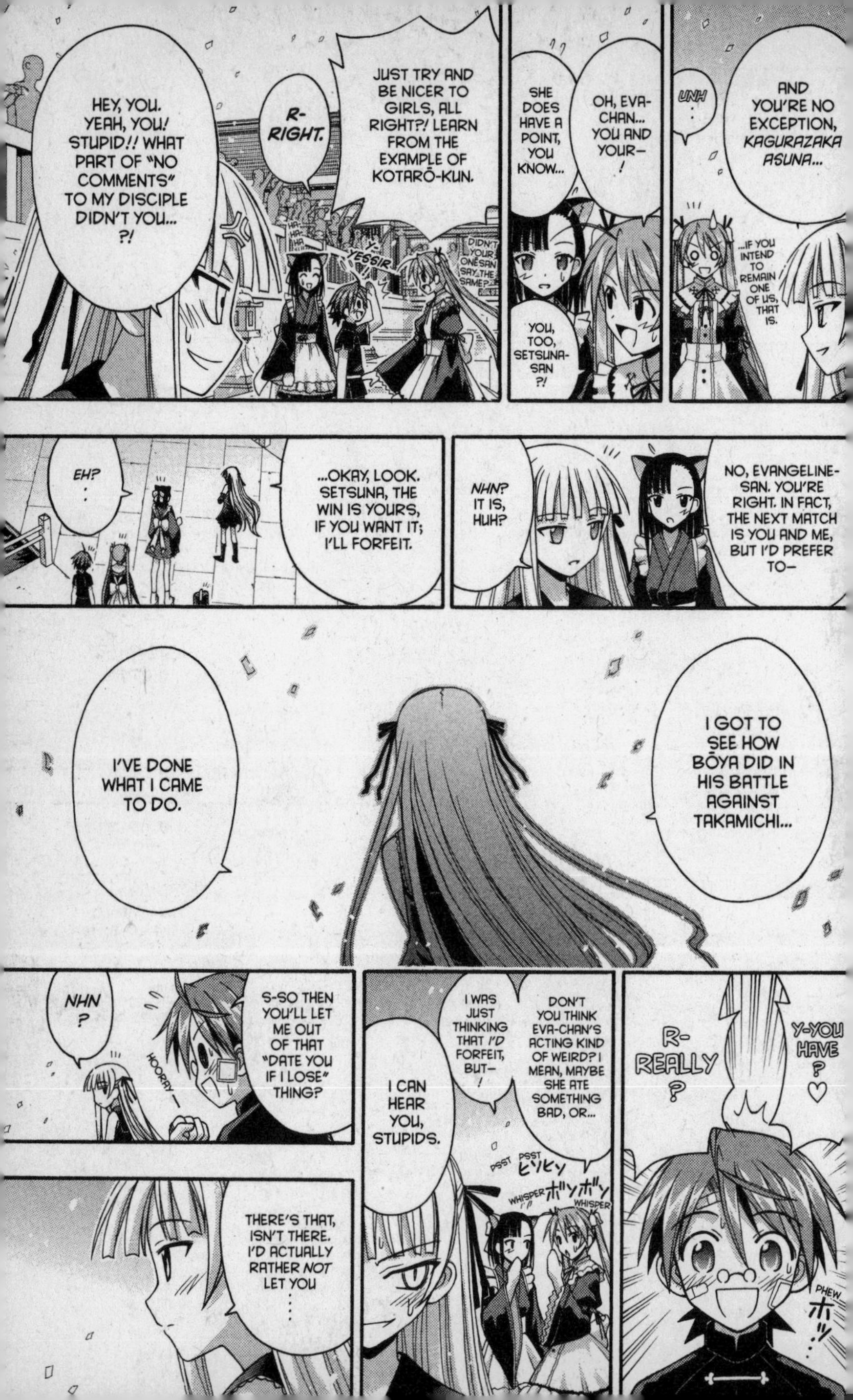
AND YOU'RE NO EXCEPTION, KAGURAZAKA ASUNA...
...IF YOU INTEND TO REMAIN ONE OF US, THAT IS.
UNH
OH, EVA-CHAN... YOU AND YOUR—!
SHE DOES HAVE A POINT, YOU KNOW...
YOU, TOO, SETSUNA-SAN?!
JUST TRY AND BE NICER TO GIRLS, ALL RIGHT?! LEARN FROM THE EXAMPLE OF KOTARŌ-KUN.
R-RIGHT.
DIDN'T YOUR ONĒSAN SAY THE SAME?
Y-YESSIR
HA HA HA
HEY, YOU. YEAH, YOU! STUPID!! WHAT PART OF "NO COMMENTS" TO MY DISCIPLE DIDN'T YOU...?!
NO, EVANGELINE-SAN. YOU'RE RIGHT. IN FACT, THE NEXT MATCH IS YOU AND ME, BUT I'D PREFER TO—
NHN? IT IS, HUH?
...OKAY, LOOK. SETSUNA, THE WIN IS YOURS, IF YOU WANT IT; I'LL FORFEIT.
EH?
I GOT TO SEE HOW BŌYA DID IN HIS BATTLE AGAINST TAKAMICHI...
I'VE DONE WHAT I CAME TO DO.
Y-YOU HAVE? ♥
R-REALLY?
PHEW ホッ
DON'T YOU THINK EVA-CHAN'S ACTING KIND OF WEIRD? I MEAN, MAYBE SHE ATE SOMETHING BAD, OR...
I WAS JUST THINKING THAT I'D FORFEIT, BUT—!
PSST PSST ヒソヒソ
WHISPER ボソボソ WHISPER
I CAN HEAR YOU, STUPIDS.
S-SO THEN YOU'LL LET ME OUT OF THAT "DATE YOU IF I LOSE" THING?
HOORAY
NHN?
THERE'S THAT, ISN'T THERE. I'D ACTUALLY RATHER NOT LET YOU ....

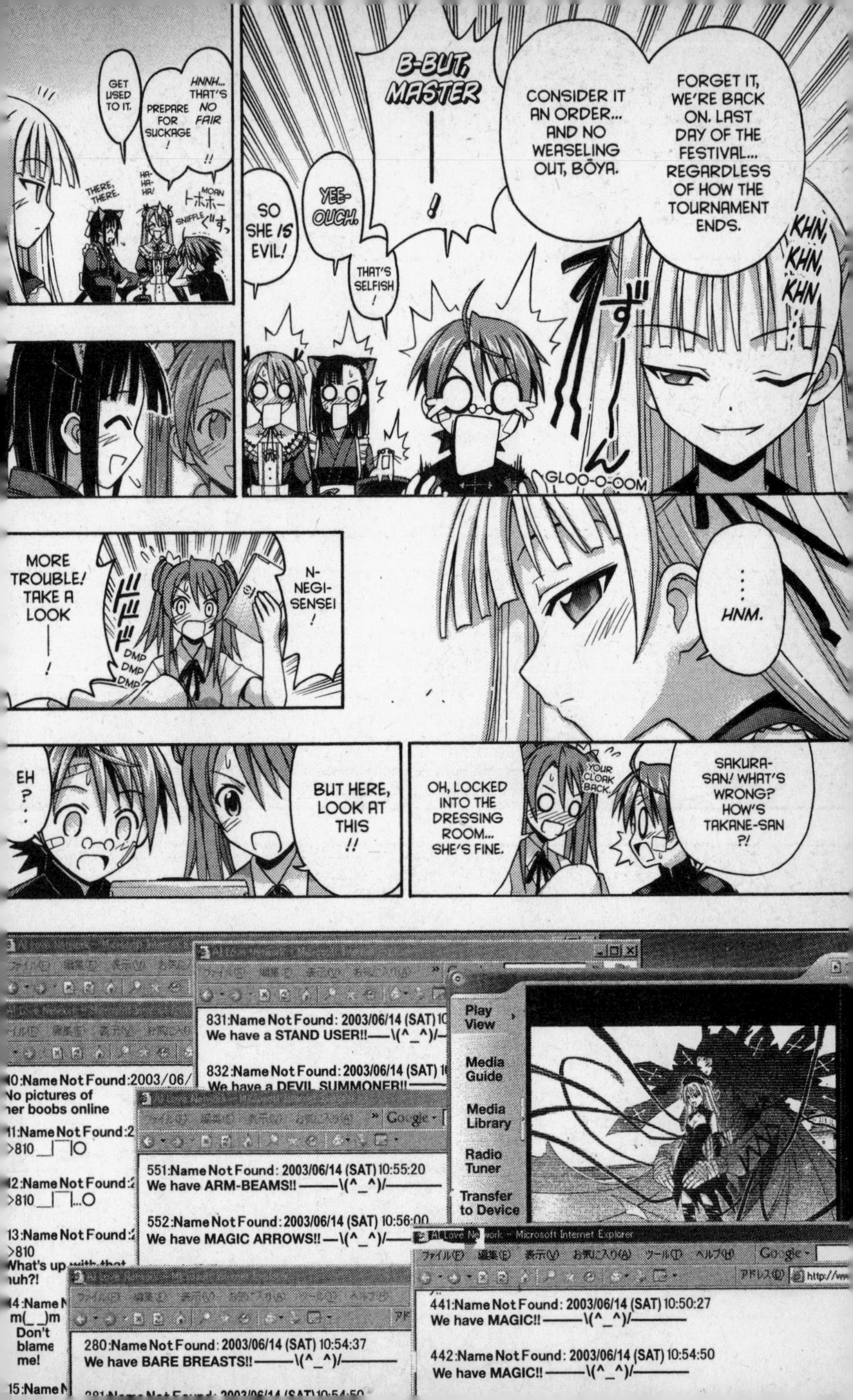
FORGET IT, WE'RE BACK ON. LAST DAY OF THE FESTIVAL... REGARDLESS OF HOW THE TOURNAMENT ENDS.
CONSIDER IT AN ORDER... AND NO WEASELING OUT, BŌYA.
KHN, KHN, KHN...
B-BUT, MASTER—!
YEE-OUCH.
SO SHE IS EVIL!
THAT'S SELFISH!
ずーん
GLOO-O-OOM
HNNH... THAT'S NO FAIR—!!
GET USED TO IT.
PREPARE FOR SUCKAGE!
THERE, THERE.
HA-HA-HA!
MOAN トホホー
SNIFFLE ぐすっ
...HNM.
N-NEGI-SENSEI!
MORE TROUBLE! TAKE A LOOK—!
ドドド
DMP DMP DMP
SAKURA-SAN! WHAT'S WRONG? HOW'S TAKANE-SAN?!
YOUR CLOAK BACK.
OH, LOCKED INTO THE DRESSING ROOM... SHE'S FINE.
BUT HERE, LOOK AT THIS!!
EH?...
Play View
Media Guide
Media Library
Radio Tuner
Transfer to Device
831:Name Not Found: 2003/06/14 (SAT) 1
We have a STAND USER!!—\(^_^)/—
832:Name Not Found: 2003/06/14 (SAT) 1
We have a DEVIL SUMMONER!!
10:Name Not Found:2003/06/
No pictures of her boobs online
11:Name Not Found:2
>810 _|￣|○
12:Name Not Found:2
>810 _|￣|...○
13:Name Not Found:2
>810
What's up with that huh?!
14:Name N
m(_ _)m
Don't blame me!
15:Name N
551:Name Not Found: 2003/06/14 (SAT) 10:55:20
We have ARM-BEAMS!! ———\(^_^)/———
552:Name Not Found: 2003/06/14 (SAT) 10:56:00
We have MAGIC ARROWS!! —\(^_^)/—
AI Love Network - Microsoft Internet Explorer
441:Name Not Found: 2003/06/14 (SAT) 10:50:27
We have MAGIC!! ———\(^_^)/———
442:Name Not Found: 2003/06/14 (SAT) 10:54:50
We have MAGIC!! ———\(^_^)/———
280:Name Not Found: 2003/06/14 (SAT) 10:54:37
We have BARE BREASTS!! ———\(^_^)/———

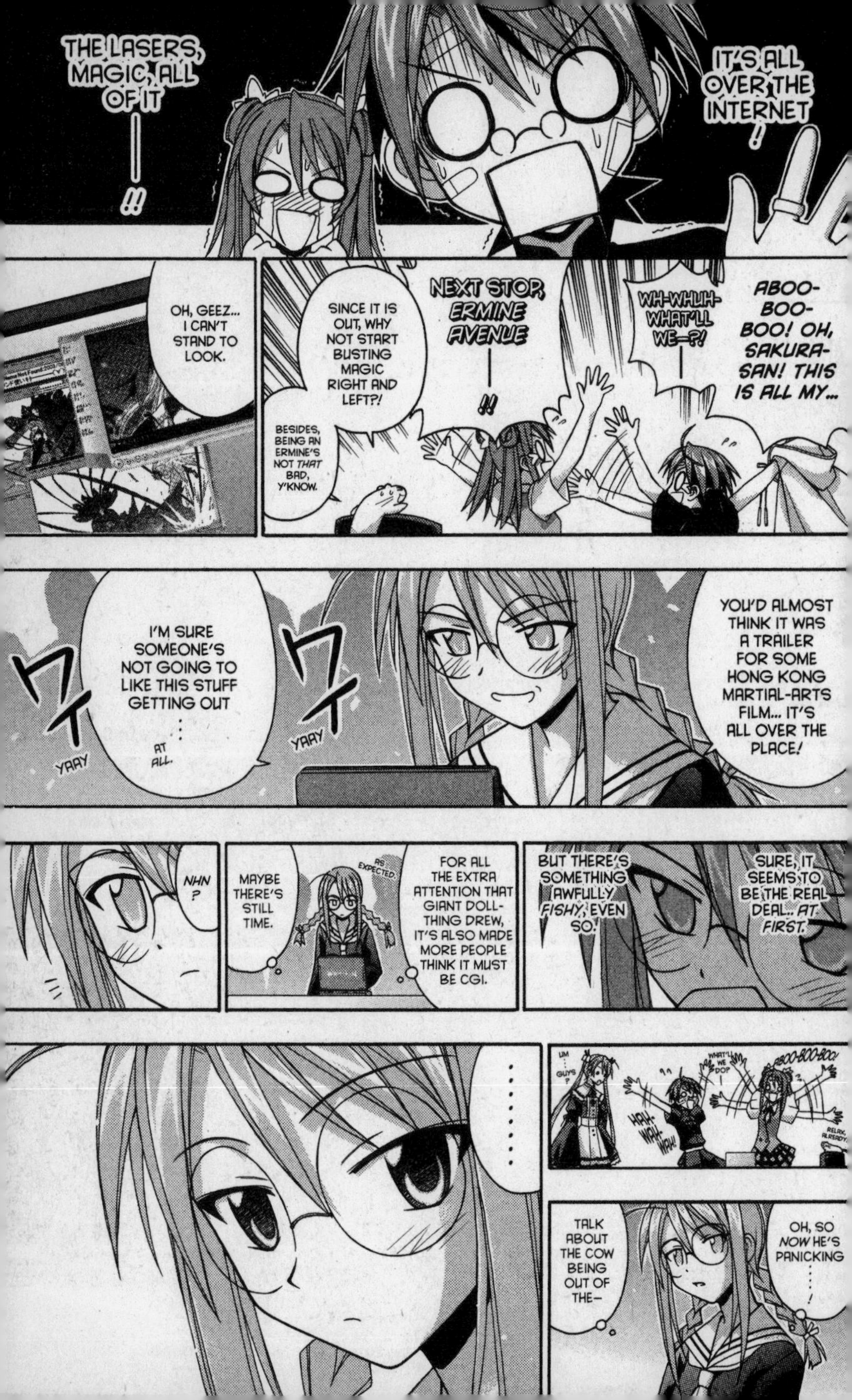
IT'S ALL OVER THE INTERNET!
THE LASERS, MAGIC, ALL OF IT——!!
ABOO-BOO-BOO! OH, SAKURA-SAN! THIS IS ALL MY...
WH-WHUH-WHAT'LL WE—?!
NEXT STOP, ERMINE AVENUE—!!
SINCE IT IS OUT, WHY NOT START BUSTING MAGIC RIGHT AND LEFT?!
BESIDES, BEING AN ERMINE'S NOT THAT BAD, Y'KNOW.
OH, GEEZ... I CAN'T STAND TO LOOK.
YOU'D ALMOST THINK IT WAS A TRAILER FOR SOME HONG KONG MARTIAL-ARTS FILM... IT'S ALL OVER THE PLACE!
YAAY
I'M SURE SOMEONE'S NOT GOING TO LIKE THIS STUFF GETTING OUT... AT ALL.
YAAY
SURE, IT SEEMS TO BE THE REAL DEAL.. AT FIRST.
BUT THERE'S SOMETHING AWFULLY FISHY, EVEN SO.
FOR ALL THE EXTRA ATTENTION THAT GIANT DOLL-THING DREW, IT'S ALSO MADE MORE PEOPLE THINK IT MUST BE CGI.
AS EXPECTED.
MAYBE THERE'S STILL TIME.
NHN?
ABOO-BOO-BOO!
WHAT'LL WE DO?!
WAH-WAH-WAH!
UM... GUYS?
RELAX, ALREADY.
OH, SO NOW HE'S PANICKING......!
TALK ABOUT THE COW BEING OUT OF THE—
......

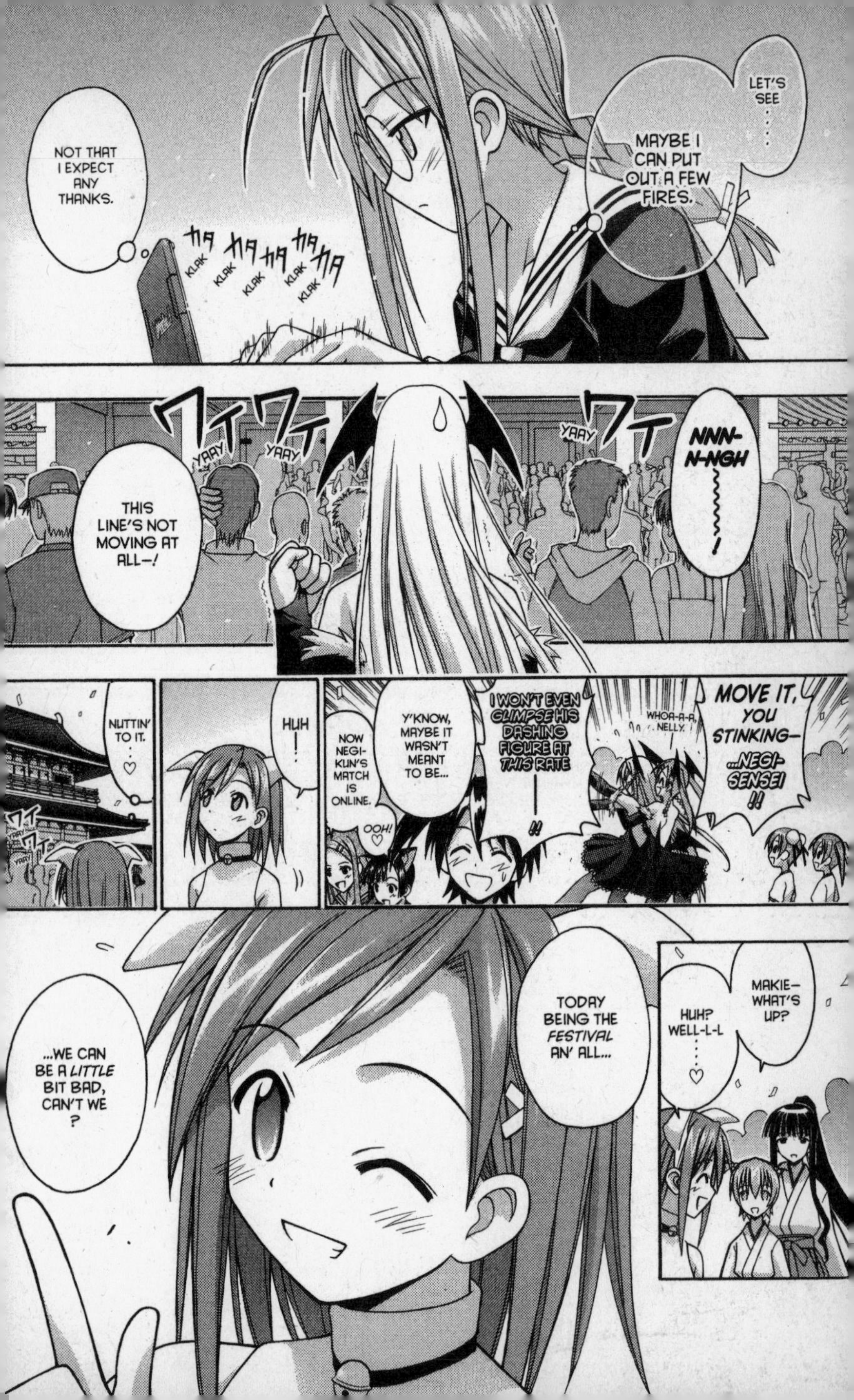
LET'S SEE . . . .
MAYBE I CAN PUT OUT A FEW FIRES.
KLAK KLAK KLAK KLAK KLAK
NOT THAT I EXPECT ANY THANKS.
NNNN-N-NGH ~~~!
YAAY YAAY YAAY
THIS LINE'S NOT MOVING AT ALL—!
MOVE IT, YOU STINKING— ...NEGI-SENSEI!!
WHOA-A-A, NELLY.
I WON'T EVEN GLIMPSE HIS DASHING FIGURE AT THIS RATE—!!
Y'KNOW, MAYBE IT WASN'T MEANT TO BE...
NOW NEGI-KUN'S MATCH IS ONLINE.
OOH! ♡
HUH!
NUTTIN' TO IT. . . . ♡
YAAY YAAY
MAKIE—WHAT'S UP?
HUH? WELL-L-L . . . . ♡
TODAY BEING THE FESTIVAL AN' ALL...
...WE CAN BE A LITTLE BIT BAD, CAN'T WE?

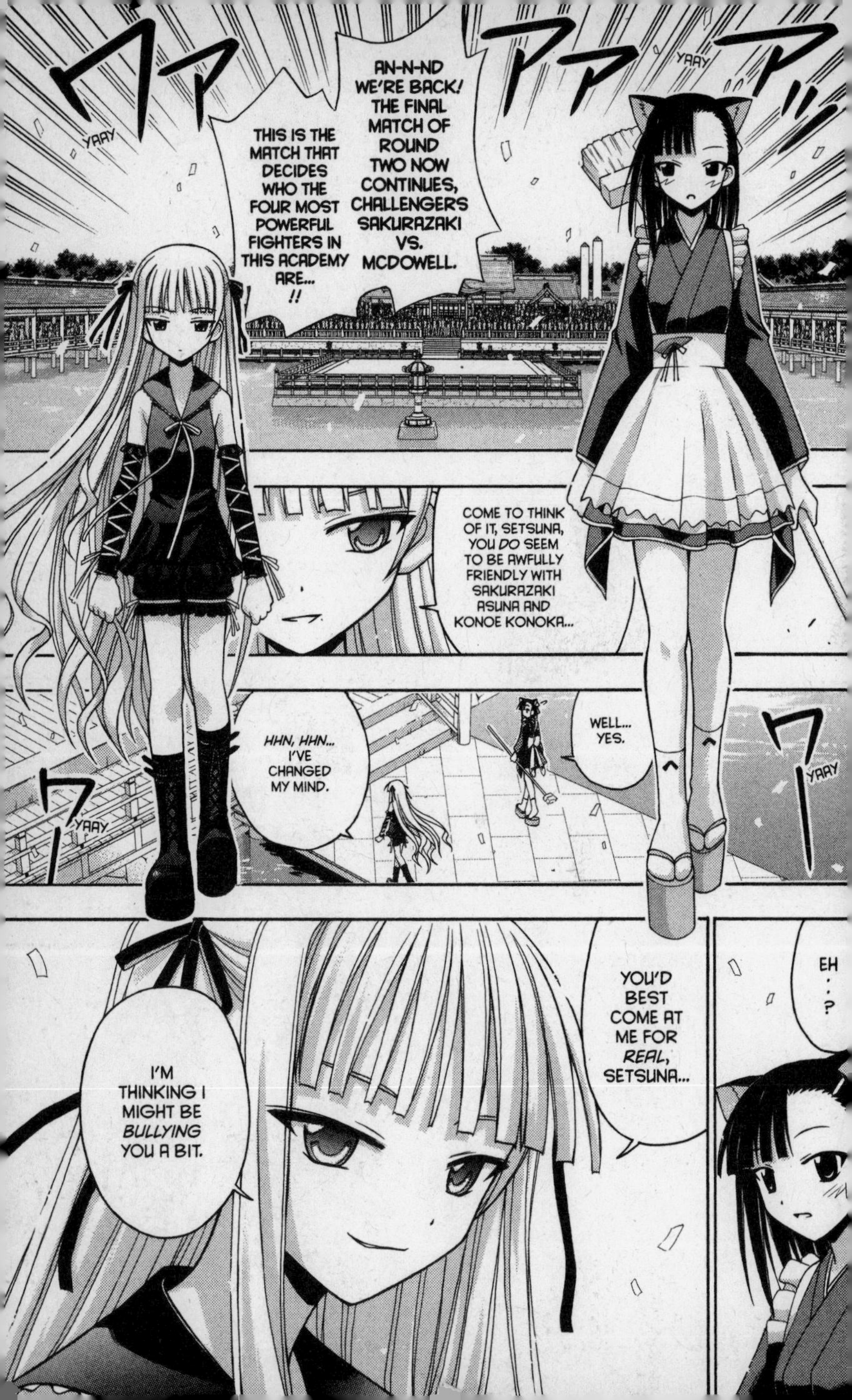
YAAY
AN-N-ND WE'RE BACK! THE FINAL MATCH OF ROUND TWO NOW CONTINUES, CHALLENGERS SAKURAZAKI VS. MCDOWELL.
THIS IS THE MATCH THAT DECIDES WHO THE FOUR MOST POWERFUL FIGHTERS IN THIS ACADEMY ARE... !!
YAAY
COME TO THINK OF IT, SETSUNA, YOU *DO* SEEM TO BE AWFULLY FRIENDLY WITH SAKURAZAKI ASUNA AND KONOE KONOKA...
YAAY
WELL... YES.
HHN, HHN... I'VE CHANGED MY MIND.
YAAY
EH...?
YOU'D BEST COME AT ME FOR *REAL*, SETSUNA...
I'M THINKING I MIGHT BE *BULLYING* YOU A BIT.

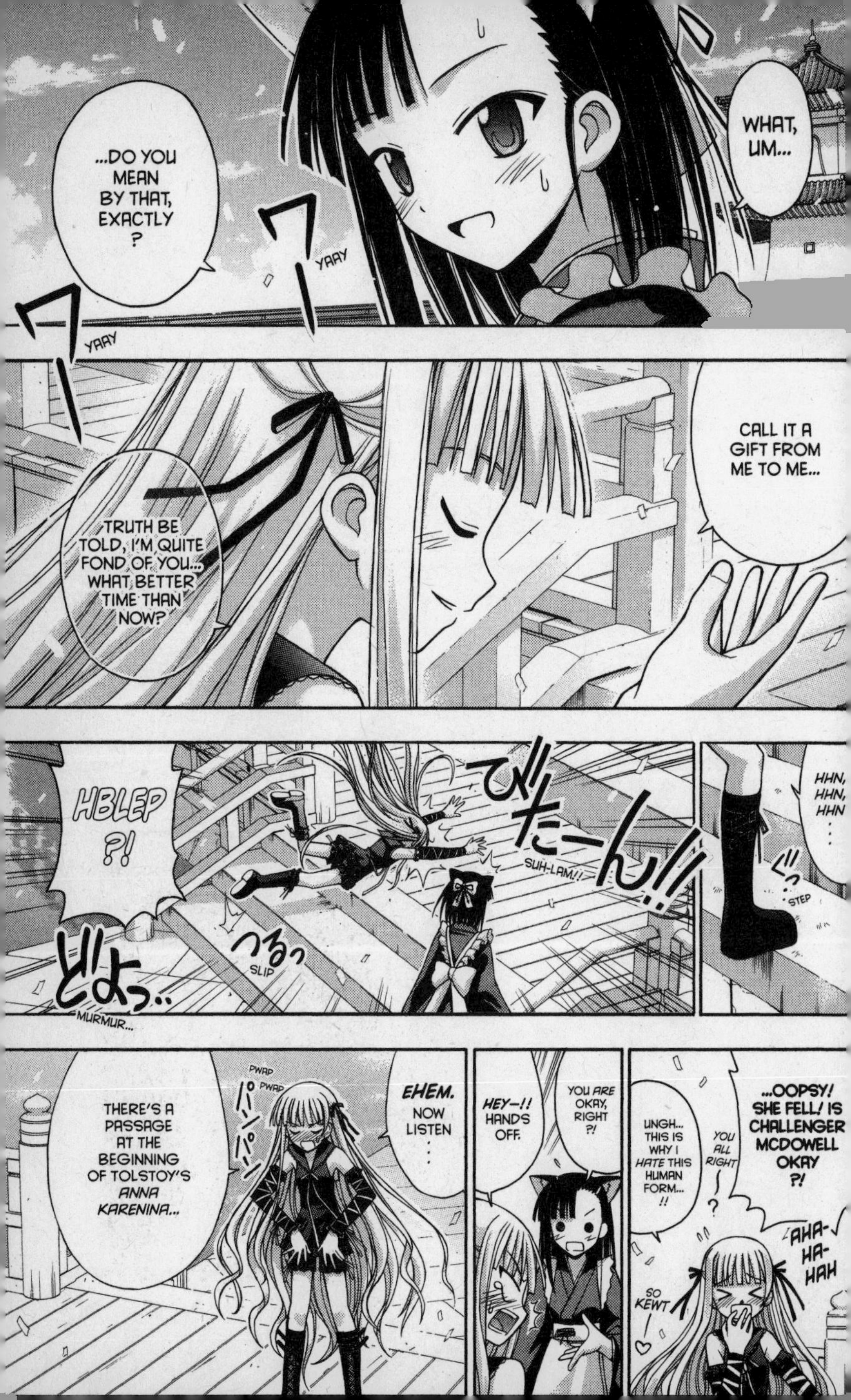
WHAT, UM...
...DO YOU MEAN BY THAT, EXACTLY?
YAAY
YAAY
CALL IT A GIFT FROM ME TO ME...
TRUTH BE TOLD, I'M QUITE FOND OF YOU... WHAT BETTER TIME THAN NOW?
HHN, HHN, HHN...
STEP
SUH-LAM!!
SLIP
HBLEP?!
MURMUR...
...OOPSY! SHE FELL! IS CHALLENGER MCDOWELL OKAY?!
AHA-HA-HAH
YOU ALL RIGHT?
SO KEWT!
UNGH... THIS IS WHY I HATE THIS HUMAN FORM...!!
YOU ARE OKAY, RIGHT?!
HEY—!! HANDS OFF.
EHEM. NOW LISTEN...
PWAP PWAP
THERE'S A PASSAGE AT THE BEGINNING OF TOLSTOY'S ANNA KARENINA...

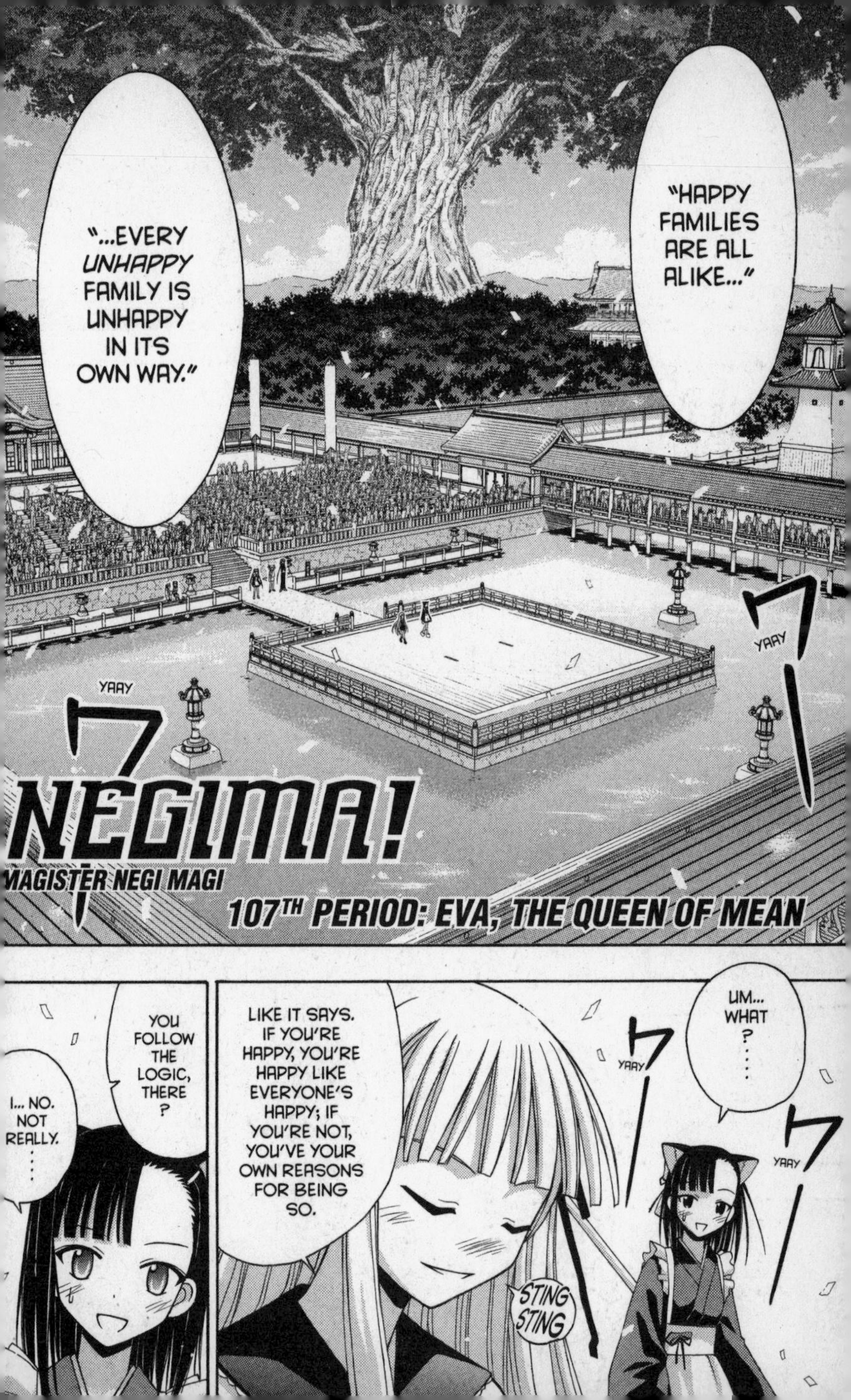
"HAPPY FAMILIES ARE ALL ALIKE..."
"...EVERY *UNHAPPY* FAMILY IS UNHAPPY IN ITS OWN WAY."
YAAY
YAAY
NEGIMA!
MAGISTER NEGI MAGI
107TH PERIOD: EVA, THE QUEEN OF MEAN
UM... WHAT ? ....
YAAY
YAAY
LIKE IT SAYS. IF YOU'RE HAPPY, YOU'RE HAPPY LIKE EVERYONE'S HAPPY; IF YOU'RE NOT, YOU'VE YOUR OWN REASONS FOR BEING SO.
STING STING
YOU FOLLOW THE LOGIC, THERE ?
I... NO. NOT REALLY. ....

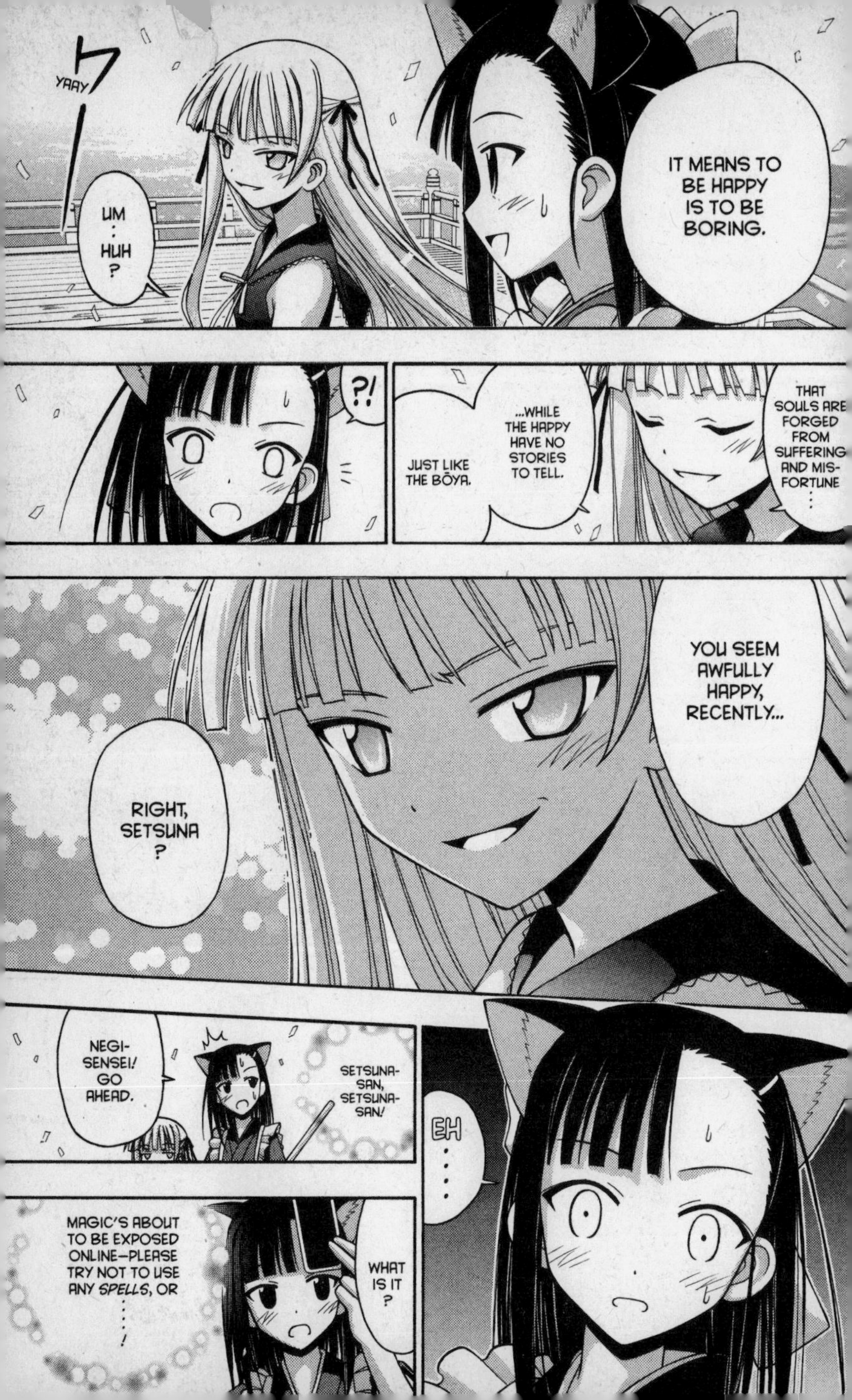
IT MEANS TO BE HAPPY IS TO BE BORING.
YAAY
UM : HUH ?
THAT SOULS ARE FORGED FROM SUFFERING AND MIS-FORTUNE . . .
...WHILE THE HAPPY HAVE NO STORIES TO TELL.
JUST LIKE THE BŌYA.
?!
YOU SEEM AWFULLY HAPPY, RECENTLY...
RIGHT, SETSUNA ?
EH . . . .
SETSUNA-SAN, SETSUNA-SAN!
NEGI-SENSEI! GO AHEAD.
WHAT IS IT ?
MAGIC'S ABOUT TO BE EXPOSED ONLINE—PLEASE TRY NOT TO USE ANY *SPELLS*, OR . . . . !

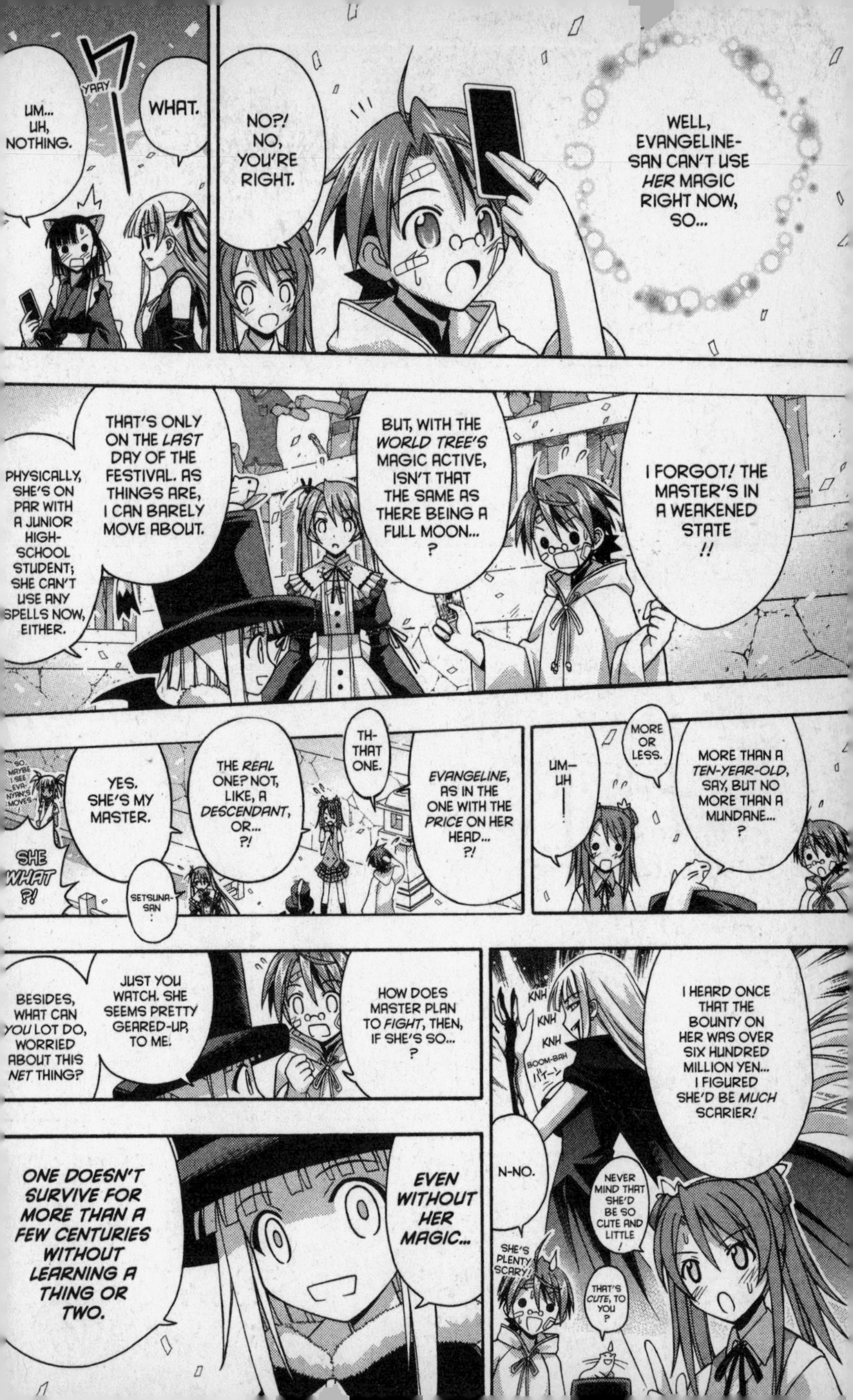
WELL, EVANGELINE-SAN CAN'T USE HER MAGIC RIGHT NOW, SO...
NO?! NO, YOU'RE RIGHT.
WHAT.
YAAY
UM... UH, NOTHING.
I FORGOT! THE MASTER'S IN A WEAKENED STATE !!
BUT, WITH THE WORLD TREE'S MAGIC ACTIVE, ISN'T THAT THE SAME AS THERE BEING A FULL MOON... ?
THAT'S ONLY ON THE LAST DAY OF THE FESTIVAL. AS THINGS ARE, I CAN BARELY MOVE ABOUT.
PHYSICALLY, SHE'S ON PAR WITH A JUNIOR HIGH-SCHOOL STUDENT; SHE CAN'T USE ANY SPELLS NOW, EITHER.
MORE THAN A TEN-YEAR-OLD, SAY, BUT NO MORE THAN A MUNDANE... ?
MORE OR LESS.
UM—UH—!
EVANGELINE, AS IN THE ONE WITH THE PRICE ON HER HEAD... ?!
TH-THAT ONE.
THE REAL ONE? NOT, LIKE, A DESCENDANT, OR... ?!
YES. SHE'S MY MASTER.
SO MAYBE I SEE EVA-NYAN'S MOVES
SHE WHAT ?!
SETSUNA-SAN...
I HEARD ONCE THAT THE BOUNTY ON HER WAS OVER SIX HUNDRED MILLION YEN... I FIGURED SHE'D BE MUCH SCARIER!
KNH
KNH
KNH
BOOM-BAH バイーン
NEVER MIND THAT SHE'D BE SO CUTE AND LITTLE!
N-NO.
SHE'S PLENTY SCARY!
THAT'S CUTE, TO YOU ?
HOW DOES MASTER PLAN TO FIGHT, THEN, IF SHE'S SO... ?
JUST YOU WATCH. SHE SEEMS PRETTY GEARED-UP, TO ME.
BESIDES, WHAT CAN YOU LOT DO, WORRIED ABOUT THIS NET THING?
EVEN WITHOUT HER MAGIC...
ONE DOESN'T SURVIVE FOR MORE THAN A FEW CENTURIES WITHOUT LEARNING A THING OR TWO.

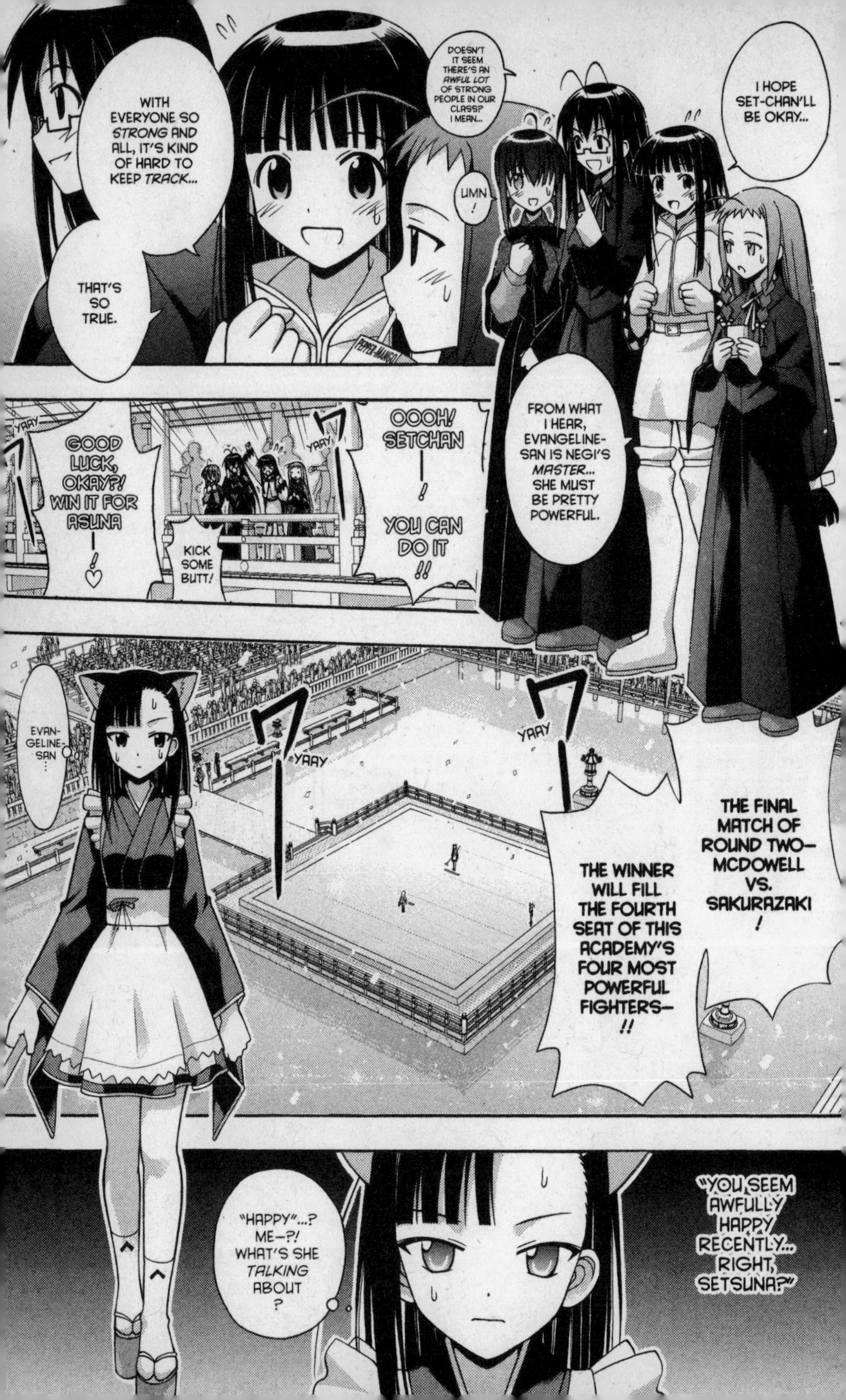
I HOPE SET-CHAN'LL BE OKAY...
DOESN'T IT SEEM THERE'S AN *AWFUL LOT* OF STRONG PEOPLE IN OUR CLASS? I MEAN...
UMN!
WITH EVERYONE SO *STRONG* AND ALL, IT'S KIND OF HARD TO KEEP *TRACK*...
THAT'S SO TRUE.
PEPPER-MANGO
FROM WHAT I HEAR, EVANGELINE-SAN IS NEGI'S *MASTER*... SHE MUST BE PRETTY POWERFUL.
OOOH! SETCHAN—!
YOU CAN DO IT!!
YAAY
KICK SOME BUTT!
YAAY
GOOD LUCK, OKAY?! WIN IT FOR ASUNA—!♡
THE FINAL MATCH OF ROUND TWO—MCDOWELL VS. SAKURAZAKI!
THE WINNER WILL FILL THE FOURTH SEAT OF THIS ACADEMY'S FOUR MOST POWERFUL FIGHTERS—!!
YAAY
YAAY
EVANGELINE-SAN...
"YOU SEEM AWFULLY HAPPY RECENTLY... RIGHT, SETSUNA?"
"HAPPY"...? ME—?! WHAT'S SHE *TALKING* ABOUT?

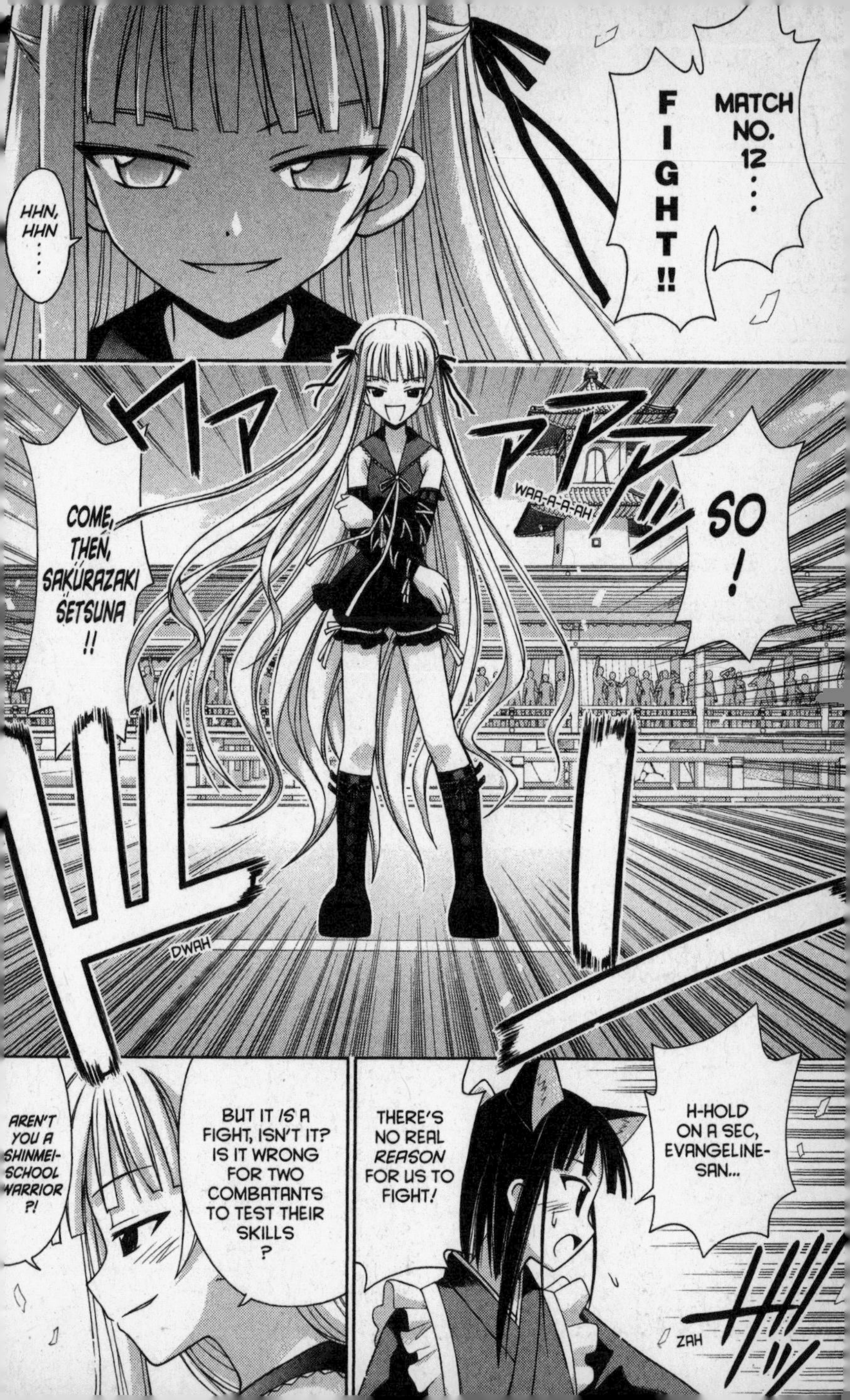
MATCH NO. 12...
FIGHT!!
HHN, HHN....
WAA-A-A-AH
SO!
COME, THEN, SAKURAZAKI SETSUNA!!
DWAH
H-HOLD ON A SEC, EVANGELINE-SAN...
THERE'S NO REAL *REASON* FOR US TO FIGHT!
ZAH
BUT IT *IS* A FIGHT, ISN'T IT? IS IT WRONG FOR TWO COMBATANTS TO TEST THEIR SKILLS?
AREN'T YOU A SHINMEI-SCHOOL WARRIOR?!

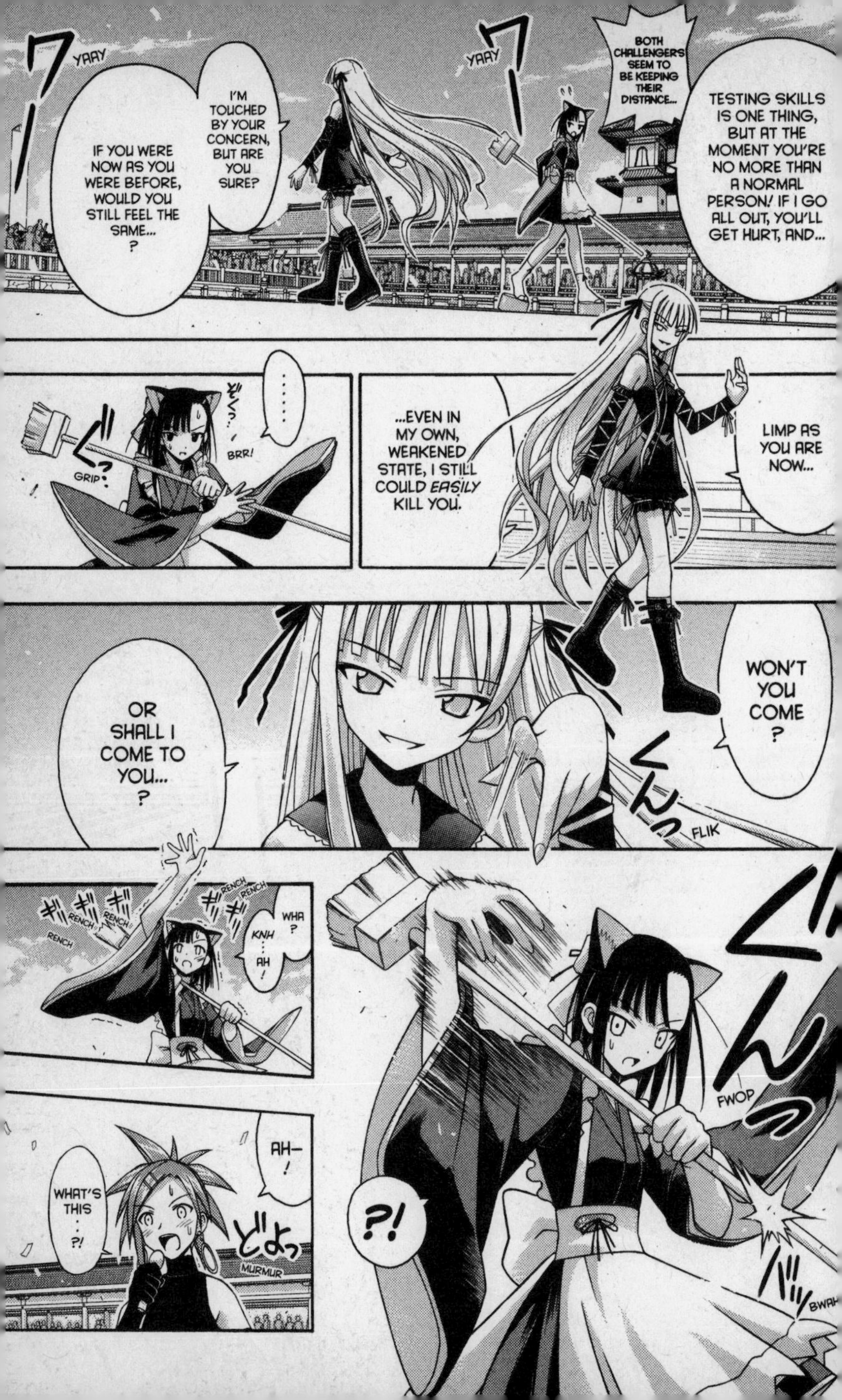

BOTH CHALLENGERS SEEM TO BE KEEPING THEIR DISTANCE...
TESTING SKILLS IS ONE THING, BUT AT THE MOMENT YOU'RE NO MORE THAN A NORMAL PERSON! IF I GO ALL OUT, YOU'LL GET HURT, AND...
YAAY
I'M TOUCHED BY YOUR CONCERN, BUT ARE YOU SURE?
IF YOU WERE NOW AS YOU WERE BEFORE, WOULD YOU STILL FEEL THE SAME...?
YAAY
LIMP AS YOU ARE NOW...
...EVEN IN MY OWN, WEAKENED STATE, I STILL COULD *EASILY* KILL YOU.
......
BRR!
GRIP
WON'T YOU COME?
FLIK
OR SHALL I COME TO YOU...?
FWOP
?!
BWAH
WHA?
KNH... AH!
RENCH
RENCH
RENCH
RENCH
RENCH
AH-!
WHAT'S THIS..?!
MURMUR

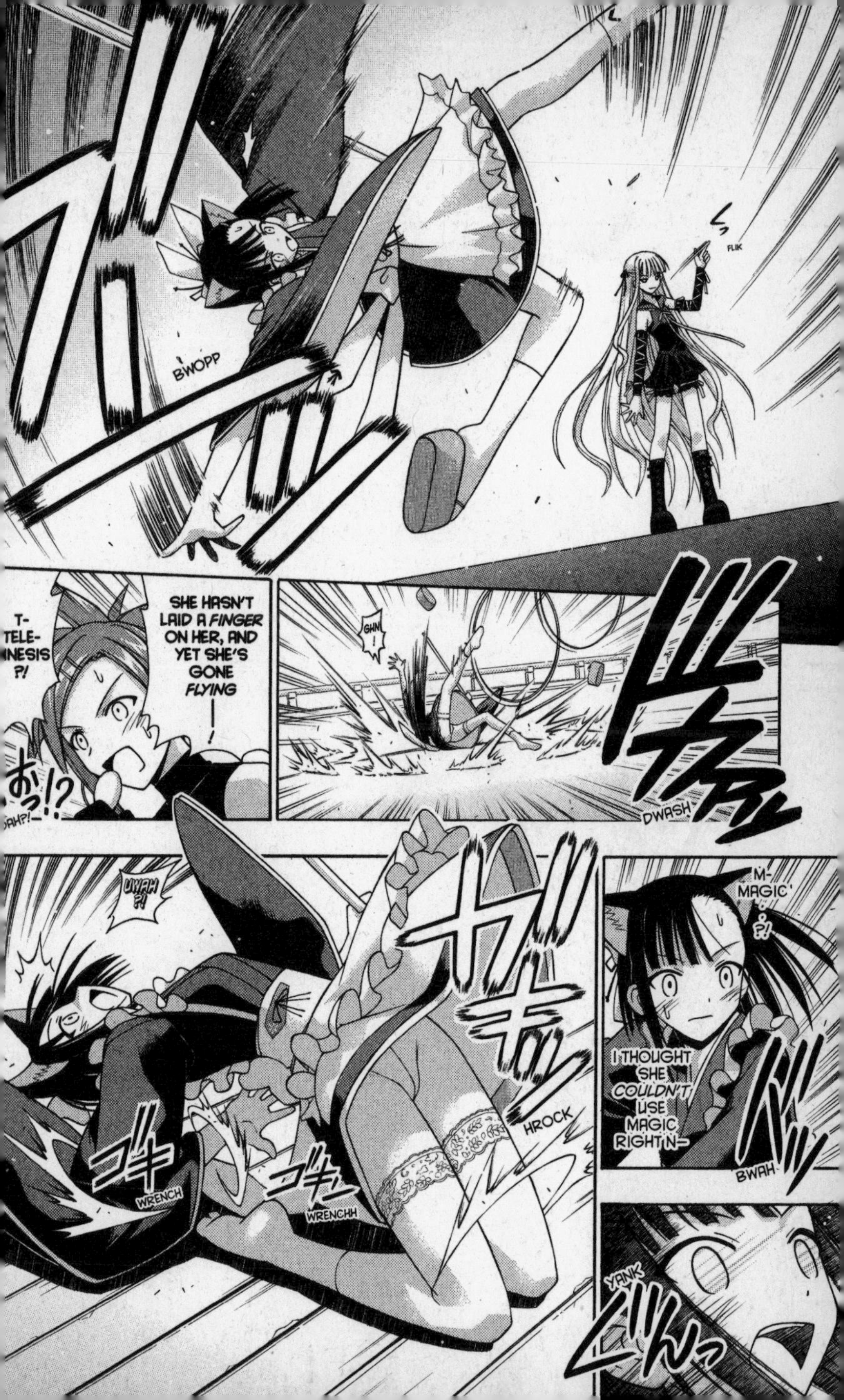
FLIK
BWOPP
GHN!
DWASH
SHE HASN'T LAID A FINGER ON HER, AND YET SHE'S GONE FLYING—!
T-TELE-NESIS?!
おっ!?
DAH?!
M-MAGIC...?!
I THOUGHT SHE COULDN'T USE MAGIC RIGHT N-
BWAH
YANK
UWAH?!
HROCK
WRENCH
WRENCHH

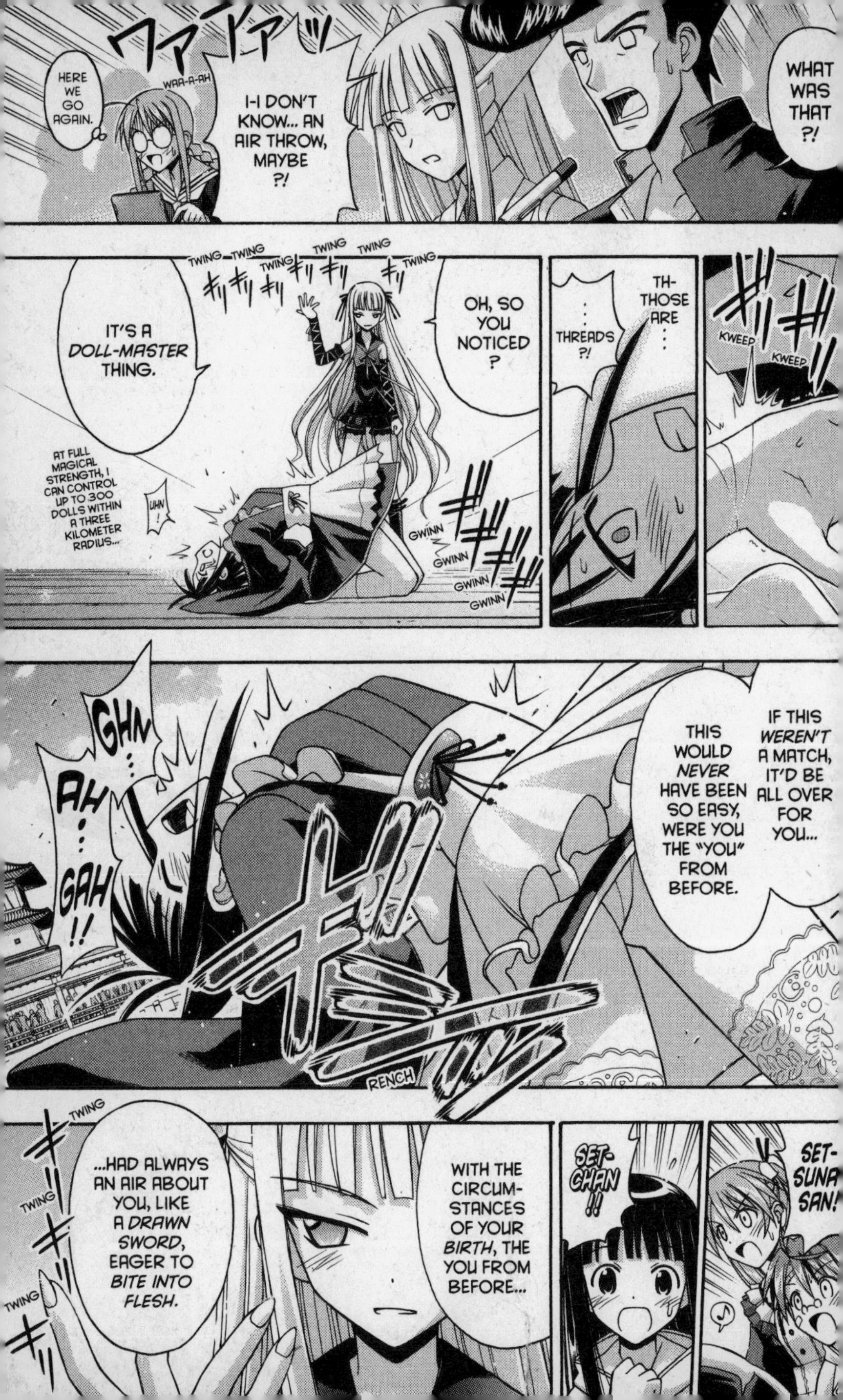
WHAT WAS THAT ?!
ワァァァッ
I-I DON'T KNOW... AN AIR THROW, MAYBE ?!
WAA-A-AH
HERE WE GO AGAIN.
KWEEP KWEEP
TH- THOSE ARE . . .
. . . THREADS ?!
TWING TWING TWING TWING TWING TWING
OH, SO YOU NOTICED ?
IT'S A *DOLL-MASTER* THING.
AT FULL MAGICAL STRENGTH, I CAN CONTROL UP TO 300 DOLLS WITHIN A THREE KILOMETER RADIUS...
UHN !
GWINN GWINN GWINN GWINN
IF THIS *WEREN'T* A MATCH, IT'D BE ALL OVER FOR YOU...
THIS WOULD *NEVER* HAVE BEEN SO EASY, WERE YOU THE "YOU" FROM BEFORE.
GHN . . . AH . . . GAH !!
RENCH
SET-SUNA SAN!
SET-CHAN !!
WITH THE CIRCUM-STANCES OF YOUR *BIRTH*, THE YOU FROM BEFORE...
...HAD ALWAYS AN AIR ABOUT YOU, LIKE A *DRAWN SWORD*, EAGER TO *BITE INTO FLESH.*
TWING TWING TWING

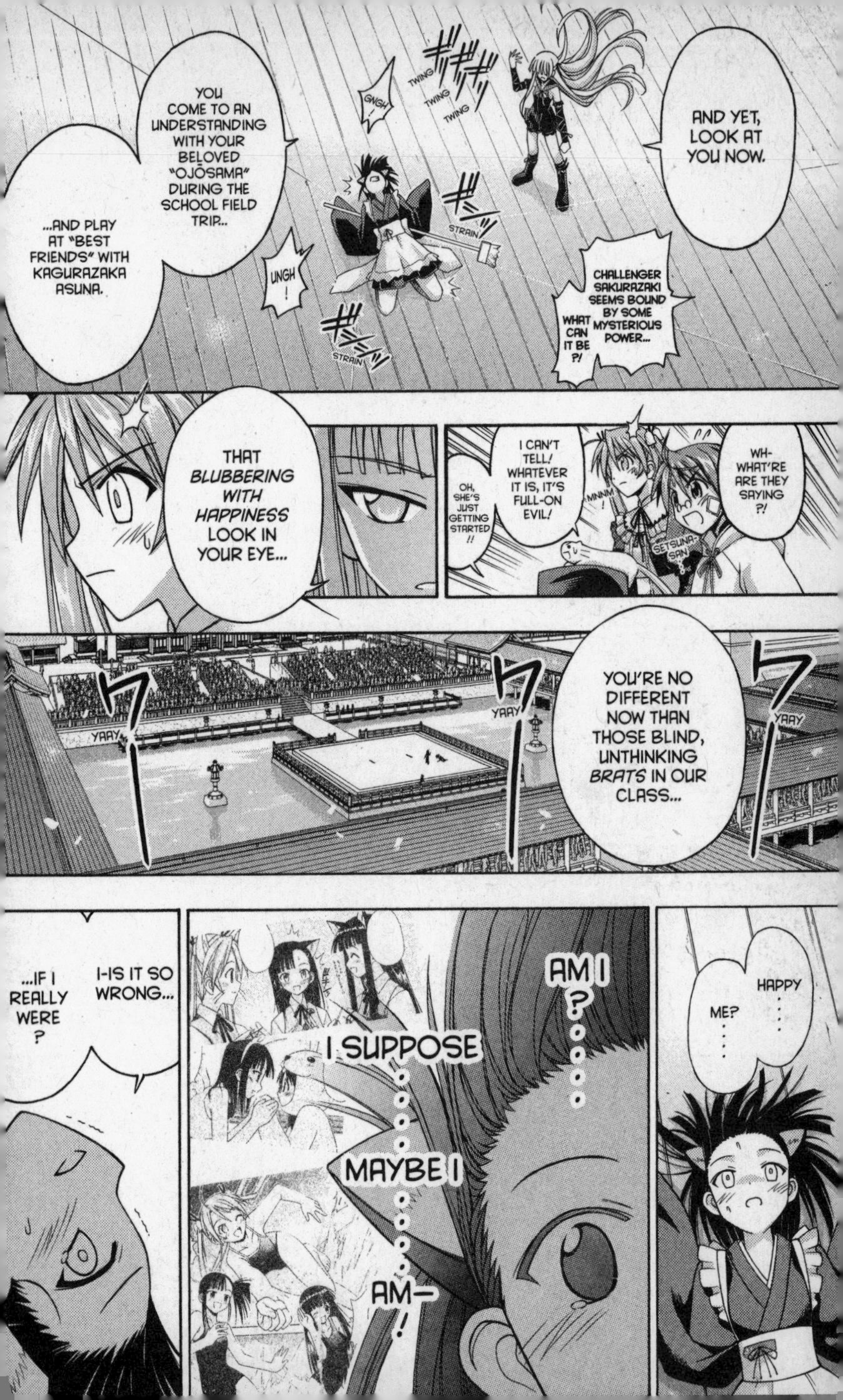
AND YET, LOOK AT YOU NOW.
CHALLENGER SAKURAZAKI SEEMS BOUND BY SOME MYSTERIOUS POWER...
WHAT CAN IT BE ?!
TWING TWING TWING
GNGH !
STRAIN
YOU COME TO AN UNDERSTANDING WITH YOUR BELOVED "OJŌSAMA" DURING THE SCHOOL FIELD TRIP...
UNGH !
STRAIN
...AND PLAY AT "BEST FRIENDS" WITH KAGURAZAKA ASUNA.
WH- WHAT'RE ARE THEY SAYING ?!
SETSUNA-SAN
MNNM !
I CAN'T TELL! WHATEVER IT IS, IT'S FULL-ON EVIL!
OH, SHE'S JUST GETTING STARTED !!
THAT *BLUBBERING WITH HAPPINESS* LOOK IN YOUR EYE...
YOU'RE NO DIFFERENT NOW THAN THOSE BLIND, UNTHINKING *BRATS* IN OUR CLASS...
YAAY
YAAY
YAAY
ME? .... HAPPY ....
AM I ? ....
I SUPPOSE ...... MAYBE I ...... AM— !
I-IS IT SO WRONG...
...IF I REALLY WERE ?

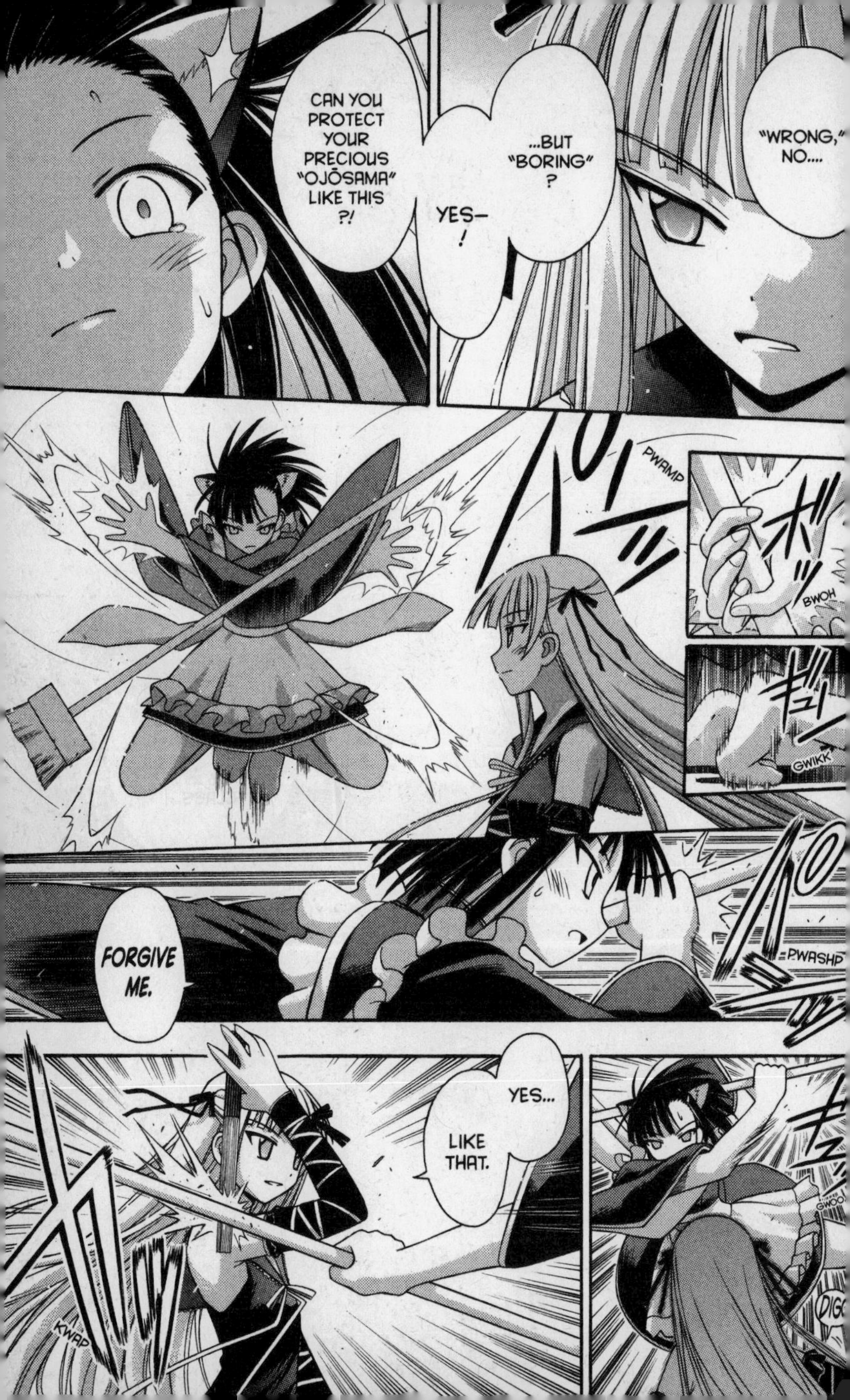

"WRONG," NO....
...BUT "BORING" ?
YES—!
CAN YOU PROTECT YOUR PRECIOUS "OJŌSAMA" LIKE THIS ?!
PWAMP
BWOH
GWIKK
PWASHP
FORGIVE ME.
GWOO
YES... LIKE THAT.
KWAP

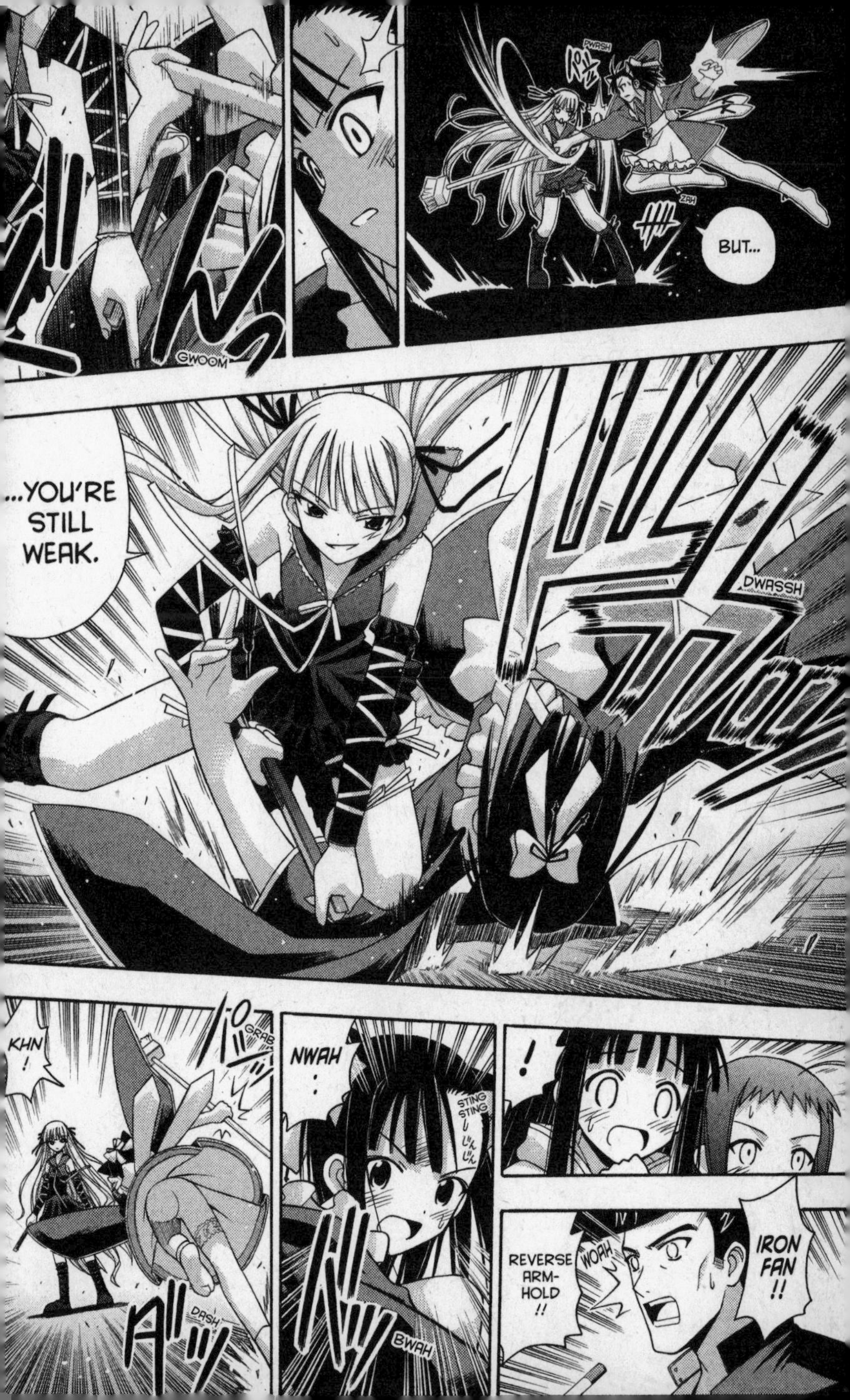
PWASH
ZAH
BUT...
GWOOM
...YOU'RE STILL WEAK.
DWASSH
!
IRON FAN!!
WOAH
REVERSE ARM-HOLD!!
NWAH...
STING STING
BWAH
GRAB
KHN!
DASH

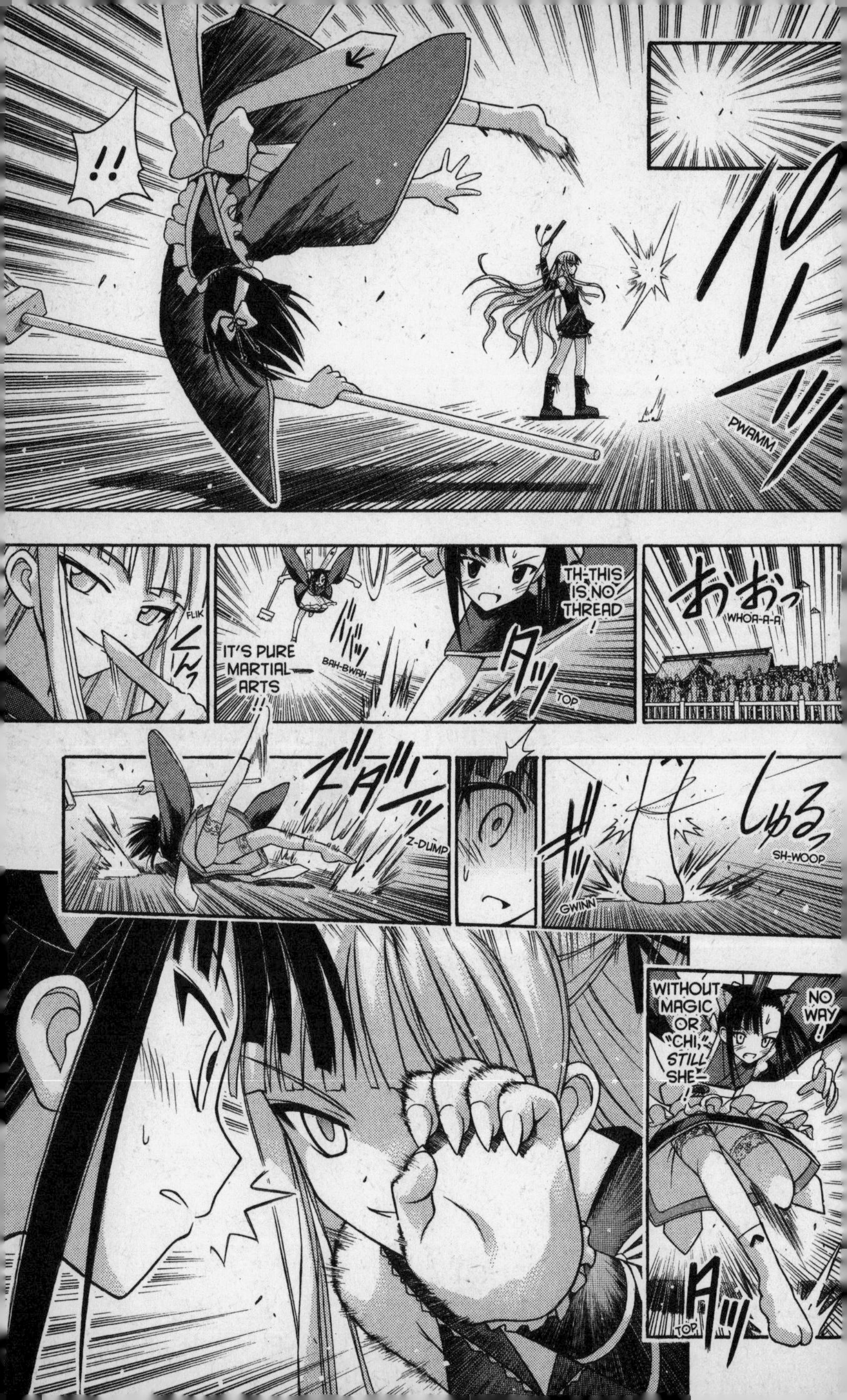
PWAMM
!!
おおっ
WHOA-A-A
TH-THIS IS NO THREAD!
TOP
BAH-BWAH
IT'S PURE MARTIAL ARTS!!
FLIK
しゅるっ
SH-WOOP
GWINN
Z-DUMP
NO WAY!
WITHOUT MAGIC OR "CHI," STILL SHE—!
TOP

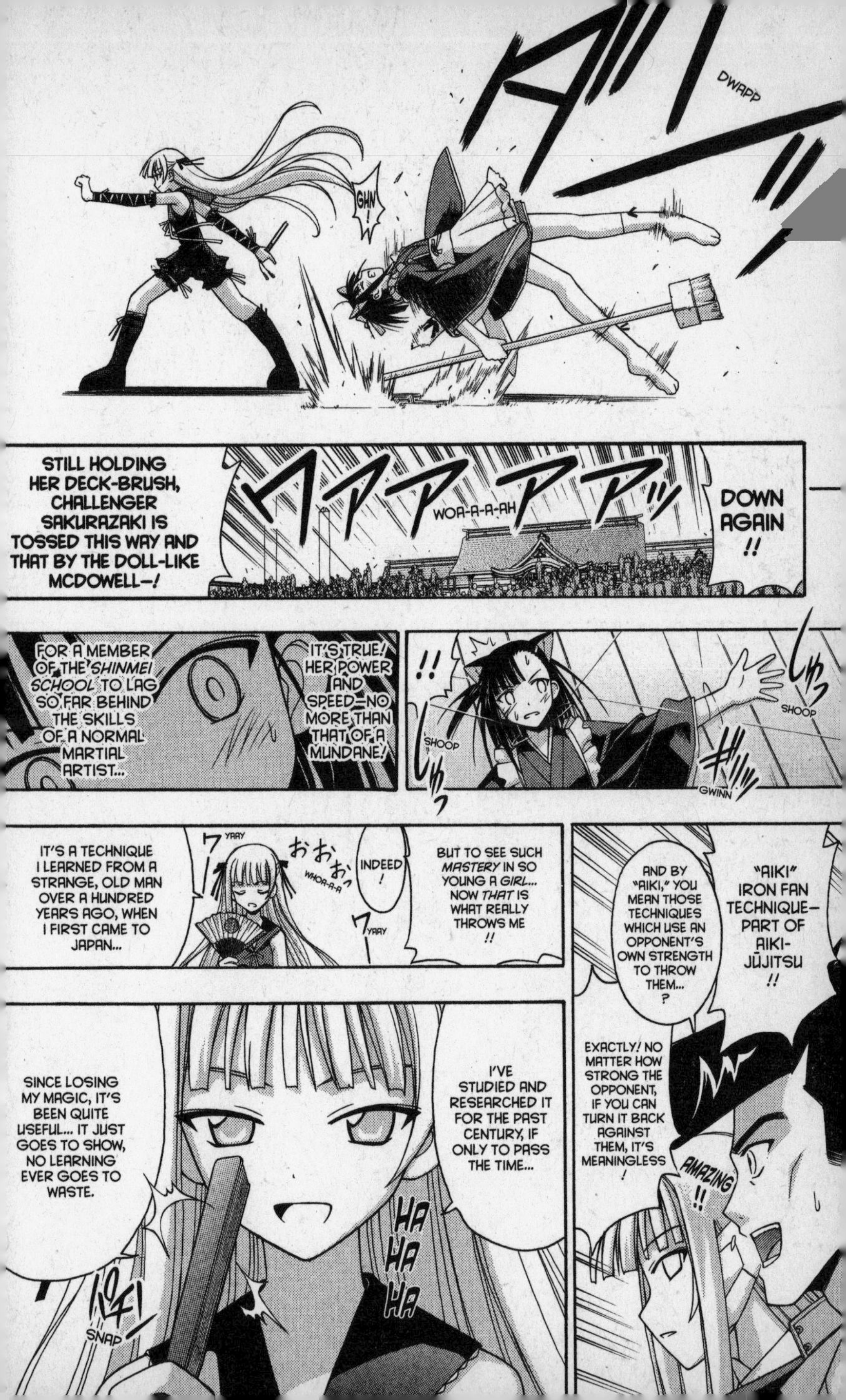

DWAPP
GHN!
DOWN AGAIN !!
WOA-A-A-AH
STILL HOLDING HER DECK-BRUSH, CHALLENGER SAKURAZAKI IS TOSSED THIS WAY AND THAT BY THE DOLL-LIKE MCDOWELL—!
SHOOP
!!
SHOOP
GWINN
IT'S TRUE! HER POWER AND SPEED—NO MORE THAN THAT OF A MUNDANE!
FOR A MEMBER OF THE *SHINMEI SCHOOL* TO LAG SO FAR BEHIND THE SKILLS OF A NORMAL MARTIAL ARTIST...
"AIKI" IRON FAN TECHNIQUE—PART OF AIKI-JŪJITSU !!
AND BY "AIKI," YOU MEAN THOSE TECHNIQUES WHICH USE AN OPPONENT'S OWN STRENGTH TO THROW THEM... ?
EXACTLY! NO MATTER HOW STRONG THE OPPONENT, IF YOU CAN TURN IT BACK AGAINST THEM, IT'S MEANINGLESS !
AMAZING !!
BUT TO SEE SUCH *MASTERY* IN SO YOUNG A *GIRL*... NOW *THAT* IS WHAT REALLY THROWS ME !!
YAAY
INDEED !
WHOA-A-A
YAAY
IT'S A TECHNIQUE I LEARNED FROM A STRANGE, OLD MAN OVER A HUNDRED YEARS AGO, WHEN I FIRST CAME TO JAPAN...
I'VE STUDIED AND RESEARCHED IT FOR THE PAST CENTURY, IF ONLY TO PASS THE TIME...
SINCE LOSING MY MAGIC, IT'S BEEN QUITE USEFUL... IT JUST GOES TO SHOW, NO LEARNING EVER GOES TO WASTE.
HA HA HA HA
SNAP

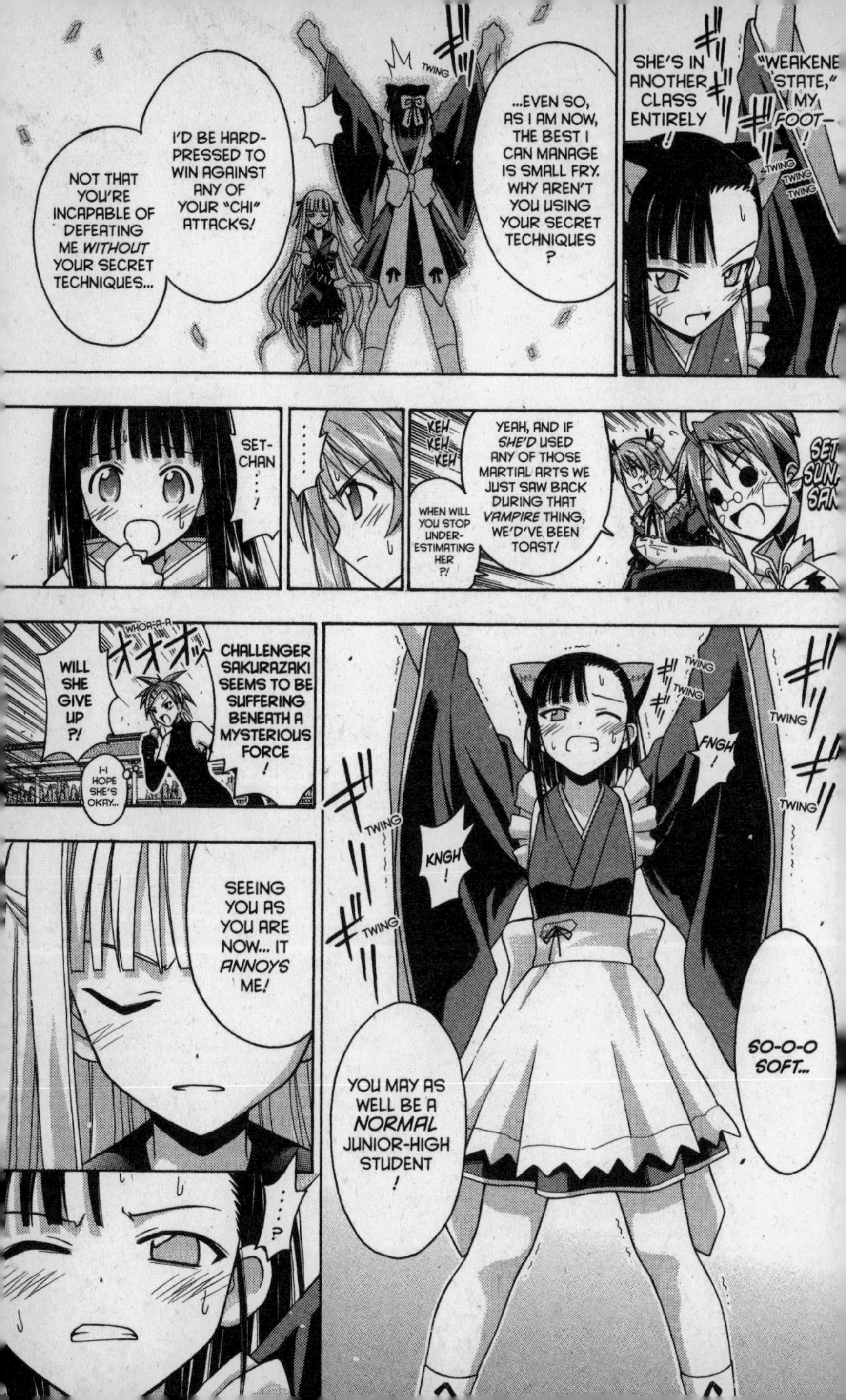
"WEAKENE STATE," MY FOOT—!
TWING TWING TWING
SHE'S IN ANOTHER CLASS ENTIRELY
...EVEN SO, AS I AM NOW, THE BEST I CAN MANAGE IS SMALL FRY. WHY AREN'T YOU USING YOUR SECRET TECHNIQUES?
TWING
I'D BE HARD-PRESSED TO WIN AGAINST ANY OF YOUR "CHI" ATTACKS!
NOT THAT YOU'RE INCAPABLE OF DEFEATING ME *WITHOUT* YOUR SECRET TECHNIQUES...
SETSUNA-SAN
YEAH, AND IF *SHE'D* USED ANY OF THOSE MARTIAL ARTS WE JUST SAW BACK DURING THAT *VAMPIRE* THING, WE'D'VE BEEN TOAST!
KEH KEH KEH
WHEN WILL YOU STOP UNDER-ESTIMATING HER?!
......
SET-CHAN...!
TWING
TWING
TWING
FNGH!
TWING
KNGH!
TWING
SO-O-O SOFT...
YOU MAY AS WELL BE A *NORMAL* JUNIOR-HIGH STUDENT!
CHALLENGER SAKURAZAKI SEEMS TO BE SUFFERING BENEATH A MYSTERIOUS FORCE!
WHOA-A-A
WILL SHE GIVE UP?!
I-I HOPE SHE'S OKAY...
SEEING YOU AS YOU ARE NOW... IT *ANNOYS* ME!
...?

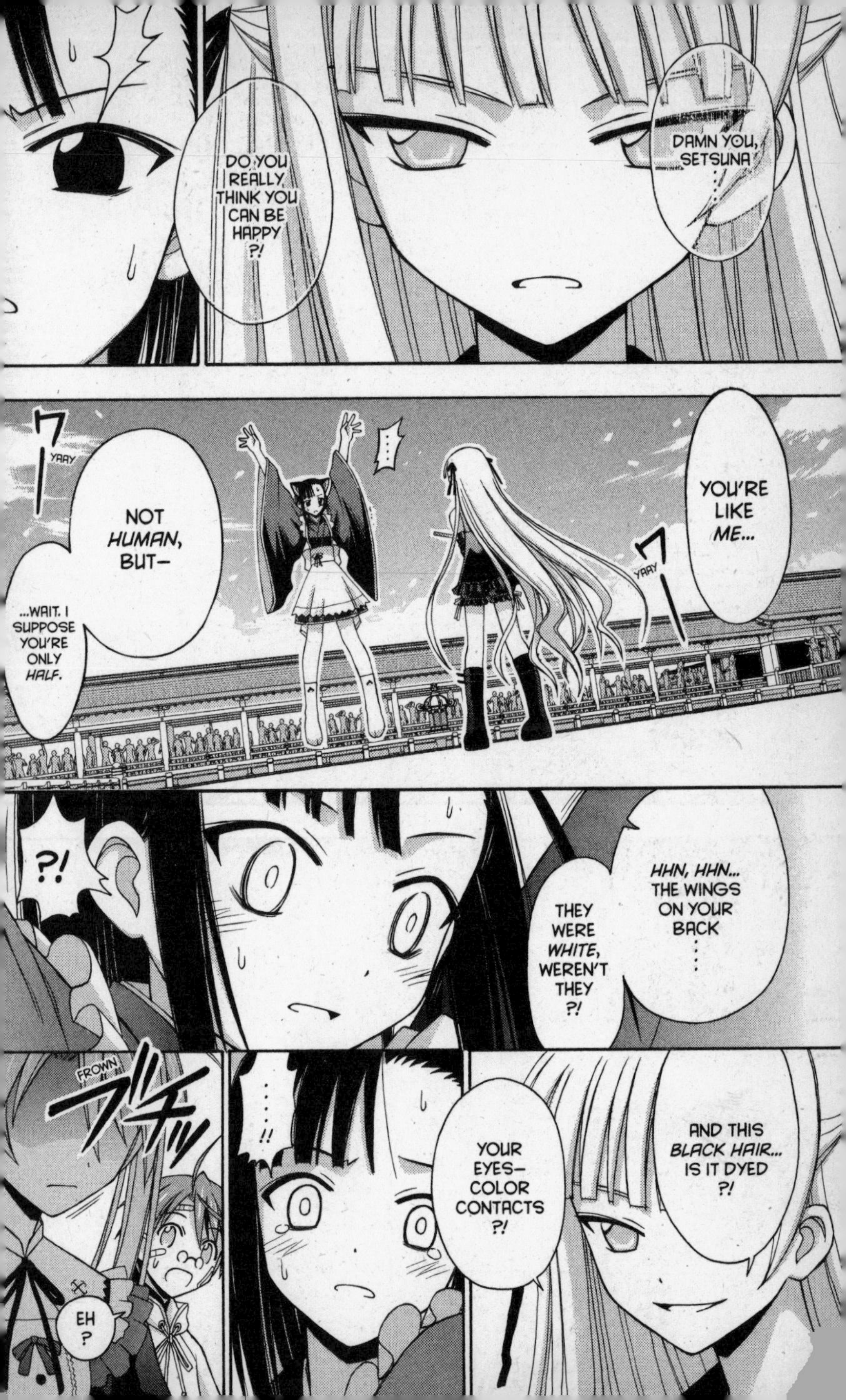
DAMN YOU, SETSUNA...
DO YOU REALLY THINK YOU CAN BE HAPPY?!
YAAY
YOU'RE LIKE ME...
YAAY
NOT *HUMAN*, BUT—
...WAIT. I SUPPOSE YOU'RE ONLY *HALF*.
HHN, HHN... THE WINGS ON YOUR BACK...
THEY WERE *WHITE*, WEREN'T THEY?!
?!
AND THIS *BLACK HAIR*... IS IT DYED?!
YOUR EYES— COLOR CONTACTS?!
......!!
FROWN
EH?

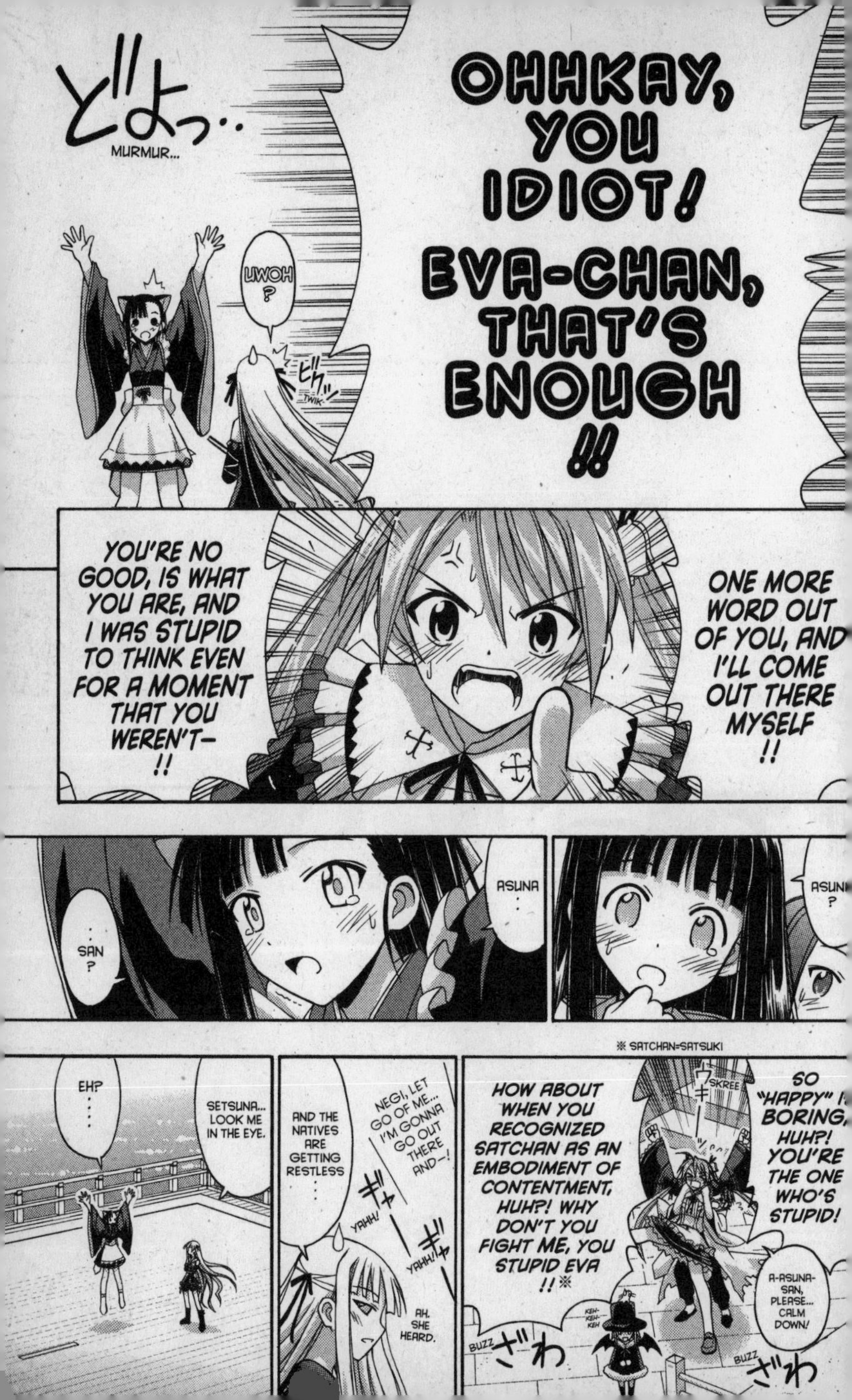
OHHKAY, YOU IDIOT! EVA-CHAN, THAT'S ENOUGH!!
どよっ‥ MURMUR...
UWOH?
ビクッ TWIK
ONE MORE WORD OUT OF YOU, AND I'LL COME OUT THERE MYSELF!!
YOU'RE NO GOOD, IS WHAT YOU ARE, AND I WAS STUPID TO THINK EVEN FOR A MOMENT THAT YOU WEREN'T—!!
ASUN ?
ASUNA... ...SAN?
※ SATCHAN=SATSUKI
SO "HAPPY" I BORING, HUH?! YOU'RE THE ONE WHO'S STUPID!
HOW ABOUT WHEN YOU RECOGNIZED SATCHAN AS AN EMBODIMENT OF CONTENTMENT, HUH?! WHY DON'T YOU FIGHT ME, YOU STUPID EVA!!※
ウキー SKREE
A-ASUNA-SAN, PLEASE... CALM DOWN!
KEH-KEH-KEH
ざわ BUZZ
ざわ BUZZ
NEGI, LET GO OF ME... I'M GONNA GO OUT THERE AND—!
AND THE NATIVES ARE GETTING RESTLESS...
ギャ YAHH!
ギャ YAHH!
AH. SHE HEARD.
EH?...
SETSUNA... LOOK ME IN THE EYE.

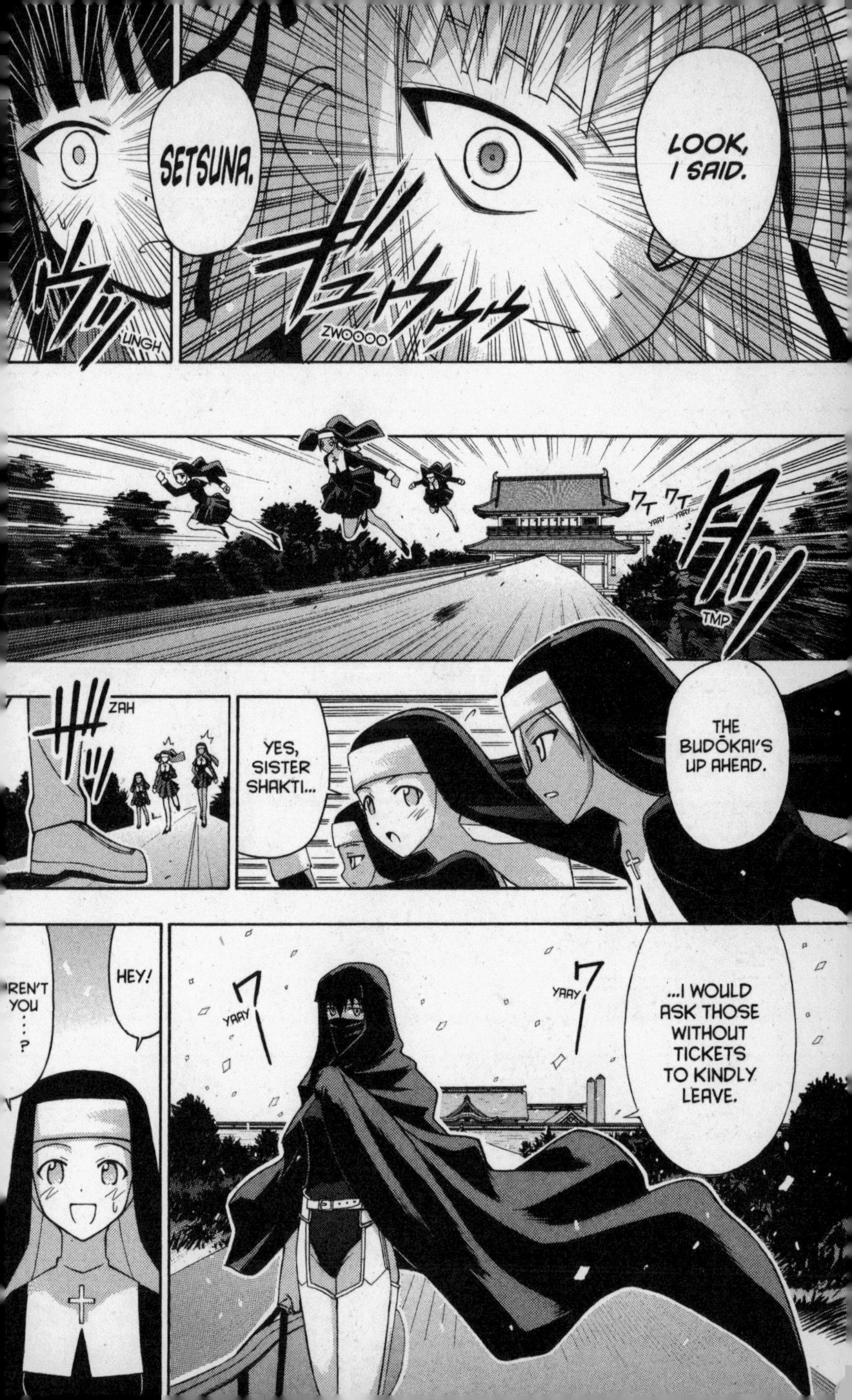

LOOK, I SAID.
ZWOOOO
SETSUNA.
UNGH
YAAY
YAAY
TMP
THE BUDŌKAI'S UP AHEAD.
YES, SISTER SHAKTI...
ZAH
...I WOULD ASK THOSE WITHOUT TICKETS TO KINDLY LEAVE.
YAAY
YAAY
HEY!
'REN'T YOU...?

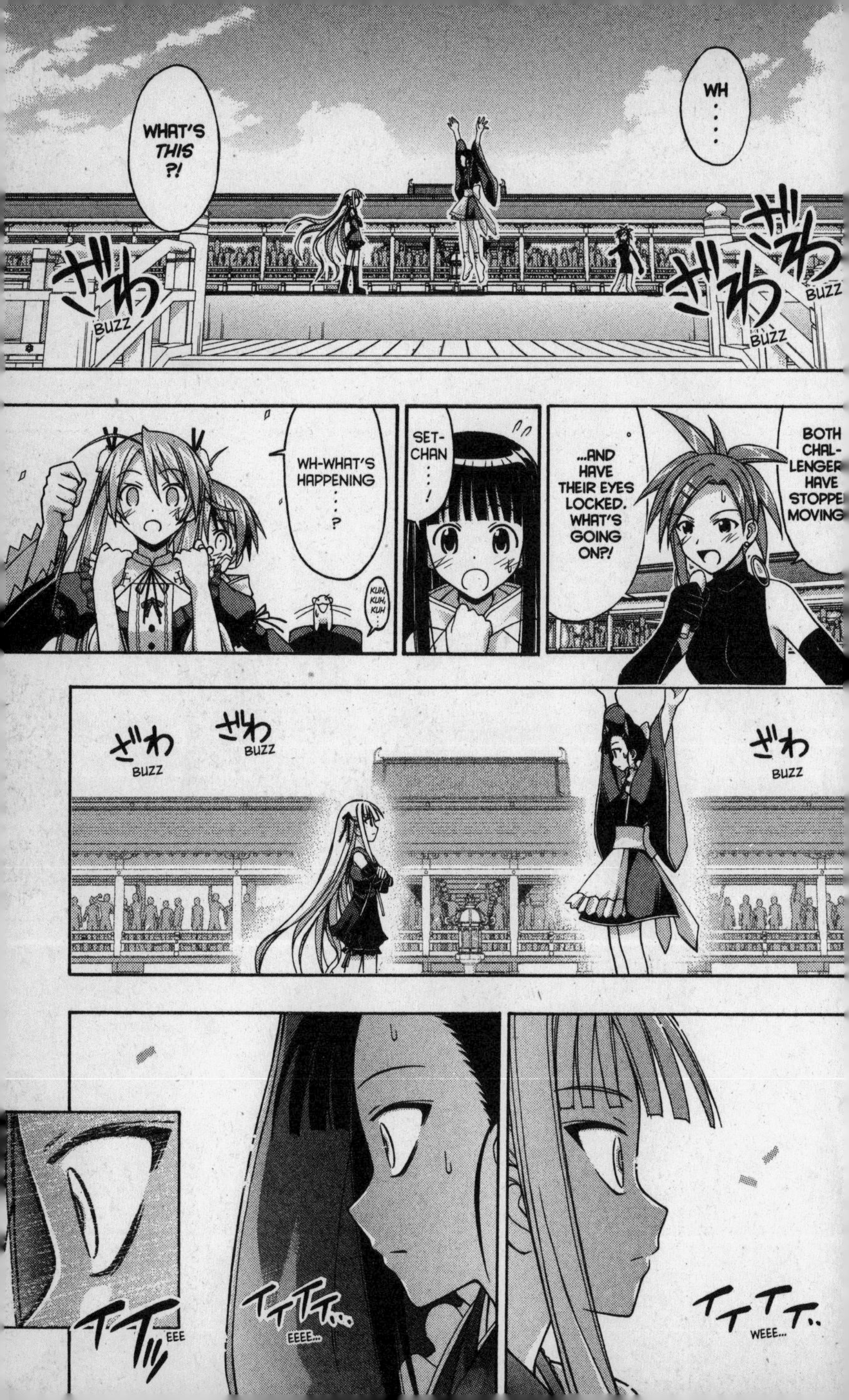
WH....
WHAT'S THIS ?!
ざわ ざわ
BUZZ BUZZ
ざわ
BUZZ
BOTH CHAL-LENGER HAVE STOPPE MOVING
...AND HAVE THEIR EYES LOCKED. WHAT'S GOING ON?!
SET-CHAN ...!
WH-WHAT'S HAPPENING ...?
KUH, KUH, KUH...
ざわ
BUZZ
ざわ
BUZZ
ざわ
BUZZ
イイイイ...
WEEE...
イイイイ...
EEEE...
イイ
EEE

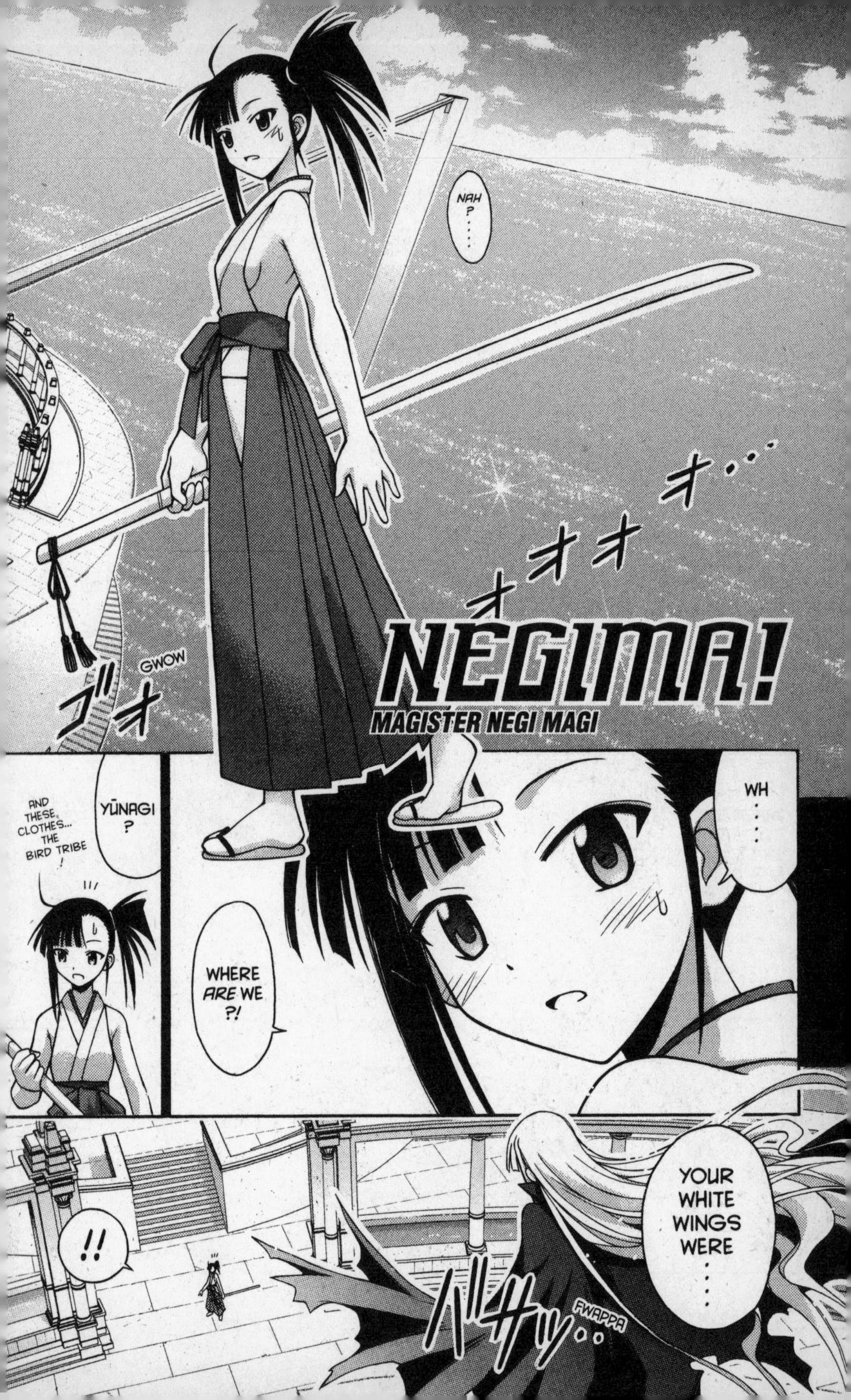

NAH?.....
オオオオ…
GWOW
ゴオ
NEGIMA!
MAGISTER NEGI MAGI
WH.....
WHERE ARE WE?!
YŪNAGI?
AND THESE CLOTHES... THE BIRD TRIBE!
YOUR WHITE WINGS WERE.....
FWAPPA
!!

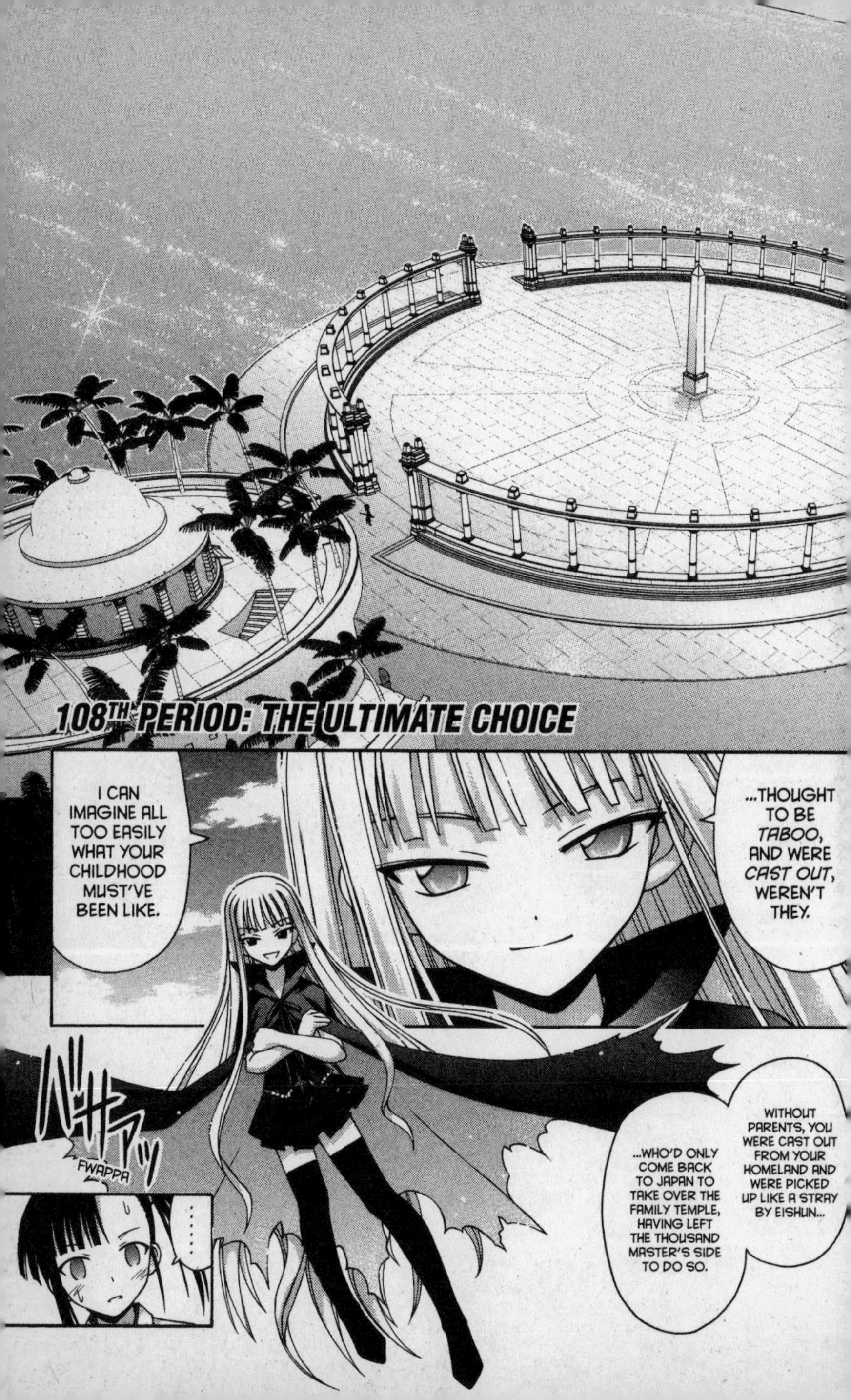
108TH PERIOD: THE ULTIMATE CHOICE
...THOUGHT TO BE TABOO, AND WERE CAST OUT, WEREN'T THEY.
I CAN IMAGINE ALL TOO EASILY WHAT YOUR CHILDHOOD MUST'VE BEEN LIKE.
WITHOUT PARENTS, YOU WERE CAST OUT FROM YOUR HOMELAND AND WERE PICKED UP LIKE A STRAY BY EISHUN...
...WHO'D ONLY COME BACK TO JAPAN TO TAKE OVER THE FAMILY TEMPLE, HAVING LEFT THE THOUSAND MASTER'S SIDE TO DO SO.
FWAPPA
......

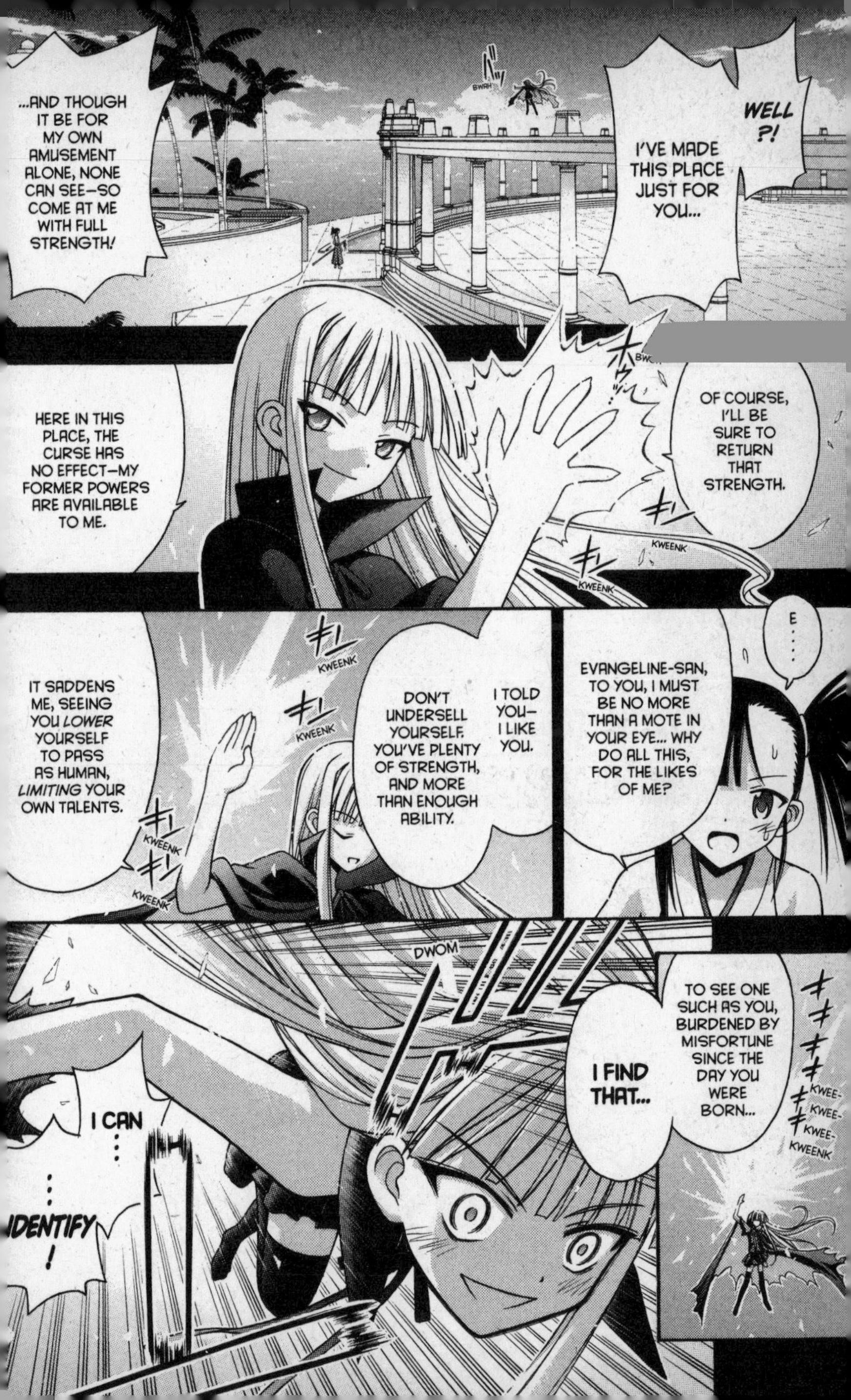
WELL?!
I'VE MADE THIS PLACE JUST FOR YOU...
BWAH
...AND THOUGH IT BE FOR MY OWN AMUSEMENT ALONE, NONE CAN SEE—SO COME AT ME WITH FULL STRENGTH!
OF COURSE, I'LL BE SURE TO RETURN THAT STRENGTH.
KWEENK
KWEENK
HERE IN THIS PLACE, THE CURSE HAS NO EFFECT—MY FORMER POWERS ARE AVAILABLE TO ME.
E....
EVANGELINE-SAN, TO YOU, I MUST BE NO MORE THAN A MOTE IN YOUR EYE... WHY DO ALL THIS, FOR THE LIKES OF ME?
I TOLD YOU— I LIKE YOU.
DON'T UNDERSELL YOURSELF. YOU'VE PLENTY OF STRENGTH, AND MORE THAN ENOUGH ABILITY.
KWEENK
KWEENK
KWEENK
KWEENK
IT SADDENS ME, SEEING YOU *LOWER* YOURSELF TO PASS AS HUMAN, *LIMITING* YOUR OWN TALENTS.
KWEE- KWEE- KWEE- KWEENK
TO SEE ONE SUCH AS YOU, BURDENED BY MISFORTUNE SINCE THE DAY YOU WERE BORN...
I FIND THAT...
DWOM
I CAN... ...IDENTIFY!

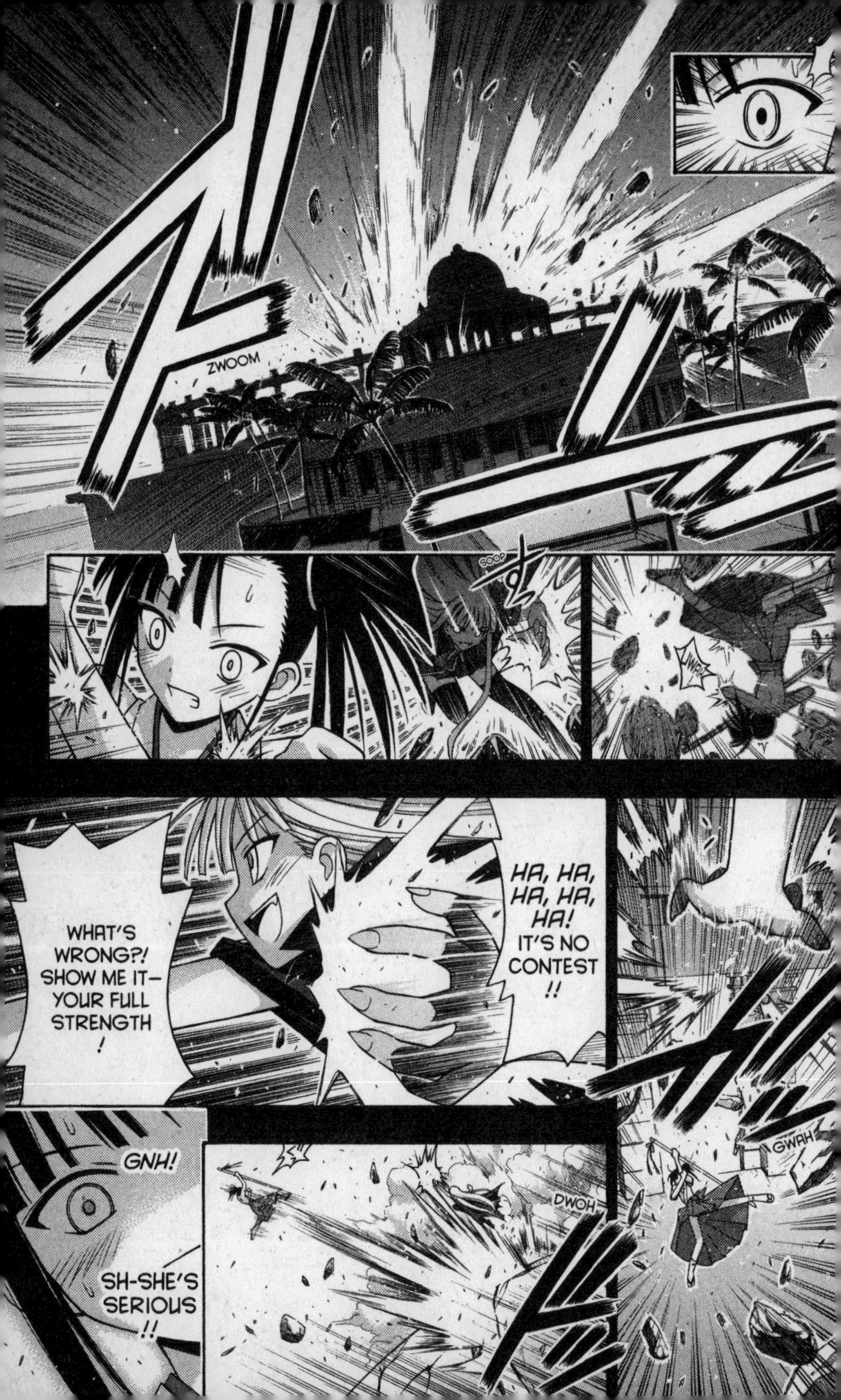
ZWOOM
UWAH
SOOP
HA, HA, HA, HA, HA! IT'S NO CONTEST !!
WHAT'S WRONG?! SHOW ME IT— YOUR FULL STRENGTH !
GWAH
DWOH
GNH!
SH-SHE'S SERIOUS !!

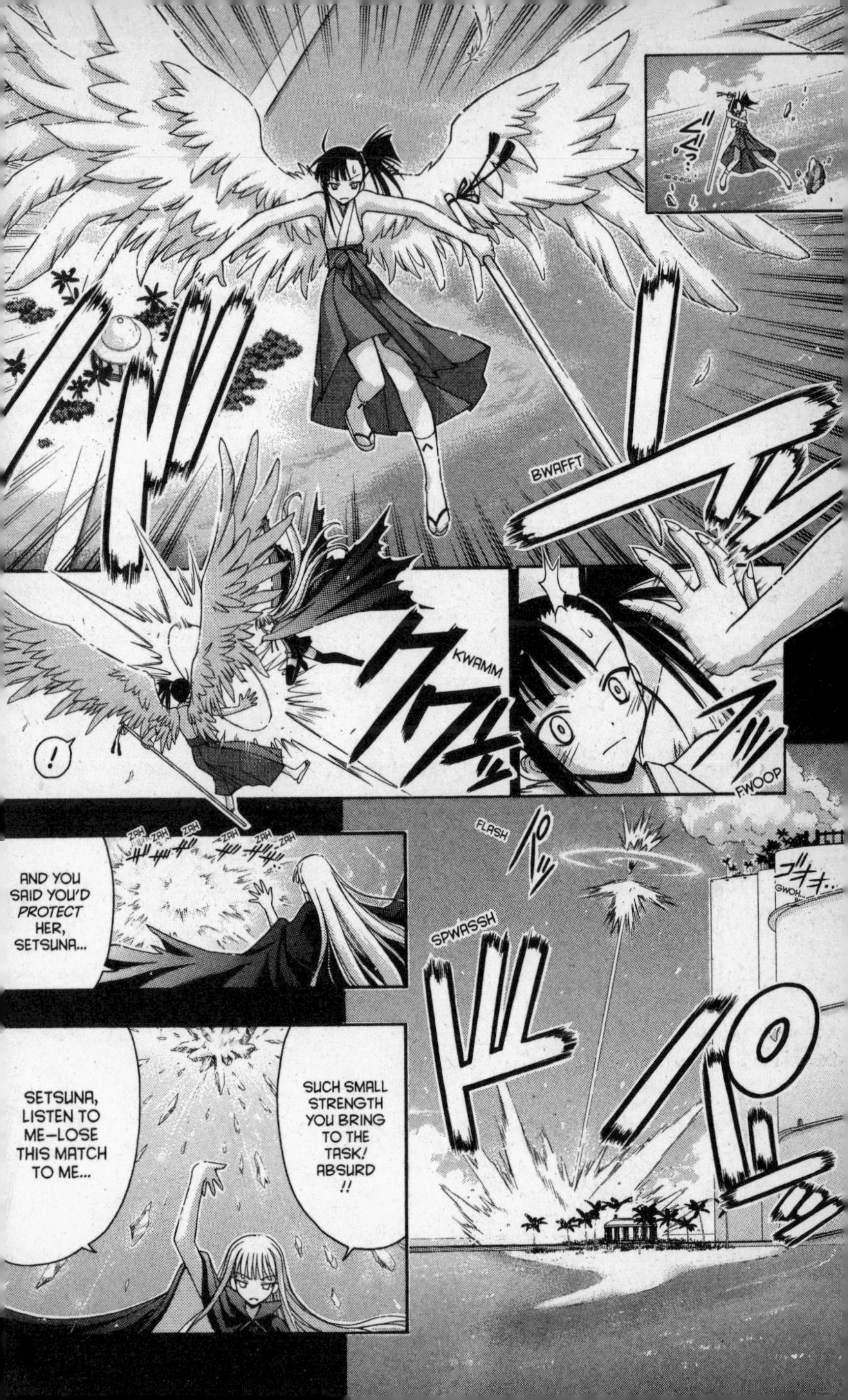
RR-R-RCH
BWAFFT
FWOOP
KWAMM
!
FLASH
GWOH...
SPWASSH
ZAH ZAH ZAH ZAH ZAH ZAH
AND YOU SAID YOU'D *PROTECT* HER, SETSUNA...
SUCH SMALL STRENGTH YOU BRING TO THE TASK! ABSURD !!
SETSUNA, LISTEN TO ME—LOSE THIS MATCH TO ME...

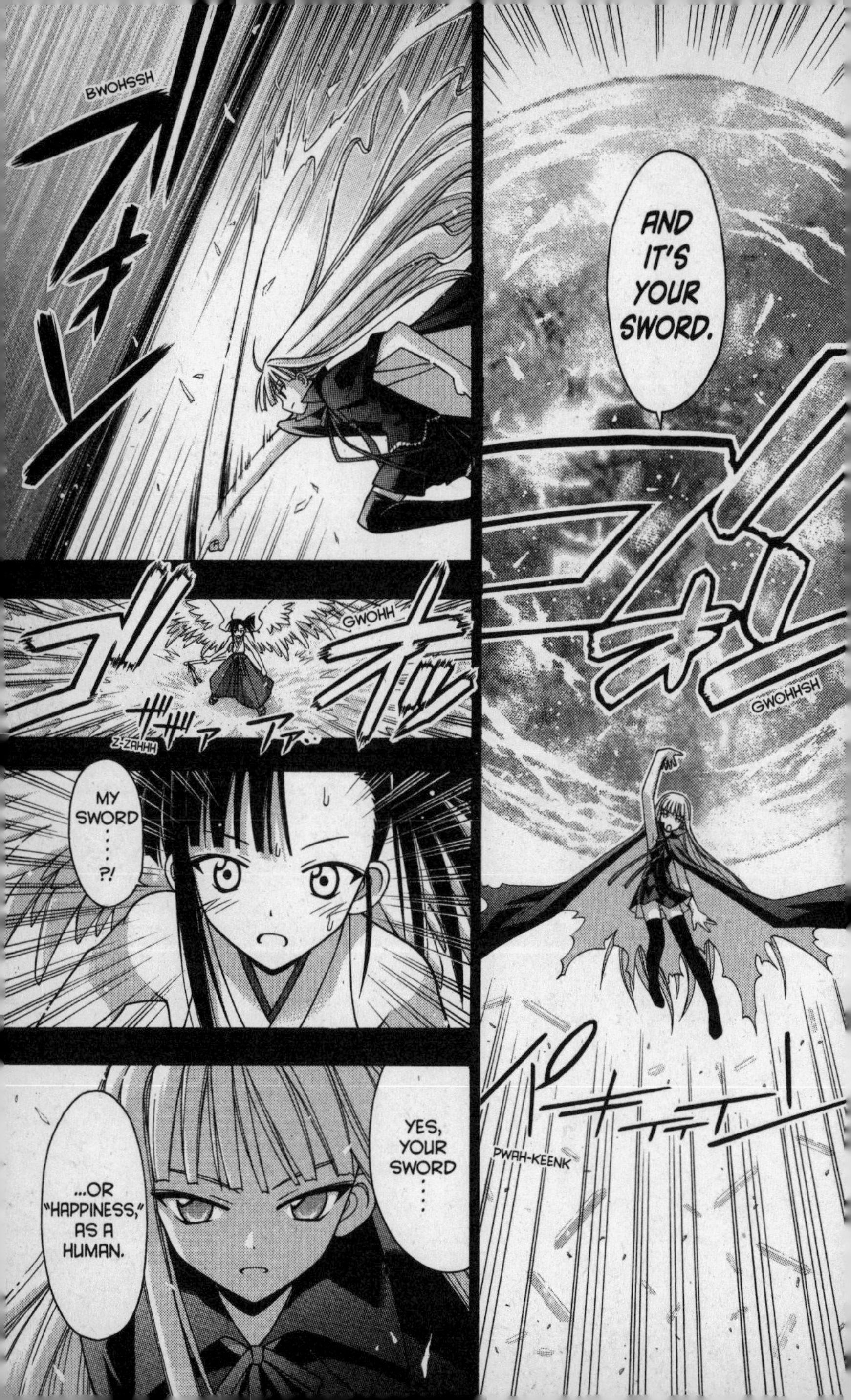
AND IT'S YOUR SWORD.
GWOHHSH
PWAH-KEENK
BWOHSSH
GWOHH
Z-ZAHHH
MY SWORD .....?!
YES, YOUR SWORD .....
...OR "HAPPINESS," AS A HUMAN.

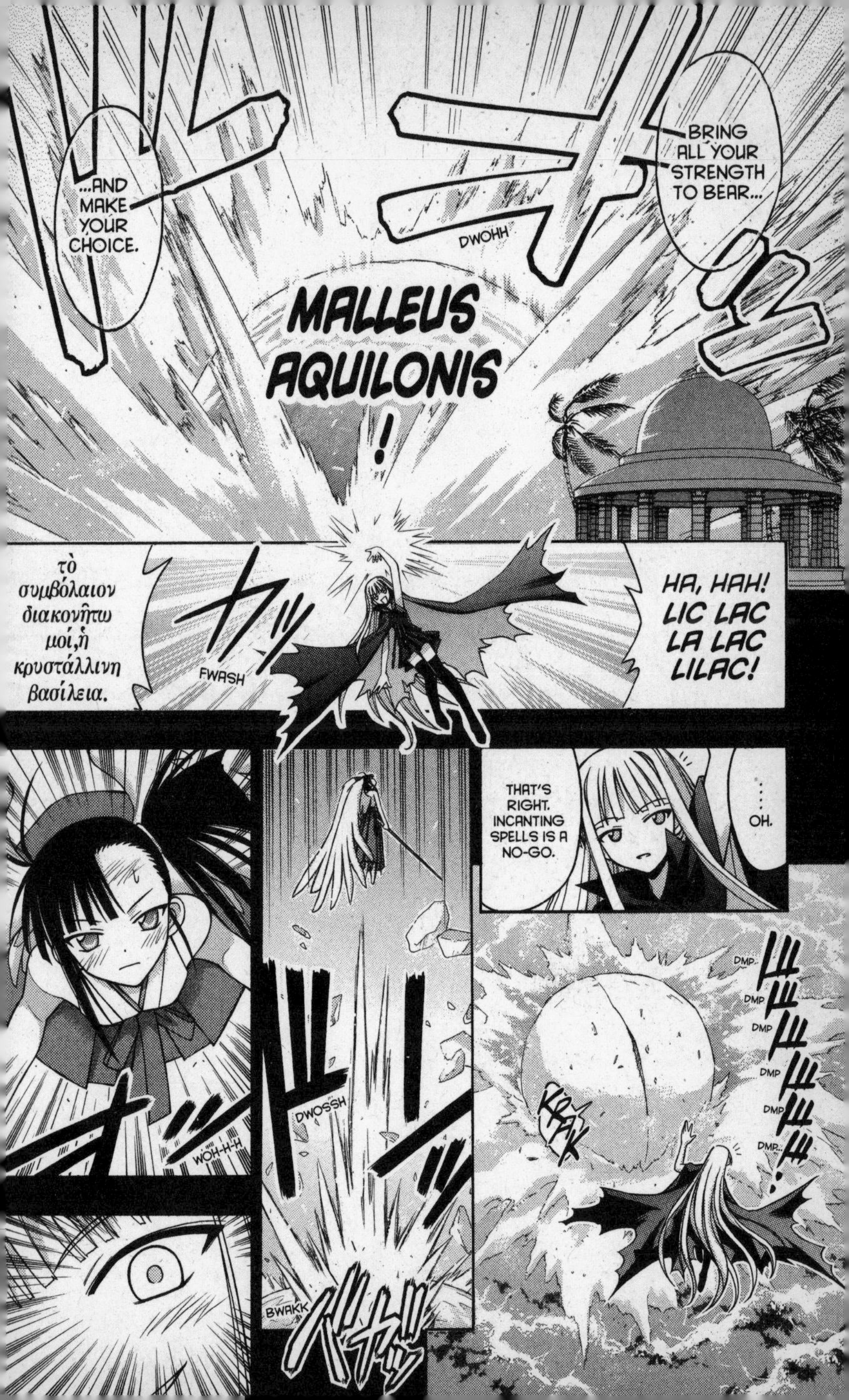
BRING ALL YOUR STRENGTH TO BEAR...
...AND MAKE YOUR CHOICE.
DWOHH
MALLEUS AQUILONIS !
HA, HAH! LIC LAC LA LAC LILAC!
FWASH
τὸ συμβόλαιον διακονῆτω μοί,ἡ κρυστάλλινη βασίλεια.
......OH.
THAT'S RIGHT. INCANTING SPELLS IS A NO-GO.
DMP DMP DMP DMP DMP DMP...!!
KRAK
DWOSSH
BWAKK
WOH-H-H

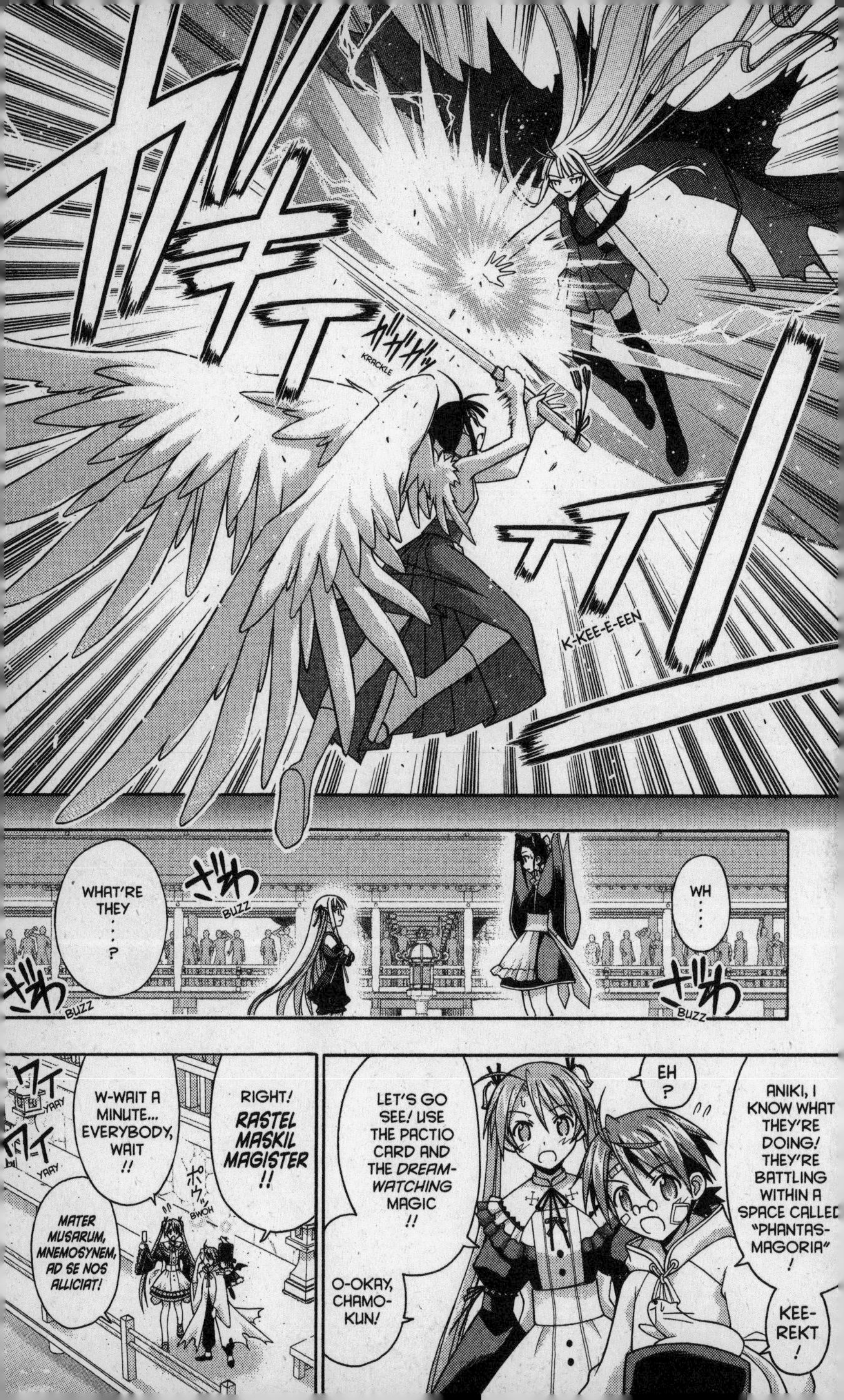
KRACKLE
K-KEE-E-EEN
WH....
BUZZ
WHAT'RE THEY . . . ?
BUZZ
BUZZ
ANIKI, I KNOW WHAT THEY'RE DOING! THEY'RE BATTLING WITHIN A SPACE CALLED "PHANTAS-MAGORIA"!
EH ?
LET'S GO SEE! USE THE PACTIO CARD AND THE DREAM-WATCHING MAGIC!!
KEE-REKT!
O-OKAY, CHAMO-KUN!
RIGHT! RASTEL MASKIL MAGISTER!!
W-WAIT A MINUTE... EVERYBODY, WAIT!!
YAAY
YAAY
BWOH
MATER MUSARUM, MNEMOSYNEM, AD SE NOS ALLICIAT!

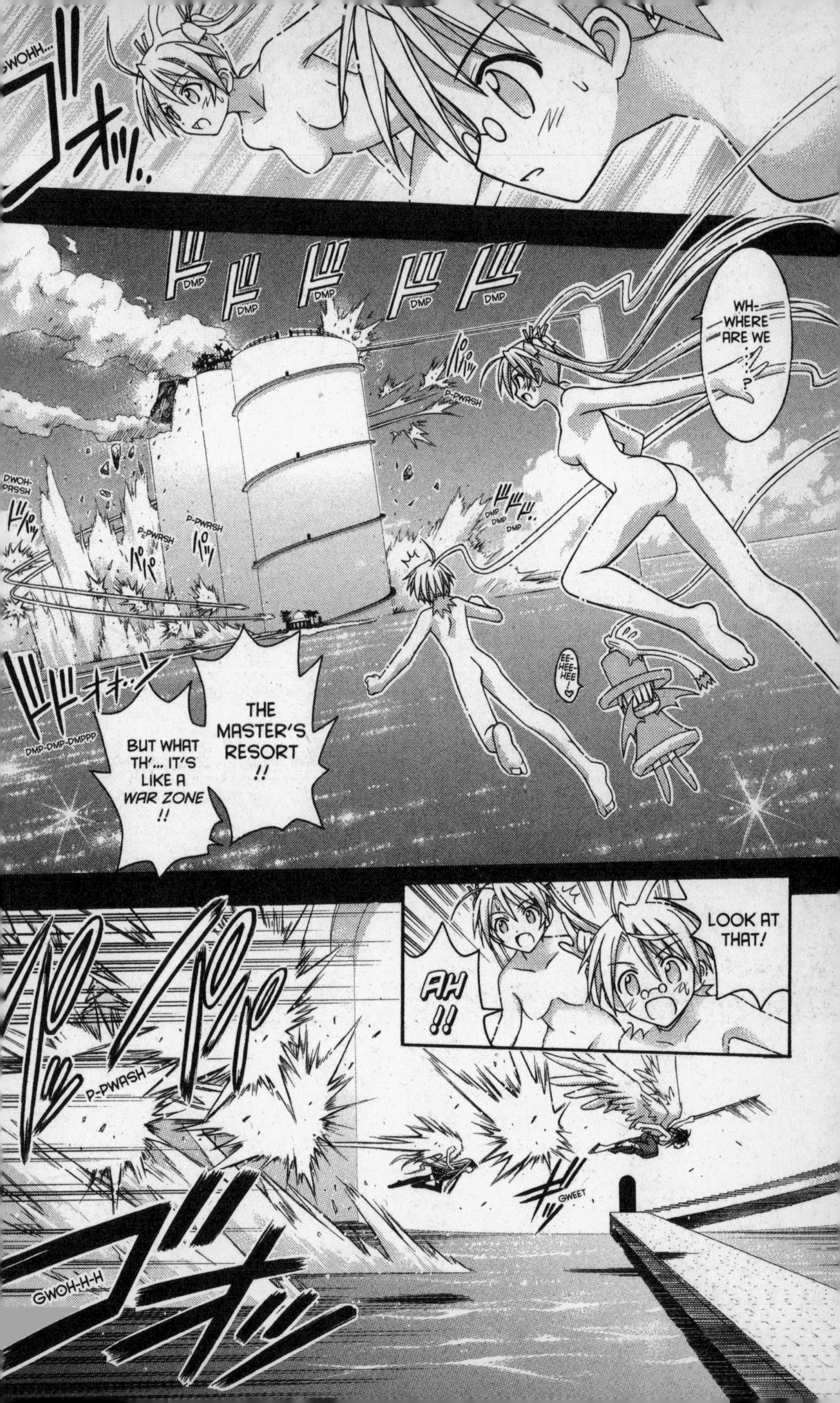
GWOHH...
WH-WHERE ARE WE ...?
DMP
DMP
DMP
DMP
DMP
P-PWASH
DMP DMP DMP
EE-HEE-HEE!
THE MASTER'S RESORT!!
BUT WHAT TH'... IT'S LIKE A WAR ZONE!!
P-PWASH
DWOH-PASSH
DMP-DMP-DMPPP
LOOK AT THAT!
AH!!
GWEET
P-PWASH
GWOH-H-H

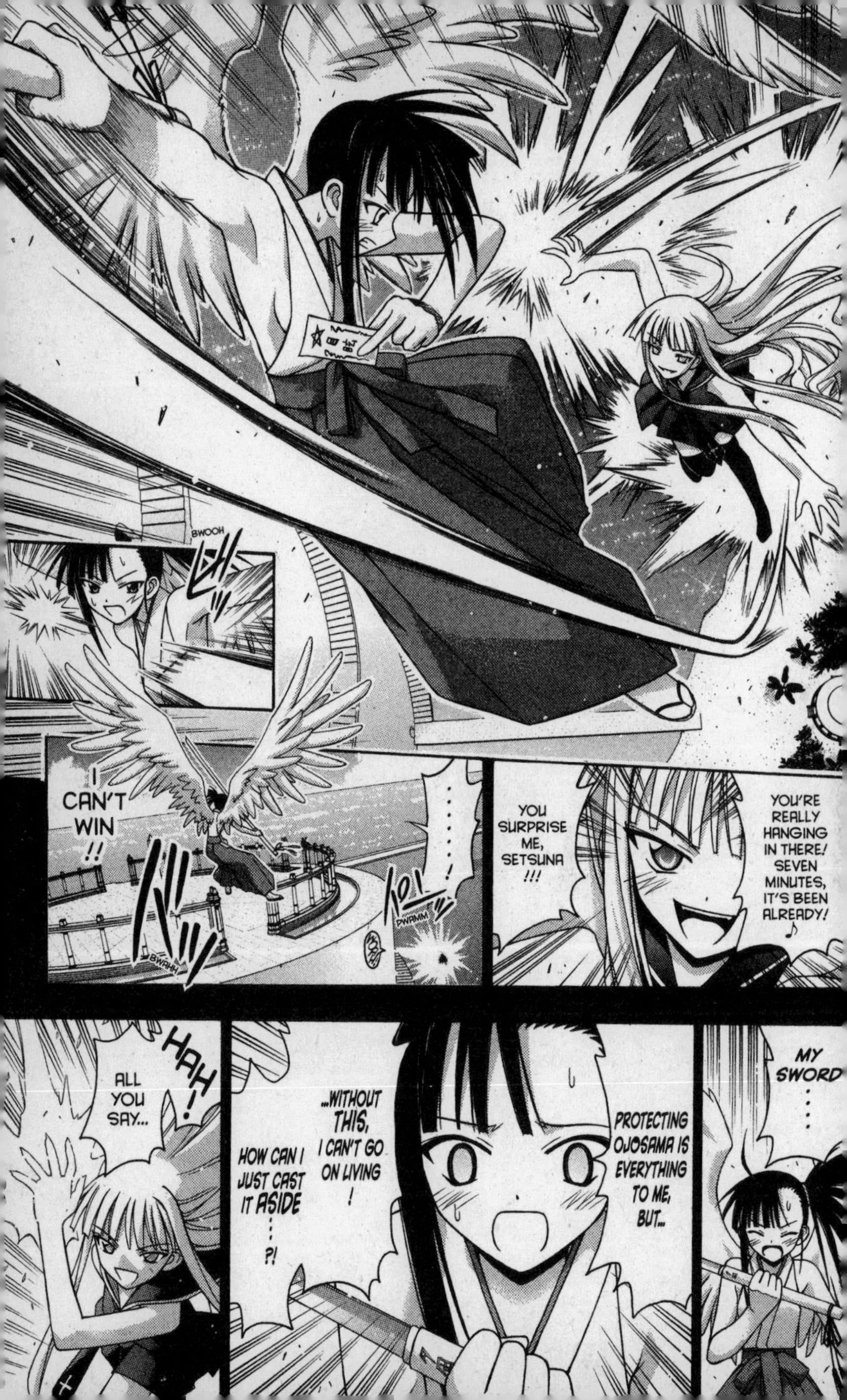
BWOOH
YOU'RE REALLY HANGING IN THERE! SEVEN MINUTES, IT'S BEEN ALREADY! ♪
YOU SURPRISE ME, SETSUNA !!!
......!
DWAMM
I CAN'T WIN !!
BWAHH
MY SWORD ....
PROTECTING OJOSAMA IS EVERYTHING TO ME, BUT...
...WITHOUT THIS, I CAN'T GO ON LIVING !
HOW CAN I JUST CAST IT ASIDE ...?!
HAH!
ALL YOU SAY...

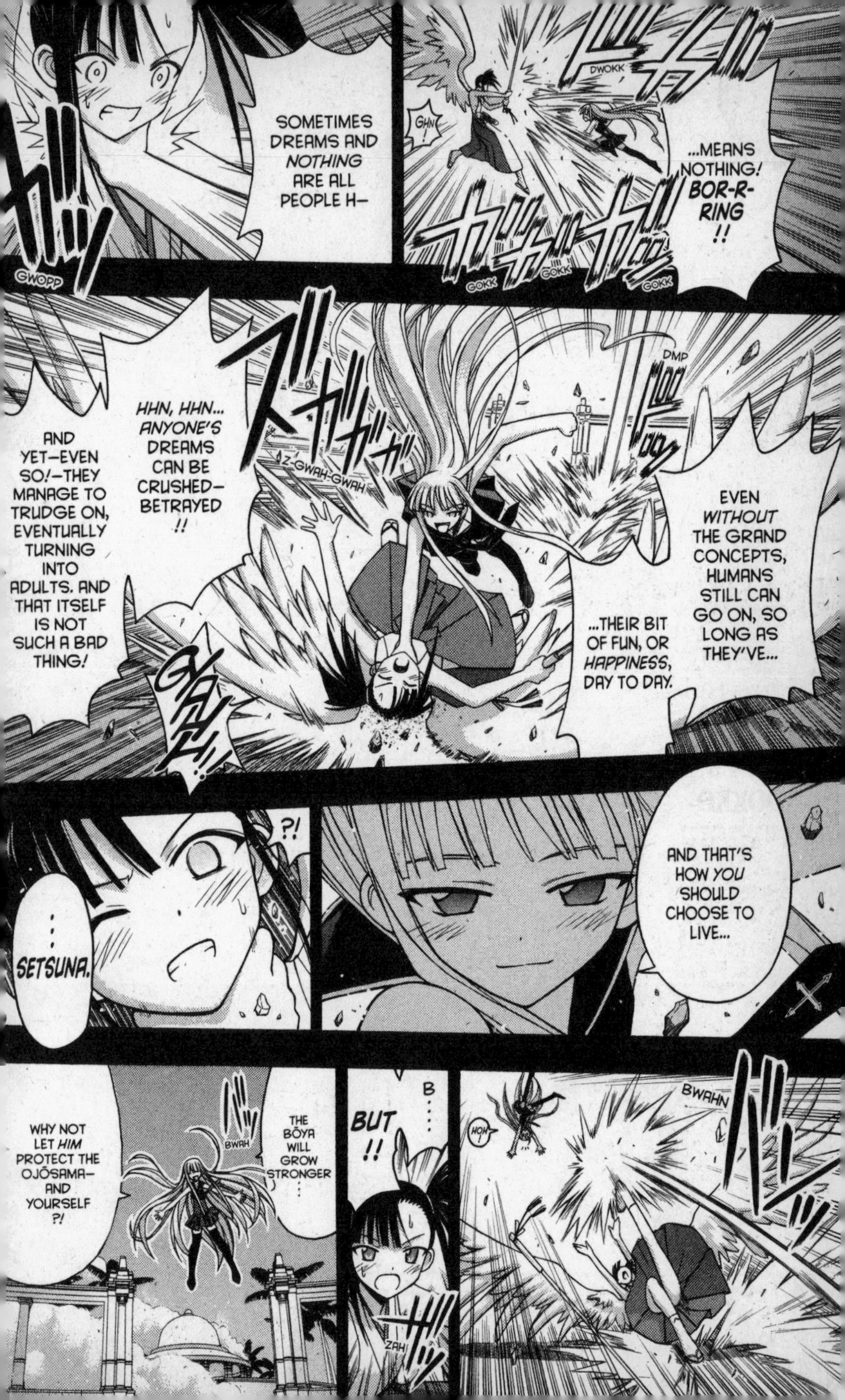
DWOKK
GHN!
...MEANS NOTHING! BOR-R-RING!!
GOKK GOKK GOKK
SOMETIMES DREAMS AND *NOTHING* ARE ALL PEOPLE H—
GWOPP
DMP
EVEN *WITHOUT* THE GRAND CONCEPTS, HUMANS STILL CAN GO ON, SO LONG AS THEY'VE...
...THEIR BIT OF FUN, OR *HAPPINESS*, DAY TO DAY.
Z-GWAH-GWAH
HHN, HHN... ANYONE'S DREAMS CAN BE CRUSHED—BETRAYED!!
AND YET—EVEN SO!—THEY MANAGE TO TRUDGE ON, EVENTUALLY TURNING INTO ADULTS. AND THAT ITSELF IS NOT SUCH A BAD THING!
AND THAT'S HOW *YOU* SHOULD CHOOSE TO LIVE...
?!
... SETSUNA.
BWAHN
HOH?
B....
BUT!!
ZAH
THE BŌYA WILL GROW STRONGER...
BWAH
WHY NOT LET *HIM* PROTECT THE OJŌSAMA—AND YOURSELF?!

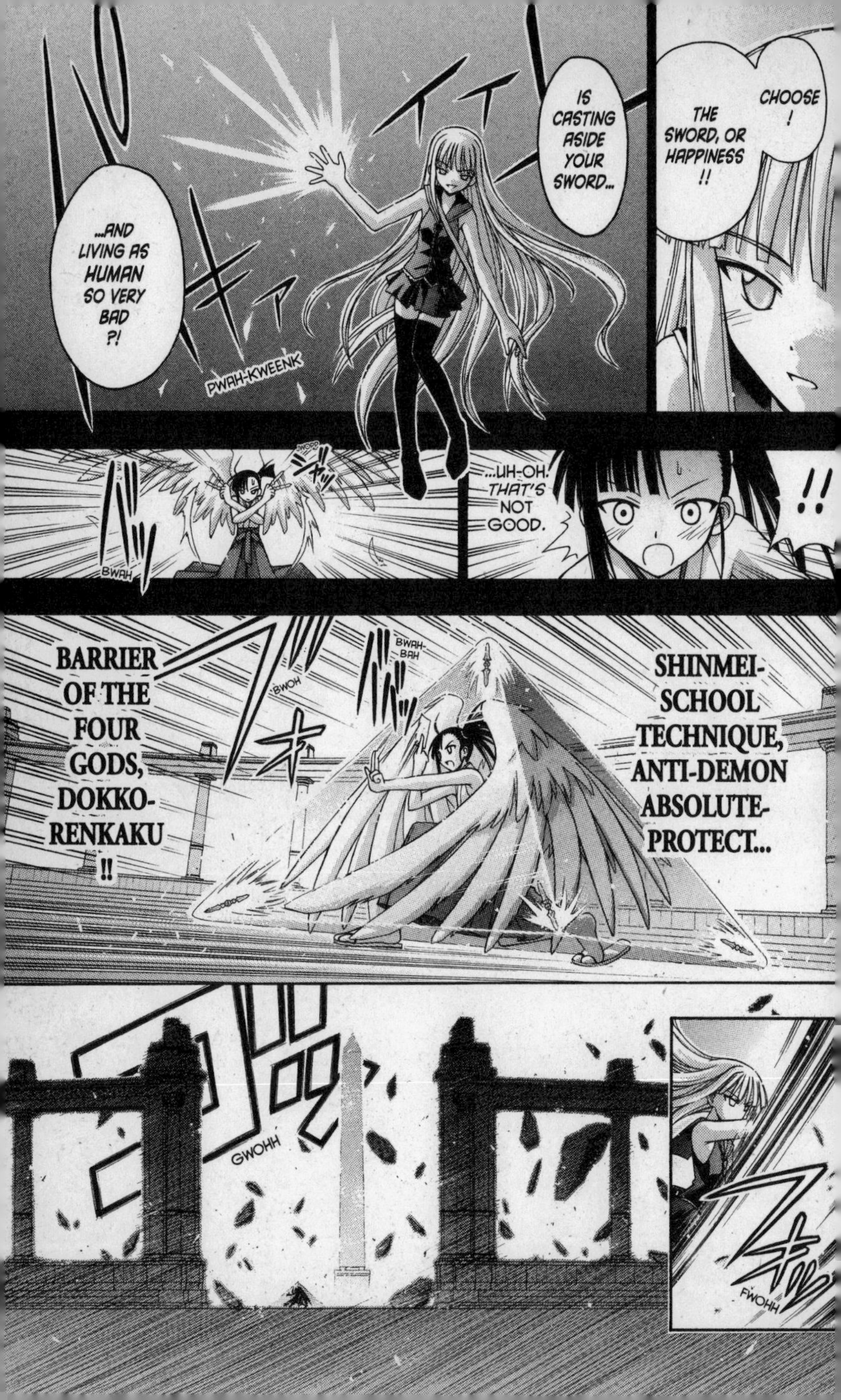
CHOOSE!
THE SWORD, OR HAPPINESS!!
IS CASTING ASIDE YOUR SWORD...
...AND LIVING AS HUMAN SO VERY BAD?!
PWAH-KWEENK
!!
...UH-OH. THAT'S NOT GOOD.
BWAH
SHINMEI-SCHOOL TECHNIQUE, ANTI-DEMON ABSOLUTE-PROTECT...
BWAH-BAH
BWOH
BARRIER OF THE FOUR GODS, DOKKO-RENKAKU!!
FWOHH
GWOHH

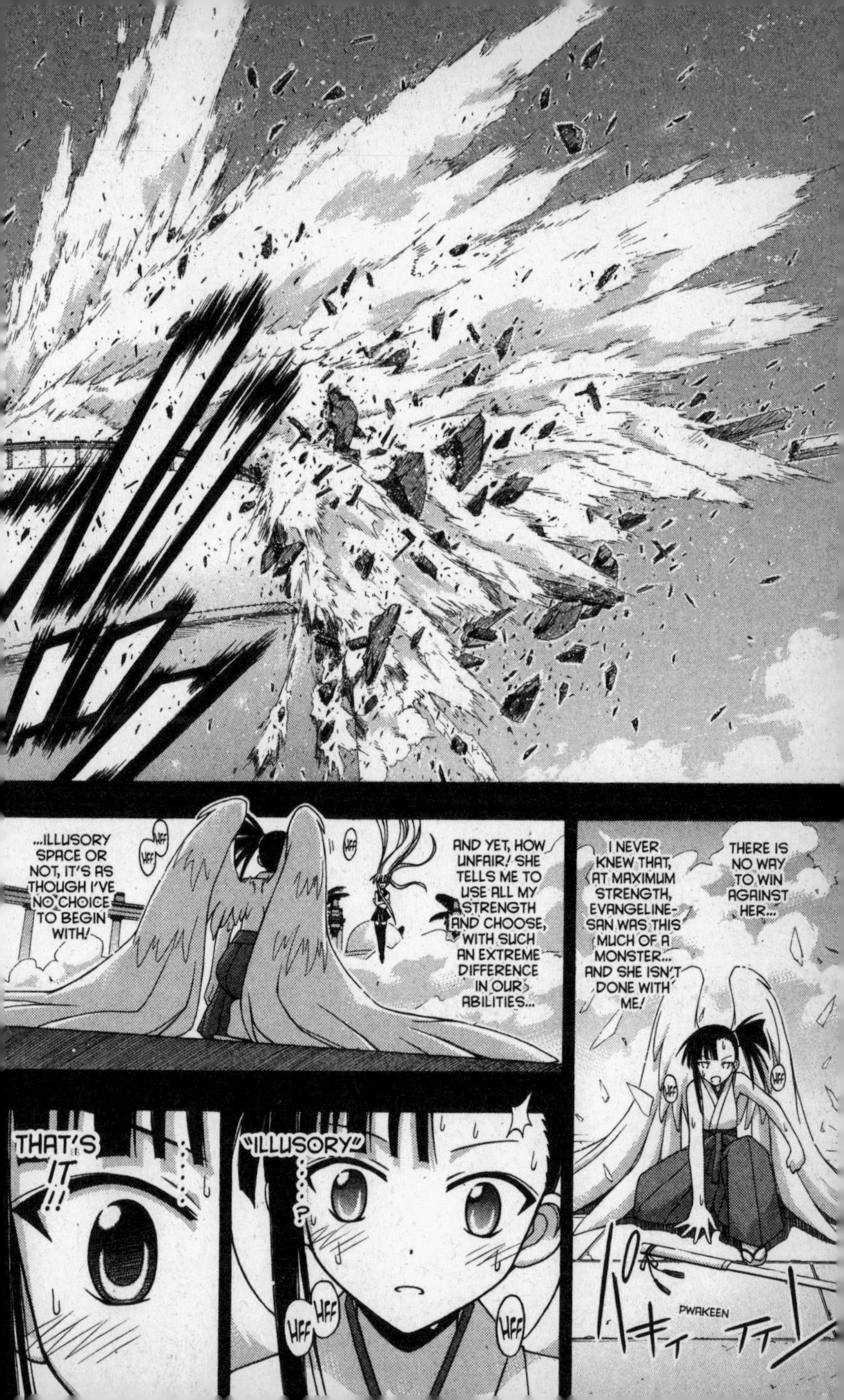
THERE IS NO WAY TO WIN AGAINST HER...
I NEVER KNEW THAT, AT MAXIMUM STRENGTH, EVANGELINE-SAN WAS THIS MUCH OF A MONSTER... AND SHE ISN'T DONE WITH ME!
HFF
HFF
PWAKEEN
AND YET, HOW UNFAIR! SHE TELLS ME TO USE ALL MY STRENGTH AND CHOOSE, WITH SUCH AN EXTREME DIFFERENCE IN OUR ABILITIES...
HFF
HUFF
HFF
...ILLUSORY SPACE OR NOT, IT'S AS THOUGH I'VE NO CHOICE TO BEGIN WITH!
"ILLUSORY"
...?
HFF
HFF
HFF
THAT'S IT!!
......

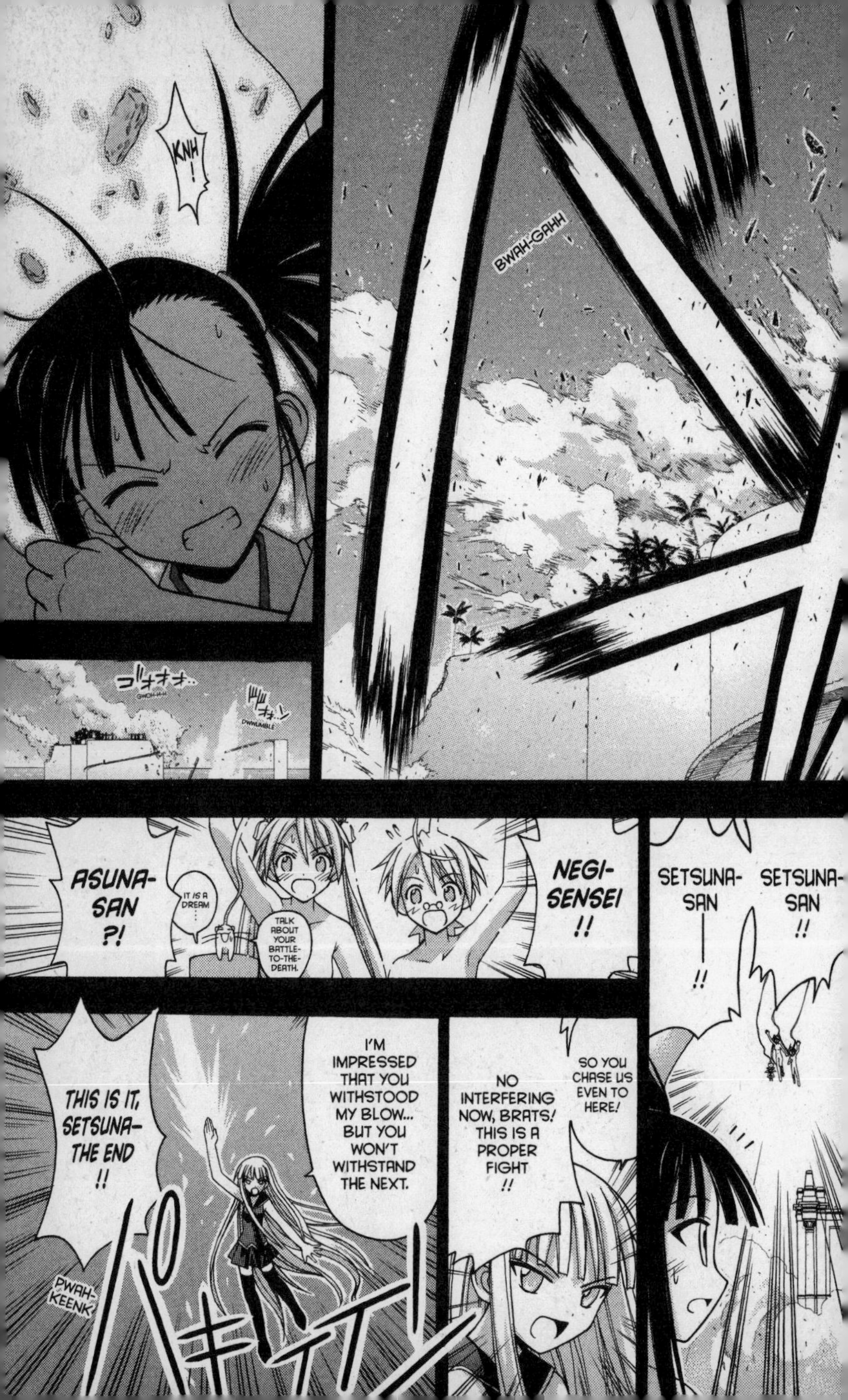
BWAH-GAHH
KNH!
ゴオオオ..
GWOH-H-H
ドゥオォン
DWUMBLE
SETSUNA-SAN !!
SETSUNA-SAN —!!
NEGI-SENSEI !!
TALK ABOUT YOUR BATTLE-TO-THE-DEATH.
IT IS A DREAM...
ASUNA-SAN ?!
SO YOU CHASE US EVEN TO HERE!
NO INTERFERING NOW, BRATS! THIS IS A PROPER FIGHT !!
I'M IMPRESSED THAT YOU WITHSTOOD MY BLOW... BUT YOU WON'T WITHSTAND THE NEXT.
THIS IS IT, SETSUNA-THE END !!
パキィィン
PWAH-KEENK

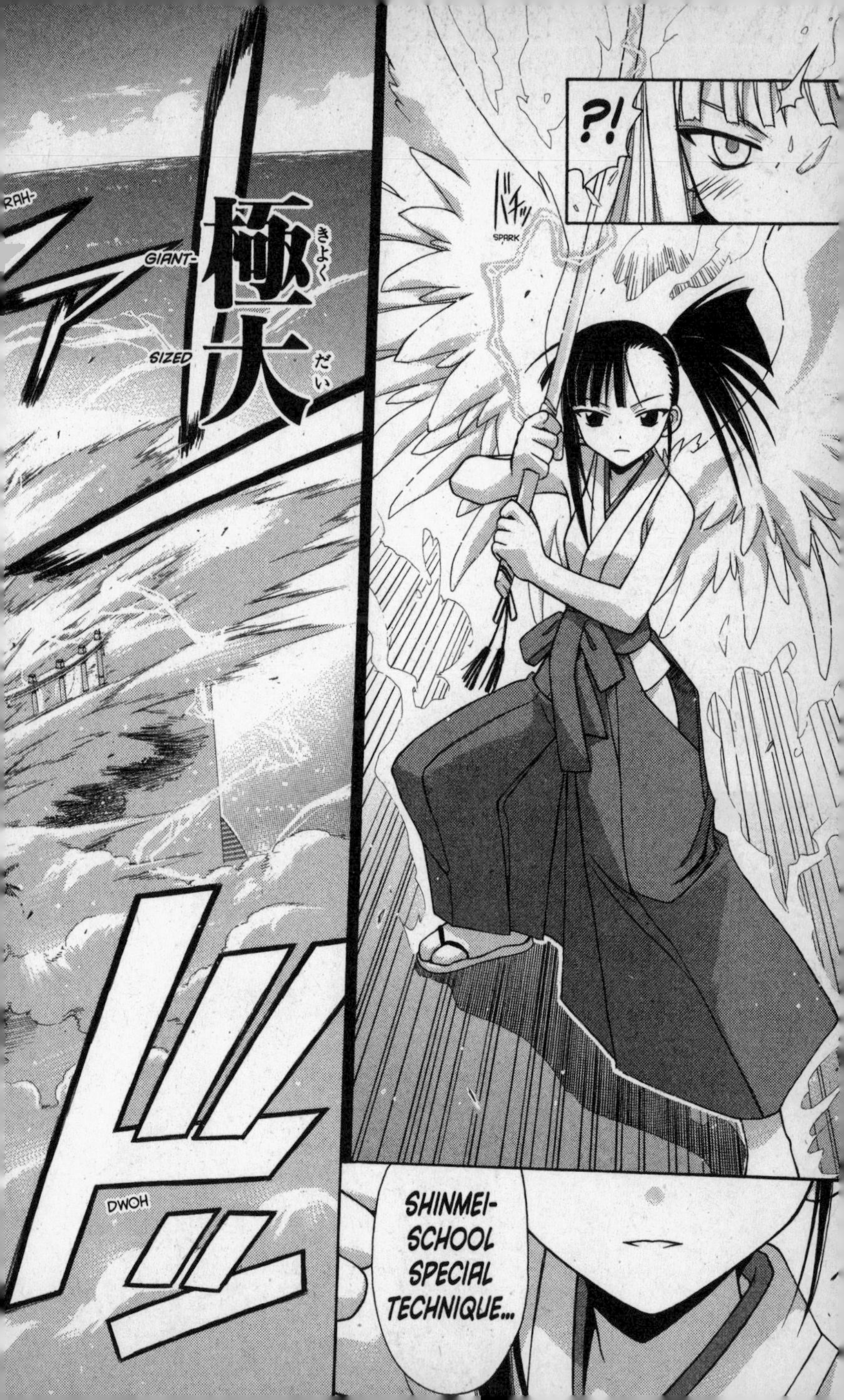
?!
SPARK
SHINMEI-SCHOOL SPECIAL TECHNIQUE...
極大
GIANT-
SIZED
RAH-
DWOH

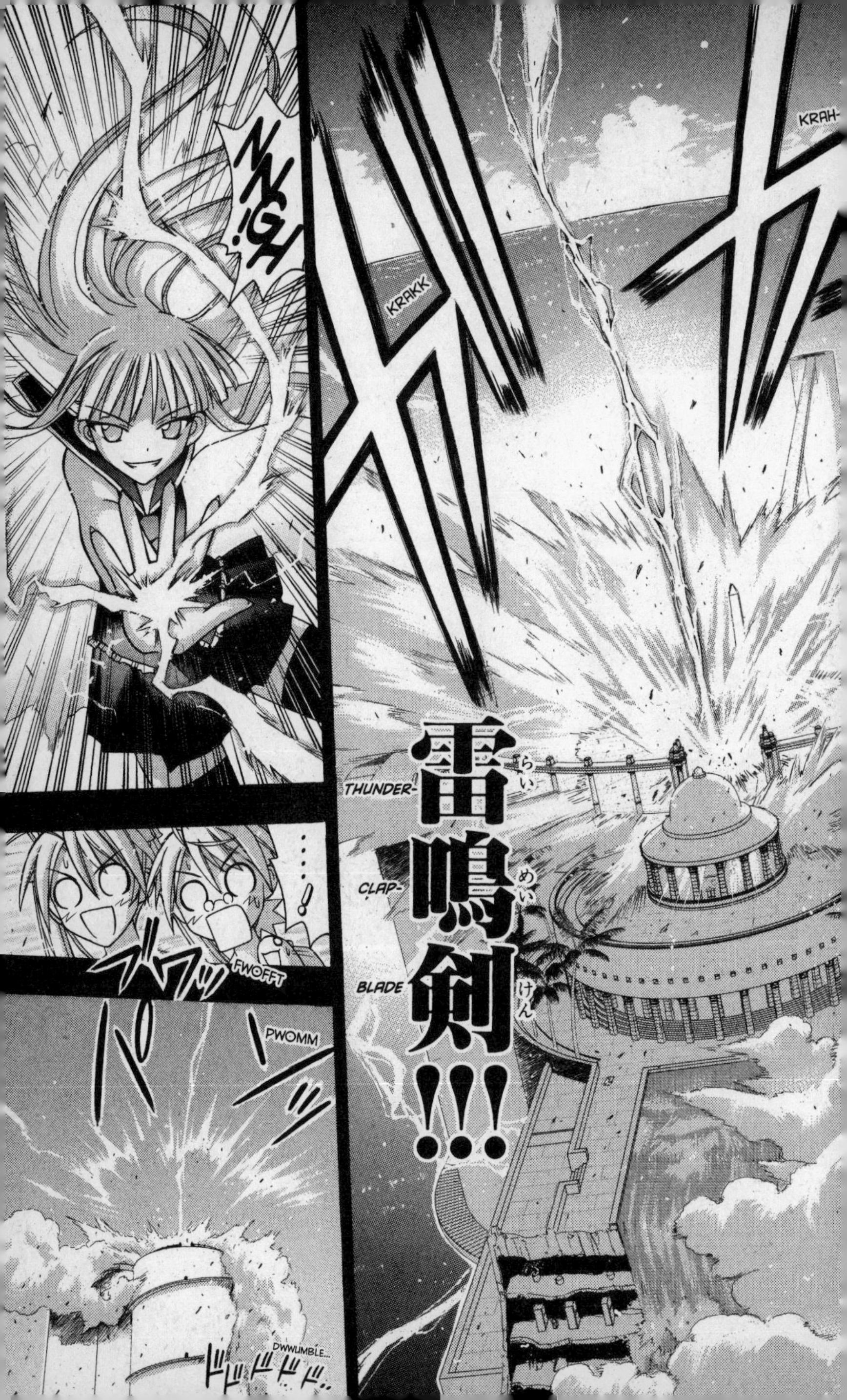
KRAH-
KRAKK
THUNDER-
CLAP-
BLADE
雷鳴剣!!!
NNGH!
.....!
FWOFFT
PWOMM
DWWUMBLE...

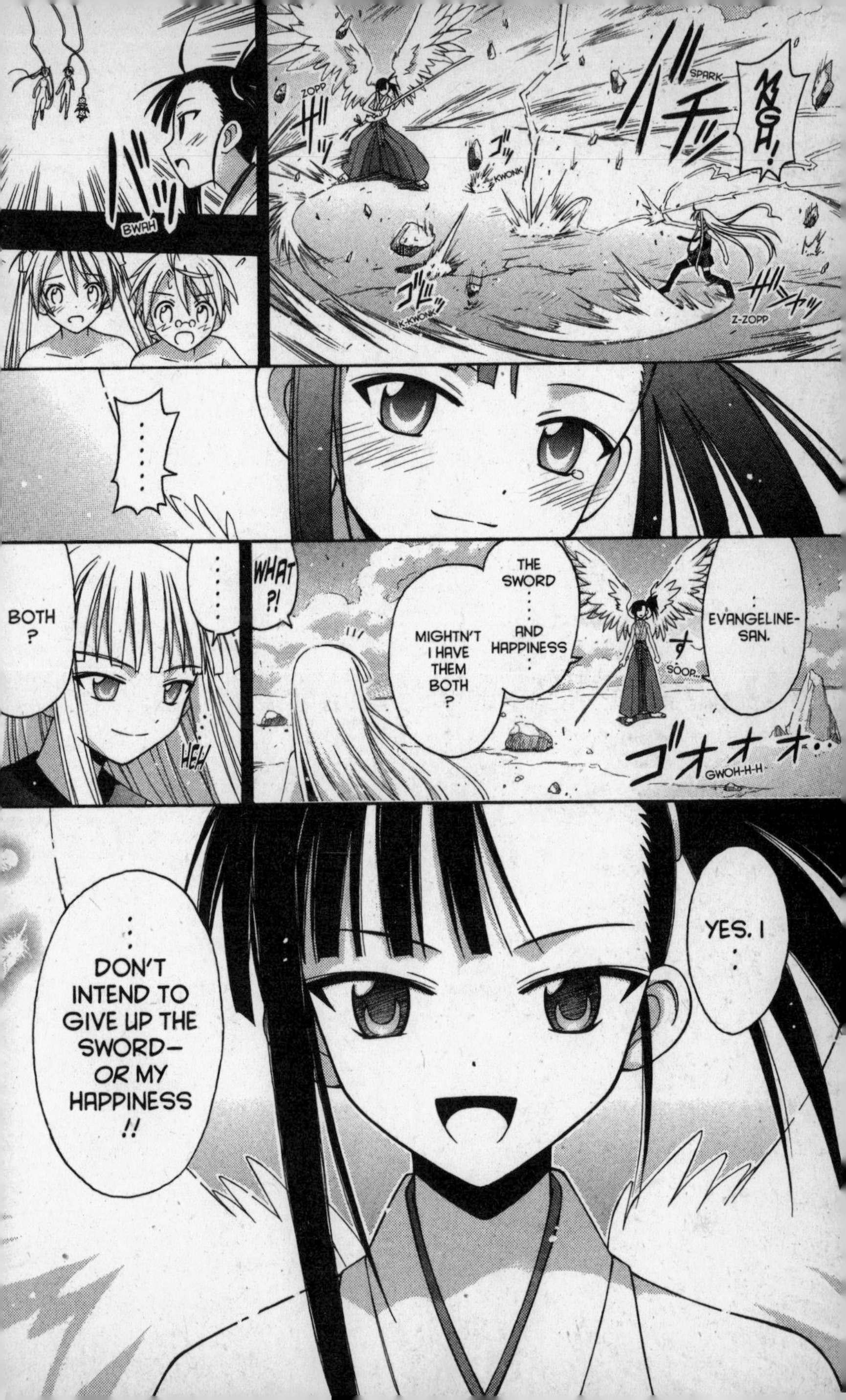
SPARK
NGH!
ZOPP
KWONK
Z-ZOPP
K-KWONK
BWAH
……
: EVANGELINE-SAN.
THE SWORD …… AND HAPPINESS …
MIGHTN'T I HAVE THEM BOTH ?
SOOP..
GWOH-H-H
WHAT ?!
……
HEH
BOTH ?
YES. I :
: DON'T INTEND TO GIVE UP THE SWORD— OR MY HAPPINESS !!

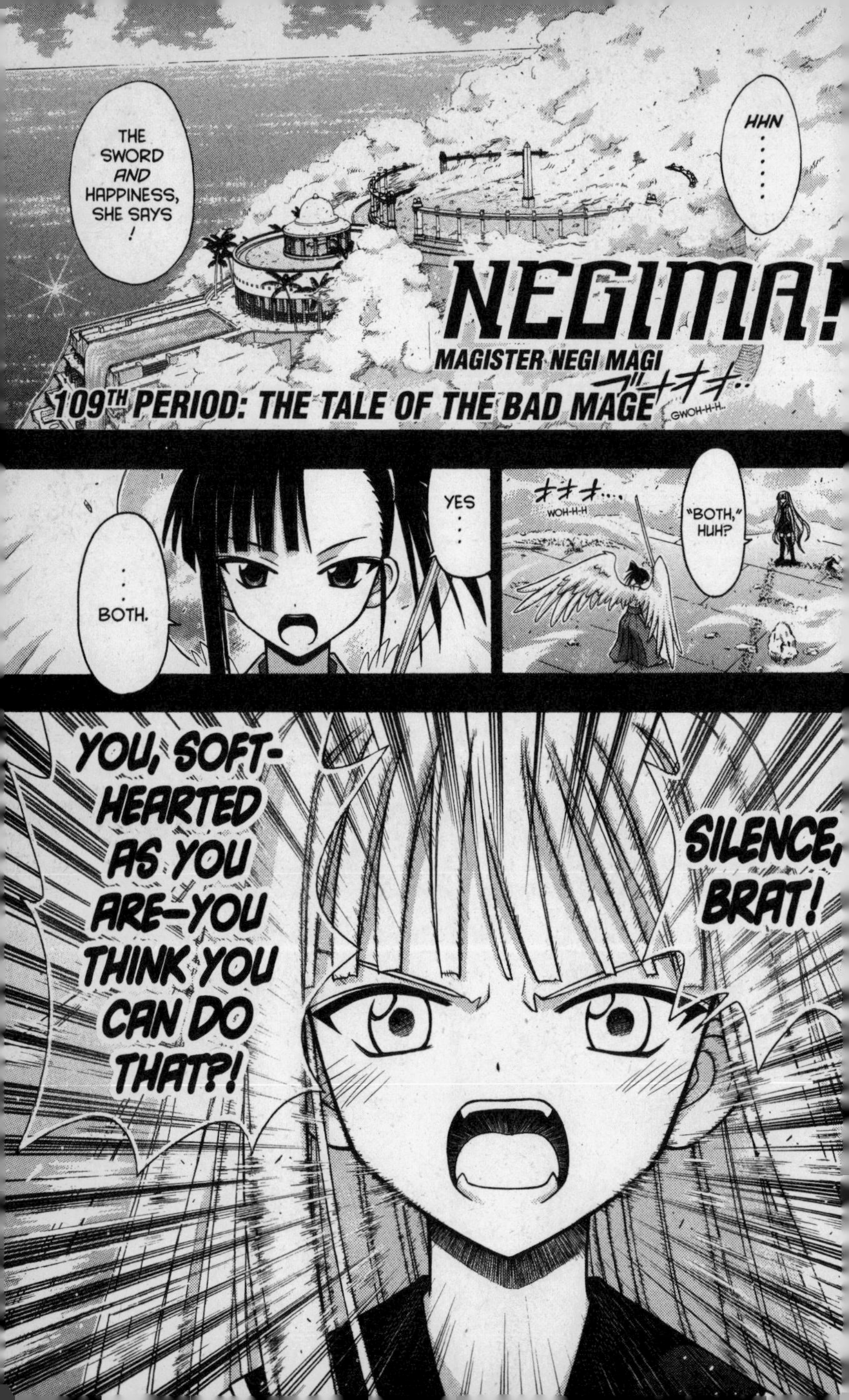
HHN......
NEGIMA!
MAGISTER NEGI MAGI
109TH PERIOD: THE TALE OF THE BAD MAGE
GWOH-H-H..
THE SWORD AND HAPPINESS, SHE SAYS!
WOH-H-H
"BOTH," HUH?
YES...
...BOTH.
SILENCE, BRAT!
YOU, SOFT-HEARTED AS YOU ARE—YOU THINK YOU CAN DO THAT?!

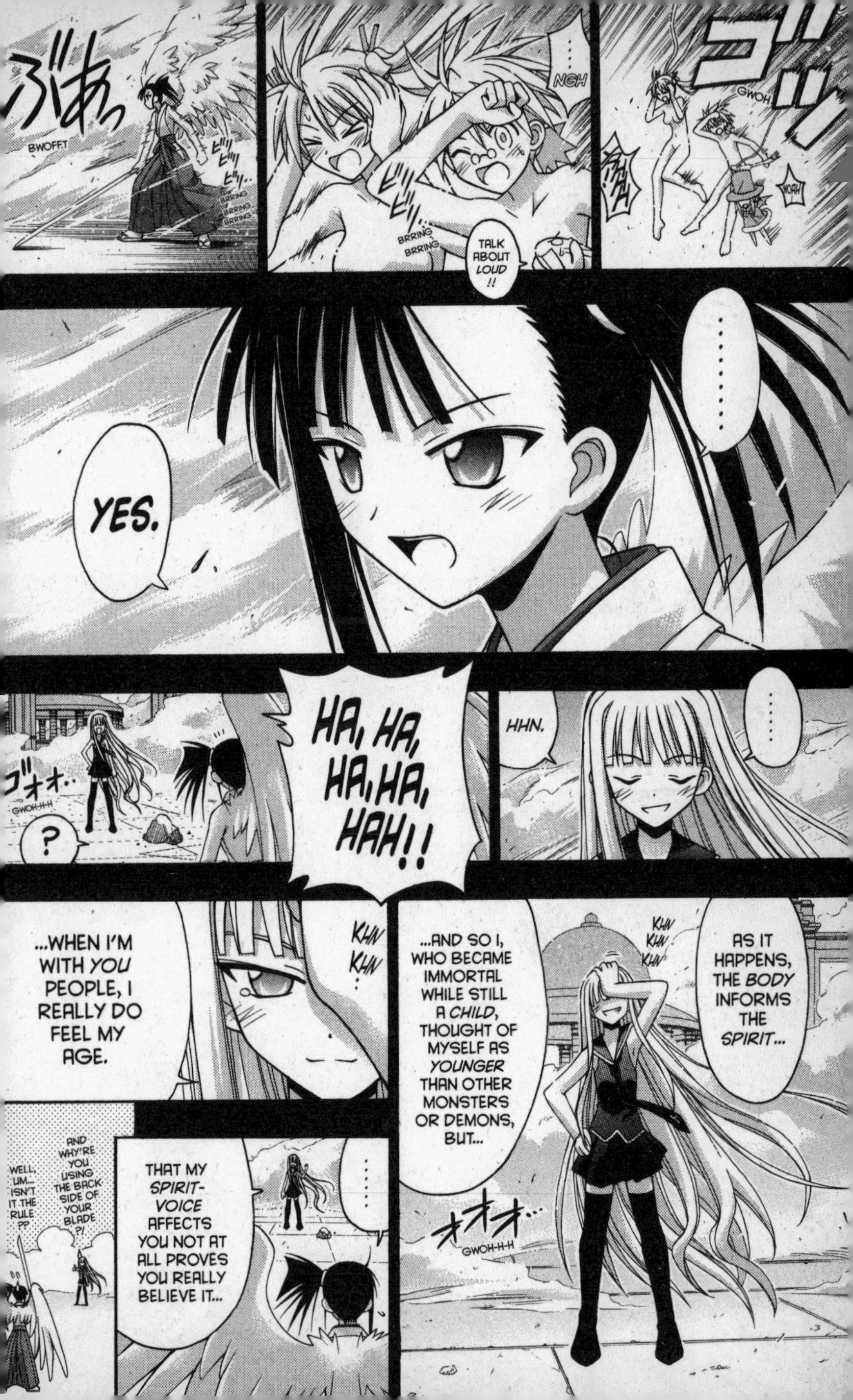

GWOH
WOAH
...
NGH
TALK ABOUT *LOUD* !!
BRRING BRRING
ぶあっ
BWOFFT
BRRING BRRING BRRING
....
YES.
.....
HHN.
HA, HA, HA, HA, HAH!!
?
GWOH-H-H
AS IT HAPPENS, THE *BODY* INFORMS THE *SPIRIT*...
KHN KHN KHN
...AND SO I, WHO BECAME IMMORTAL WHILE STILL A *CHILD*, THOUGHT OF MYSELF AS *YOUNGER* THAN OTHER MONSTERS OR DEMONS, BUT...
GWOH-H-H
KHN KHN
...WHEN I'M WITH *YOU* PEOPLE, I REALLY DO FEEL MY AGE.
....
THAT MY *SPIRIT-VOICE* AFFECTS YOU NOT AT ALL PROVES YOU REALLY BELIEVE IT...
AND WHY'RE YOU USING THE BACK-SIDE OF YOUR BLADE?!
WELL, UM... ISN'T IT THE RULE??

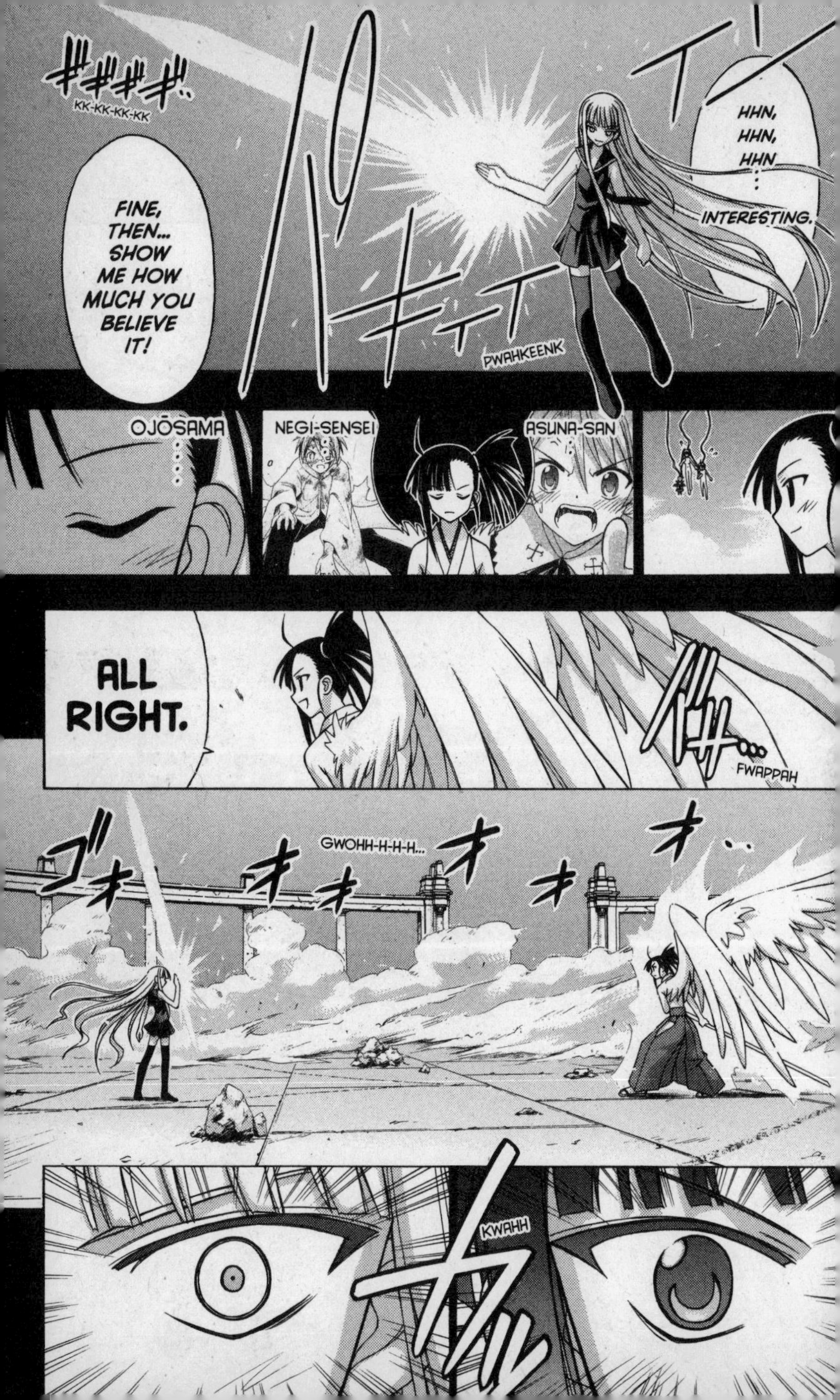
HHN, HHN, HHN...
INTERESTING.
PWAHKEENK
KK-KK-KK-KK
FINE, THEN... SHOW ME HOW MUCH YOU BELIEVE IT!
ASUNA-SAN
NEGI-SENSEI
OJŌSAMA....
FWAPPAH
ALL RIGHT.
GWOHH-H-H-H...
KWAHH

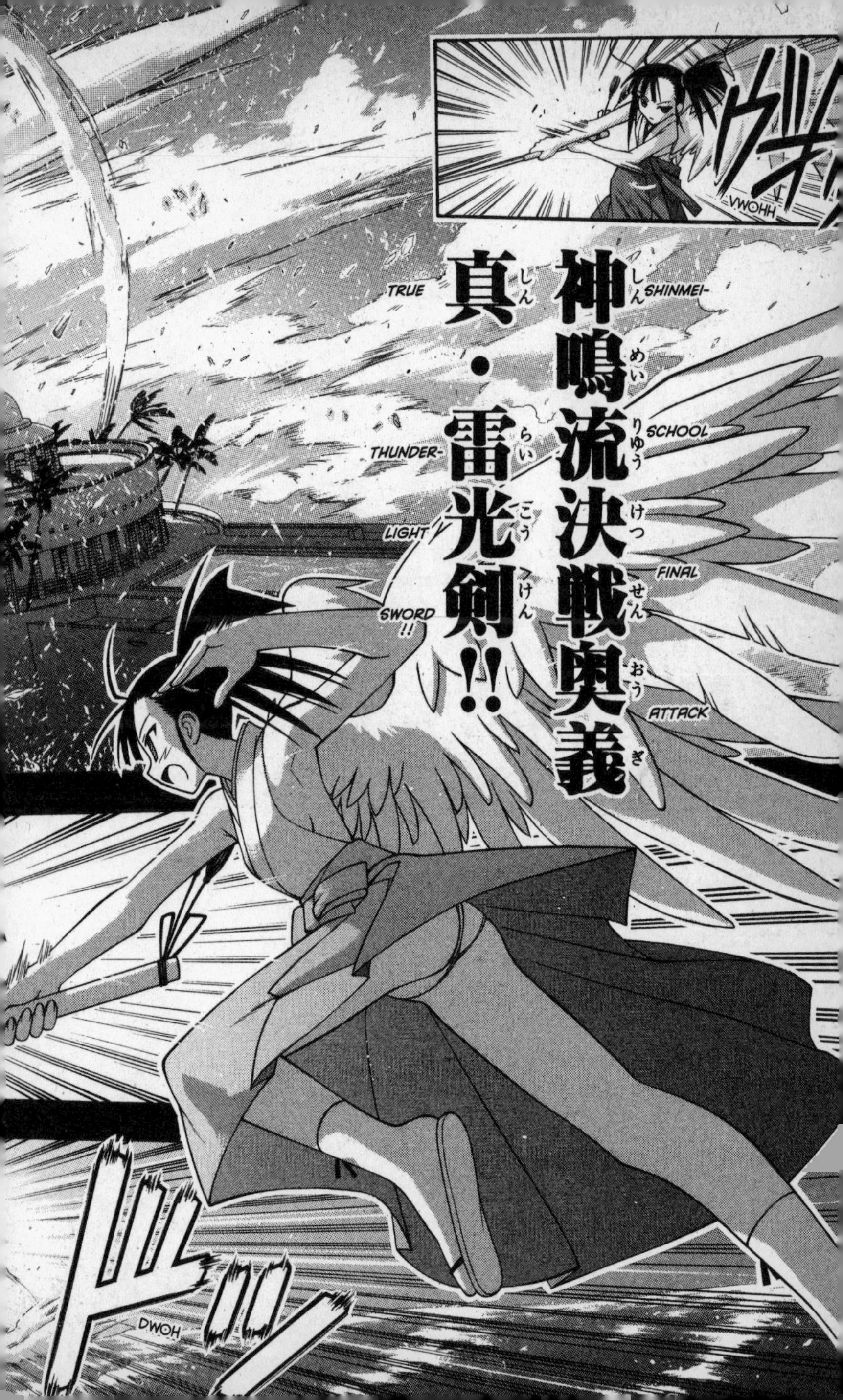
VWOHH
神鳴流決戦奥義
真・雷光剣!!
SHINMEI-SCHOOL FINAL ATTACK
TRUE THUNDER-LIGHT SWORD!!
DWOH

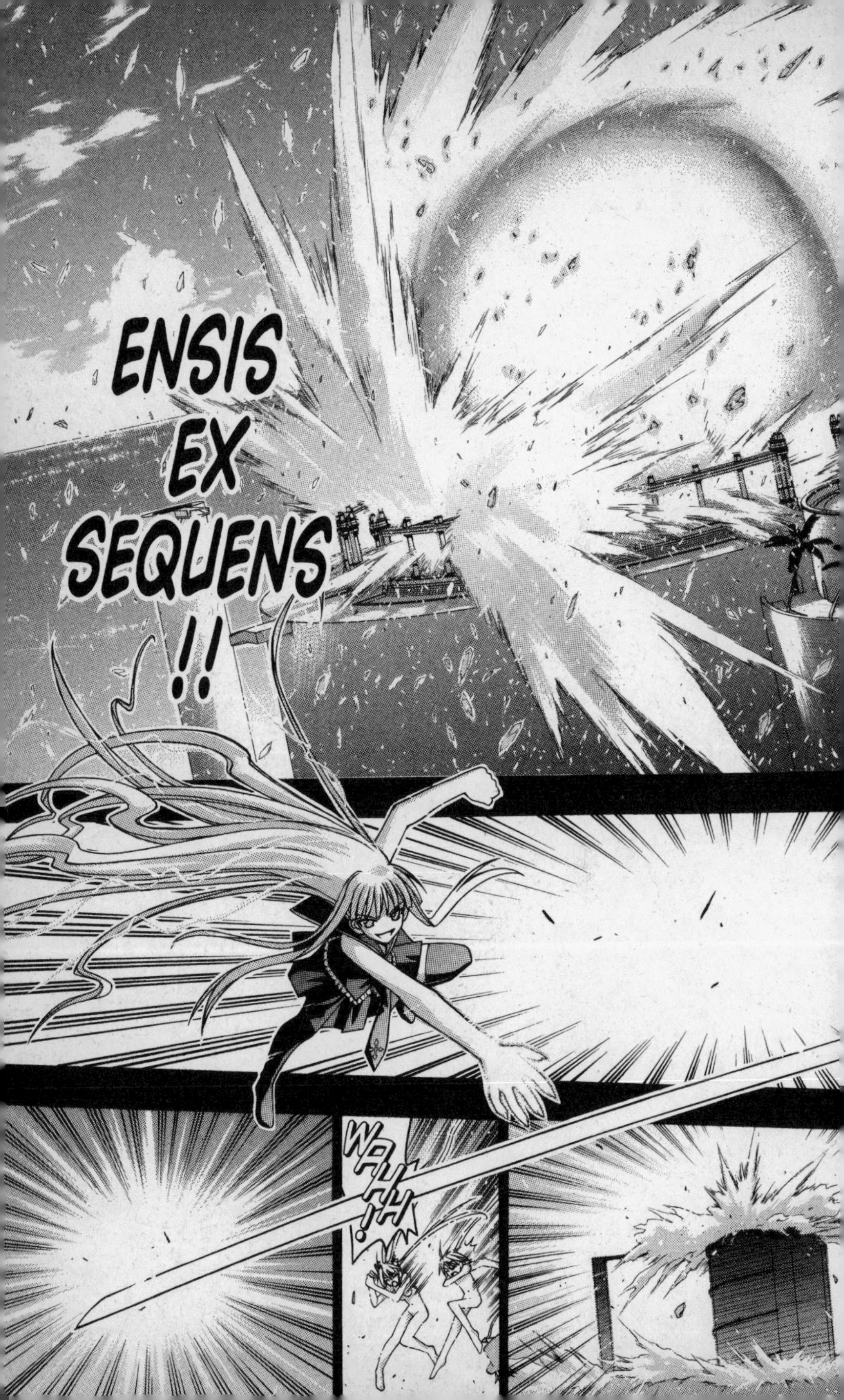
ENSIS EX SEQUENS!!
WAHH!

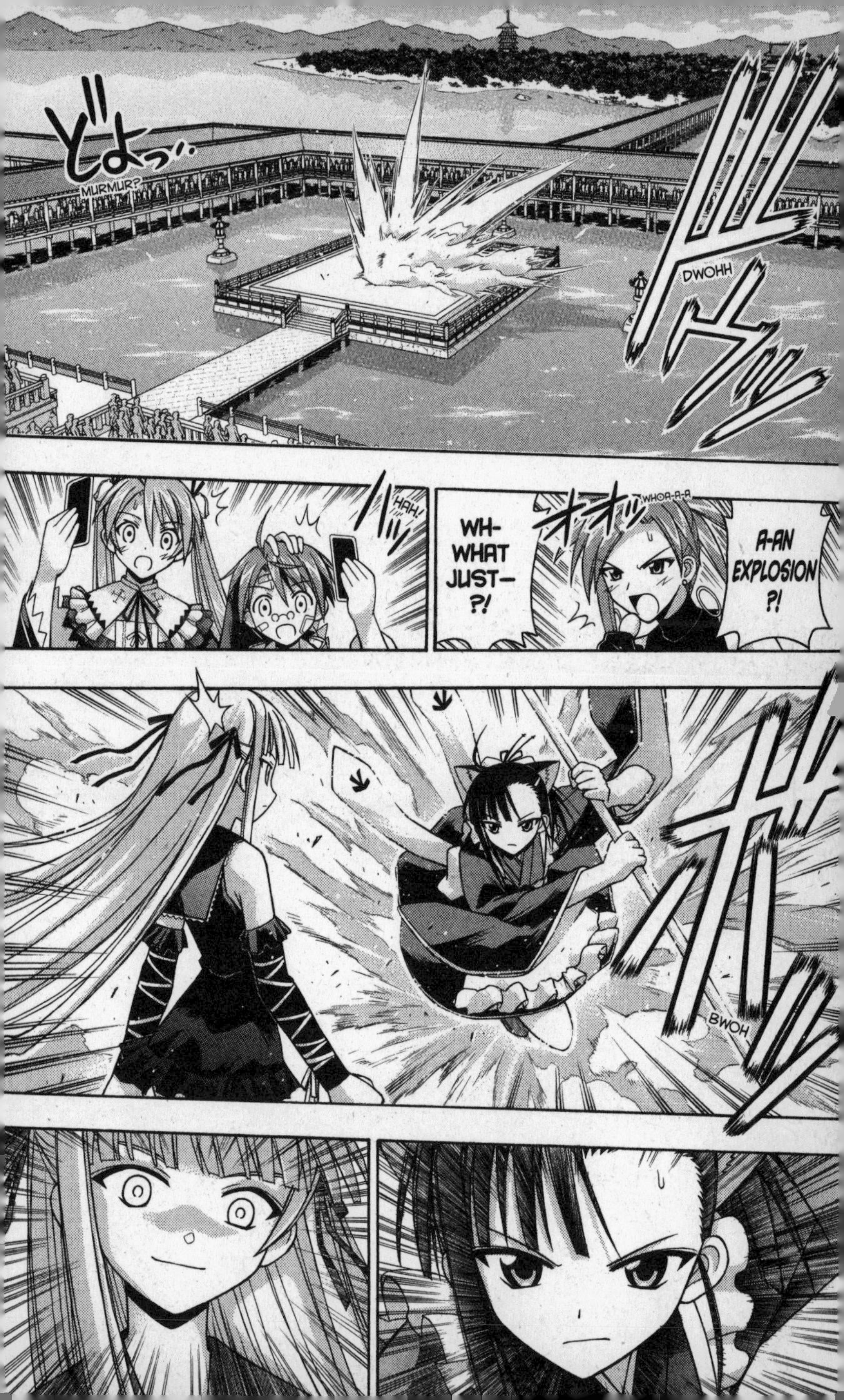

DWOHH
どよっ
MURMUR?
WHOA-A-A
A-AN EXPLOSION ?!
WH- WHAT JUST— ?!
HAH!
BWOH

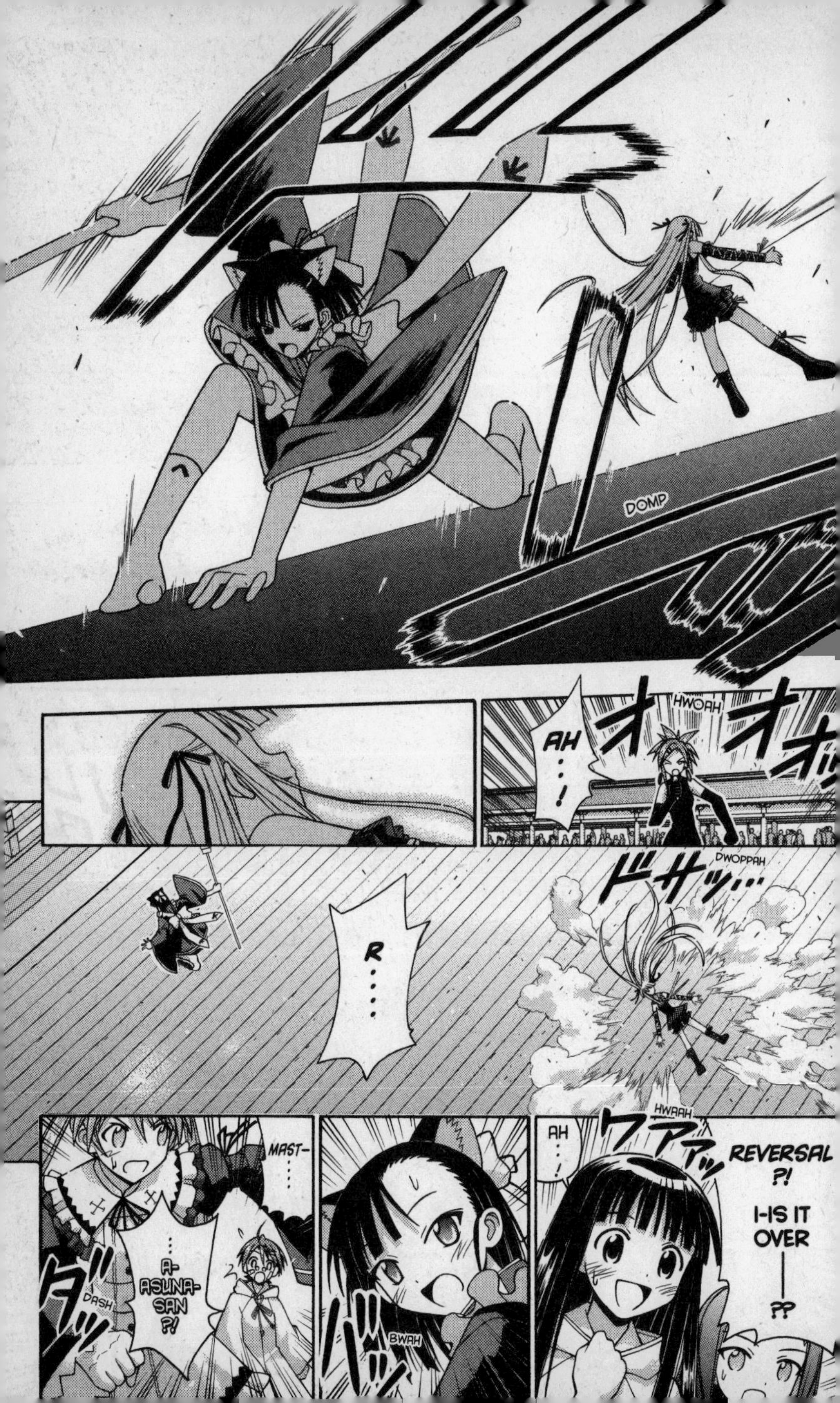
DOMP
オオオッ
HWOAH
AH...!
ドサッ
DWOPPAH
R.....
REVERSAL?!
ワアアッ
HWAAH
AH...!
I-IS IT OVER——??
BWAH
MAST-....
...A-ASUNA-SAN?!
DASH

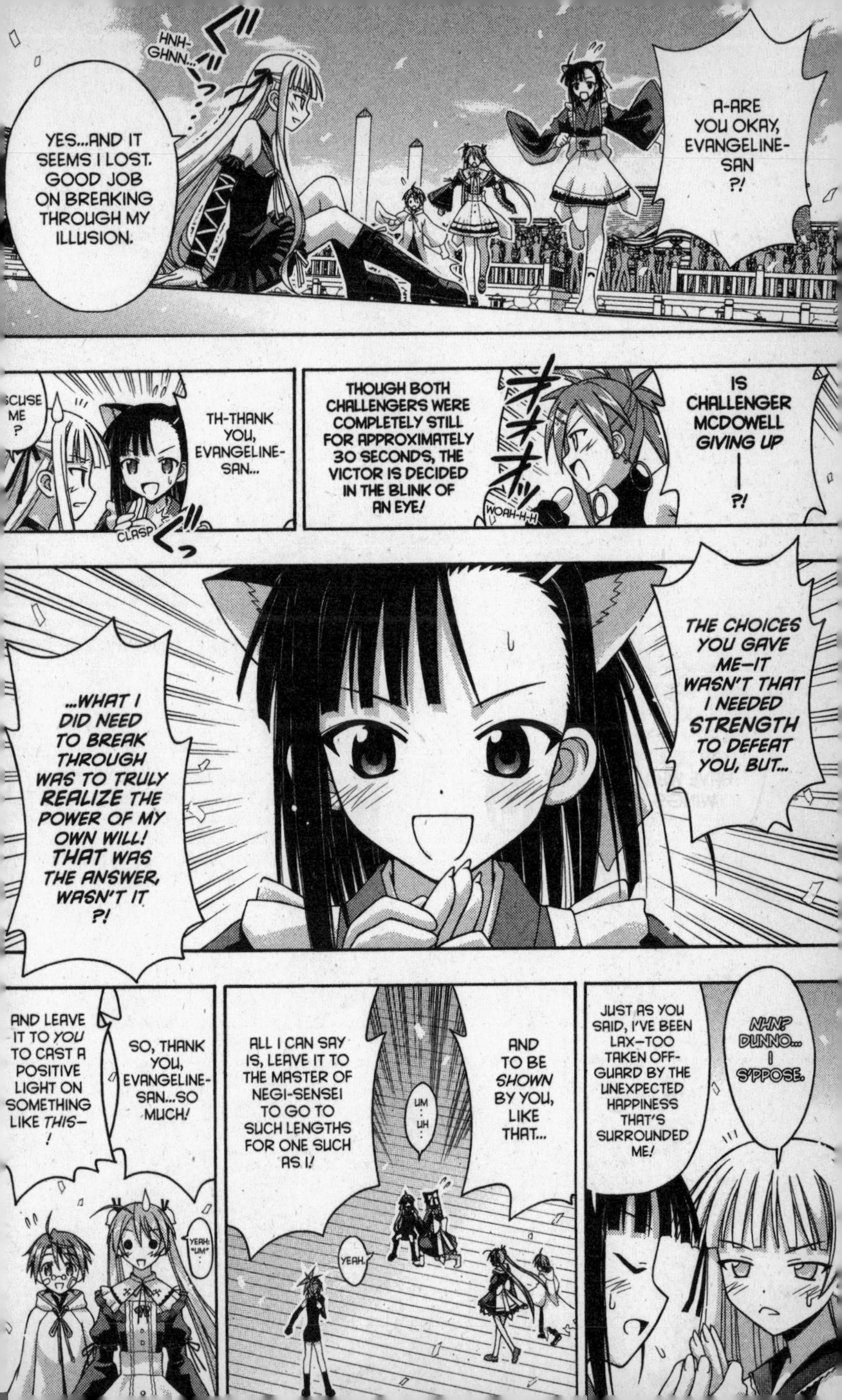
A-ARE YOU OKAY, EVANGELINE-SAN ?!
HNH-GHNN...
YES...AND IT SEEMS I LOST. GOOD JOB ON BREAKING THROUGH MY ILLUSION.
IS CHALLENGER MCDOWELL GIVING UP —?!
WOAH-H-H
THOUGH BOTH CHALLENGERS WERE COMPLETELY STILL FOR APPROXIMATELY 30 SECONDS, THE VICTOR IS DECIDED IN THE BLINK OF AN EYE!
TH-THANK YOU, EVANGELINE-SAN...
SCUSE ME ?
CLASP
THE CHOICES YOU GAVE ME—IT WASN'T THAT I NEEDED STRENGTH TO DEFEAT YOU, BUT...
...WHAT I DID NEED TO BREAK THROUGH WAS TO TRULY REALIZE THE POWER OF MY OWN WILL! THAT WAS THE ANSWER, WASN'T IT ?!
NHN? DUNNO... I S'PPOSE.
JUST AS YOU SAID, I'VE BEEN LAX—TOO TAKEN OFF-GUARD BY THE UNEXPECTED HAPPINESS THAT'S SURROUNDED ME!
AND TO BE SHOWN BY YOU, LIKE THAT...
UM... UH...
ALL I CAN SAY IS, LEAVE IT TO THE MASTER OF NEGI-SENSEI TO GO TO SUCH LENGTHS FOR ONE SUCH AS I!
YEAH.
SO, THANK YOU, EVANGELINE-SAN...SO MUCH!
AND LEAVE IT TO YOU TO CAST A POSITIVE LIGHT ON SOMETHING LIKE THIS—!
YEAH: "UM"

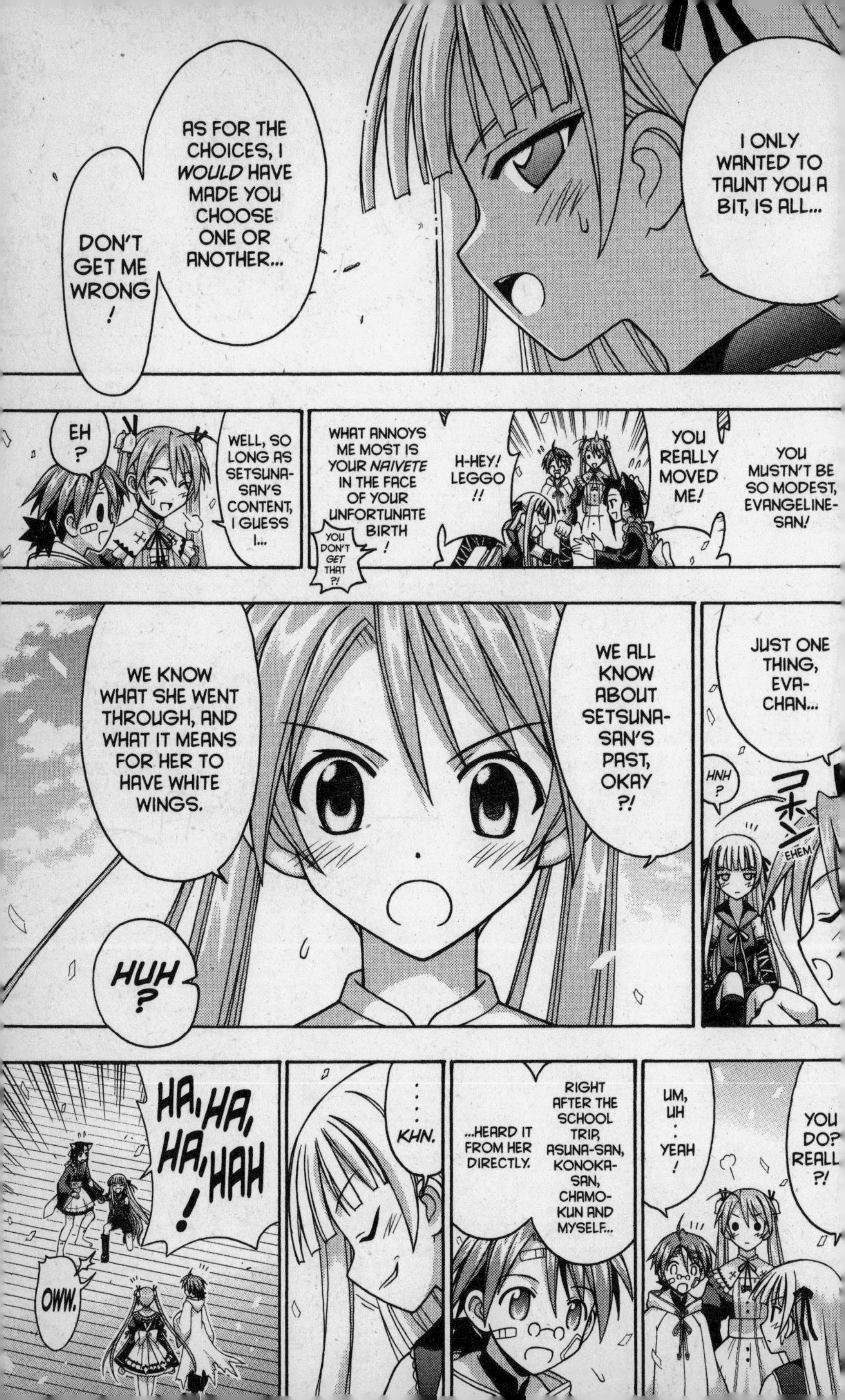
I ONLY WANTED TO TAUNT YOU A BIT, IS ALL...
AS FOR THE CHOICES, I *WOULD* HAVE MADE YOU CHOOSE ONE OR ANOTHER...
DON'T GET ME WRONG!
YOU MUSTN'T BE SO MODEST, EVANGELINE-SAN!
YOU REALLY MOVED ME!
H-HEY! LEGGO!!
WHAT ANNOYS ME MOST IS YOUR *NAIVETE* IN THE FACE OF YOUR UNFORTUNATE BIRTH!
YOU DON'T *GET* THAT?!
WELL, SO LONG AS SETSUNA-SAN'S CONTENT, I GUESS I...
EH?
JUST ONE THING, EVA-CHAN...
HNH?
コホン
EHEM
WE ALL KNOW ABOUT SETSUNA-SAN'S PAST, OKAY?!
WE KNOW WHAT SHE WENT THROUGH, AND WHAT IT MEANS FOR HER TO HAVE WHITE WINGS.
HUH?
YOU DO? REALL ?!
UM, UH... YEAH!
RIGHT AFTER THE SCHOOL TRIP, ASUNA-SAN, KONOKA-SAN, CHAMO-KUN AND MYSELF...
...HEARD IT FROM HER DIRECTLY.
......
KHN.
HA, HA, HA, HAH!
OWW.

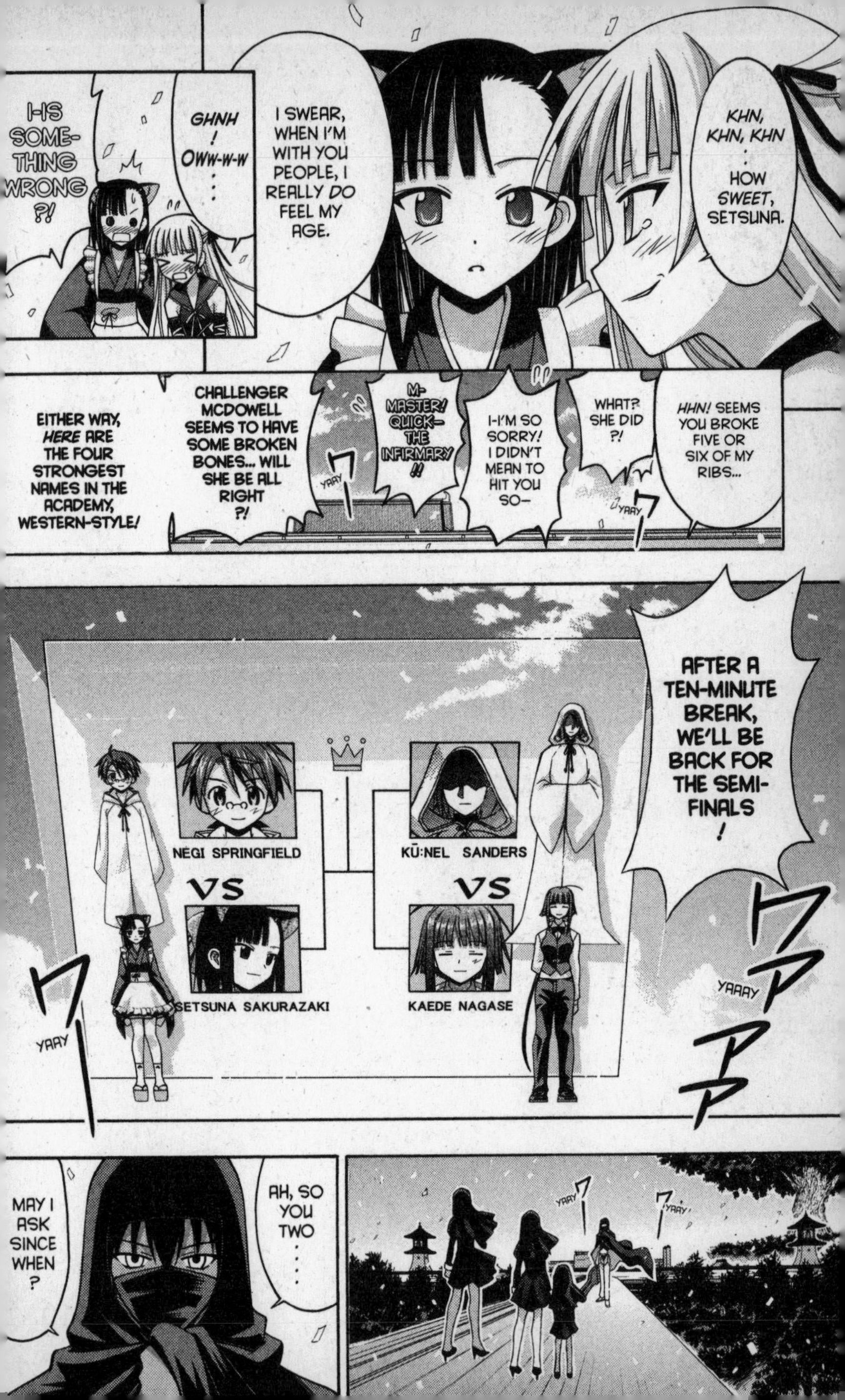

KHN, KHN, KHN... HOW *SWEET*, SETSUNA.
I SWEAR, WHEN I'M WITH YOU PEOPLE, I REALLY *DO* FEEL MY AGE.
GHNH! OWW-W-W...
I-IS SOME-THING WRONG?!
HHN! SEEMS YOU BROKE FIVE OR SIX OF MY RIBS...
YAAY
WHAT? SHE DID?!
I-I'M SO SORRY! I DIDN'T MEAN TO HIT YOU SO—
M-MASTER! QUICK— THE INFIRMARY!!
YAAY
CHALLENGER MCDOWELL SEEMS TO HAVE SOME BROKEN BONES... WILL SHE BE ALL RIGHT?!
EITHER WAY, *HERE* ARE THE FOUR STRONGEST NAMES IN THE ACADEMY, WESTERN-STYLE!
AFTER A TEN-MINUTE BREAK, WE'LL BE BACK FOR THE SEMI-FINALS!
YAAAY
KŪ:NEL SANDERS
VS
KAEDE NAGASE
NEGI SPRINGFIELD
VS
SETSUNA SAKURAZAKI
YAAY
YAAY
YAAY
AH, SO YOU TWO...
MAY I ASK SINCE WHEN?

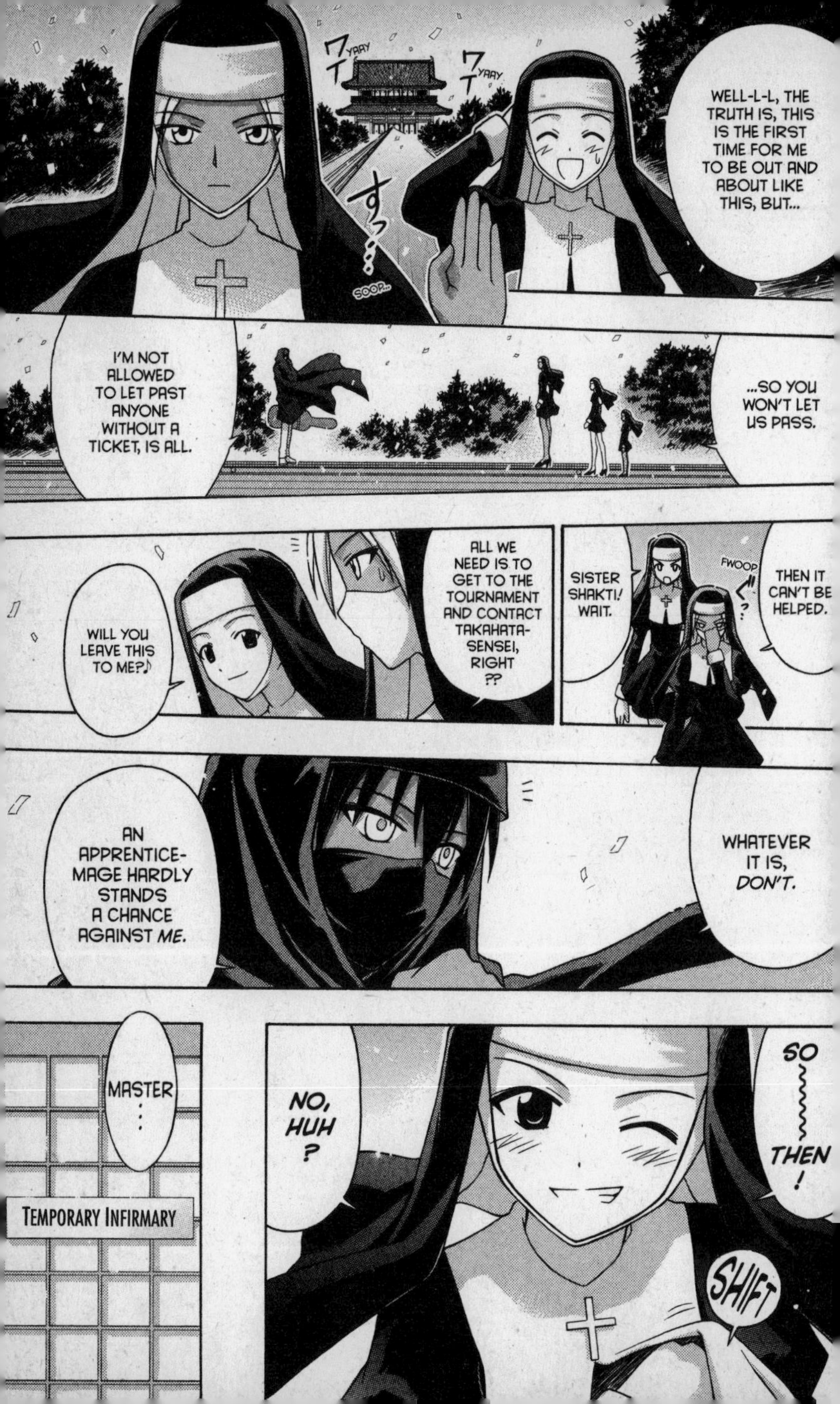
WELL-L-L, THE TRUTH IS, THIS IS THE FIRST TIME FOR ME TO BE OUT AND ABOUT LIKE THIS, BUT...
YAAY
YAAY
SOOP...
...SO YOU WON'T LET US PASS.
I'M NOT ALLOWED TO LET PAST ANYONE WITHOUT A TICKET, IS ALL.
THEN IT CAN'T BE HELPED.
FWOOP
SISTER SHAKTI! WAIT.
ALL WE NEED IS TO GET TO THE TOURNAMENT AND CONTACT TAKAHATA-SENSEI, RIGHT ??
WILL YOU LEAVE THIS TO ME?♪
WHATEVER IT IS, *DON'T.*
AN APPRENTICE-MAGE HARDLY STANDS A CHANCE AGAINST *ME.*
SO~ THEN!
NO, HUH?
SHIFT
MASTER...
TEMPORARY INFIRMARY

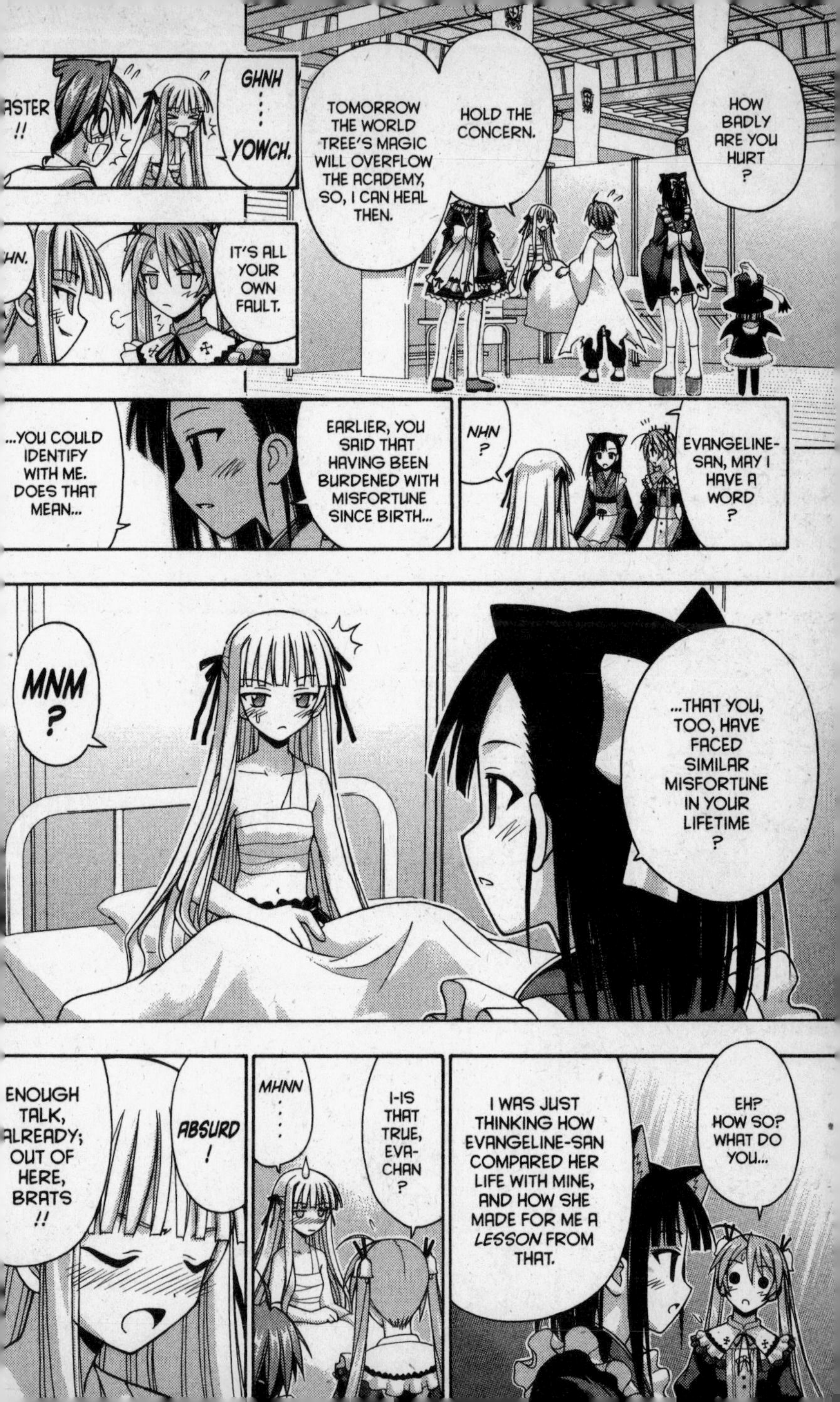
HOW BADLY ARE YOU HURT?
HOLD THE CONCERN.
TOMORROW THE WORLD TREE'S MAGIC WILL OVERFLOW THE ACADEMY, SO, I CAN HEAL THEN.
GHNH ... YOWCH.
ASTER !!
IT'S ALL YOUR OWN FAULT.
HN.
EVANGELINE-SAN, MAY I HAVE A WORD?
NHN?
EARLIER, YOU SAID THAT HAVING BEEN BURDENED WITH MISFORTUNE SINCE BIRTH...
...YOU COULD IDENTIFY WITH ME. DOES THAT MEAN...
...THAT YOU, TOO, HAVE FACED SIMILAR MISFORTUNE IN YOUR LIFETIME?
MNM?
EH? HOW SO? WHAT DO YOU...
I WAS JUST THINKING HOW EVANGELINE-SAN COMPARED HER LIFE WITH MINE, AND HOW SHE MADE FOR ME A *LESSON* FROM THAT.
I-IS THAT TRUE, EVA-CHAN?
MHNN ...
ABSURD!
ENOUGH TALK, ALREADY; OUT OF HERE, BRATS !!

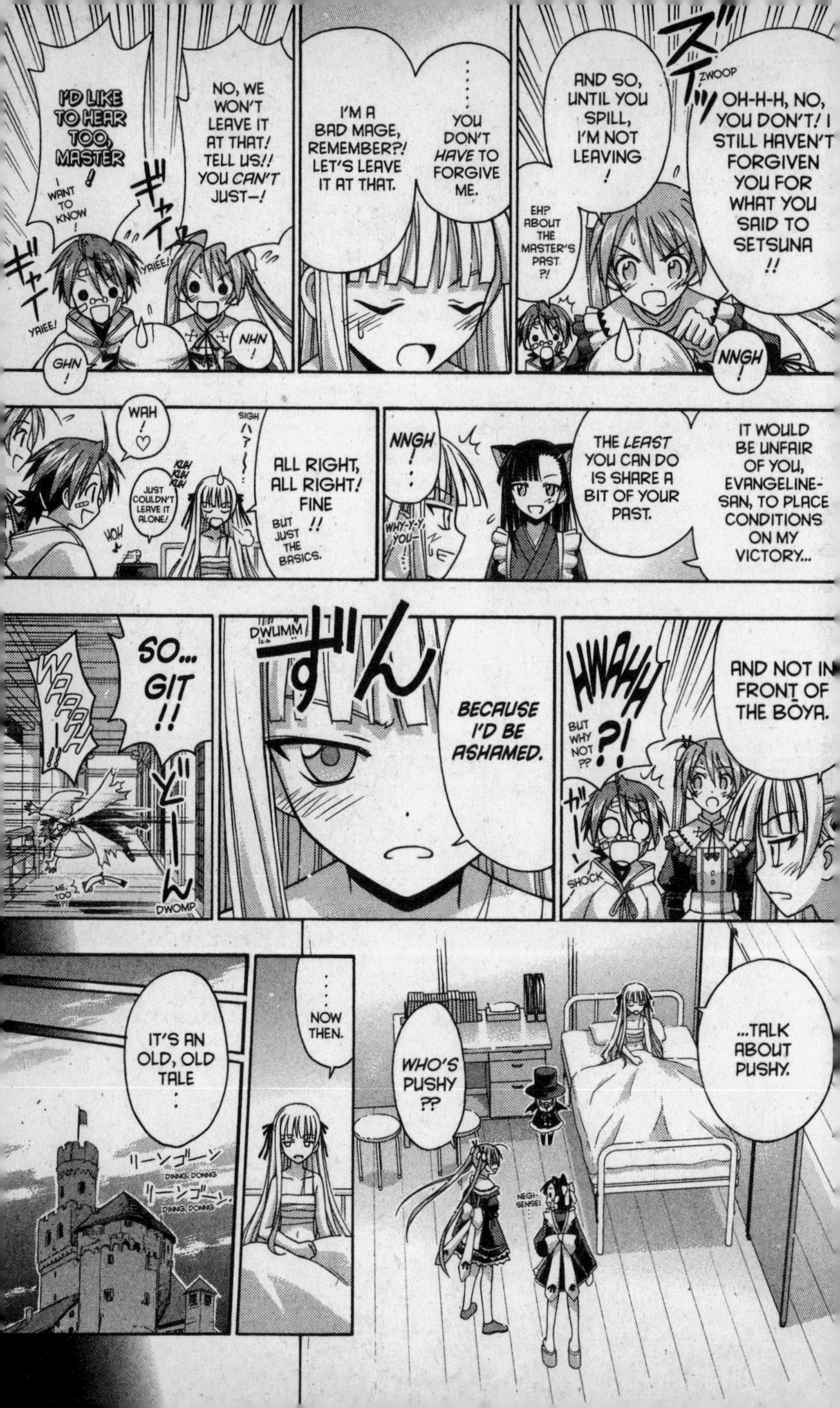
ZWOOP
OH-H-H, NO, YOU DON'T! I STILL HAVEN'T FORGIVEN YOU FOR WHAT YOU SAID TO SETSUNA!!
AND SO, UNTIL YOU SPILL, I'M NOT LEAVING!
EH? ABOUT THE MASTER'S PAST?!
NNGH!
......YOU DON'T *HAVE* TO FORGIVE ME.
I'M A BAD MAGE, REMEMBER?! LET'S LEAVE IT AT THAT.
NO, WE WON'T LEAVE IT AT THAT! TELL US!! YOU *CAN'T* JUST—!
YRIEE!
NHN!
I'D LIKE TO HEAR TOO, MASTER!
I WANT TO KNOW!
YRIEE!
GHN!
IT WOULD BE UNFAIR OF YOU, EVANGELINE-SAN, TO PLACE CONDITIONS ON MY VICTORY...
THE *LEAST* YOU CAN DO IS SHARE A BIT OF YOUR PAST.
NNGH!...
WHY-Y-Y, YOU—!
SIGH
ALL RIGHT, ALL RIGHT! FINE!!
BUT JUST THE BASICS.
WAH! ♡
KUH KUH KUH
JUST COULDN'T LEAVE IT ALONE!
HOH
AND NOT IN FRONT OF THE BŌYA.
HWAHH?!
BUT WHY NOT??
SHOCK
DWUMM
BECAUSE I'D BE ASHAMED.
SO... GIT!!
WAAAAH!!
ME, TOO?!
DWOMP
...TALK ABOUT PUSHY.
WHO'S PUSHY??
NEGI-SENSEI...
......NOW THEN.
IT'S AN OLD, OLD TALE...
DING, DONG
DING, DONG

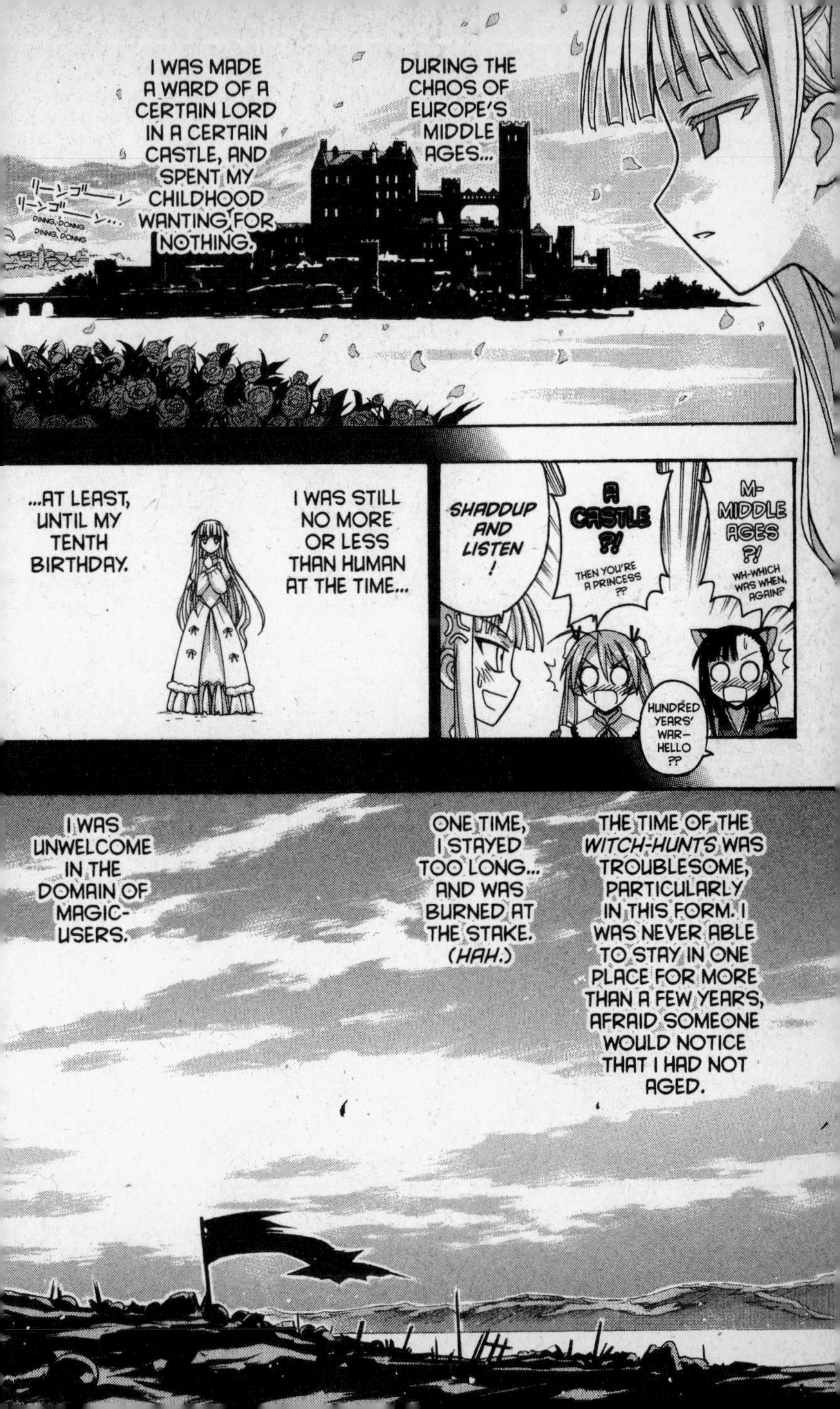
DURING THE CHAOS OF EUROPE'S MIDDLE AGES...
I WAS MADE A WARD OF A CERTAIN LORD IN A CERTAIN CASTLE, AND SPENT MY CHILDHOOD WANTING FOR NOTHING.
リーンゴーン リーンゴーン…
DINNG, DONNG DINNG, DONNG
M-MIDDLE AGES ?!
WH-WHICH WAS WHEN, AGAIN?
A CASTLE ?!
THEN YOU'RE A PRINCESS ??
SHADDUP AND LISTEN !
HUNDRED YEARS' WAR— HELLO ??
I WAS STILL NO MORE OR LESS THAN HUMAN AT THE TIME...
...AT LEAST, UNTIL MY TENTH BIRTHDAY.
THE TIME OF THE *WITCH-HUNTS* WAS TROUBLESOME, PARTICULARLY IN THIS FORM. I WAS NEVER ABLE TO STAY IN ONE PLACE FOR MORE THAN A FEW YEARS, AFRAID SOMEONE WOULD NOTICE THAT I HAD NOT AGED.
ONE TIME, I STAYED TOO LONG... AND WAS BURNED AT THE STAKE. (*HAH.*)
I WAS UNWELCOME IN THE DOMAIN OF MAGIC-USERS.

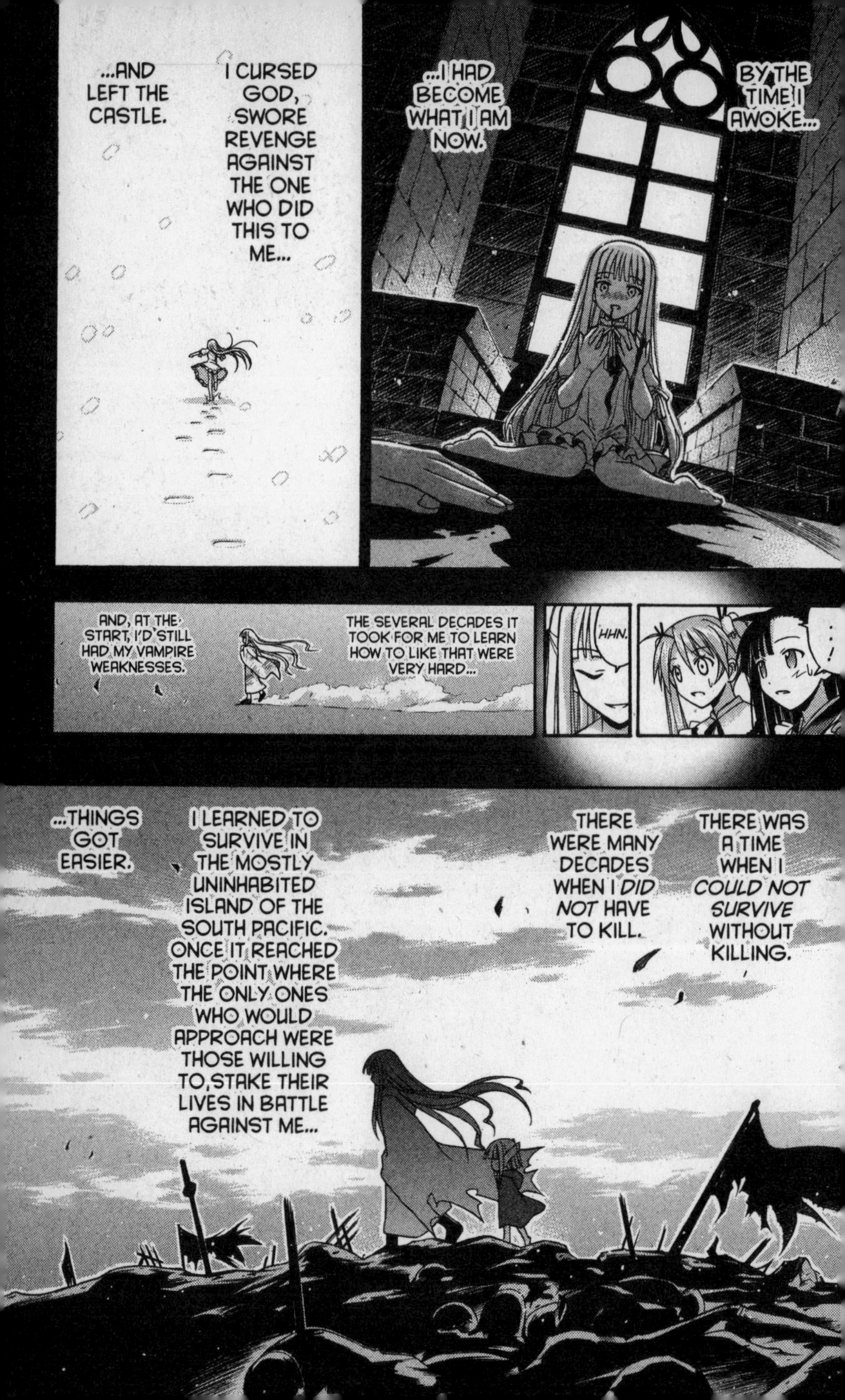
BY THE TIME I AWOKE...
...I HAD BECOME WHAT I AM NOW.
I CURSED GOD, SWORE REVENGE AGAINST THE ONE WHO DID THIS TO ME...
...AND LEFT THE CASTLE.
HHN.
THE SEVERAL DECADES IT TOOK FOR ME TO LEARN HOW TO LIKE THAT WERE VERY HARD...
AND, AT THE START, I'D STILL HAD MY VAMPIRE WEAKNESSES.
THERE WAS A TIME WHEN I *COULD NOT SURVIVE* WITHOUT KILLING.
THERE WERE MANY DECADES WHEN I *DID NOT* HAVE TO KILL.
I LEARNED TO SURVIVE IN THE MOSTLY UNINHABITED ISLAND OF THE SOUTH PACIFIC. ONCE IT REACHED THE POINT WHERE THE ONLY ONES WHO WOULD APPROACH WERE THOSE WILLING TO STAKE THEIR LIVES IN BATTLE AGAINST ME...
...THINGS GOT EASIER.

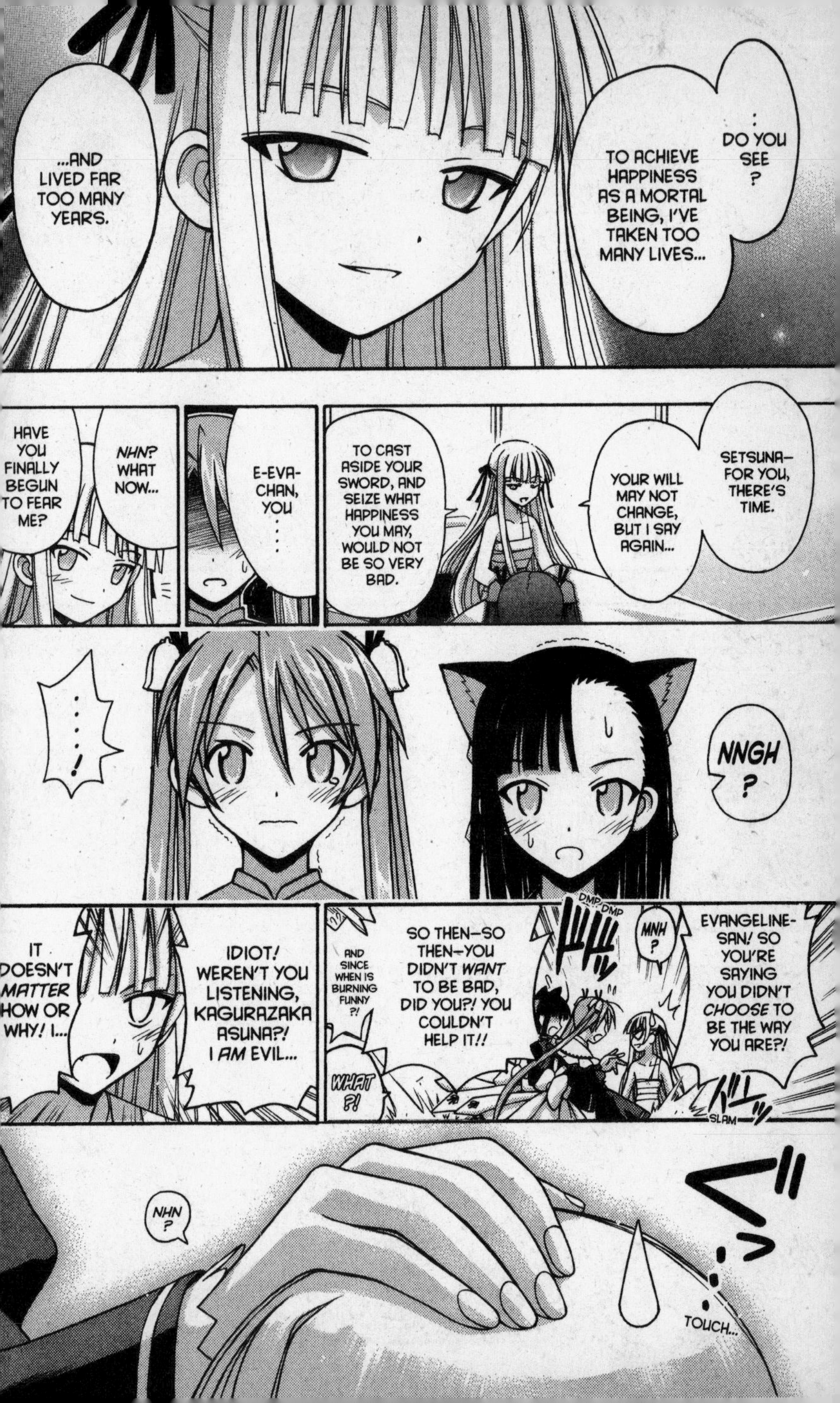
TO ACHIEVE HAPPINESS AS A MORTAL BEING, I'VE TAKEN TOO MANY LIVES...
...AND LIVED FAR TOO MANY YEARS.
: DO YOU SEE ?
SETSUNA— FOR YOU, THERE'S TIME.
YOUR WILL MAY NOT CHANGE, BUT I SAY AGAIN...
TO CAST ASIDE YOUR SWORD, AND SEIZE WHAT HAPPINESS YOU MAY, WOULD NOT BE SO VERY BAD.
E-EVA-CHAN, YOU ....
NHN? WHAT NOW...
HAVE YOU FINALLY BEGUN TO FEAR ME?
NNGH ?
....!
EVANGELINE-SAN! SO YOU'RE SAYING YOU DIDN'T CHOOSE TO BE THE WAY YOU ARE?!
SLAM
MNH ?
DMP DMP
SO THEN—SO THEN—YOU DIDN'T WANT TO BE BAD, DID YOU?! YOU COULDN'T HELP IT!!
AND SINCE WHEN IS BURNING FUNNY ?!
WHAT ?!
IDIOT! WEREN'T YOU LISTENING, KAGURAZAKA ASUNA?! I AM EVIL...
IT DOESN'T MATTER HOW OR WHY! I...
TOUCH...
NHN ?

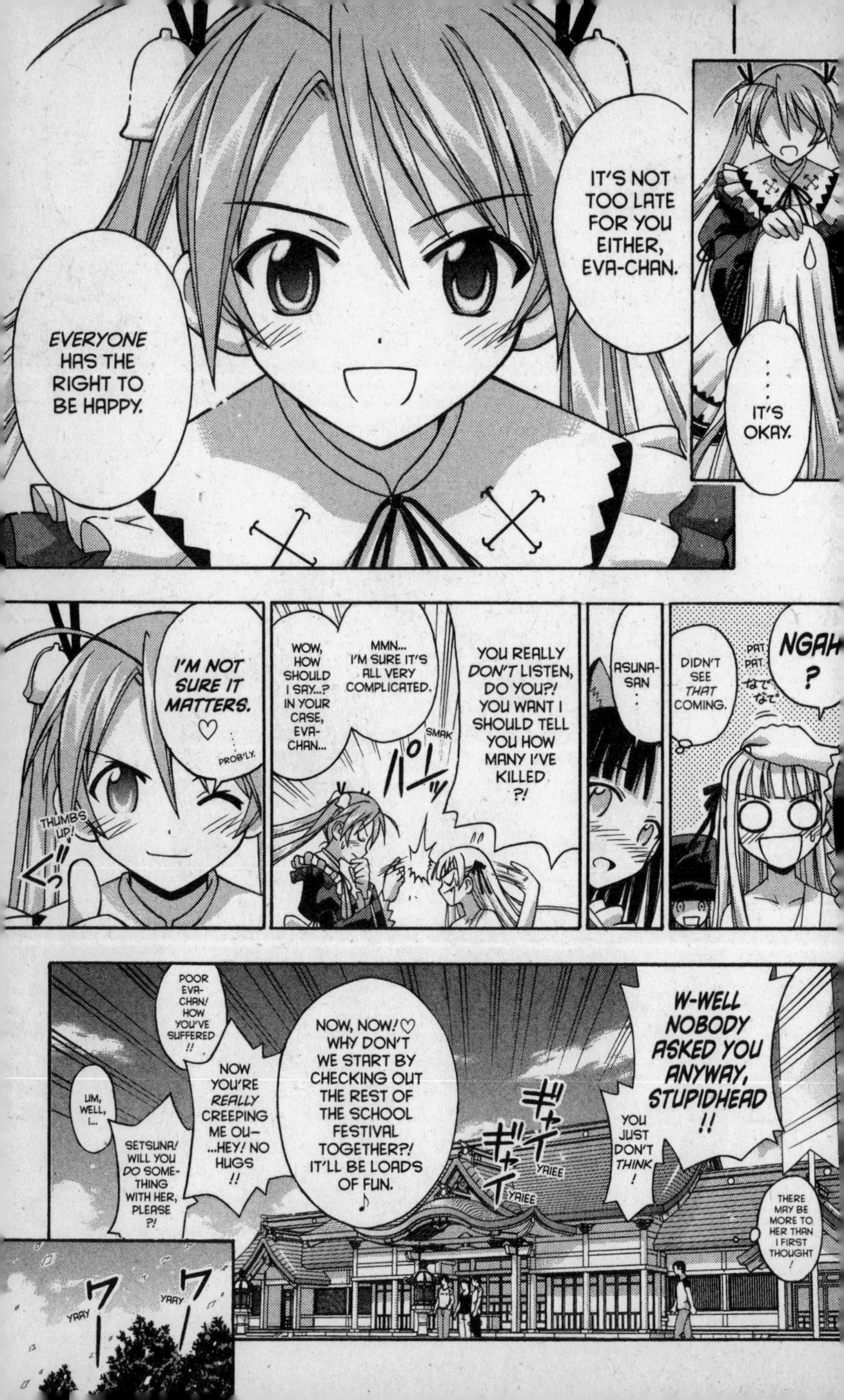
......IT'S OKAY.
IT'S NOT TOO LATE FOR YOU EITHER, EVA-CHAN.
EVERYONE HAS THE RIGHT TO BE HAPPY.
NGAH?
PAT PAT
なでなで
DIDN'T SEE *THAT* COMING.
ASUNA-SAN...
YOU REALLY *DON'T* LISTEN, DO YOU?! YOU WANT I SHOULD TELL YOU HOW MANY I'VE KILLED?!
SMAK
MMN... I'M SURE IT'S ALL VERY COMPLICATED.
WOW, HOW SHOULD I SAY...? IN YOUR CASE, EVA-CHAN...
I'M NOT SURE IT MATTERS. ♡
...PROB'LY.
THUMBS UP!
W-WELL NOBODY ASKED YOU ANYWAY, STUPIDHEAD!!
YOU JUST DON'T *THINK*!
THERE MAY BE MORE TO HER THAN I FIRST THOUGHT!
YAIEE
YAIEE
NOW, NOW! ♡ WHY DON'T WE START BY CHECKING OUT THE REST OF THE SCHOOL FESTIVAL TOGETHER?! IT'LL BE LOADS OF FUN. ♪
POOR EVA-CHAN! HOW YOU'VE SUFFERED!!
NOW YOU'RE *REALLY* CREEPING ME OU— ...HEY! NO HUGS!!
UM, WELL, I...
SETSUNA! WILL YOU *DO* SOMETHING WITH HER, PLEASE?!
YAAY
YAAY

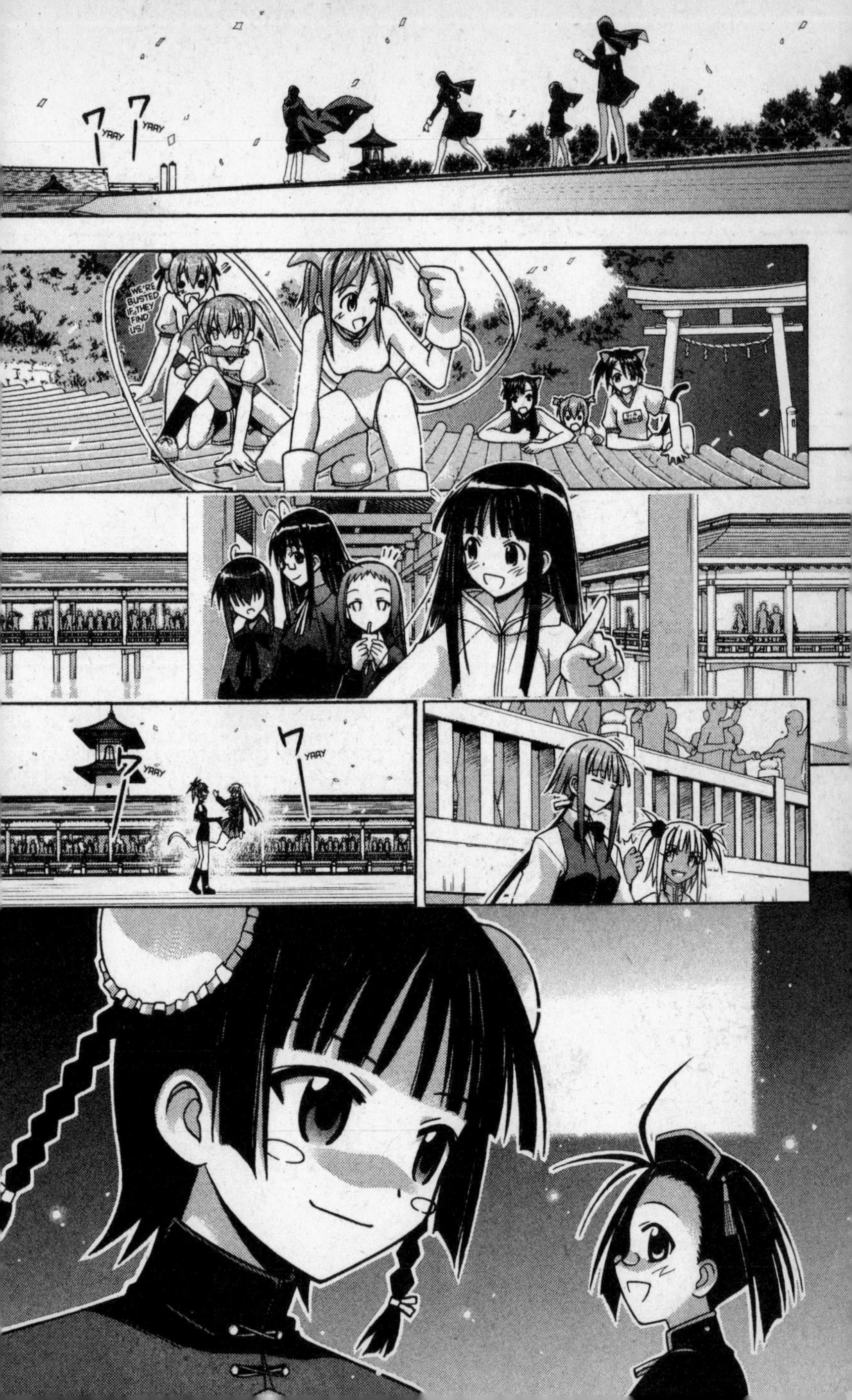
YAAY
YAAY
WE'RE BUSTED IF THEY FIND US!
YAAY
YAAY

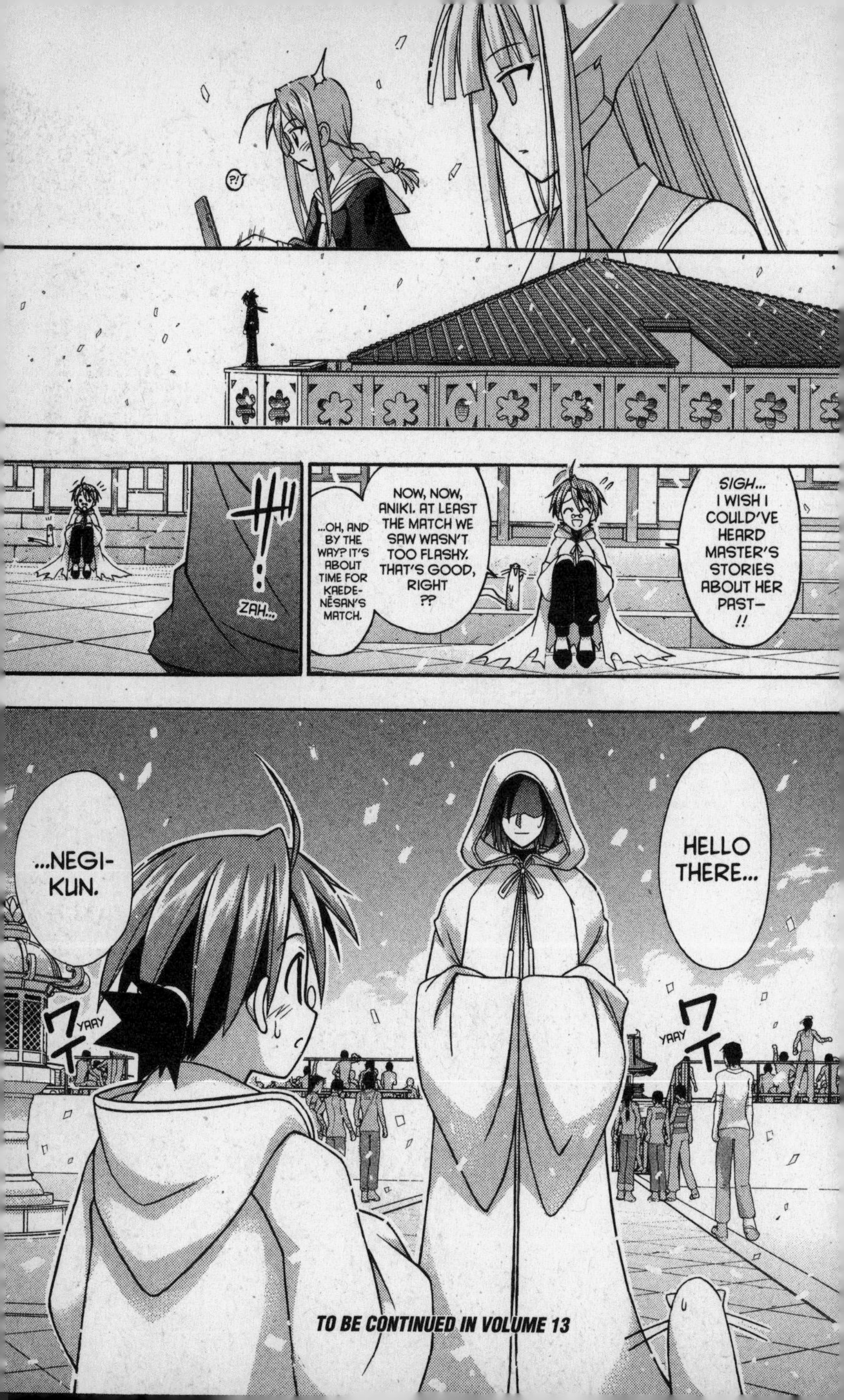
?!
SIGH... I WISH I COULD'VE HEARD MASTER'S STORIES ABOUT HER PAST—!!
NOW, NOW, ANIKI. AT LEAST THE MATCH WE SAW WASN'T TOO FLASHY. THAT'S GOOD, RIGHT ??
...OH, AND BY THE WAY? IT'S ABOUT TIME FOR KAEDE-NĒSAN'S MATCH.
ZAH...
HELLO THERE...
...NEGI-KUN.
YAAY
YAAY

TO BE CONTINUED IN VOLUME 13

-STAFF-

Ken Akamatsu
Takashi Takemoto
Kenichi Nakamura
Masaki Ohyama
Keiichi Yamashita
Tadashi Maki
Tohru Mitsuhashi

Thanks to
Ran Ayanaga

3-D BACKGROUNDS EXPLANATION CORNER

• UNDERGROUND SEWER

SCENE NAME: SEWER   POLYGON COUNT: 111,765

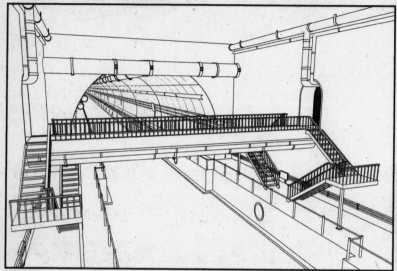

ALTHOUGH THE UNDERGROUND SEWER HERE APPEARED AT THE END OF *LAST* VOLUME, WE DIDN'T GET TO FEATURE IT THERE, SO LET'S DO IT HERE. A SECTION OF THE ENORMOUS UNDERGROUND SEWER SYSTEM THAT LIES BENEATH THE CITY-LIKE MAHORA ACADEMY, CHAO SEEMS TO BE USING AT LEAST A SECTION OF IT FOR HER OWN PERSONAL USE COMING AND GOING FROM HER SECRET HIDEOUT INSIDE THE TATSUMIYA SHRINE AS SHE PLEASES. OTHER AREAS ARE SAID TO EXIST AS WELL—A SECRET RESEARCH FACILITY, A WAREHOUSE....

ON A SIDE NOTE, AS WITH THE ACTUAL CITY-CAMPUS OF MAHORA ACADEMY, THE UNDERGROUND SEWERS ARE MODELED AFTER THOSE FOUND IN EUROPE. OF COURSE, WE *DO* REARRANGE THEM A BIT.

RIGHT, THEN. IN THIS INSTALLMENT WE'LL COVER THE ACTUAL PROCEDURE WE WENT THROUGH TO COME UP WITH THE BACKGROUNDS FOR THIS SCENE. IN CASES WHERE THE PANEL IS TO FEATURE THE BACKGROUND MORE THAN THE CHARACTERS, WE START BY FINDING THE ANGLE THAT MAKES THINGS LOOK COOLEST. WHY DON'T WE MOVE IT AROUND NOW, AND SEE IF WE CAN'T FIND THE ANGLE WE WANT. (HEH.)

HMM, LET'S SEE... WHICH ANGLE LOOKS BEST? MAYBE WE SHOULD MOVE IN A BIT CLOSER.

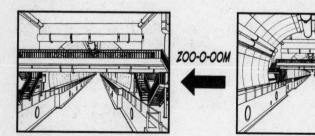

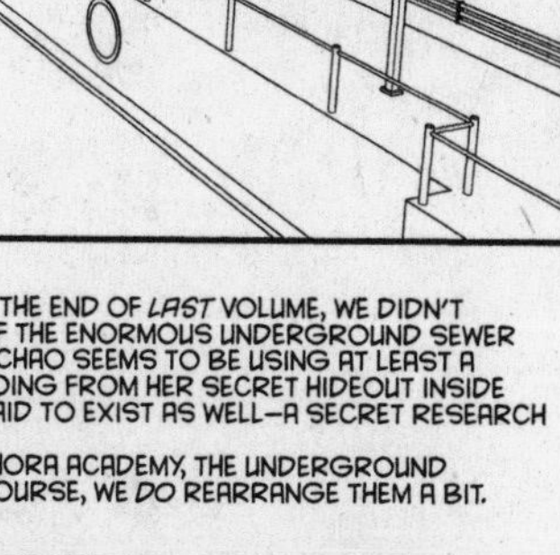

ZOO-O-OOM

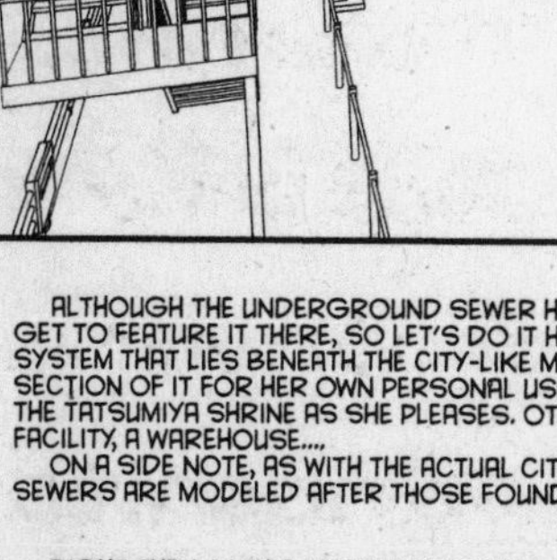

NOW WE'RE CLOSER. KIND OF BORING, THOUGH, ISN'T IT? LOOKING HEAD-ON?

MAYBE IT'LL SEEM MORE COOL IF WE LOOK UP AT IT FROM A LOWER ANGLE. WAIT—FROM HERE, IT'S HARD TO SEE THE ENTRANCE TO THE SEWER-TUNNEL....

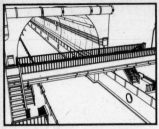

ROTA-A-ATE

MMM, LOOKING DOWN IS PRETTY GOOD. BUT IT WOULD BE NICER IF WE COULD SEE MORE OF WHAT WE'RE LOOKING AT.

WE HAVE MORE OPTIONS THAN JUST PULLING BACK THE CAMERA FOR THESE SORTS OF THINGS—WE CAN ALSO ADJUST THE VIEWING ANGLE. AS ILLUSTRATED BELOW, WE CAN FOCUS THE LENS TO COVER AREAS WE WANT TO HIGHLIGHT. CAN YOU TELL THAT THE FORCED PERSPECTIVE OF THE IMAGE ON THE LEFT MAKES FOR A MORE DRAMATIC SCENE?

TELEPHOTO LENS

WIDE-ANGLE LENS

ONCE CAMERA POSITION AND ANGLE HAS BEEN DECIDED UPON, WE CAN CREATE LINE ART AND PRINT IT OUT—THE RESULT OF WHICH IS THE FIRST ILLUSTRATION ON THE PREVIOUS PAGE. THIS IS HOW PRODUCTION OF PANELS WITH 3-D MODELED BACKGROUNDS IS BEGUN; I HOPE IT'S BEEN BOTH ENTERTAINING AND INFORMATIVE.

ANGLE CHANGES CAN BE MADE FREELY AFTER THE 3-D MODEL'S BEEN MADE, ALLOWING US THE ADVANTAGE OF TRYING OUT SEVERAL VARIATIONS BEFORE DECIDING WHAT WORKS BEST IN A PANEL. IT ALSO CUTS DOWN ON THE AMOUNT OF WORK.

AN INCONVENIENT TRUTH OF LINE-ART PRINTOUTS OF CG BACKGROUNDS IS THAT THEY ARE TOO CLEAN, AND LOOK UNNATURAL IF USED WITHOUT A BIT OF DETAIL WORK. IN THIS CASE, WE HAD TO "DINGY" UP THE SCENE TO MAKE IT LOOK MORE LIKE A SEWER SYSTEM; THIS KIND OF DETAIL WORK MUST ALWAYS BE DONE BY HAND. COMPARE THIS TO THE PICTURE ON THE PREVIOUS PAGE, AND YOU SHOULD BE ABLE TO TELL THE AMOUNT OF ADDITIONAL WORK REQUIRED TO MAKE A COMPLETED PANEL LOOK LIKE THIS.

ULTIMATELY, IF YOU WANT TO CREATE A NICE LOOKING BACKGROUND, I SUPPOSE WHAT THIS MEANS IS THAT YOU CAN'T AVOID THE EXTRA WORK. (^_^;)

ゴオオオオ…

NOW LET'S RETURN TO MORE EXPLANATIONS OF THE OTHER 3-D BACKGROUNDS.

● BELL TOWER

SCENE NAME: TOWER POLYGON COUNT: 15,995

THE BELL TOWER IN THE SCENE
WHERE KOTARŌ SHEDS TEARS
AFTER LOSING IN HIS MATCH
IS ONE MAHORA ACADEMY
STRUCTURE THAT REALLY STANDS
OUT BECAUSE OF ITS RELATIVE
HEIGHT.

THE BASIS FOR THIS
STRUCTURE IS THE GIOTTO BELL
TOWER IN FLORENCE; ITS DETAILS
HAVE MORE OR LESS BEEN
DUPLICATED HERE.

WE USED ONLY THE UPPER
PORTION OF THE TOWER, SO WE
HAVEN'T GOTTEN AROUND TO
COMPLETING THE BOTTOM YET.
(^_^;)

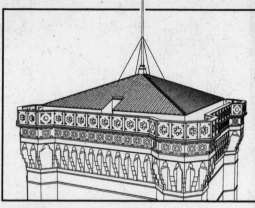

● TEMPORARY DRESSING-ROOM

SCENE NAME: SMALL ROOM POLYGON COUNT: 9,583

THE SMALL ROOM WHERE ASUNA AND
SETSUNA GET DRESSED FOR THEIR
MATCH WAS ALSO MODELED IN 3-D.

SURE, IT WAS ONLY USED FOR FOUR
PANELS, SO WHY NOT HIGHLIGHT IT HERE,
RIGHT? (^_^;)

I HAVE THE FEELING WE'LL BE GETTING QUITE
↓ A BIT OF USE FROM THIS TABLE (*HEH*).

—BONUS—

TO COPE WITH THE EVER-INCREASING NUMBER OF SPECTATORS
AT THE MAHORA "BUDOKAI" MARTIAL ARTS TOURNAMENT, ADDITIONAL
SEATING HAD TO BE PREPARED—AND FAST. THE FACT THAT THESE
BLEACHERS WERE CONSTRUCTED WITHIN TENS OF MINUTES SPEAKS
VERY HIGHLY OF THE INCREDIBLE SPEED AND TECHNIQUE POSSESSED
BY THE MAHORA CONSTRUCTION CLUB, DON'T YOU THINK? (HEH.)

19:00~20:00: ON TO DAY TWO

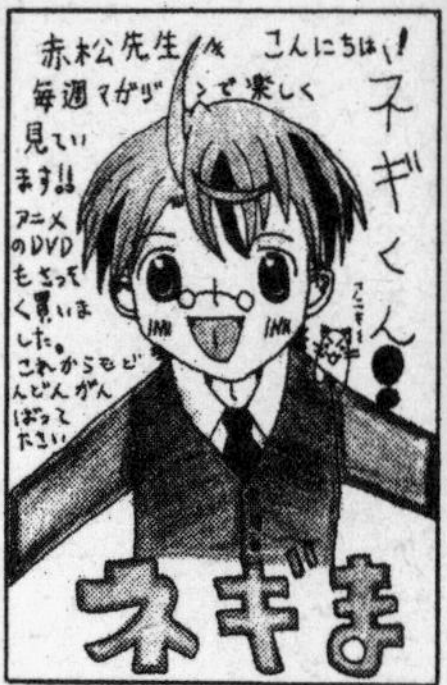
赤松先生へ こんにちは！
毎週マガジンで楽しく見ています!!
ネギくん
ネギま

THE EXPRESSION ON CHAMO'S FACE IS JUST LOVELY (HEH).

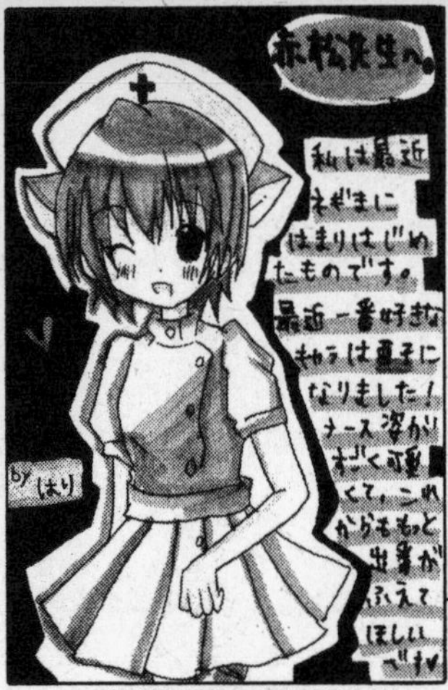
赤松先生へ。
私は最近ネギまにはまりはじめたものです。最近一番好きなキャラは亜子になりました！ナース姿がすごく可愛くて、これからもっと出番がふえてほしいです♥
by はり

TH-THE NURSE'S UNIFORM ON AKO IS VERY NICE! (*LAUGH.*)

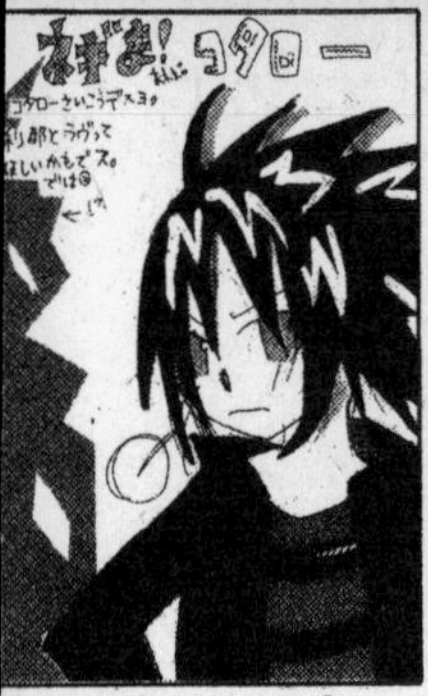
ネギま！

A VERY COOL KOTARŌ. (^^)

MAGISTER NEGI MAGI

NEGIMA!
FAN ART CORNER

THIS VOLUME'S INSTALLMENT IS EXTRA-LARGE! (^^) WE'VE BROKEN THE 100-CHAPTER MARK AND WE'RE STILL GOING STRONG (*HEH*). PLEASE CONTINUE TO SEND IN YOUR ENCOURAGING LETTERS AND PICTURES! (^^)

TEXT: ASSISTANT MAX

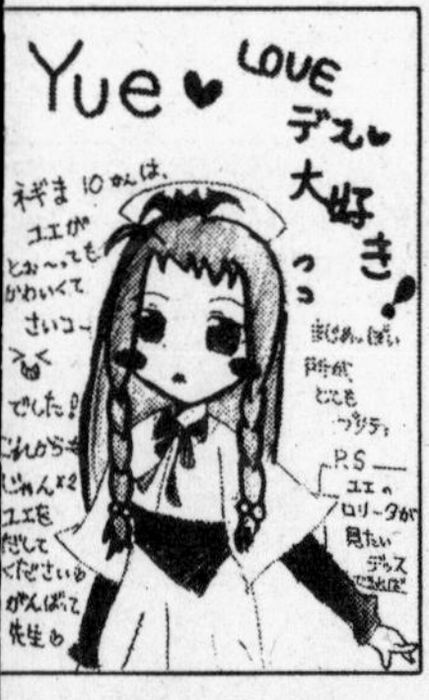
Yue♥
LOVE
デス♥
大好き！

THIS ENDEARING ILLO OF YUE IS WONDERFUL.

"HAPPY MATERIAL" IS A GREAT SONG, ISN'T IT. (^_^) ♪

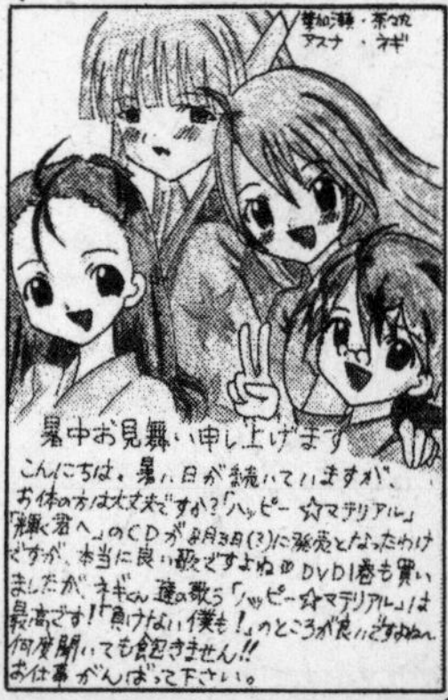
暑中お見舞い申し上げます
こんにちは。暑い日が続いていますが、お体の方は大丈夫ですか？「ハッピー☆マテリアル」「輝く君へ」のCDが発売となったわけですが、本当に良い歌ですよね DVD1巻も買いましたが、ネギくん達の歌う「ハッピー☆マテリアル」は最高です！「負けない僕も！」のところが良いですよね。何度聞いても飽きません!!
お仕事がんばって下さい。

YOU REALLY MOVED US WITH THE DIALOGUE IN THE BALLOON (*HEH*).

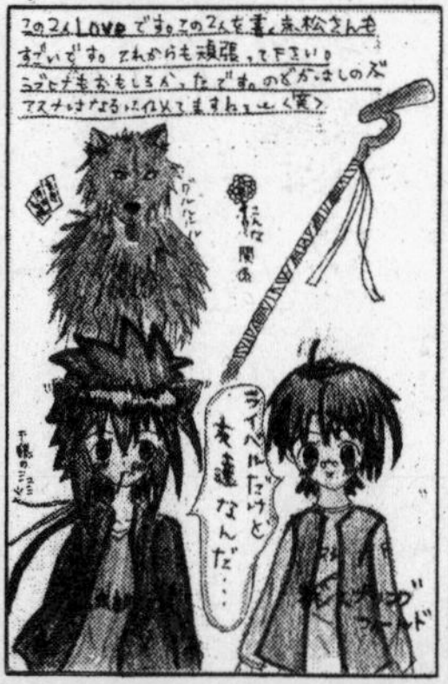
ライバルだけど友達なんだ…

SETSUNA LOOKS VERY "LOLITA" IN THIS PICTURE (*HEH*). STILL, WE LOVE IT (*LAUGHS*).

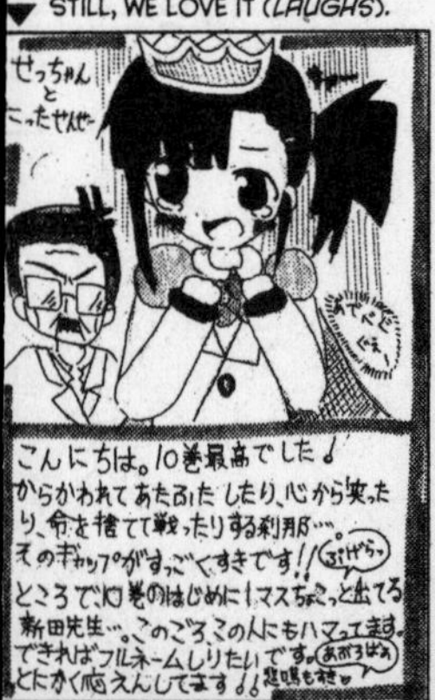
せっちゃん と
こんにちは。10巻最高でした！
からかわれてあたふたしたり、心から笑ったり、命を捨てて戦ったりする刹那…。
そのギャップがすごくすきです!!
ところで、10巻のはじめにちょこっと出てる新田先生…。このごろこの人にもハマってます。
できればフルネームしりたいです。
とにかく応えんしてます！

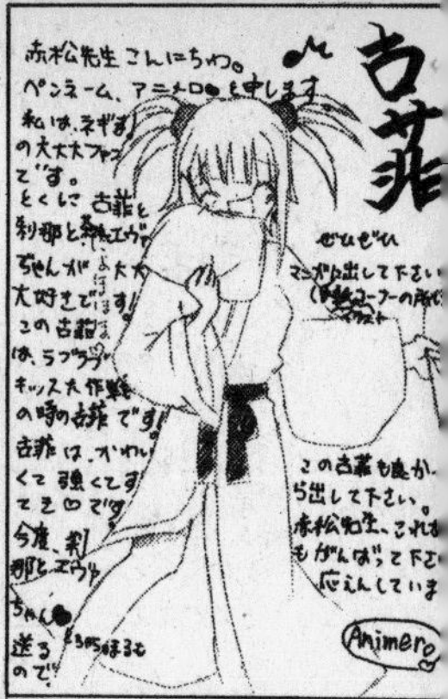
古菲
Animero

▲ DOESN'T KŪ FEI LOOK VALIANT HERE? (^^)

WE LOVE HOW ASUNA'S PEEKING FROM AROUND A CORNER IN THE BACKGROUND (*HEH*). ▼

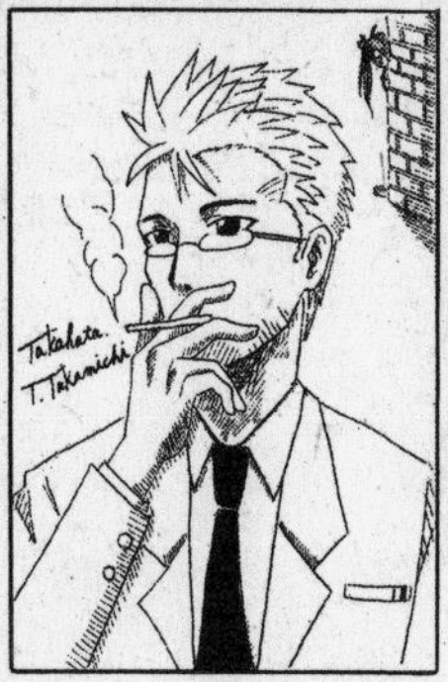
Takahata. T. Takamichi

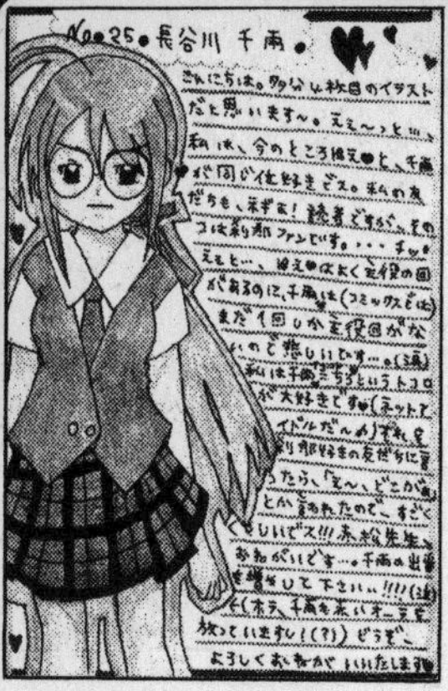
No. 25 長谷川 千雨

◀ WE'D LIKE TO SEE MORE OF CHISAME IN ACTION, AS WELL.

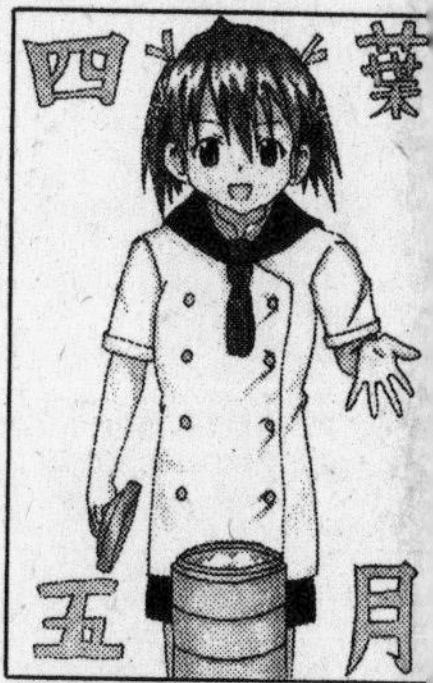
四葉
五月

▲ LET'S BUILD SATSUKI'S POPULARITY TOO, WHILE WE'RE AT IT! (^^)

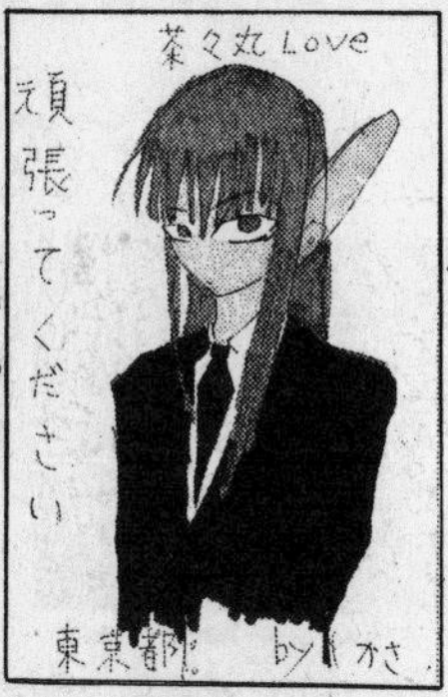
茶々丸LOVE
頑張ってくださ い

◀ LOVE THE WAY CHACHAMARU LOOKS SO "READY FOR ACTION."

WHAT IS THAT THING BEHIND THE NARUTAKI SISTERS...?! (*LAUGHS.*) ▼

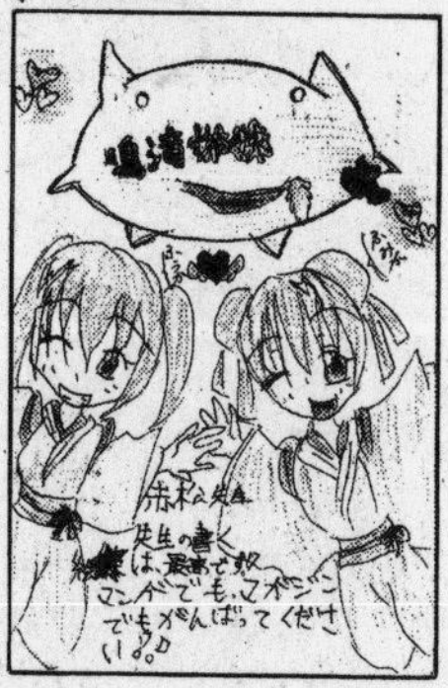

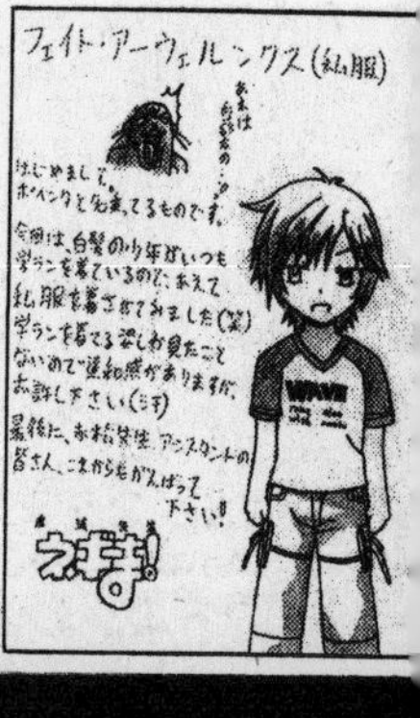
フェイト・アーウェルンクス(私服)

TALK ABOUT RARE—A PICTURE OF FATE! (^^) ▶

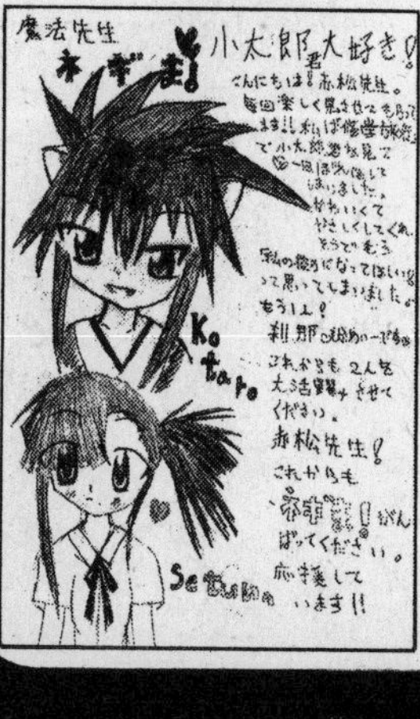
魔法先生 ネギま!
小太郎君大好き!
Kotaro

◀ KOTARŌ SURE IS POPULAR, LATELY. (^^)

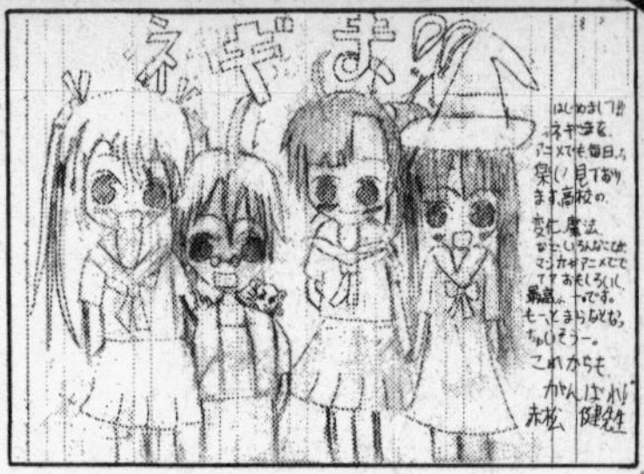
ネギま!
これからも
がんばれ!
赤松 健先生

▲ WE LIKE THE MOOD OF THIS ILLUSTRATION A LOT. (^^)

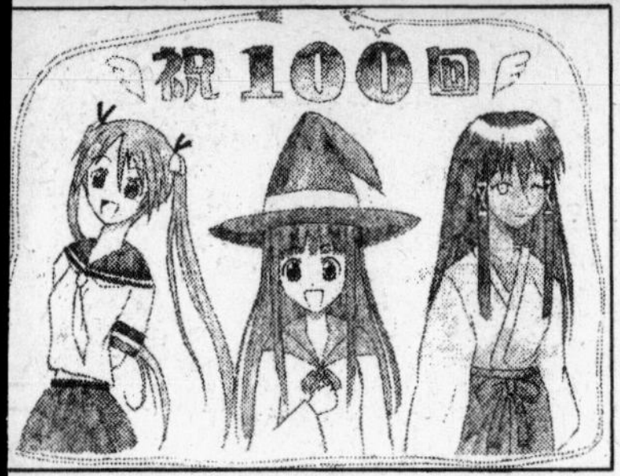
祝100回

▲ ARIGATŌ—! (^^)

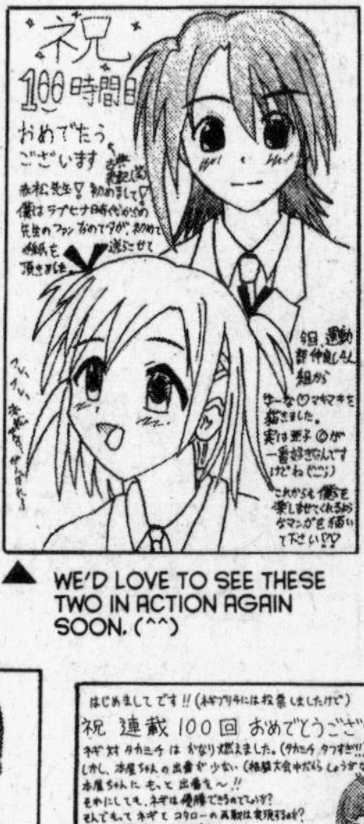
祝
100時間目
おめでとう
ございます

▲ WE'D LOVE TO SEE THESE TWO IN ACTION AGAIN SOON. (^^)

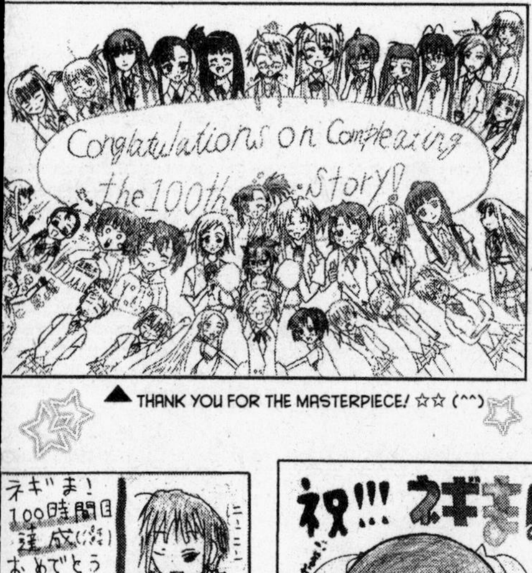
Conglatulations on Compleating the 100th Story!

▲ THANK YOU FOR THE MASTERPIECE! ☆☆ (^^)

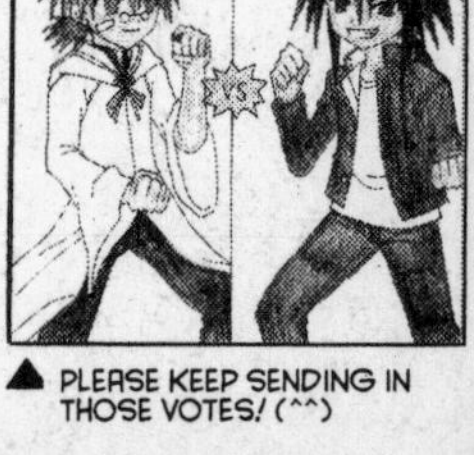
はじめましてです!!
祝 連載100回 おめでとうございます!

▲ PLEASE KEEP SENDING IN THOSE VOTES! (^^)

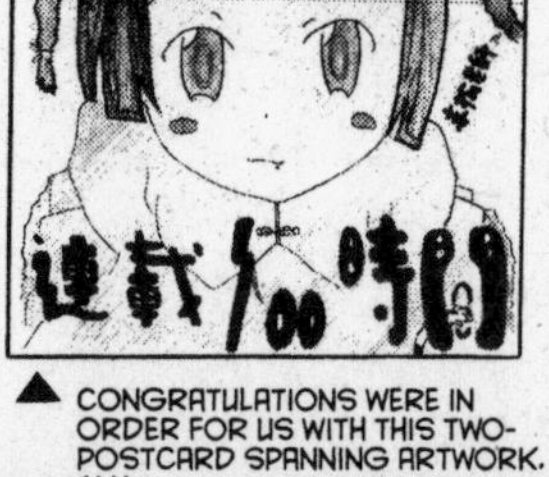
祝!!! ネギま!
連載100時間

▲ CONGRATULATIONS WERE IN ORDER FOR US WITH THIS TWO-POSTCARD SPANNING ARTWORK. (^^)

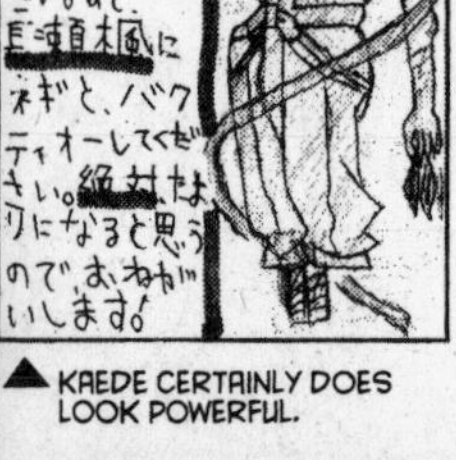
ネギま!
100時間目
おめでとう
ございます。

▲ KAEDE CERTAINLY DOES LOOK POWERFUL.

NEGI MA!

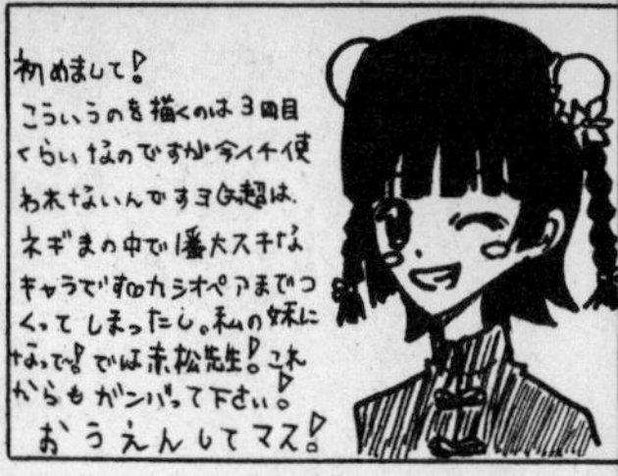
初めまして!
こういうのを描くのは3回目
くらいなのですが今イチ使
われないんですヨ(泣)超は、
ネギまの中で一番大スキな
キャラです!カシオペアまでつ
くってしまったし。私の妹に
なって!では赤松先生!これ
からもガンバって下さい。
おうえんしてマス!

IT MIGHT BE FUN, HAVING SOMEONE LIKE CHAO FOR YOUR SISTER.

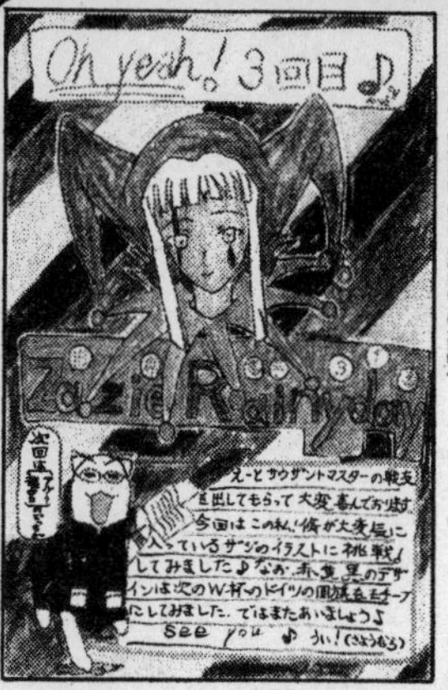
Oh yeah! 3回目♪
Zazie Rainyday
see you ♪

LET'S START A ZAZIE-BOOM! (HEH).

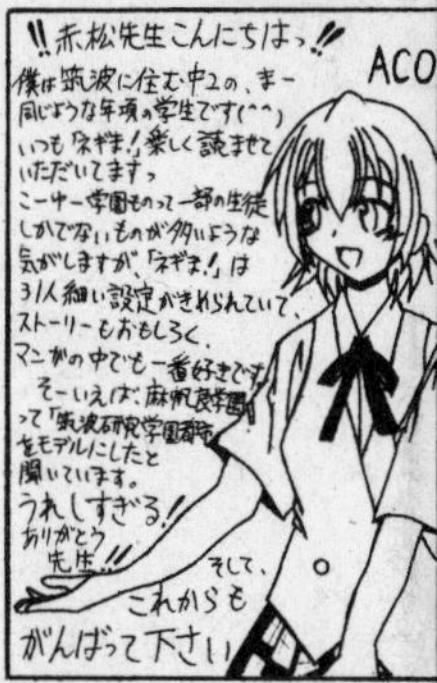
!!赤松先生こんにちは。!!
僕は筑波に住む中2の、ま〜
同じような年頃の学生です(^^)
いつも「ネギま!」楽しく読ませて
いただいてます。
気がしますが、「ネギま!」は
ストーリーもおもしろく、
マンガの中でも一番好きです!
をモデルにしたと
聞いています。
うれしすぎる!
ありがとう
先生!!
そして、
これからも
がんばって下さい
ACO

THANKS FOR YOUR MAHORAFEST SUPPORT (LAUGHS).

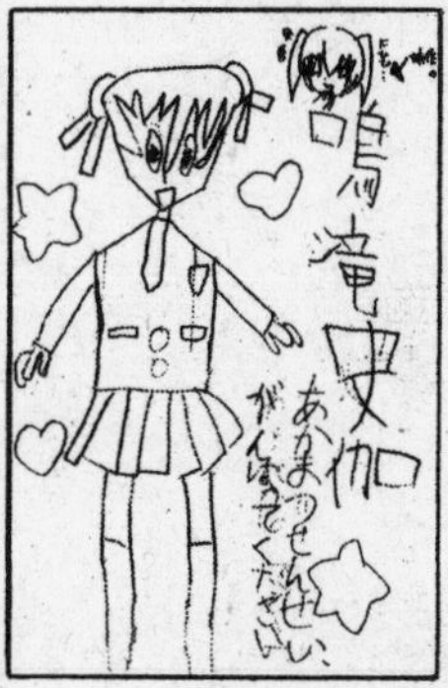
鳴滝史伽
あかまつせんせいがんばってください

FUMIKA LOOKS GREAT.

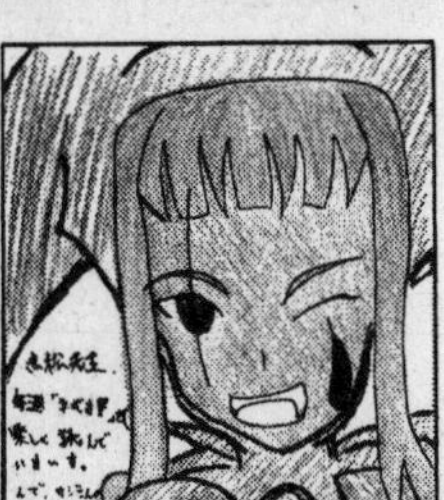
赤松先生。
毎週「ネギま!」楽しく読んでいます。
これからもガンバって
くださいね。

IS THE DAY OF "ZAZIE IN ACTION" NEAR...?!

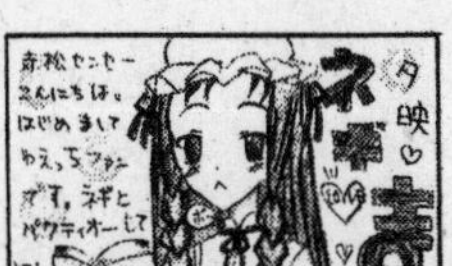
赤松センセーこんにちは。
はじめまして
これからもがんばって
下さい
赤松センセー

WITH HER INCREASING POPULARITY, YOU CAN COUNT ON SEEING HER MORE OFTEN!

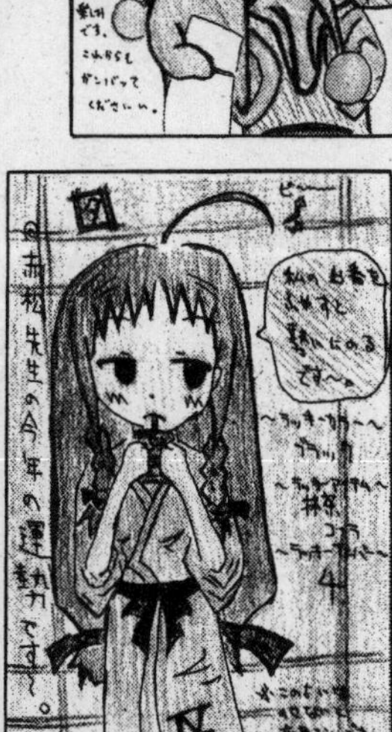
私の出番を
赤松先生の今年の運勢です。
〜ラッキーカラー〜

TALK ABOUT "LUCKY GIRL YUE"...!

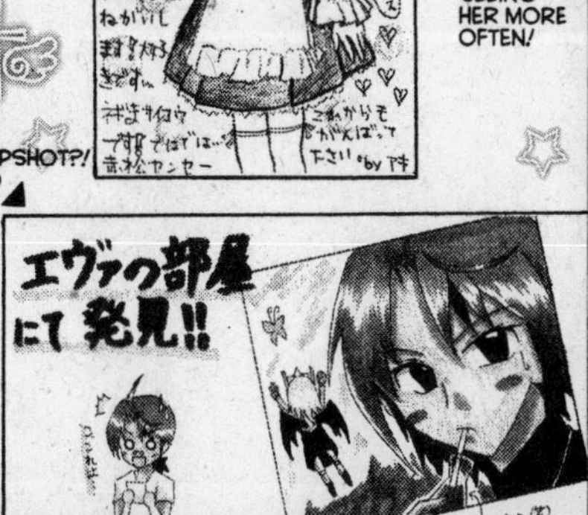
エヴァの部屋
にて発見!!

A SNAPSHOT?! (HEH.)

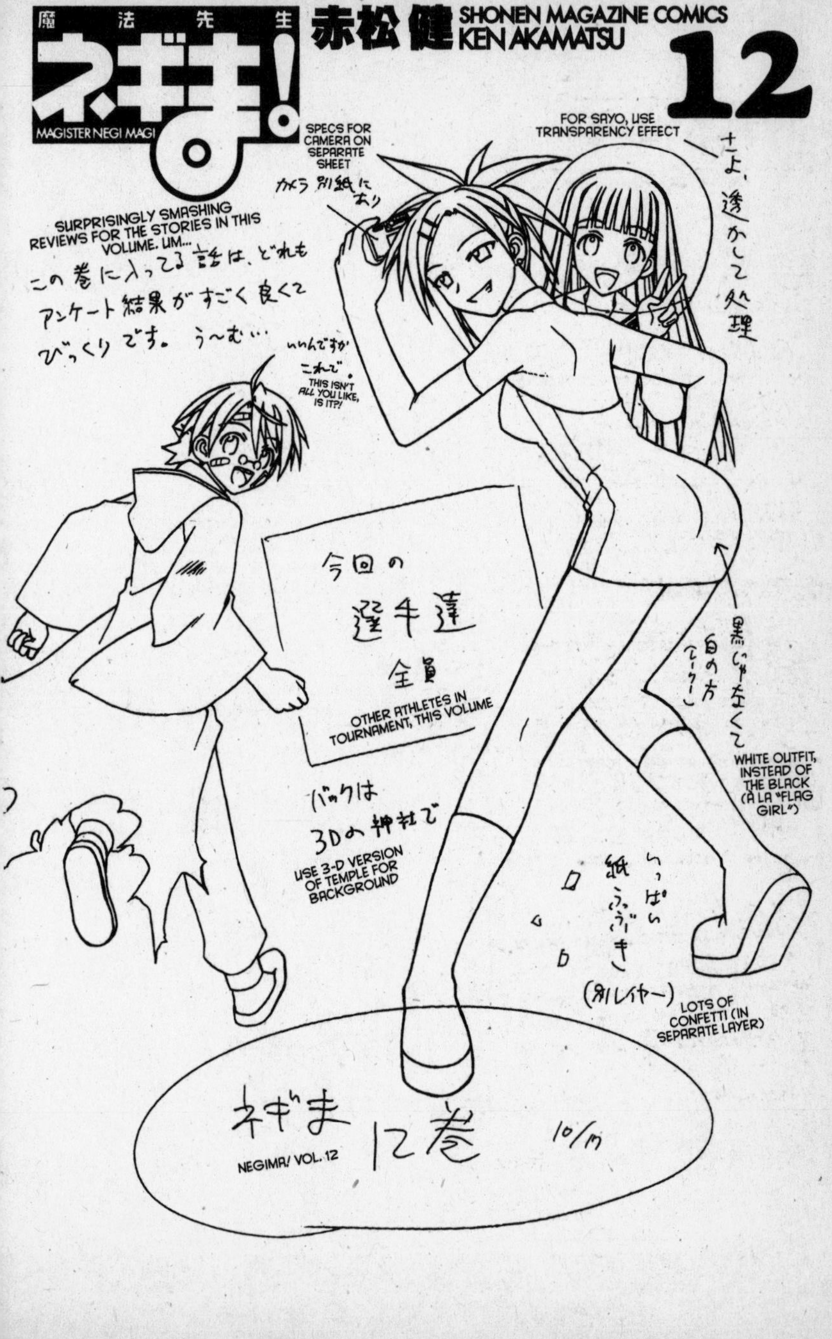
魔法先生
ネギま!
MAGISTER NEGI MAGI
赤松健
SHONEN MAGAZINE COMICS
KEN AKAMATSU
12
SURPRISINGLY SMASHING REVIEWS FOR THE STORIES IN THIS VOLUME. UM...
この巻に入ってる話は、どれもアンケート結果がすごく良くてびっくりです。う〜む…
SPECS FOR CAMERA ON SEPARATE SHEET
カメラ 別紙にあり
FOR SAYO, USE TRANSPARENCY EFFECT
サヨ、透かして処理
いいんですかこれで。
THIS ISN'T ALL YOU LIKE, IS IT?!
今回の選手達全員
OTHER ATHLETES IN TOURNAMENT, THIS VOLUME
黒じゃなくて白の方
WHITE OUTFIT, INSTEAD OF THE BLACK (À LA "FLAG GIRL")
バックは3Dの神社で
USE 3-D VERSION OF TEMPLE FOR BACKGROUND
いっぱい紙ふぶき
(別レイヤー)
LOTS OF CONFETTI (IN SEPARATE LAYER)
ネギま12巻
10/17
NEGIMA! VOL. 12

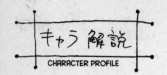

キャラ解説

CHARACTER PROFILE

㉕ 長谷川 千雨

㉕ HASEGAWA, CHISAME

個人的に 親近感を おぼえる

CHISE IS ACTUALLY ONE CHARACTER TO WHOM I FEEL A

千雨です。(笑)

CONNECTION ON A PERSONAL LEVEL

(趣味とか ほとんど

私と同じだし…)

(HEH—MOSTLY 'CAUSE WE SHARE THE SAME HOBBIES...).

成瀬川に 似ていますが

SHE MAY SEEM SIMILAR TO NARUSEGAWA...

別人です。ツリ目だし。

BUT SHE ISN'T. HER EYES ARE DEFINITELY
MORE UPWARD-SLANTING.

…ネギのことが

...DOES SHE HAVE A THING FOR NEGI? AT THIS

好きなのでしょうか、

POINT, I MYSELF AM NOT SURE, AND YET,

今のところ 分かりませんが、

INITIALLY-STANDOFFISH-THEN-ALL-TOO-DOCILE

もろ ツンデレっぽい キャラなので

"TSUNDERE"-TYPE THAT SHE IS, I CAN'T HELP

将来が 心配です。(^^;)

BUT FEAR FOR HER FUTURE. (^^;)

最後まで 意地をはれ！ ちう！

CHŪ! DON'T LET 'EM GRIND YOU DOWN, Y' HEAR?!

声優は 志村由美さん。

...HER VOICE-ACTOR IS SHIMURA YUMI. EVER SINCE

キャラCDの頃から ぴったりだ！

HEARING HER ON THE DRAMA CDS, I THOUGHT, "PERFECT!"

と思ってました。 新人とは思えない…

HARD TO BELIEVE SHE'S NEW TO VOICE-ACTING....

すごく 良いです。

SHE'S REALLY GOOD.

赤松

(AKAMATSU)

LEXICON MAGICUM NEGIMARIUM

—*NEGIMA!* VOLUME 12—

[101st Period]

■咸卦

KANKAHŌ (A.K.A. "XIANGUA")

One of the 64 hexagrams of the *I Ching*. The meaning of *Kan* or "Xian" is the conjoined forces of yin and yang *qi* (or "chi"). The reading of the Hsing Hexagram is, "Your focus and energy are scattered. Bring together that which belongs together. Reach out and join others. Someone or something has the vital piece of the puzzle." In the philosophical treatise *Reflections of Things at Hand*, there is a passage that alludes to "rising" or "soft" *qi* as having the attribute of yang, while yin is "descending" and "hard."

According to writings on Chinese medicine, the *qi* found outside the body is that of yang, and *chi* within the body is that of yin. Therefore, as stated by Chamo in the Thirty-ninth and Ninety-second Periods of *Negima!*, magical power = yang *qi* and *chi* = ying *qi*. Together, the two types of *qi* or "chi" may be referred to as *Kan* (Xian), and the ability to combine the attributes of magical power and *chī* as *Kankaho* (Xiangua).

Normally, because they are of opposing attributes, these two types of power repel each other. In the books of the *I Ching*, the ability to bring the two together is likened to being able to join the Heavens and the Earth, making all things possible—the ability, in other words, to generate a tremendous amount of power.

In writings on *Kan*, the ability may also be thought of as relating to that of marriage. In this instance, the conjoining is of the male yang aspect to that of the female yin. In Latin, *Pactio* may also have a meaning of "marriage," or the joining of two opposites. When Asuna uses the Kankahō, then, she is multiplying yang (magical power/male/Negi) by yin (*chi*/female/Asuna), resulting in a fusion which allows her to expel an explosion-like release of power.

As for he who calls himself "Kū:nel," when he advises Asuna to void herself of thought, it may be considered to be a reference to further writings on the *I Ching*, in which there is a passage that says, "Atop a mountain there is blessing; it is the *Kan* (Xian). To achieve it, one must let go and free oneself." This may well lead to the conclusion that Kū:nel is learned in the magicks of the East, as well. Evangeline, who prefers for *Kankahō* the Greek term "*συνταξιζ αντικειμενοιν*," means a "union of two opposing individuals."

[105th Period]

NOCTURNA NIGREDNIS

("Nocturne of the Darkened Garb")

The ultimate technique of a Shadow Master—one who controls the manifestations of one's own shadows. By conjuring a large "Shadow Puppet," the Shadow Master is protected by the body of the Shadow, allowing the caster to enter into close-range combat. As it is indeed a close-range combat technique, the Shadow may be summoned instantly and, afterward, would allow the caster to remain without additional protection from his or her Minister/Ministra.

Before the advent of the modern-day scientific art of optics, things such as mirrors and shadows were long thought to have been in some way magical. In fact, shadows were once believed to be another incarnation of the person casting it. In *Archetypes and the Collective Unconscious*, Carl Gustav Jung referred to shadows as denied psychic material—from which one might infer the connection of shadows to other worlds.

In the Eightieth and Eighty-fourth Periods of *Negima!*, Takane's Shadow Puppets are able to manifest from the cast shadow of anyone. As far back as the Fifty-first Period, Evangeline is able to move from Mahora Academy to Kyoto through a shadow—yet another manifestation of their power.

In that shadows are essentially a part of ourselves, mimicking our every move, Takane's Shadow Puppet moving the way it does (i.e., identically to Takane) is an example of this line of thinking.

■位相
TOPOLOGIA

A branch of mathematics concerned with those properties of geometric configurations (such as point sets) that are unaltered by elastic deformations (as in stretching, or twisting) and are homeomorphisms.

"Topology" also refers to a particular mathematical object studied in this area. In this sense, a topology is a family of open sets that contain the empty set as well as the entire space, and is closed under the operations of union and finite intersection.

It has often been said that a topologist is a person who cannot tell a doughnut from a coffee cup with a handle—in that both are solids with a single hole. Because it does not distinguish between a circle and a square (a circle formed of a rubber band may be stretched into the shape of a square), topology has sometimes been called "rubber-sheet geometry," although it does distinguish between a circle and a figure-eight (one cannot stretch a figure-eight into a circle without tearing). The spaces studied in topology are called "topological spaces."

When Chao says that the magical world exists in a different phase than that of the other world, what she means in this sense by the "magical world" and the "other world" cannot be inferred with any degree of accuracy, in that so little explanation is given by her within the story's actual dialogue.

Do note that, in quantum mechanics, in order to describe those mechanics, an object and its energy output may be placed on a coordinate in topological space, but ought not be thought of as a true "location"... meaning, what Chao describes as topologia and this are probably not the same thing.

[108th Period]

■白鳥
BYAKU-U
("White Bird")

Since the most ancient days of Japan's history, large, white-winged creatures have been considered good omens. In the twenty-fifth volume of the *Nihon Shōki* ("Chronicles of Japan"), the mythical tales of the phoenix, *kirin*, *byaku-ji*, and the *byaku-u*, as well as those of other creatures and their perceived good-omen appearances, are told (an albino crow may also be interpreted as a positive omen). In the twenty-first scroll of the *Engishiki* ("Ceremonies of the *Engi* Era"), the white winged-creature is described not only as good, but as the essence of the sun, reflecting upon them the highly spiritual position "Spirit of the Sun."

Traditionally, those with high spiritual classifications have been feared for their power and avoided. In anthropological terms, this is called a taboo. Be it good or bad, people tend to avoid taboos. Ernst Cassirer (1874–1945) elaborates on this concept in his book,

An Essay on Man. "*Sawaranu kami ni tatari-nashi*," a Japanese idiom equivalent to the English "Let sleeping dogs lie," comes from this culture of taboos.

According to Cassirer, to look upon a taboo individual is similar to looking (inappropriately) on a high priest or a member of royalty—in other words, dangerous. In a society where the culture of taboo exists, the common person avoids the taboo individual. The reason Setsuna distances herself from her people is similar to this—her white wings made her different (albeit very powerful). As a side note, it should be noted that those with blue and red wings are similarly looked upon as good omens, as is a bird with three legs.

■「『氷神の戦鎚』」
MALLEUS AQUILONIS
("Japanese War-Hammer of the Ice God")

Spell that creates a large mass of ice and crashes it down upon its intended target. (In the story, it is performed as an unincanted spell.) When the ice melts—and not dry ice, but ice made with regular water—it absorbs 79.65 cal/g of heat energy…so, if a large enough mass of ice were to be created, it would decrease the ambient temperature of the surrounding area significantly.

Formed as they are by molecular bonds weaker than those of crystals of oxidized silicone, ice crystals lose much of their kinetic energy when broken apart after colliding with their target. In that sense, unless a ball of ice with a great deal of mass is created, one cannot expect damage to be very high. As for why the spell appears so extravagant, that is because of its need for a sufficiently large mass of ice to be formed.

Aside from the fact that it gathers an impressive amount of mass, then, a spell such as this—which creates a large amount of ice and then propels it—is rather a simple temperature-control magic, and therefore is not particularly difficult to master.

In Latin, the word *malleus* means "hammer," with Aquilonis making it a genus of Aquilon, the God of the North Wind.

■ 幻想世界
PHANTASMAGORIA
(Φαντασμαγορία)

In Ancient Greek, Φαντασμα means "illusion," while -αγορία means "movement." In modern terms, perhaps the idea would be that of a magical-illusion projector.

Φαντασμα or "phantasma" itself comes from the Greek word Φαινειν, meaning "to shed light." In this case, however, it is more an illusion which one experiences fully, rather than one only seen.

■「『エクスキューショーナー・ソード』」
ENSIS EXSEQUENS
("Sword of the Executioner")

Meaning "executioner's sword" in Latin, the Ensis Exsequens spell is one which instantly converts matter into a solid (or liquid into a gas) which then is conveyed via a violent phase transition to attack an opponent (in the story, the spell is unincanted). On some matter, the spell has no effect, but an object or individual thusly phase-shifted instantly into a gas would be just as instantly vaporized. Depending upon the spell's area of effect, then, the outcome might be very destructive, indeed, with anything in its effective range essentially wiped out of existence.

Although it may be normal upon hearing the term "vaporized" for one to expect a sudden increase in temperature, matter that is transported via phase transition actually absorbs an incredible amount of heat energy, so much so that surrounding temperatures suddenly drop. (At 1AT, a steamlike vapor with a temperature of -25°C develops.) This powerful spell has an additional effect—even if the brunt of the spell is avoided, the target still has the extremely low temperature left in its wake to deal with.

Most magic that utilizes cold does so by lowering the temperature of an object; this creates a corresponding condensation effect. Ensis Exsequens, on the other hand, causes extreme cold by initiating phase transition by means of the sudden transformation of solids into gasses. For spells as high level as this, only mages of Evangeline's ability (or above) would be able to master it.

■魔女狩り
INQUISITIO MALEFICARUM
("Witch Inquisition")

From the Middle Ages to Early Modern Europe, the Inquisitio Maleficarum is sometimes regarded as an activity performed by Christians looking to get rid of those thought in their eyes to be heretics. Many were put to death, accused of having made a pact with Satan. Although the Christian order would come to be vilified for these acts, they were not sanctioned by the Church.

Even so, it is written in Deuteronomy 18:10–12 that, "No one shall be found among you who makes a son or daughter pass through fire, or who practices divination, or is a soothsayer, or an augur, or a sorcerer, or one who casts spells, or who consults ghosts or spirits, or who seeks oracles from the dead. For whoever does these things is abhorrent to the Lord; it is because of such abhorrent practices that the Lord your God is driving them out before you." Clearly, the practice of magic was not sanctioned in the time of Christ.

As an organization proper, however, from the time of the Ancient to the Middle Ages, the Christian Church did not hunt witches per se. Certainly, to cast out people not familiar to them was an aspect of the culture of small farming communities, and the hunting of witches during the Middle Ages may in fact have come from the paranoia of the people. For the Church to make efforts to calm people in such times is common. For example, in 1080, Pope Gregory VII sent a letter to the King of Denmark admonishing him for his policy of executing suspected witches.

In 1485, James Sprenger (1439–95) and Heinrich Kramer (?–1505) wrote *Malleus Maleficarum* and positioned witches as enemies of the Christian Church (heretics), legitimizing the hunting of witches in the eyes of the faithful. (The Middle Ages ended in 1453, so this would have been the Early Modern Age.) After this point, witch hunts would go on gaining in momentum, reaching a peak in the seventeenth century.

Changes in the Church's position would not come about until the topic of witch hunts would become a tool for politicians. For example, France's King Philip IV the Fair accused the Knights Templar of heresy and seized the considerable Templar treasury, breaking up the Templar monastic banking system, in order to control it himself (1312). Then, during the Hundred Years' War, Joan of Arc was executed as a witch (1431). In acts such as these, politics played an undeniable part in witch hunts, going so far as to legitimize them even further as the Church continued to view witches as enemies of the order. In time, the power of the Church in these matters would fade away…although that was only eventually.

About the Creator

Negima! is only Ken Akamatsu's third manga, although he started working in the field in 1994 with *AI Ga Tomaranai* (released in the United States with the title *A.I. Love You).* Like all of Akamatsu's work to date, it was published in Kodansha's *Shonen Magazine. AI Ga Tomaranai* ran for five years before concluding in 1999. In 1998, however, Akamatsu began the work that would make him one of the most popular manga artists in Japan: *Love Hina. Love Hina* ran for four years, and before its conclusion in 2002, it would cause Akamatsu to be granted the prestigious Manga of the Year award from Kodansha, as well as going on to become one of the best-selling manga in the United States.

Translation Notes

Japanese is a tricky language for most westerners, and translation is often more art than science. For your edification and reading pleasure, here are notes on some of the places where we could have gone in a different direction in our translation of the work, or where a Japanese cultural reference is used.

Asuna's "Maid" Outfit, page 24

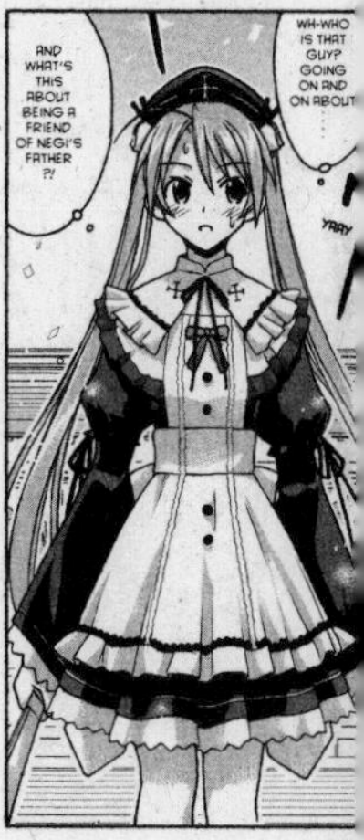
WH-WHO IS THAT GUY? GOING ON AND ON ABOUT
AND WHAT'S THIS ABOUT BEING A FRIEND OF NEGI'S FATHER ?!
YAAY

The gothic maid outfit worn by Asuna in this volume is an actual costume designed by milky ange, a specialty retailer based in Kobe, Japan. The design is used by *Negima!* creator Akamatsu with permission from the company. In this case, the name of the particular outfit seen in the comic is "Antique Sister Maid—Brady." If you're itching to get on a plane or even just online to go and buy one for yourself, bad news—it's in the "sold out" section.

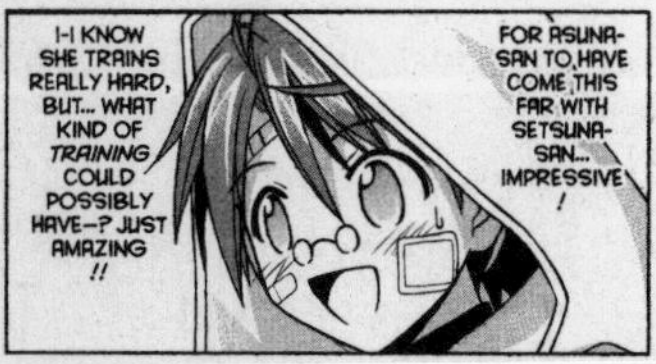
FOR ASUNA-SAN TO HAVE COME THIS FAR WITH SETSUNA-SAN... IMPRESSIVE!
I-I KNOW SHE TRAINS REALLY HARD, BUT... WHAT KIND OF *TRAINING* COULD POSSIBLY HAVE—? JUST AMAZING !!

Asuna's Boost of Sudden Power, page 43

Because the battle between Asuna and Setsuna (page 43, panel 6) was being watched by Negi so intently, the amount of magical power forwarded by Negi to an embattled Asuna was more than either of them might have anticipated, says creator Akamatsu. In other words, it wasn't just that Negi was watching the battle, but that he was concentrating on it so singlemindedly, that Asuna experienced the sudden boost in power (page 44, panel 1).

Sister Shakti, page 95

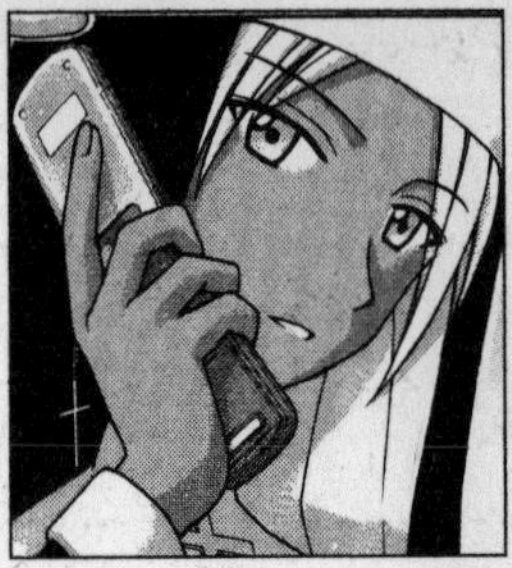

...And so it turns out that the identity of the mage in the nun's habit is new character Sister Shakti! Defined by Merriam-Webster as the "dynamic energy of a Hindu god personified as his female consort," or more broadly as "cosmic energy as conceived in Hindu thought," another way of defining *shakti* might be the divine cosmic energy which projects, maintains, and dissolves the universe. Cosmic stuff!

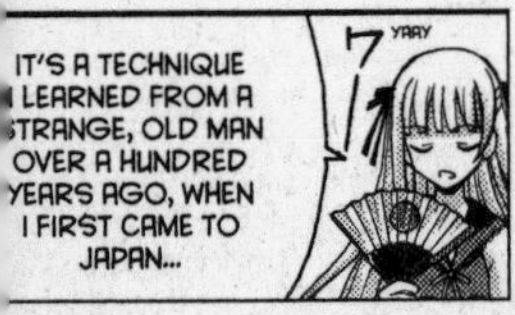
IT'S A TECHNIQUE I LEARNED FROM A STRANGE, OLD MAN OVER A HUNDRED YEARS AGO, WHEN I FIRST CAME TO JAPAN...
YAAY

Strange Old Man, page 138

The man from whom Evangeline learned her martial arts (when she first came to Japan—"a hundred years ago," as she tell it) is most likely to be famed martial-arts master Takeda Sokaku (1859-1943). A last-generation samurai mostly remembered as a reviver of *Daitō-ryū Aikijutsu*, one of Takeda's prominent students was the founder of Aikidō, Ueshiba Morihei.

"Tsundere," Back Cover Text (Beneath Dust Jacket)

A word used to describe Chisame on the beneath-dust-jacket back cover of the original Japanese *tankōbon* or collected-weeklies volume, *tsundere* is a slang word often encountered in Japanese "dating simulation" games...you know, the kind that tend to be rated "Ages 18 and Up." Used to describe an archetypal anime/manga girl who's standoffish at the start (sometimes obnoxiously so, as in *The Taming of the Shrew*'s "Kate") and then, once "mastered," is only all too docile, *tsundere* comes etymologically from the Japanese sound effect of an "upturned nose (*tsun*), with the *–dere* from the onomatopoetic *dere-dere*—being a mushy, fawning, or misty-eyed sort of sound.

Preview of Volume Thirteen

We're pleased to present you with a preview from *Negima!* volume 13. This volume will be available in English on February 27, 2007, but for now you'll have to make do with Japanese!

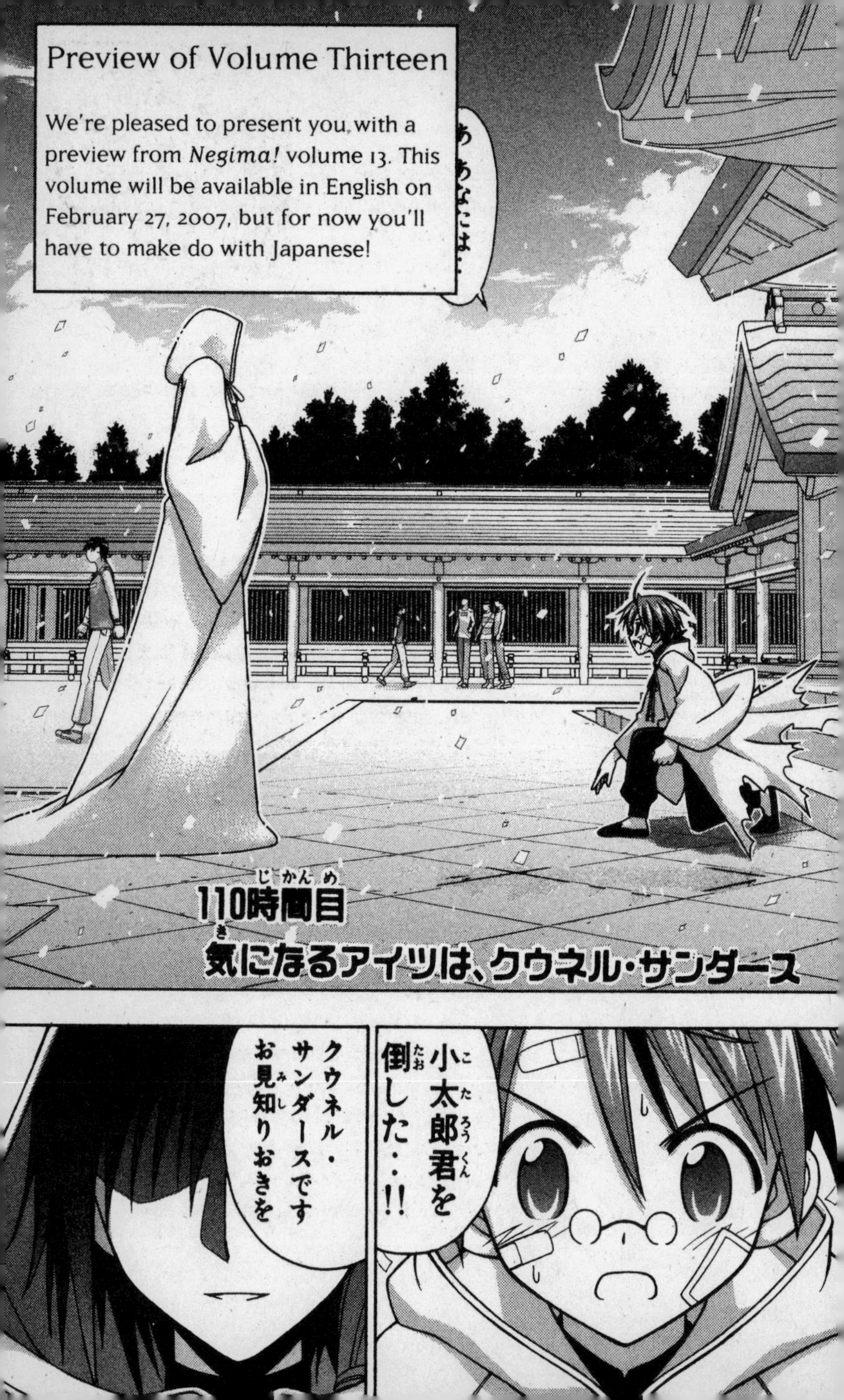
あ あなたは…
110時間目
気になるアイツは、クウネル・サンダース
小太郎君を倒した…!!
クウネル・サンダースです お見知りおきを

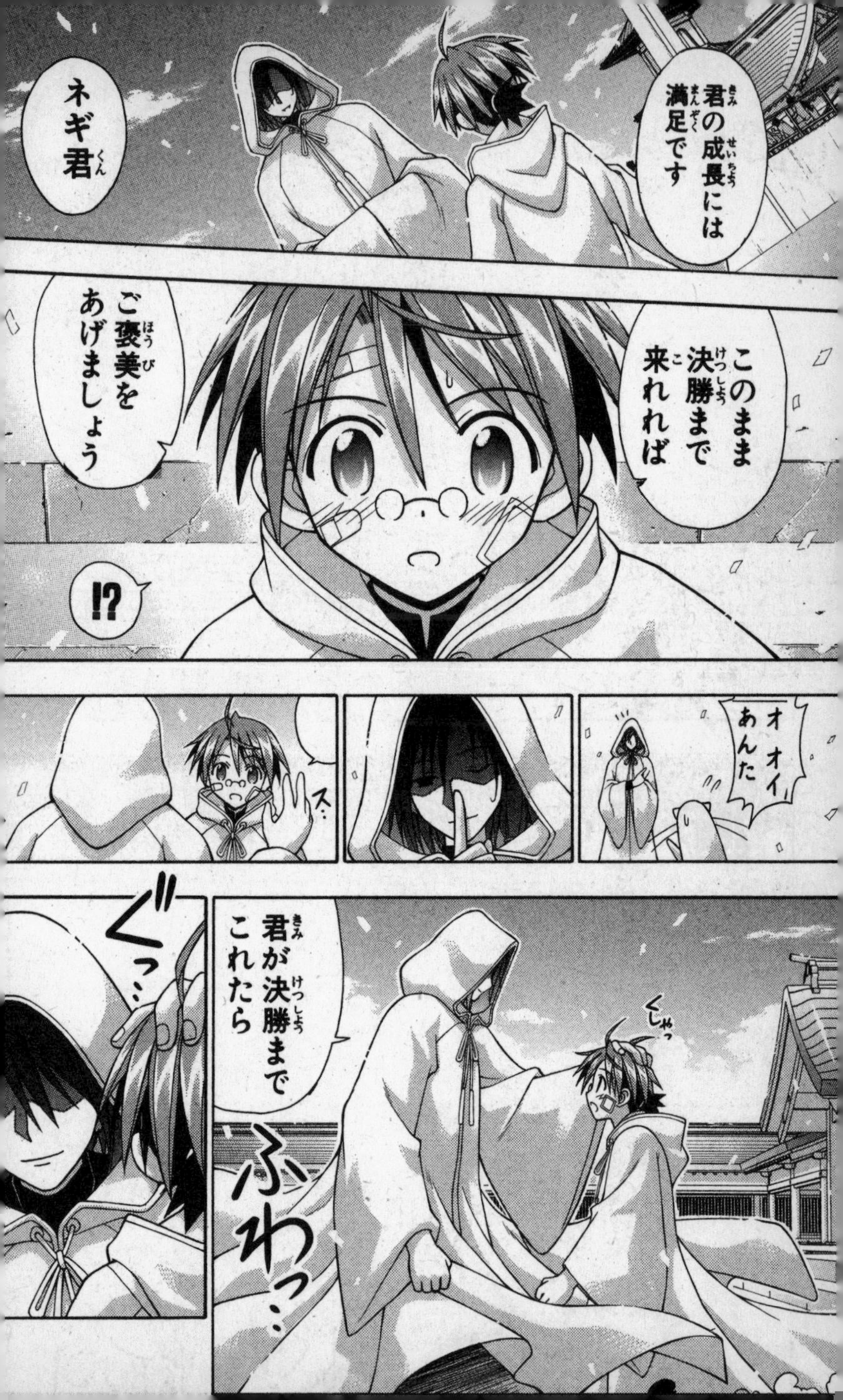
君の成長には満足です
ネギ君
このまま決勝まで来れれば
ご褒美をあげましょう
!?
オオイあんた
ス…
君が決勝まで これたら
くしゃっ
ふわっ…
ぐっ…

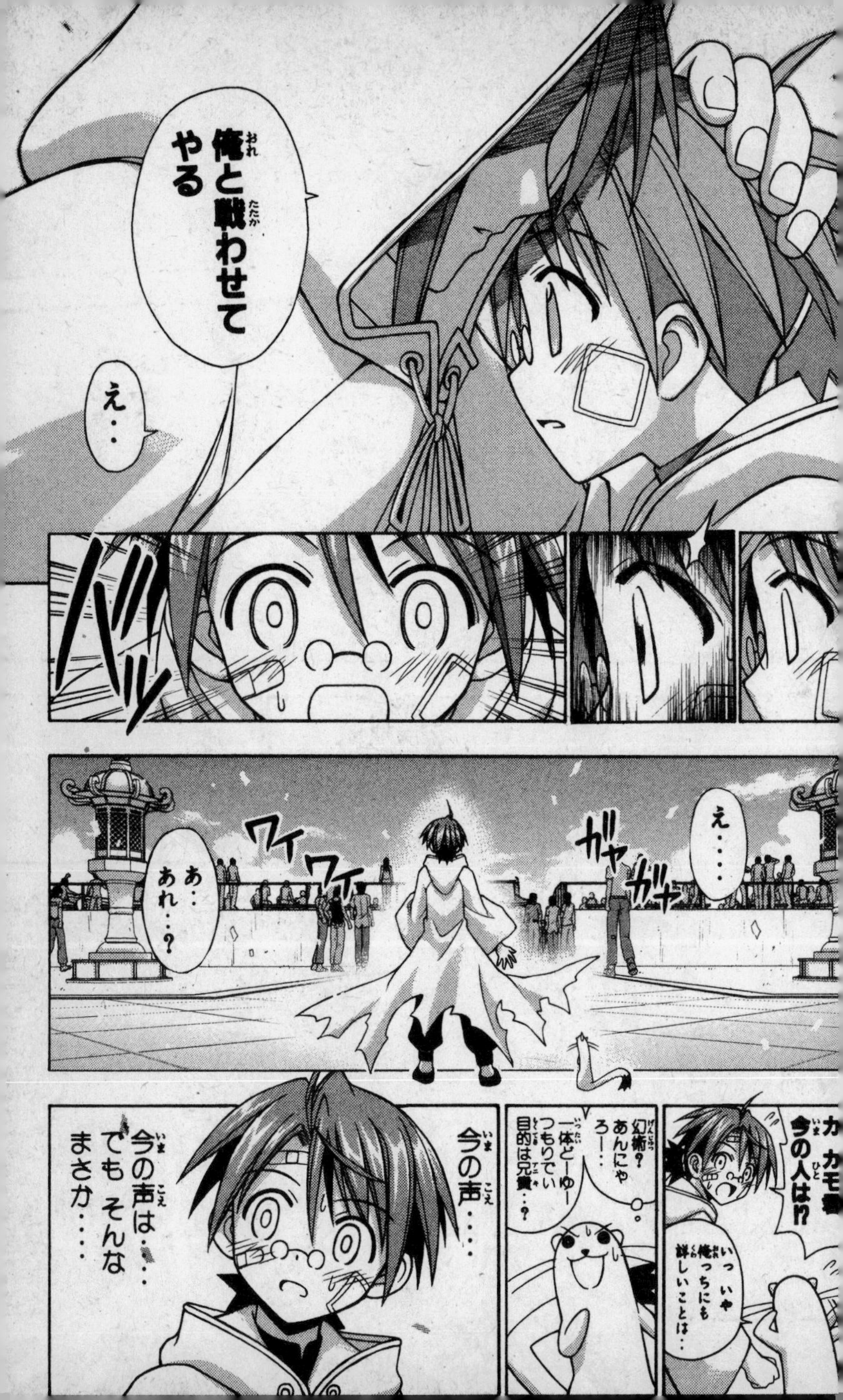
俺と戦わせてやる
え・・
バッ
え・・・・
ガヤ ガヤ
ワイ ワイ
あ・・あれ・・?
カ カモ君 今の人は!?
いっいや 俺っちにも詳しいことは・・・
幻術? あんにゃろー・・
一体どーゆーつもりで 目的は兄貴・・・?
今の声・・・・
今の声は・・・ でも そんな まさか・・・・

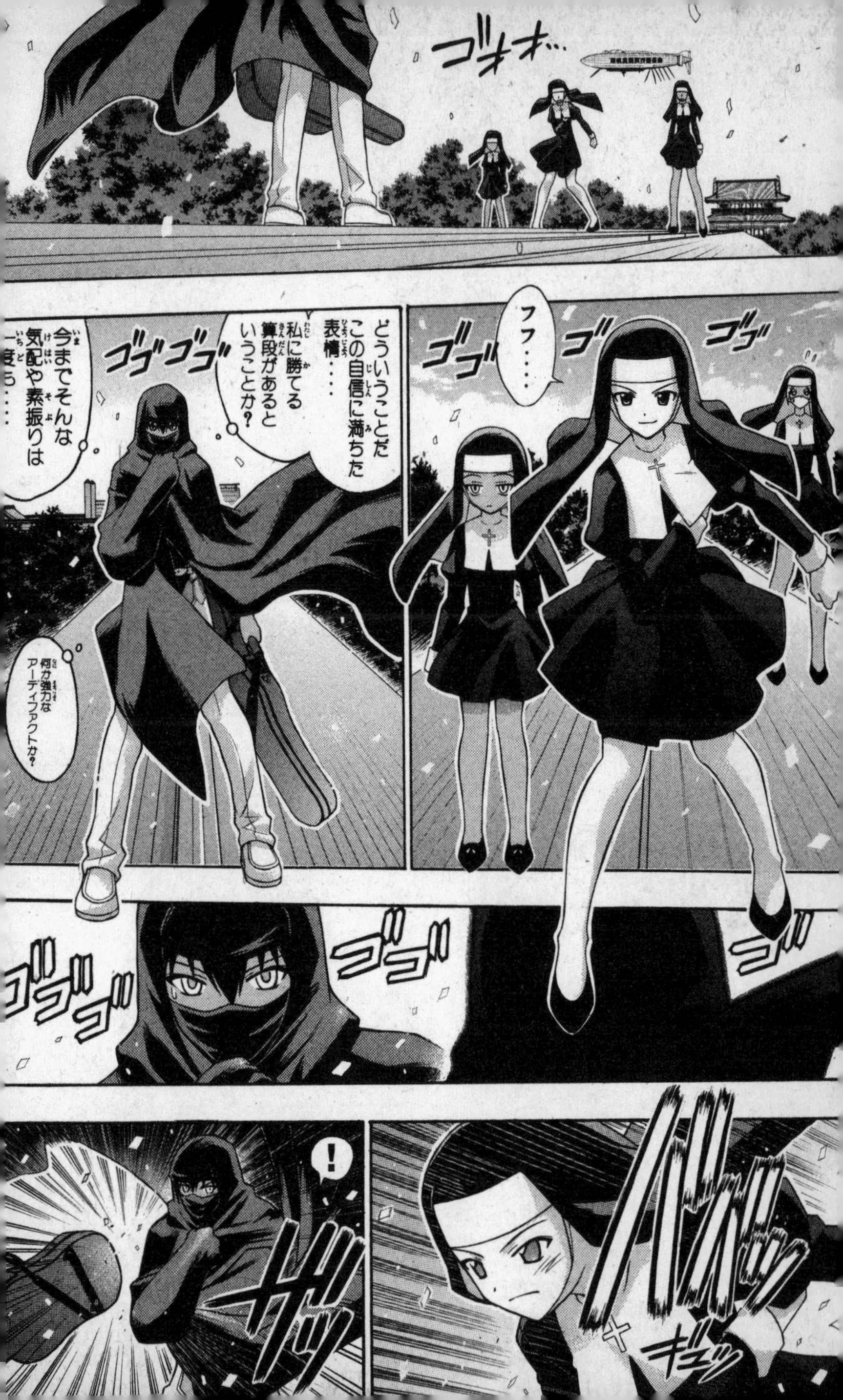
ゴオオ…
ゴゴ
ゴ
ゴゴ
フフ……
ゴゴゴゴ
どういうことだ この自信に満ちた表情……
私に勝てる算段があるということか？
今までそんな気配や素振りは一度も……
何か強力なアーティファクトか？
ゴゴ
ゴゴ
ゴゴゴ
バババッ
ギュッ
!
ザッ

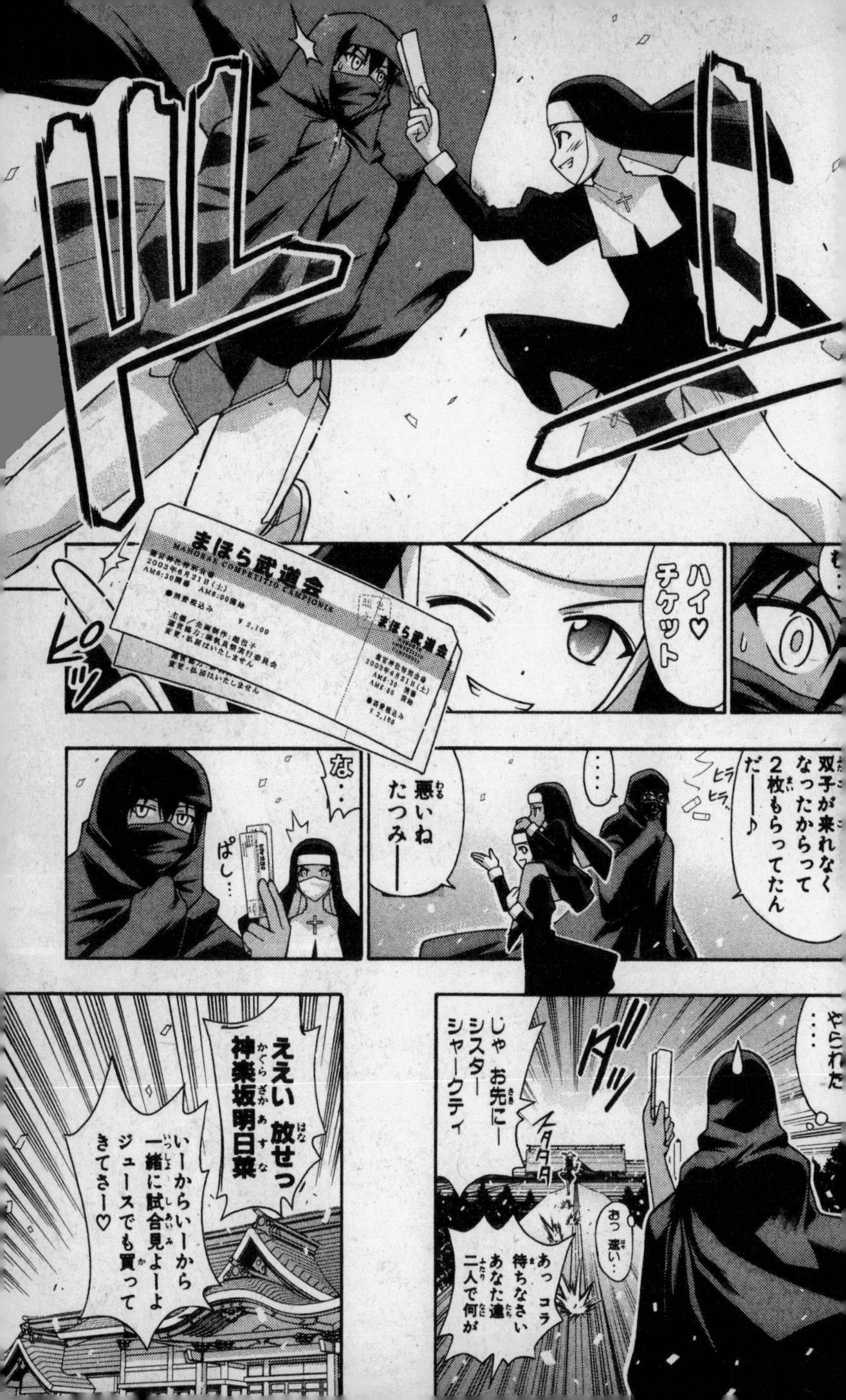
む…
ハイ♡チケット
ピッ
まほら武道会
まほら武道会
双子が来れなくなったからって2枚もらってたんだー♪
ヒラ ヒラ
……
悪いねたつみー
な…
ぱし…
やられた……
ダッ
じゃ お先にー シスターシャークティ
タタタ
あっ コラ 待ちなさい あなた達二人で何が
おっ 速い…
ええい 放せっ 神楽坂明日菜
いーからいーから一緒に試合見よーよ ジュースでも買ってきてさー♡

TOMARE!

[STOP!]

You're going the wrong way!

Manga is a completely different
type of reading experience.

To start at the *beginning*,
go to the *end*!

That's right! Authentic manga is read the traditional Japanese way—
from right to left. Exactly the *opposite* of how American books are
read. It's easy to follow: Just go to the other end of the book, and read
each page—and each panel—from right side to left side, starting at
the top right. Now you're experiencing manga as it was meant to be.